MICHAEL DAVITT:
FREELANCE RADICAL AND FRONDEUR

For Rosanna and Ultán

MICHAEL DAVITT

Freelance Radical and Frondeur

LAURENCE MARLEY

FOUR COURTS PRESS

Set in 10 pt on 13 pt Janson Text for
FOUR COURTS PRESS LTD
7 Malpas Street, Dublin 8, Ireland
e-mail: info@four-courts-press.ie
http://www.four-courts-press.ie
and in North America by
FOUR COURTS PRESS
c/o ISBS, 920 N.E. 58th Avenue, Suite 300, Portland, OR 97213.

A catalogue record for this title
is available from the British Library.

ISBN 978–1–84682–066–3

SPECIAL ACKNOWLEDGMENT

**This publication was grant-aided by the Publications Fund
of the National University of Ireland, Galway.**

Printed in England
by MPG Books, Bodmin, Cornwall.

Contents

Illustrations

CREDITS

Abbreviations

CAC	Churchill Archive Cambridge
CT	*Connaught Telegraph*
DA	Davitt archive
DP	Davitt papers
DMS	Davitt Museum, Straide
DPB	*Devoy's Post Bag*, ed. W. O'Brien and D. Ryan (2 vols, Dublin, 1979)
DRD	D.R. Daniel papers
EHR	*English Historical Review*
ET	*Evening Telegraph*
FJ	*Freeman's Journal*
FTLU	Federated Trade and Labour Union
GAA	Gaelic Athletic Association
HGP	Henry George papers
HLLRA	Highland Land Law Reform Association
IDTLA	Irish Democratic Trade and Labour Federation
IESH	*Irish Economic and Social History*
IHS	*Irish Historical Studies*
ILP	Independent Labour Party
INL	Irish National League
INLGB	Irish National League of Great Britain
IRB	Irish Republican Brotherhood
JDP	John Dillon papers
JRLUM	John Ryland's Library, University of Manchester
JRP	John Redmond papers
LW	*Labour World*
LRC	Labour Representation Committee
LRCP	Labour Representation Committee papers
NLW	National Library of Wales
NUDL	National Union of Dock Labourers
NYPL	New York Public Library
RHST	*Royal Historical Society Transactions*
RIC	Royal Irish Constabulary
RJP	Rosamund Jacobs papers
SDF	Social Democatic Federation
SHR	*Scottish Historical Review*

SLRL	Scottish Land Restoration League
SLP	Scottish Labour Party
SP	Stead papers
SSP	Francis Sheehy Skeffington papers
TDSP	T.D. Sullivan papers
TCD	Trinity College Dublin, Manuscripts Department
UIL	United Irish League
WHR	*Welsh Historical Review*

Acknowledgments

Fᴵᴿˢᵀ ᴏꜰ ᴀʟʟ, I would like to extend my gratitude to the staff of the following institutions and archives: the Davitt Museum, Straide, Co. Mayo, particularly the Michael Davitt Memorial Association; National Library of Ireland, Dublin; John Ryland's Library, University of Manchester; Churchill Archive, Cambridge; National Library of Wales, Aberystwyth; New York Public Library; the James Hardiman Library, National University of Ireland, Galway, with special thanks to Marie Boran; and The Board of Trinity College Dublin for granting me permission to publish quotations from manuscripts in the Davitt and John Dillon papers. I must also express my sincere thanks to the Davitt family, particularly Maurice, Brian and Fr Tom Davitt, who were helpful and supportive in the early days when I was involved in research for the doctoral thesis on which this book is based.

Thanks are also due to my family, especially my mother, Kate, and my brother Setanta. It is a matter of deep regret to me that my late father, Larry, is not here to read this book; he would, I know, have taken great pleasure in receiving a copy.

My gratitude also to others who helped me in one way or another along the way: Dr Emmet O'Connor and Dr Caitriona Clear for their early comments and suggestions; Dr John Dunleavy, with whom I had a number of interesting and useful conversations, especially about the early Davitt; Dr John Cunningham, who was generous with his time when I was in the final stages of preparing the book for publication; Renate Mitchell, for patiently translating a short Russian work on Davitt; Dr Andrew Newby who was generous with his own material; Martin Fanning at Four Courts Press for his patience and his general help and guidance; Mary and Vincent McCafferty; Joe McGowan; John McHugh; Damien Mooney; and Fr Aidan Troy, who kindly set aside a room for me in the peace and quiet of Holy Cross Monastery, Ardoyne, where I could work, undisturbed, on the final chapter. I must also acknowledge my debt to Dr Carla King, whose excellent work in editing Davitt's writings has provided an invaluable resource for scholars undertaking research on Davitt.

I owe a very special word of thanks to Professor Gearóid Ó Tuathaigh, my former doctoral supervisor, who encouraged and supported me during each stage of my research on Davitt, and who took time to discuss and read drafts of this study. His invaluable insights, guidance, sound advice – and also his good humour – made working under his supervision both a pleasure and a privilege.

My greatest debt is to Rosanna, not only for her patience, tolerance and practical support while I was in the midst of what seemed like a never-ending writing and editing process, but also for her encouragement, especially during the past year. It made all the difference in bringing this work to fruition. The book is dedicated, with love and affection, to her and to our son, Ultán.

Preface

DURING THE IRISH land war of 1879–82, Michael Davitt, whose moral authority and organizational prowess in leading that agrarian campaign earned him the legendary title 'the father of the Land League', was still only in his mid-thirties. For almost a quarter of a century after the Kilmainham 'treaty' (1882), he remained extremely politically active, not only in Ireland but also in British labour politics and on the international stage. Unlike Parnell, he was a prolific writer, a working journalist, newspaper editor, and the author of six major works. He travelled widely – in Europe, Palestine, Egypt, South Africa, North America and Australasia – and was well known to such diverse figures as the veteran Hungarian leader, Louis Kossuth, the Chinese revolutionary leader, Sun Yat Sen, US president, Theodore Roosevelt, Mark Twain, Leo Tolstoy and Oscar Wilde. Yet on the centenary year of his death, he remained popularly known mainly for his leadership of the land war, pivotal though that was. Indeed, while his early life and his role in mobilizing the tenantry have been well documented, his later political career after 1882 has attracted relatively little scholarly attention.

There have been two substantial works on Davitt. Francis Sheehy Skeffington's biography, *Michael Davitt: revolutionary agitator and labour leader*, was written in 1907, shortly after Davitt's death. This work, as stated in its preface, was intended only as 'a primer of Davitt' rather than an exhaustive study. Nevertheless, it has certain shortcomings, even as an introduction to its subject. It was written without the support of Davitt's widow and is based mainly on published sources. More importantly, Sheehy Skeffington was unashamedly sympathetic to Davitt's politics, and viewed him as the 'prophet of the future Ireland'. Although the work is valuable, in that it provides an overview of Davitt's whole life and political career, it is essentially hagiographical in nature. In contrast, T.W. Moody's contextual biography, *Davitt and Irish revolution, 1846–82* (1982), is a detailed, scholarly work, which had been in gestation for many years as its author worked on an array of primary material placed at his disposal. As Pauric Travers has only recently observed, it was the knowledge that Moody was working on such a study that proved sufficient 'to dissuade a generation of young Irish scholars from studying Davitt'.[1] However, while making a hugely significant contribution to Irish historiography, the Moody work is incomplete. A twenty-four-page epilogue provides an overview of Davitt's later years, but as its title indicates, the book only substantially covers the period up until the end of the land war. It is, moreover, largely a study of Davitt's political life, with little on his political thought.

In an article published in the *Royal Historical Society Transactions* in 1953, entitled 'Michael Davitt and the British Labour Movement, 1882–1906', Moody did deal with one of the most important aspects of Davitt's later career. It was, however, a short piece and nothing more substantial on this area has been published since. Davitt's political role and his activism have, to some extent, featured in works on political/legislative developments in Ireland, particularly in political biographies of his contemporaries; on agrarian radicalism; and on labour politics. In particular, Carla King's more recent writings have shed much light on his later career; and the publication of Davitt's collected writings, edited by King, has proven an invaluable addition to an already substantial body of primary material.[2] However, given the diversity of Davitt's political engagements and activities in the years after the Kilmainham accord, and the fact that many of his political ideas were only formulated or developed towards the end of the land war, a thoroughgoing exposition, not only of his activism but particularly also his political thought, remains necessary. Such an undertaking has demanded a new, revised contextualization, including, for example, a consideration of his career in the context of comparative labour history. Indeed, his relationship with and impact upon the British labour movement has, significantly, not only been neglected in Irish historical scholarship but also in British labour historiography.

Davitt's name has been invoked and claimed by different traditions, from the leader of the Blueshirts, Eoin O'Duffy, in the 1930s, to the former leader of the British Labour Party, Michael Foot, who was, in fact, named after Davitt. Without seeking in any way to diminish Davitt's significance as an historical figure, it is important, therefore, that he be restored to a proper

1 Pauric Travers, 'Davitt after the Land League' in Carla King (ed.), *Famine, land and culture in Ireland* (Dublin, 2000), p. 84. More recent doctoral dissertations on Davitt, or touching on aspects of Davitt's political life, are evidence that this inhibition no longer applies. See Laura McNeil, 'Land, labor and liberation: Michael Davitt and the Irish question in the age of British democratic reform, 1898–1906', PhD thesis (Boston College, 2002), and Andrew Newby, '"Shoulder to shoulder?" Scottish and Irish land reformers in the Highlands of Scotland', (PhD thesis, University of Edinburgh, 2001). 2 See, for example, King, 'Michael Davitt, Irish nationalism and the British empire in the late nineteenth century', in Peter Gray (ed.), *Victoria's Ireland? Irishness and Britishness, 1837–1901* (Dublin, 2004); King (ed.), *Michael Davitt: collected writings, 1868–1906*, vols 1–8 (Bristol, 2001). See also King's edited publication of Davitt's *Jottings in Solitary* (Dublin, 2003).

historical context. I have attempted in this book to chart not just the trajectory of his activism in the years after the land war but also the evolution of his political ideas, an area which has generally been neglected. Many of the questions asked about Davitt's later political career – whether he was, for example, a constitutional nationalist rather than a separatist; or whether he was a socialist or social democrat – have usually been put in narrow terms. I argue, however, that he must be understood in a broader context, as an internationalist; not in a strict, ideological sense, but more so as a universal figure, driven by an egalitarianism which had as much to do with his early influences in industrial Lancashire as with his identification with the west of Ireland. The most effective way in which he could act on his own political instincts from 1882 onwards was as a freelance activist, and by understanding these instincts we can best appreciate his political alignments during his later years, even with Parnell and the conservative wing of Irish nationalism; his desire for social reform and political justice; the extent of his radicalism; and also his inconsistencies and contradictions.

1 / Struggle and self-discovery: the early Davitt

O WING TO THE CIRCUMSTANCES OF Davitt's early childhood in Ireland and his youth in industrial England, and to his experiences as a political prisoner in the 1870s, he came to possess a moral capital which he could later draw upon to mobilize and inspire peasants and industrial workers alike, and which afforded him considerable leverage in dealing with political opponents, particularly his later rivals within the Irish nationalist movement. By his early thirties he was widely viewed, in Ireland and beyond, as the archetypical victim of both Irish landlordism and British industrialism; and more than any other Irish nationalist of his day, he appealed to the Irish diaspora, especially immigrants who had fresh and painful memories of exile. When John Boyle O'Reilly, editor of the Boston *Pilot* and former Fenian arms agent, remarked that Davitt's influence and power were 'unique, beautiful',[1] it was to Davitt's moral authority that he alluded, an authority based on an early life of hardship and suffering which was pregnant with political symbolism.

From the mid-nineteenth century, Irish nationalists, even many of those of a moderate hue, looked upon the Famine of 1845–9, with its huge human cost and massive social dislocation, as the ultimate indictment of British rule in Ireland.[2] It was in the midst of this calamity that Davitt was born on 25 March 1846 in the village of Straide, Co. Mayo, to Martin Davitt, a small tenant farmer, and his wife Catherine (*née* Kielty). In this particular year, the pota-

---

1 O'Reilly to Davitt, 12 June 1882, DP, TCD, MS 9488/3607. 2 In its most coherent form, this was argued by James Fintan Lalor; see David N. Buckley, *James Fintan Lalor: radical* (Cork, 1990), pp 29–43. The Young Irelander and later Fenian, John Mitchel, argued, in a much more visceral way, that the Famine was a calculated act of genocide by the British government, and that its relief measures amounted to nothing more than 'contrivances for slaughter'; see Mitchel, *The last conquest of Ireland (perhaps)*, ed. Patrick Maume (Dubin, 2005), pp 102, 219. Davitt concurred with the assessment that while the potato blight was a natural phenomenon, the English government caused the Famine itself. He also apportioned blame to the Catholic clergy for failing to condemn the landlord system; see Davitt, *The fall of feudalism in Ireland* (London and New York, 1904), pp 50, 66. In fact, Davitt was apparently the first to refer to the Famine as a 'holocaust'; see David Krause, 'The conscience of Ireland: Lalor, Davitt and Sheehy Skeffington', *Éire-Ireland*, 28:1 (spring, 1993), 13, fn. 12.

to, the crop on which labourers, cottiers and poor smallholders had become increasingly and dangerously dependent, was shown to have succumbed on a large scale to the blight first detected at a local level in the autumn of 1845.[3] The failure of the crop throughout the country had a major impact during the winter of 1846–7, and this resulted in widespread distress and suffering. The Whig administration under Lord John Russell, which had only recently replaced Peel's Tory government, was single-minded in its commitment to *laissez-faire*, the prevailing economic ideology of the day, and it insisted that Irish landlords should be left with the responsibility for local relief, a disastrous approach to an evolving national crisis. Over the course of 1847, the full extent and gruesome nature of the tragedy became all too apparent. Joel Mokyr has estimated that in Mayo, where there was not only a heavy dependency on the potato but also already high levels of poverty, the mortality rate ultimately reached somewhere between 100,000 and 120,000, the highest of any county in Ireland.[4] As Sheehy-Skeffington remarked, 'The horrors of the famine broke over [Davitt's] infancy'.[5]

Yet the Davitts themselves, though only smallholders living on a few acres, managed to weather the storm. They had some livestock, and Davitt later heard it said that the family was in 'easy circumstances' during the second and more serious appearance of the blight (although, as he noted some years later while reflecting on his family's fortunes, his 'father being but a tenant-at-will was not calculated to make such circumstances very "easy"').[6] Under the public works scheme, legislated for in 1846 as a form of relief, Martin Davitt was also appointed as an overseer of road works in the district between Castlebar and Straide. He held this position for a while, but, after apparently losing the job to a 'jealous neighbour', he was forced, by the need to pay rent and arrears, to travel to England in the summer of 1849 to work as a harvester.[7] During his time as a seasonal labourer in England he did not earn enough to resolve his financial difficulties, and after failing to satisfy the landlord's demands for the payment of arrears by the following year, he and his family were evicted from their homestead in 1850, probably some time around September. By this stage, Martin and his wife had four children: Mary, who was Michael's senior by five years; and Anne and Sabina, born in 1848 and 1850 respectively, the latter only two months before the eviction. The eviction scene itself was something which left an indelible impression on Davitt. In 1881 he wrote,

3 Christine Kinealy, *This great calamity: the Irish famine, 1845–52* (Dublin, 2006), p. 71. 4 Mokyr's unpublished estimates are cited in Donald E. Jordan, *Land and popular politics in Ireland: county Mayo from the plantation to the Land War* (Cambridge, 1984), p. 108, fn. 18. 5 Sheehy Skeffington, *Michael Davitt*, p. 17. 6 Davitt, *Jottings in solitary*, ed. Carla King (Dublin, 2003), p. 5. 7 T.W. Moody, *Davitt and Irish revolution, 1846–82* (Oxford, 1982), p. 8.

[Failing] to wipe off all arrears, we were one morning thrown out on the roadside and our little house and home pulled down before our eyes by the reigning institution: the 'Crowbar Brigade'. I was then but four and a half years old yet I have a distinct remembrance (doubtless strengthened by the frequent narration of events by my parents in after years) of that morning's scene: The remnant of our household furniture flung about the road, the roof of our house falling in and the thatch taking fire, my mother and father looking on with four young children.[8]

The Davitts were, of course, not the only family to suffer this fate. After September 1847, landlords increasingly resorted to eviction, and to the demolition of cabins, as a means of avoiding the payment of rates to which they were liable on holdings valued under £4, a significant financial burden for many landlords whose properties had not yielded rents since the beginning of the blight.[9]

Like others in the same state of near destitution, Martin and Catherine Davitt turned to the workhouse for relief. Central to the 1838 Poor Law, the workhouse was a draconian institution, based on a conservative ideology of self-help, and certainly not designed to deal with major social distress in an emergency crisis. With its strict, penal regime, it was dreaded by the Irish poor, and a stigma was attached to those who became inmates. The local Swinford workhouse, to which the Davitts presented themselves immediately after their eviction, was one of 130 such buildings constructed throughout the country in the 1840s. Such was the prejudice against entering these institutions that many people were initially prepared to suffer their own poverty rather than enter the system. Yet as the Famine progressed, and pride gave way to the instinct for survival, the workhouses were filled beyond their capacity as throngs of paupers desperately sought admission. Even after an amendment to the Poor Law in June 1847, the workhouses were still wholly inadequate in dealing with the crisis, financed as they were by local rates: they were overcrowded, disease-ridden, and mortality was high not only among the inmates but also among the staff.[10] One of the aspects of life under the regime which particularly instilled fear in the poverty-stricken was the separation of family members; and when Catherine Davitt learned of the regulation which required that male children over three years of age be kept separate from their mothers, she resolved to take her chances with her family on the roadside, rather than submit to such an unnatural arrangement. The family spent no more than an hour in the Swinford workhouse, but Martin Davitt could never again bring himself to refer to the event, such was his sense of shame.[11]

---

8 Davitt, *Jottings*, p. 6. 9 Kinealy, *This great calamity*, p. 190. 10 John O'Connor, *The workhouses of Ireland* (Dublin, 1995), pp 120–54. 11 Davitt, *Jottings*, p. 8.

Having turned their backs on this institution, the Davitts opted for emigration, the course chosen by over 200,000 others that year, many of whom were just as desperate to put some distance between themselves and their poverty in Ireland, even if it involved braving a difficult crossing to England in autumn or winter weather.[12] Martin and Catherine Davitt set out for Dublin, sharing the journey with another emigrating family who had transport in the form of a horse and cart. From Dublin, they sailed to Liverpool where they landed on 1 November, less than two months after their eviction.[13] Huge numbers of Irish emigrants passed through the port of Liverpool, but not everyone who left Ireland's shores was from the same farming class or in the same financial state. In the earlier part of the nineteenth century most emigrants came from the province of Ulster, not the poorer west; and during the Famine itself, large numbers of better-off farmers were part of the exodus.[14] In 1847 this was remarked upon by the *Liverpool Times*, which identified two distinct groups among the Irish: the 'emigrants of hope', those with some capital who were ultimately destined for North America in search of better conditions of living and more promising opportunities; and the 'emigrants of despair', those, like the Davitts, who were emigrating out of economic necessity and fear.[15] Of the latter, a Catholic priest, Fr Cahill, who preached in Liverpool in 1853, observed, 'the very nature of their case sends them to this country naked, and hungry, and friendless, and exterminated, and broken hearted [...] This is the sickbed of Ireland, the hospital of Ireland, the churchyard of Ireland'.[16]

In Liverpool, the Davitt family availed of the hospitality of some friends before starting out, on foot, for their destination, the east Lancashire town of Haslingden, seventeen miles north of Manchester.[17] The attraction of this small textile town for Martin Davitt was that former neighbours from Straide had reported positively on the prospects for employment there.[18] Indeed, the factory industries of Lancashire, particularly the cotton industry, provided employment for whole families, including younger children,[19] and during the Famine there was a high rate of family migration, not only to Lancashire but also to other parts of industrial Britain.[20] On arriving in Haslingden, homeless and exposed to the harsh winter weather, the Davitts were soon taken in by James

---

12 It was estimated that 213,649 persons emigrated from Ireland in 1850, although the rate peaked in 1852; see Kinealy, *This great calamity*, p. 298. 13 In *Jottings* (p. 10), Davitt inaccurately states that the family reached Liverpool in 1851, rather than 1850. 14 Kinealy, *This great calamity*, pp 298–9. 15 Cited in Graham Davis, 'The Irish in Britain, 1815–1939', in Andy Bielenberg (ed.), *The Irish diaspora* (Essex, 2000), p. 19. 16 Quoted in David Fitzpatrick, '"A peculiar tramping people": the Irish in Britain, 1801–70', in W.E. Vaughan (ed.), *A new history of Ireland*; v, *Ireland under the union*, 1 (Oxford, 1989), p. 628. 17 Davitt, *Jottings*, p. 10, note 13. 18 Moody, *Davitt*, p. 10. 19 Frank Neal, 'Irish settlement in the north-east and north-west of England in the mid-nineteenth century' in Roger Swift and Sheridan Gilley (eds), *The Irish in Victorian Britain: the local dimension* (Dublin, 1999), p. 91. 20 Fitzpatrick, '"A peculiar tramping people"', p. 629.

Bonner, a tin-plate worker from Co. Armagh, whom Davitt later described as 'the good Samaritan'.[21] Subsequently, they secured a place as lodgers in the residence of Irish immigrant Owen Egan, a cap-hawker, who already lived in cramped conditions in his small, two-storey house with his wife, their six children and another lodger, who was also Irish. Many of the Irish immigrants in Haslingden became involved in the hawker's trade, and it was as fruit-hawkers that Martin and Catherine Davitt initially earned a living, enabling them, after several months there, to rent their own house in Rock Hall, an area of the town in which there was a heavy concentration of Irish families.[22]

In settling in Britain, the Irish did not always confine themselves, nor were they restricted, to exclusively Irish districts. David Fitzpatrick points out that 'even the "Irish quarters" were seldom exclusively Irish'.[23] Nevertheless, the Irish did tend to group together in distinctive communities, not only because they were following routes established by pre-Famine economic migrants from Ireland, but also because the small Irish communities to which they gravitated gave them a sense of belonging and a sense of security in a largely antagonistic host society. Anti-Irish sentiment had deep, historical roots,[24] but one of the most immediate causes of native hostility during the nineteenth century was the fear, felt mostly by the unskilled labourers of the British working class, that the Irish would glut the British labour market and lower the rate of wages. As M.A.G. Ó Tuathaigh has observed, there was a rational basis to this resentment: the Irish were willing to work longer and for less pay, and were sometimes used as strike-breakers. However, Ó Tuathaigh has cast doubt on E.H. Hunt's contention that Irish immigration affected wage rates in Britain to the extent that it tended to increase inter-regional wage variations.[25] Hunt's argument has also been challenged by Fitzpatrick and Cormac Ó Gráda, both of whom point to the Irish immigrants' gravitation towards areas of high wages, a fact which, in itself, would not account for an increase in the wage differential between various regions.[26]

Economic factors aside, there was also a strong degree of anti-Catholic feeling in Britain which compounded the Irish immigrants' sense of embat-

---

21 Davitt, *Jottings*, p. 12. 22 Moody, *Davitt*, pp 11–12. 23 Fitzpatrick, '"A peculiar tramping people"', p. 635. 24 In his twelfth-century work, *Expugnatio Hibernica*, Giraldus Cambrensis, argued, in his justification of the Anglo-Norman conquest of Ireland, that the 'misdemeanours and vile practices' of the barbarous Irish 'demanded' invasion and conquest; *Expugnatio Hibernica* (ed.) A.B. Scott and F.X. Martin (Dublin, 1978), p. 233. On the Elizabethan mind-set towards Ireland, see Nicholas Canny, *Making Ireland British, 1580–1650* (Oxford, 2003), pp 42–58. 25 Ó Tuathaigh, 'The Irish in nineteenth-century Britain: problems of integration', *RHST*, 5th series, 31, 1981, p. 161; Hunt, *Regional wage variations in Britain, 1850–1914* (Oxford, 1973), pp 296–7. 26 Ó Gráda, 'Some aspects of nineteenth-century Irish emigration' in L.M. Cullen and T.C. Smout (eds), *Comparative aspects of Scottish and Irish economic and social history, 1600–1900* (Edinburgh, 1977), p. 71, fn. 6; Fitzpatrick, '"A peculiar tramping people"', pp 642–3.

tlement. An uncompromising Protestantism, and an attendant anti-Catholicism, was central to the forging of a national identity in Britain from the early eighteenth century. In this political and cultural development, Catholics were considered alien and suspect, and were often used as scapegoats during political or social crises. Linda Colley notes, for instance, that it was 'no accident' that the anti-Catholic Gordon Riots in London in 1780 occasioned the first collaboration between English and Scottish artisans in major protest; or that Catholic emancipation in 1829 drew huge numbers of Welshmen and women into a nationwide petitioning campaign for the first time.[27] It must be stressed, however, that anti-Irish feeling was not simply a dimension of religious prejudice against Catholics, for British Catholics were also alarmed by the flood of Irish immigrants in the nineteenth century, particularly during the Famine. Still, religious prejudice was a factor in the antagonism between the Irish and large sections of the host community, and it tended to reinforce the racial stereotypes of the Irish which became particularly evident in popular discourse and in the cartoons of *Punch* and other journals from the 1840s.[28]

Not all images of the Irish were negative; but cartoons, in which 'Paddy' was depicted as a menacing brute with simian or fiendish features, became increasingly more evident during the main periods of social and political unrest in Ireland, certainly from the time of the Repeal agitation.[29] Ó'Tuathaigh states, then, that it was not only the Catholicism of the vast majority of Irish immigrants but also their identification with the broad political agenda of Irish nationalism which set them apart from native British society, and made them more inclined to gather in small colonies reflecting their own cultural and political identity.[30] Indeed, the Davitts became very much a part of the Irish community in Haslingden, which, on their arrival, numbered almost one thousand, roughly ten per cent of the town's overall population.[31] Martin Davitt was bi-lingual with a good standard of English literacy, and at his house in Rock Hall he wrote letters for other members of the community and held classes in reading and writing English. Yet it was Irish that was principally spoken in Rock Hall, and, like others of their generation, Martin and Catherine Davitt not only imparted their native tongue to their children but also other

27 Colley, *Britons: forging the nation, 1707–1837* (London, 1996), p. 24.   **28** The nature of anti-Irish sentiment, and the degree to which it was or was not racist, has been the matter of some debate; see S. Gilley, 'English attitudes to the Irish in England, 1780–1900' in *Immigrants and minorities in British society*, C. Holmes (ed.) (London, 1978), pp 81–110; Ó Tuathaigh, 'The Irish in nineteenth-century Britain', pp 159–63; and L.P. Curtis Jr, *Apes and angels: the Irishman in Victorian caricature* (Washington and London, 1997), pp 191–2.   **29** Curtis, *Apes and angels*, pp 31–4.   **30** Ó Tuathaigh, 'The Irish in nineteenth-century Britain', pp 163–4.   **31** John Dunleavy, *Davitt's Haslingden* (Haslingden, 2006), p. 6.

aspects of their cultural heritage. The *céilí* was the main form of entertainment in the community, and Davitt himself could remember social evenings in the house of their neighbour, Molly Madden, where, assembled around the fire, friends and neighbours would be treated to folk tales, such as stories about the 'good people', or fairies.[32]

A belief in fairies and other supernatural entities was prevalent in Irish peasant culture throughout much of the nineteenth century. As S.J. Connolly has shown, such beliefs cannot always be easily explained as innocent folk tradition. There were, for instance, cases in which desperate parents, convinced that their child had been abducted by fairies and replaced by a 'changeling', would subject the child to forms of abuse in an attempt to banish the unearthly entity and thereby reclaim the real child.[33] Davitt became familiar with such tales during the evenings of story-telling in Haslingden. The fairies, he later wrote, 'were very real entities to every soul in that little community of exiles from the West. Had [the fairies] not, to the knowledge of the oldest members, been frequently known to have exchanged infants at birth in many parts of Mayo?'. He recounts that one night he found his mother, 'after the evening tales', hastily putting her children to bed, before returning to the blazing fire, where she laid four plates – one containing bread, one meal, one butter, and a jug of milk placed on the last – 'in case of a chance visit by the fairies that night'. From Davitt's perspective, writing years later, such peasant beliefs were a 'temporary relief from the trials of misfortune',[34] misfortune which he largely attributed to the excesses of Irish landlordism and British rule.

It was, indeed, the graphic tales of the horrors of the Famine and of a peasantry brutalized by landlordism that really fired the imagination of those present during the evening gatherings in Haslingden. 'Faces would pale, and eyes would flash, in the fire-light' as accounts were related by those with first-hand experience. As a boy, Davitt himself would often retire to bed after such evenings and dream of avenging his family's eviction and forced exile, and 'wonder […] whether I should be big enough to give [the Irish landlord] a licking'.[35] In his later political speeches and writings, he would often place strong emphasis on the need for the Irish nation to assert its 'manhood' in the face of British rule. Resistance to oppression and to structures of power and privilege was, in his view, almost a moral imperative. It was in this context that he made what was, on the face of it, a remarkably callous statement on the Famine dead:

> There is possibly no chapter in the wide records of human suffering and wrong so full of shame – measureless, unadulterated, sickening

32 'Autobiographical notes', DP, TCD, MS 9460/16–18. **33** Connolly, *Priests and people in pre-famine Ireland, 1780–1845* (Dublin, 2001), pp 113–14. **34** As above, fn. 32. **35** DP, TCD, MS 9640/22.

shame – as that which tells us of […] a million people – including, pre-
sumably, two hundred thousand adult men – lying down to die in a land
out of which forty-five millions' worth of food was being exported, in
one year alone, for rent – the product of their own soil – and making
no effort, combined or otherwise, to assert even the animal's right of
existence – the right to live by the necessities of its nature. It stands
unparalleled in human history, with nothing approaching it to the complete surrender of all the ordinary attributes of manhood by almost a
whole nation, in the face of an artificial famine.

He even went so far as to remark that those who perished during the Famine
were of no great loss to the Irish nation.[36] These ruthless comments were more
a measure of Davitt's hatred of British rule. Nevertheless, he still held that, by
failing to revolt against the ravages of a famine born out of political misrule and
injustice, the peasantry had failed to demonstrate an indomitability and moral
courage which was peculiar to the Celtic race.[37] Of the Celtic spirit, he wrote,

Ireland, even in her darkest period of suffering and oppression, could
not a least [*sic*] produce from amongst her own people […] a
Schopenhauer, a Nietzsche, or even an Ibsen. Neither racial nor other
Celtic traits encourage a philosophy, which raises the question of
whether life is worth living.[38]

Even though the Famine was largely over by 1849, emigration continued;
in fact, the Emigration Commissioners estimated that 368,764 persons left
Ireland in 1852.[39] Martin and Catherine Davitt saw little prospect, therefore,
of a viable life for themselves or their children back in their native Mayo.
Having settled into immigrant life in Haslingden, they had another child,
James, in 1853 (although he did not survive beyond the age of two). By this
stage, Martin Davitt had gained employment as a farm labourer, and would
later become a mason's labourer.[40] He and his wife seem to have managed to
secure successive jobs outside the factory system. However, from the age of
12, their eldest child, Mary, went to work in a cotton-mill, a truly Dickensian
working environment which would also claim her siblings as child labourers. Factory reform legislation in the first half of the nineteenth century had
limited the working hours of children between the ages of 9 and 13 to eight
hours a day. Young child workers between these ages were required to attend
school for part of the day, leaving the remaining hours available for work as

36 Davitt, *The fall*, pp 47–8, 66. 37 Ibid., p. 53. 38 DP, TCD, MS 9460/7. 39 Kinealy, *This great calamity*, p. 298. 40 Moody, *Davitt*, p. 13.

'half-timers' in the textile factories. Older children between the ages of 13 and 18 worked a total of 10½ hours between 6.00 a.m. and 6.00 p.m., with a shorter day on Saturdays.[41] At 9 years of age, the young Davitt was enrolled at a junior school and could have entered employment as a 'half-timer', of which there were 32,000 in Britain in 1850.[42] However, he rebelled against his early schooling, and, after posing as a 13-year-old, he was taken on as a full-time bobbin tender at John Parkinson's Ewood Bridge cotton mill, a couple of miles outside Haslingden. Thus began his career as a child textile labourer, starting on a wage of 2s. 6d. a week.[43]

The use of child labour in Britain's mills has, as F.M.L. Thompson points out, directly influenced the popular image of the Industrial Revolution as a dark, sordid episode. Despite the humanitarian zeal of social reformers in the early nineteenth century, children were still open to abuse, both physically at the hands of employers or superiors (for which there is ample evidence),[44] and also through exposure to an exacting, unforgiving industrial regime which demanded long hours in an unhealthy environment, and in which workers' safety was sacrificed in the pursuit of efficiency and productivity. In fact, in the second cotton factory where the young Davitt worked, Lawrence Whitaker's Holden mill, again just outside Haslingden, a boy named John Ginty, who was a neighbour of the Davitts in Rock Hall, was killed after sustaining a head injury in an accidental encounter with a belt shaft. He was one of several of Michael's peers to sustain serious injuries; indeed, in Britain's industrial towns, many boys and young men bore the physical signs of having been maimed or disabled in such accidents. After the death of John Ginty, Martin and Catherine Davitt moved their son on to the nearby Stellfoxe's Victoria cotton mill at Baxenden. In this factory, Michael was employed in the spinning-room, joining threads which had broken in the spinning process, and for this he earned five shillings a week. However, it was while working here that he himself, aged 11 years, became one of the many children to suffer a serious physical trauma while employed in the British industrial system. After being forcibly put to work on a machine which he was too young to operate, he had his right arm caught and crushed between cog-wheels, an injury so severe that amputation of the limb was later required in order to save his life.[45]

Though Michael's injury left him with a serious disability, the incident proved fortunate in the long term. Free from the grinding pressures of industrial life, he was given the opportunity to continue with his education after a cotton mill proprietor and prominent Methodist, John Dean, offered to pay

41 Edward Royle, *Modern Britain: a social history, 1750–1985* (London, 1987), pp 192–5. 42 F.M.L. Thompson, *The rise of respectable society: a social history of Victorian Britain, 1830–1900* (London, 1988), p. 81. 43 Moody, *Davitt*, p. 15. 44 Thompson, *The rise*, p. 23. 45 Moody, *Davitt*, pp 16–18.

for his tuition at the local Wesleyan school in Haslingden, which was under the direction of a highly respected teacher, George Poskett. It was here that Michael would spend the next four years, in an environment conducive to intellectual development, and one which gave him a sound basis for his later life as a man of letters.[46] While a pupil at Poskett's school, he also attended evening classes in the local Mechanics' Institute, one of the many such educational establishments for artisans and labourers, which had resulted from the work of Sir James Kay-Shuttleworth, the founder of popular education in England. In Haslingden, a local physician, Dr John Binns, had been instrumental in having a library, newsroom and lecture hall added to a new building as a way of reviving the Institute in the area,[47] and it was here that Davitt, during his teenage years, had access to a wide range of books, and to leading newspapers, reviews and periodicals. The institutes played an important role in the social – and as Davitt later believed, moral – development of the working class in the north of England. He recalled,

> Round this establishment [Haslingden's institute] might be seen every evening, after labour, men from the factories and workshops who like [me had?] an ambition to make self-help and leisure from toil supply to some extent [...] an education beyond our worldly means to attain. 'The Mechanics', as the place was familiarly termed, soon became the line which separated the sober[,] industrious and intelligent working man of the locality from the rest of that class which (at that time) spent large portions of its earnings in public houses after each 'pay day'.[48]

Davitt's autodidactic reading not only satisfied his youthful curiosity but undoubtedly also contributed to his early political education. This education was also significantly influenced by the English radicals whom he would have encountered in Haslingden and surrounding areas in these early years. Guest speakers were frequently invited by Binns to address the Institute, and among them were prominent social reformers and former Chartists;[49] it was probably here, in fact, that Davitt heard the veteran Chartist, Ernest Jones, speak, 'the first man after my father whom I ever heard denouncing landlordism, not only in Ireland but in England'.[50] Jones, who was a practising barrister in Manchester in the early 1860s, was the leading figure in the working-class movement in Lancashire at that time. His appeal for unity between Irish nationalism and British democracy, and statements of his, such as 'Those who

46 Ibid., p. 19; Dunleavy, *Davitt's Haslingden*, pp 12–13. 47 Dunleavy, *Davitt's Haslingden*, pp 14–15. 48 Davitt, *Jottings*, p. 86. 49 Dunleavy, *Davitt's Haslingden*, p. 15. 50 Davitt, *The Times-Parnell commission: speech delivered by Michael Davitt in defence of the Land League* (London, 1890), p. 30.

ejected the cottar in Ireland created the pauper in Great Britain', made a huge impression on Davitt in his formative years. Indeed, Davitt's early experiences of factory life had given him an affinity with the labouring masses in Britain, despite the regular upsurges of Irish-baiting and sectarianism with which he and other Irish immigrants in Lancashire had to contend.[51] Even during his time in Poskett's Wesleyan school – where, as it happens, around half of the pupils were 'half-timers' – he gained a richer experience than most Irish or, indeed, English Catholics, and it impressed him that not once in his four years at the school did he ever hear his headmaster express a sectarian sentiment.[52]

Despite this affinity, however, Davitt always very much identified with the small Irish Catholic enclave in Haslingden from which he came, and the trajectory of his political activism from his late teens does not indicate an 'assimilation' into mainstream working-class life in Britain.[53] During sectarian riots, which were a feature of life not only for the Irish diaspora in Britain but also in North America during the nineteenth century,[54] he took an active part in the defence of his area. On one occasion in 1868, when he was in his early twenties, he drew a Colt revolver to see off an advancing Protestant crowd intent on destroying the local Catholic church.[55] He later looked back with pride on his early days as part of the embattled immigrant community in Haslingden. The phrase, 'nemo me impune lacessit',[56] could not, he insisted, be more appropriately said of any section of the Irish diaspora than the 'Irishrie of the North of England', who distinguished themselves by their strong nationalism and 'indomitable pluck', the very same spirit which was 'abundantly illustrated in the daring' Fenian enterprises in that part of England.[57]

Davitt himself joined the Irish Republican Brotherhood (IRB) in 1865 at the age of 19, with the full knowledge and backing of his parents.[58] In being 'agin the government' in this new, clandestine role, he was in many ways following in his father's footsteps, Martin Davitt having been connected with a secret Ribbon society in Mayo in the 1830s.[59] Perhaps on account of the 'pluck' for which he was now becoming known, Michael, despite his disability, was appointed the senior figure, or 'centre', of the Rossendale 'circle' of the IRB

51 Moody, *Davitt*, pp 21–2. 52 Ibid., p. 19; Dunleavy, *Davitt's Haslingden*, pp 12–13. 53 W.J. Lowe, *The Irish in mid-Victorian Lancashire: the shaping of a working-class community* (New York, 1989), maintains that during the two decades after the Irish Famine, the second-generation Irish in Lancashire showed signs of having become assimilated into mainstream working-class life, pp 109–44, pp 145–78. 54 See Donald M. MacRaild, 'Crossing migrant frontiers: comparative reflections on Irish migrants in Britain and the United States during the nineteenth century' in Donald M. MacRaild (ed.), *The great famine and beyond: Irish migrants in Britain in the nineteenth and twentieth centuries* (Dublin, 2000), pp 57–63. 55 Moody, *Davitt*, pp 52–3. 56 'No one strikes me with impunity'. 57 Davitt, *Jottings*, pp 13–14. 58 Moody, *Davitt*, p. 44. Davitt no doubt became associated with Fenianism at an even earlier point; see Davitt, *The Times-Parnell comm*, p. 20. 59 Quoted in Carla King, *Michael Davitt* (Dundalk, 1999), pp 11–12.

not long after joining the organization, a position which put him in command of around fifty men. There was no great surprise in his decision to join the republican movement; many young Irish immigrants in Lancashire had been recruited into its ranks. Frank Harran, who lived near the Davitts in Haslingden, later remarked that 'every smart, respectable young fellow' among the Irish in the town was a member.[60] Davitt certainly fitted this description. After leaving the Wesleyan school in 1861 he had secured employment as an errand boy with the postmaster of Haslingden, Henry Cockcroft, who, in conjunction with his post office, also ran a small printing and stationary establishment. Shortly after commencing employment, Davitt was promoted to book-keeper in the business, and would later be given greater responsibilities in both the postal department and the printing-house.[61] At this time he was what could be described as an upwardly mobile young man; he was, indeed, one of the best educated among his peers in the town.[62] He became a good friend of the Cockcroft family, and was highly praised by Henry Cockcroft himself, especially for the ability which he demonstrated in operating the printing press with one arm.[63]

While employed here, Davitt quietly went about his Fenian business. He increasingly gave more time to his clandestine activities, and in February 1867 he led a detachment of IRB men from Haslingden on a daring, albeit unsuccessful, mission to raid an arsenal at Chester castle. This military operation, which involved Fenians from throughout the north of England, was aborted at the eleventh hour after having been compromised by a Fenian informer, the Liverpool-based J.J. Corydon, who was also responsible for providing the police with information on the ill-fated IRB insurrection in Dublin the following month, and who would later give evidence against Davitt.[64] By the summer of 1868 Davitt had become so heavily involved in the republican movement that he resigned from his post at Cockcroft's in order to devote his energies full time to his new, high-ranking position as organizing secretary and arms-agent of the IRB in England and Scotland. Posing as a hawker over the next two years, he toured various centres of Irish population throughout Britain, putting his intelligence and organizational skills to use in raising support and funds for the procurement of arms.[65] Particularly during his tours in Scotland, he would make contacts that would serve him well in his later political life. As Máirtín Ó Catháin has noted, 'Whether in secret conclave with

60 Quoted in Moody, *Davitt*, p. 44. 61 Ibid., pp 19–20. 62 Only one other young man from the Irish community attended classes in the Mechanics' Institute in Haslingden while Davitt was there; Davitt, *Jottings*, p. 87. 63 Moody, *Davitt*, p. 20; Dunleavy, *Davitt's Haslingden*, pp 13–14. 64 Shin-ichi Takagami, 'The fenian rising in Dublin, March 1867', *IHS*, 29: 115 (1995), 345; Moody, *Davitt*, pp 49, 91–107; John Newsinger, *Fenianism in mid-Victorian Britain* (London, 1994), pp 53–4. 65 Moody, *Davitt*, p. 53.

artisans in an empty warehouse in Glasgow's dilapidated and fever-ridden Bridgegate district or in a pub or temperance hall […] in rural Lanarkshire, Davitt was unconsciously making himself into a myth'.[66]

Always security-conscious and careful in his movements, Davitt was convinced that the police were entirely ignorant of his Fenian activities in these early years.[67] What he did not know was that he had come under the notice of the authorities in the months after the Chester castle episode, and that by January 1869 Dublin Castle had opened a file on him. The intelligence was, however, quite fragmented and his position within the organization was not fully appreciated; even the name on his file was spelt incorrectly.[68] It was not until the end of 1869 that he really came under heavy police surveillance, directly through his correspondence and association with Arthur Forrester, a fellow Fenian who had taken part in the Chester castle operation and who was also an arms-agent, although not as senior as Davitt. Given the problems which the movement had had with informers among its ranks, Forrester argued that 'exemplary measures' should be taken against those suspected as police agents. In December 1869, after a young Fenian from Salford, named Burke, had aroused his deep suspicions, Forrester wrote to Davitt, informing him that he had enough of a case against Burke to warrant his execution. Davitt, according to his own later accounts, strongly believed that the case had no merit. However, convinced that Forrester was fixed on an independent and immediate course of action, and that he was averse to persuasion otherwise, he wrote back, appearing to agree with the assassination bid but impressing upon Forrester the prudence of awaiting the approval of the organization's leadership. Davitt always later maintained, both publicly and privately, that the letter was designed to prevent precipitate action against Burke and therefore save his life.[69] The urgency with which Davitt replied to Forrester and the manner in which the letter was phrased certainly lends support to this claim, not to mention his later consistent testimonies to that effect. Writing to Forrester many years later, he remarked,

> No man knew me more intimately while in the fenian movement than
> you did, and if you can recall the persons and incidents, the suspicions,
> the hasty accusations incidental to meetings and conventions in the
> north of England in our boy-conspirator days […] you will, I think,
> remember also how strenuously and consistently I always opposed the
> rude suggestions, begot of morbid suspicion, about extreme measures,
> punishments, &c., for alleged treasons to the organisation.[70]

---

66 Máirtín Ó Catháin, 'Michael Davitt and Scotland', *Saothar*, 25 (1999), 19. **67** See Davitt's letter to Arthur Forrester, 3 Aug. 1894, DP, TCD, MS 9341/437. **68** Moody, *Davitt*, pp 55–6. **69** Davitt, *The Times-Parnell comm*, pp 38–9; indeed, he claimed that the supreme council of the IRB was opposed, in principle, to such executions, p. 21. **70** As above, fn. 67.

Despite Davitt's later vehement denials that he had been central to a murder plot, the 'pen letter', as it became known,[71] proved useful to his political opponents during much of his later political career.[72]

In the immediate circumstances of 1869-70, the letter seriously compromised his underground activities. Less than twenty-four hours after he had sent it, it was seized by police in Liverpool when they arrested Forrester, who was also caught in possession of a number of revolvers. Forrester was, of course, not now in a position to assassinate Burke; but the incident had brought Davitt, and even the rest of his family, under the scrutiny of the police at a time when he was heavily engaged in gun-running.[73] So immersed was Davitt in these conspiratorial activities that in the early months of 1870 he prevailed upon his parents and his sisters, Anne and Sabina, to move to America to join Mary, who had emigrated to Scranton, Pennsylvania, five years earlier.[74] By this stage, the police were closing in on him, building vital intelligence on an elaborate gun-trafficking operation of his which was based in Birmingham. In fact, it was only weeks after his parents' departure for New York that he and John Wilson, a gunsmith from Birmingham with whom he had been dealing, were separately arrested on 14 May at Paddington railway station, London, and subsequently charged with treason-felony. At their later trial, held in the Old Bailey in July, the informer, Corydon, was produced by the prosecution to prove Davitt's involvement in the IRB and specifically to try to connect him with the Chester castle raid. More damning, however, was the 'pen' letter, not necessarily in itself, but more so because Forrester, now released from prison and called as a witness by the defence, perjured himself, quite transparently, by denying his attendance at Fenian meetings and by stating that Davitt was not the original author of the letter, thereby giving the document added significance as a piece of evidence before the judge. The political climate at the time did not augur well for the two defendants either. Just over a year earlier, the new Liberal prime minister, W.E. Gladstone, had released forty-nine Fenian prisoners in response to a popular amnesty campaign in Ireland. The significance of the gesture meant, however, that those subsequently convicted of subversive offences would face severe sentences. As it transpired, Davitt and Wilson were both found guilty on 18 July. Davitt received fifteen years' penal servitude and Wilson, despite having had no involvement in the IRB, received seven years.[75]

The amnesty movement, which began in 1868 and which became embodied in the Amnesty Association from June 1869, had gained considerable strength by the time of Davitt's conviction. It was nominally under the lead-

71 It was known as such because, in the letter, 'pen' was the code-word for 'revolver'. 72 See Moody, 'Michael Davitt and the "pen" letter', *IHS*, 4:15 (1945), pp 224–53. 73 Moody, *Davitt*, pp 61–7. 74 Ibid., pp 23, 79. 75 Ibid., pp 67–100, 121.

ership of Isaac Butt, a gifted lawyer and later MP for Limerick, but the organizational brains behind the movement was the Association's secretary, John
Nolan, a leading Dublin republican and member of the IRB's supreme council.[76] Amnesty agitation was not the preserve of Fenians, but the Association
attracted many urban rank-and-file members of the IRB. Within a few, short
years its branches were widespread, making it a hugely significant umbrella
organization in political mobilization; indeed, the nationalist fervour which
it excited ultimately served to precipitate the emergence of the home rule movement under Butt. In the latter part of 1869, following the release of the Fenian
prisoners, Nolan had organized a series of massive amnesty rallies, one of which,
at Cabra, Dublin, attracted an estimated 200,000 people.[77] Protesters had come
from around the country to hear the demand for the release of more prisoners, a message keenly felt by Irish Gladstonian Liberals. Gladstone, for his part,
wanted to push ahead with early releases.[78] However, despite the popular
protests in Ireland, he was determined that he would not be coerced – and certainly would not be seen to be coerced – into taking such steps. Eventually,
in January 1871, against the backdrop of an opportune lull in the amnesty campaign, the government sanctioned the discharge of yet more Fenians, among
them such figures as John O'Leary, John Devoy and Jeremiah O'Donovan
Rossa, albeit on the condition that they live outside the United Kingdom.[79]

Having secured the freedom of these prisoners, the Amnesty Association
continued to agitate for the release of around twenty remaining Irish republican convicts, including Davitt. In the view of the government, these inmates
could not be recognized as political prisoners because of the gravity of their
offences. The arbitrary line drawn here between political and criminal offences
was a point on which amnesty campaigners and home rule MPs vigorously
challenged the government. Another main plank of the campaign was the
demand for an independent investigation into the treatment of prisoners. This
was a particularly sensitive issue for the government, given that in 1870 a commission of inquiry had found grounds to support allegations of mistreatment
of Fenian inmates, particularly in the case of O'Donovan Rossa. It was through
the agitation around this issue that Davitt would become a symbolic figure in
the amnesty campaign during the 1870s, owing to his repeated claims that he
was subjected to ill-treatment precisely because of his Irish political offences,
and that he was denied the privileges enjoyed by other ordinary prisoners with
whom he was classed and among whom he worked. His case was popularized
by leading Fenians, including Nolan. Butt also took an early interest in the

76 Ibid., pp 120–1; Davitt, *The fall*, pp 86, 97–9. **77** Owen McGee, *The IRB: the Irish Republican Brotherhood from the Land League to Sinn Féin* (Dublin, 2005), pp 40–8. **78** Roy Jenkins, *Gladstone* (London, 1995), p. 342. **79** R.V. Comerford, *The fenians in context* (Dublin, 1998), pp 170–85.

conditions of his incarceration. And from 1874 a vigorous parliamentary campaign was led by John O'Connor Power, MP for Mayo, who was later ably supported by Charles Stewart Parnell from 1875.[80] Davitt had known O'Connor Power, who was also from an Irish immigrant background in Lancashire, in his earlier days when they were both Fenians.[81]

Following his trial, Davitt had been moved to Millbank penitentiary in London, near Westminster, where he was classified with the rest of the prison population. As such, he was placed in solitary confinement and employed in the mind-numbing work of oakum picking. He was occupied in this task for at least ten hours a day, seated on a bucket, the single article of furniture in his stone-floored cell, and only breaking from the tedium of the work for prayers in the chapel, exercise in the yard, and to eat the meals which constituted a very basic diet. The institution's rules forbade conversation among the prisoners, and the loneliness which Davitt felt here was compounded by the 'solemn tones' of the nearby Westminster tower clock, which were a constant reminder of how slowly time was 'creeping along'.[82] After ten months here, during which time he feared for his own sanity, he was moved to Dartmoor prison in Devon, and it was here that he would serve most of his sentence.

Conditions in Dartmoor were worse than he had found them in any of the prisons where he was held during the 1870s. Prisoners were kept in narrow, poorly lit corrugated-iron cells with virtually no ventilation, save that which was provided by a space of several inches at the bottom of the door. Davitt later recounted that at times he would have to kneel at the foot of the door in order to catch a breath. The air that he did access carried the fetid smell of fellow prisoners and the stench of their excrement which the prison authorities kept in tubs at the end of each landing, sometimes for days at a time, for use as manure. The food ration of Dartmoor was similar in quantity to that of Millbank, but the quality was, as Davitt put it, 'simply execrable'. The food was often inedible, rotten and infested with cockroaches. Davitt claimed, in fact, that prisoners were so tormented by hunger that they would consume almost anything:

> It is quite a common occurrence in Dartmoor [he wrote] for men to be reported and punished for eating candles, boot oil, and other repulsive articles; and notwithstanding that a highly offensive smell is purposely given to prison candles to prevent their being eaten instead of burned,

---

80 Moody, *Davitt*, pp 155–6, 175–7; Davitt, *The fall*, p. 93. 81 Ibid., pp 47–8. 82 Davitt, *The prison life of Michael Davitt, related by himself* (London, 1878). This was later published in pamphlet form as *The prison life of Michael Davitt, related by himself, together with his evidence before the house of lord [sic] commission on convict prison life* (Dublin, 1882), repr. in Carla King (ed.), *Michael Davitt: collected writings* (Bristol, 2001), vol. i, pp 49–53; see also T.W. Moody, 'Michael Davitt in penal servitude, 1870–77', *Studies*, 30:120 (1941), 16–30.

men are driven by a system of half starvation into an animal-like voracity, and anything that a dog would eat is nowise repugnant to their taste. I have seen men eat old poultices found buried in heaps of rubbish I was assisting in carting away, and have seen bits of candle pulled out of the prison cesspool and eaten, after the human soil was wiped off them![83]

On entering Dartmoor, Davitt was put to work stone-breaking, in a shed with about eighty other men. With the use of only one arm, however, his hand blistered quickly, and he was alternatively attached to the 'cart-party', a team of eight prisoners, all harnessed, pulling a heavy cart laden with prison materials, from stones to manure. The harness which Davitt was forced to wear in this work caused an injury to the stump of his amputated arm, and, on doctor's orders, he was returned to breaking granite. This did not benefit his health, for in winter weather he was forced to work outside, in the cold and damp. He was convinced, indeed, that it was through his experience of forced labour at Dartmoor that his health was irreparably damaged. In the winter of 1872-3 he complained to the doctor of symptoms which he believed were indicative of heart and lung disease, although, on examination, the doctor could make no such diagnosis.[84] One particular form of prison work which Davitt attributed to his feelings of ill-health was the breaking of putrefying bones which were to be used as fertilizer: 'The stench arising from their decomposition, together with the noxious exhalations from the action of the sun's rays on the cesspool outside, no words could adequately express – [the 'bone shed'] was a veritable charnel house'.[85]

As a Fenian prisoner, Davitt was kept under close observation, more so than other inmates, and was regularly subjected to strip-searches. He was refused permission to associate with another Fenian, Thomas Chambers, during the routine walk in the prison yard on Sundays, even though association with a fellow inmate was a privilege enjoyed by ordinary prisoners during this period of exercise. Davitt's sense of isolation and his view that he was being persecuted was heightened by the fact that his frequent requests for permission to receive visits from friends and associates were denied. Close relatives could visit; but, then, his family was in America, and he himself was not prepared to have his mother make such an onerous journey to England for the sake of a short prison visit.[86] He always felt the weight of responsibility for having led his parents and sisters to leave England for America in 1870. When he learned of his father's death in Pennsylvania in December 1871 he was tormented with guilt and remorse. Aged 25, and only months into his term of

83 Ibid., p. 59. 84 Moody, *Davitt*, p. 154. 85 Davitt, *Prison life*, pp 60–1. 86 Moody, *Davitt*, p. 153.

imprisonment in Dartmoor, he experienced a particularly low point of despondency. However, he always seemed better able to serve his time stoically, and, using the same influence that had ensured his family's departure in the first place, he continued to dissuade his mother from undertaking the trip back across the Atlantic.[87]

In September 1872, his plight as a prisoner was made known to the public in a letter which he managed to have smuggled out of Dartmoor, and which was subsequently released to the press in Britain and Ireland. In it, he outlined his experiences of prison life thus far, and gave instances which he believed confirmed a policy of victimization by the prison authorities, including strip-searches, the denial of visits, and the forced labour in the 'cart-party' which, he maintained, left his bone protruding through the stump of his amputated arm.[88] The letter won him considerable publicity, and the home secretary, H.A. Bruce, ordered an inquiry into his allegations. However, when it was officially concluded that there was no evidence to support the claims, the Amnesty Association pushed for an independent tribunal to investigate the case.[89] Davitt challenged the official view that he was treated like any other prisoner. He later pointed out that, despite a record of good conduct, he was subjected to a form of punishment which was nothing more 'than a gratuitous piece of petty tyranny'.[90] While Moody has acknowledged that Davitt was routinely subjected to the vindictiveness of warders, he nevertheless asserts that there is no evidence of any intent on the part of the home office or the prison governor to single Davitt out for special punishment. It was owing to Davitt's status as a high-risk inmate, Moody explains, that he was kept under close scrutiny, separated from Chambers, and denied visits with friends, at least during most of his time in Dartmoor.[91] But, for Davitt, it was precisely this treatment which effectively amounted to victimization, given that he was supposed to have been treated as an ordinary prisoner. His protests essentially pointed to the anomaly of his having been classified along with the general convict population while being subjected to special treatment because of his political associations. On his charges of official victimization, Moody himself considers it odd that O'Connor Power was able to visit a Fenian in Portsmouth jail in 1874 but was refused permission to see Davitt in Dartmoor during that year.[92]

By the mid-1870s, the amnesty campaign, which was now mainly centred around parliamentary agitation, had attracted the support of English radicals and Liberals. Power and Parnell employed obstructionist tactics in parliament to highlight the issue during the spring and summer of 1877, Power using Davitt's letters to reinforce his argument. Even Gladstone, as leader of

---

87 Ibid., pp 167–8. **88** *FJ*, 3 Sept. 1872. **89** Moody, *Davitt*, pp 175–6. **90** Davitt, *Prison life*, p. 70. **91** Moody, *Davitt*, p. 156. **92** Ibid., pp 156–7, 159–60.

the opposition, now declared himself firmly in favour of a full amnesty. It was in this political climate that, after more than seven years' imprisonment, Davitt found himself released on 19 December 1877, not on the amnesty terms extended to the previous Fenians prisoners, but on the basis of a conditional licence.[93] On his emergence from Dartmoor he was in quite a poor physical state. He weighed only eight stone, ten pounds, 'not, I think, the proper weight for a man six feet high, and at the age of thirty one'.[94] Several other Fenians, released only weeks after him, showed similar signs of weakness and fatigue. One of them, Charles McCarthy, actually collapsed and died of heart failure within a matter of days.[95] In the months after his discharge, Davitt became prominent in the controversy surrounding McCarthy's death, and threw himself into the continuing agitation for the release of remaining prisoners. However, his experiences in Dartmoor led him to campaign not only on the question of Irish political prisoners but also on the wider issue of prison reform.

In June 1878 he made a submission before the Kimberley commission, which was investigating the working of the Penal Servitude Acts and the management of prisons. Davitt himself was questioned on some of his previous published allegations, which amounted to an indictment of the prison system, especially the regime in Dartmoor. During the course of this examination he qualified some of his claims: he now stated that he had observed only one man eating rotten poultices, although it was clear from the statements made by the governor of Dartmoor, W.V.F Harris, during the commission's hearings, that the practice was not confined to one case. Generally, many of Davitt's charges (besides his own claims of personal victimization) were sustained in the commission's findings, which were later presented in Lord Kimberley's report in July 1879. In fact, while the report found the penal servitude system adequate, it nevertheless recommended certain reforms, including some of those suggested by Davitt (although he was not directly referred to), notably his recommendation that first-time offenders should be segregated from more seasoned convicts.[96] The psychology of prisoners and the issue of penal servitude was something in which Davitt always maintained an interest,[97] especially in the latter part of the 1890s when, as an MP, he himself investigated conditions in British prisons. At that time, he was praised for his efforts by Oscar Wilde, who had famously served two years hard labour after being found guilty of homosexual offences in 1895. 'No one knows better than yourself', Wilde wrote to Davitt, 'how terrible life in an English prison is, and what cruelties result from the stupidity of officialdom'.[98]

93 Ibid., pp 179–80. **94** Davitt, *Prison life*, p. 63. **95** Moody, *Davitt*, pp 189–90. **96** Moody, *Davitt*, pp 189–90, 209–20; Davitt, *Prison life*, pp 78–80. **97** For Davitt's views on the various types of prisoner represented in prison life, see *Leaves from a prison diary, or, lectures to a 'solitary' audience* (London, 1885), vol. i. **98** Wilde to Davitt, May–June 1897, DP, TCD, MS 9448/3604.

Davitt's case had been the *cause célèbre* of the amnesty campaign through-out the 1870s.[99] Largely unknown before his conviction, he gained notoriety through his prison letters from 1872 onwards and, after his release, through his own fuller account of the conditions of his incarceration, as outlined in *The prison life of Michael Davitt, as related by himself* (1878). Moody points out that in the history of Fenianism many other Irish republicans had had har-rowing jail experiences, but none who survived and later went on to assume a significant political role, with the exception of the 1916 leader, Tom Clarke, was as isolated as Davitt or incarcerated for such a lengthy period.[1] Davitt's experiences were a matter of public record by the time of his release. But it was during his appearances on public platforms in Ireland and Britain in the months after his discharge, and later in America, that he made an even greater impact. He cut a striking figure on the platform: tall and lean with dark hair and penetrating eyes, and bearing the sign of his disability which, as Sheehy Skeffington put it, 'was the symbol of his maimed life [...] Through it [...] the multitude [could] visualize the supreme torments this man had undergone, the grandeur of the suffering that had fostered his grandeur of soul'.[2] It was this image, besides his obvious organizational skills, that shaped his later icon-ic status as 'the father of the Land League'.

It is highly unlikely that Davitt had any preconceived ideas about a land agitation campaign in Ireland before his release from Dartmoor, despite later claims to the contrary;[3] he certainly could not have foreseen his subsequent political role at the helm of that agrarian movement which began in Mayo in 1879. He was even uncertain about his employment opportunities imme-diately after his release, and was considering employment as a commercial traveller for a liquor merchant in Dublin,[4] a not uncommon occupation for a Fenian.[5] When, in January 1878, he visited his native Straide, it was for the first time in twenty-seven years.[6] The environment was essentially new to him, given his upbringing in England; indeed, his background in industrial Lancashire was even evident by his accent. He had, of course, grown up lis-tening to his parents' recollections of their earlier days in Mayo and of their experiences of eviction and emigration; but the post-Famine Ireland to which he himself returned as an adult was a society that had already undergone sig-nificant social and cultural transformation. Changes had taken place in the

99 Moody, *Davitt*, p. 175. 1 Ibid., p. 181. 2 Sheehy Skeffington, *Michael Davitt*, p. 23. 3 Davitt, *Times-Parnell comm*, p. 2 4 Moody, *Davitt*, p. 194. 5 In *Nationalist revolutionaries in Ireland, 1858–1922* (Oxford, 1987), Tom Garvin notes that, 'Of 81 IRB organizers, leaders and activists under police surveillance between 1880 and 1902 [one ...] fifth were travelling salesmen, often in the liquor trade, commercial agents or middlemen', p. 38. A job which involved visiting drink-ing establishments with familiar republican clientele might perhaps have been something with which Davitt felt comfortable, despite a strong personal aversion to alcohol. 6 Moody, *Davitt*, p. 192.

country's social structure, and the tenant class from which his family had come was gradually decreasing relative to the larger farming group within the agricultural community.[7] While in prison, he must have learned that the land question was again finding its way into political discourse: in 1876 Butt proposed legislation that would concede the 'three fs' – fair rent, fixity of tenure and free sale – the focal point of the land reform movement in the decades after the Famine; and during a speech in the house of commons in May 1877, Parnell ventured the view that peasant proprietorship was necessary in order to settle the land question.[8] However, on his release, Davitt gave no indication whatsoever of having considered agitation along agrarian lines.

John Devoy later wrote that Davitt came out of prison no less an orthodox Fenian than when he had gone in, and would not have been embraced by the IRB leadership, as he was, if he had held anything other than plain Fenian views.[9] It is true that Davitt lost no time in rejoining the organization, and was quickly elected to its supreme council as the representative for the north of England. However, while he was still very much a staunch Fenian, he clearly seems to have been open to new political possibilities. In Dartmoor, he had been 'curious' about Parnell and those others involved in obstructionist tactics in parliament, and almost immediately after his release he met Parnell in London and was much impressed by him.[10] Indeed, in his speeches on platforms in Ireland and throughout Britain in the spring of 1878 – during which he got a taste for public speaking – Davitt not only addressed the amnesty issue but also emphasized the importance of a closer understanding between 'honest home rulers' and separatists. At a meeting in Glasgow in April, which was presided over by an old Fenian associate and the IRB representative for Scotland, John Torley, he expressed these very sentiments. His speech made a lasting impression on the leading home ruler in the city, John Ferguson, a Presbyterian and native of Belfast, who also addressed the gathering. In fact, from this point, Ferguson developed a strong admiration for Davitt, and both would later become, and remain, close friends and allies. But for Fenians in Glasgow, and in nearby Govan where another meeting was held shortly afterwards, Davitt's talk of harmony among nationalists of different traditions must have caused some confusion, especially during the latter meeting, given that Thomas Chambers, who was released shortly after Davitt, and who also met Parnell,[11] delivered an unmistakably physical-force message.[12]

Davitt later claimed that within weeks of the Govan meeting, while travelling by train from London to Liverpool *en route* to an amnesty meeting, he

---

7 See J. Lee, *The modernization of Irish society, 1848–1918* (Dublin, 1989), pp 2–3. 8 Moody, *Davitt*, pp 127, 209–10. 9 Devoy, 'Michael Davitt's career', pt. i, *Gaelic American*, 9 June 1906. 10 Davitt, *The fall*, pp 110–11. 11 *DPB*, vol. i, p. 298. 12 Moody, *Davitt*, pp 180, 201; Ó Catháin, 'Michael Davitt and Scotland', p. 20.

asked Parnell to join the IRB, not with a view to subscribing to the 'silly oath of secrecy', but to becoming part of a reformed organization, still armed and made ready for insurrection by a select group of experienced men, but now with an 'open movement', agitating on constitutional lines, as its first line of defence. The movement would, he explained, organize popular campaigns on a broad range of social and political issues. It would also be represented in parliament by an Irish party, recruited, 'as far as possible', from men with separatist convictions, and operating along obstructionist lines, which would ultimately make a demand, 'once the country was sufficiently organized', for the repeal of the Union. In the event of this 'ultimatum' being refused, the Irish members would return to Ireland and convene their own informal legislative assembly. Parnell, it is claimed, declined the invitation to join the proposed organization.[13] In fact, Parnell himself left no recollection of this exchange of views with Davitt, and there is no evidence, other than Davitt's own account, that the conversation ever took place. But given that they both addressed an amnesty meeting in Lancashire on the date indicated, and that they may very well have shared the train journey to Liverpool, it is entirely plausible that they did converse on pressing political issues. What is much harder to accept, however, is Davitt's statement that in the course of the conversation he recommended 'a war against landlordism'. Such an idea had not, certainly by this stage, featured in any of his public pronouncements. In writing his account twenty-five years later, he probably, as Moody has suggested, antedated by a year the proposal which he was to make to Parnell in 1879.[14]

Davitt was, to be sure, exploring new strategies for advancing the nationalist cause during the spring of 1878, but he was doing so tentatively, and the land question was evidently not part of his thinking. It was only after a visit to the United States in the latter part of the year that his ideas began to take a coherent form; in fact, the American visit was crucial to his political development. He had been planning to take the trip across the Atlantic after his release in order to be reunited with his family. His mother and his sisters, Anne and Sabina, had moved from Scranton to Manayunk, a suburb of Philadelphia, after his father's death, and it was his intention to bring his mother and Sabina, who was unmarried, back to Ireland.[15] Yet the visit to the US also allowed him the opportunity to make contact with the American Fenian organization, Clan na Gael, led by Dr William Carroll, a Donegal-born Presbyterian living in Philadelphia, and which had among its ranks Fenian notables, such as Devoy, O'Donovan Rossa, and Thomas Clarke Luby. Carroll himself had already encouraged Davitt to visit America to give a series of lectures.[16] However, Davitt was not known for any specific plan at this juncture. His own later claim

13 Davitt, *The fall*, pp 111–12. 14 Moody, *Davitt*, p. 208. 15 Ibid., 194. 16 Ibid., p. 221.

that he had left Ireland after securing the support of two radical IRB associates, Thomas Brennan and Patrick Egan, for a new strategy based on co-operation between constitutionalists and separatists around land agitation, is not borne out by the evidence.[17]

When Davitt eventually got to see his family in early August, the demands that came with his increasing political importance intruded from the start. On the day of his arrival in Manayunk, Devoy, whom he had met in New York days earlier, brought him to Carroll's house in Philadelphia where a meeting of Clan na Gael was taking place. Here Davitt was prevailed upon to undertake an extended lecturing tour.[18] It was in Philadelphia itself that he gave his first lecture, in the Concert Hall, on 16 September, to an '[a]ppreciative audience of about 1,000'.[19] He declared that his imprisonment had not 'caused me to deviate one iota from my original ideas or from the track I have previously pursued for the salvation of my country'. At the same time, he praised Parnell for his robust conduct in Westminster. Neither in this speech, nor in his next, which was held a week later in the Cooper Institute, New York, did he mention the land question; or, if he did, it can only have been, as Moody remarks, merely 'incidental'.[20] This is significant, because it was at the Cooper Institute that Devoy proposed a resolution, following Davitt's speech, which connected the land and the national questions, and which called for state ownership of the land under an Irish republic. At a later meeting in Brooklyn, on 13 October, Davitt himself did give a speech in which he explicitly outlined a framework for Fenian collaboration with constitutionalists, notably on agrarian agitation. Yet he stated his case in much less radical terms than Devoy. In fact, Devoy is probably accurate in his later statement that by the time of the Brooklyn meeting, Davitt's ideas on the land question were no more advanced than 'Butt's "three fs" [...] with some provision of his own to curb evictions'.[21]

Still, what is clear – and this is reflected in Devoy's later account[22] – is that Davitt was being radicalized in his encounter with American Fenianism, especially in terms of the 'new departure' thinking. When he toured the American mid-west during October and early November, it was this line of thinking which he promoted in his meetings with fellow Fenians.[23] By the time he had set out on his return journey to the east coast on 4 November, the new policy had actually been made public by Clan na Gael, although without his knowledge. He soon learnt that the New York *Herald* had published a telegram by Devoy to a veteran Fenian in Dublin, in which a new policy had been formulated, whereby Irish republicans and constitutionalists would co-operate in working towards

17 See Davitt's letter to R. Barry O'Brien, 6 Dec. 1893, DP, TCD, MS 9377/1063. **18** Moody, *Davitt*, p. 225. **19** Davittt's diary, 16 Sept. 1878, DP, TCD, MS 9528/33. **20** Moody, *Davitt*, pp 233–4. **21** Devoy, 'Michael Davitt's career', part ii, *Gaelic American*, 16 June 1906. **22** See Moody, *Davitt*, pp 234, 239–40. **23** Ibid., p. 248.

Irish self-government in tandem with vigorous agitation for radical land reform. This development had come about because Devoy and others in Clan na Gael had received news of Parnell's recent re-election as president of the Home Rule Confederation of Great Britain, against Butt's wishes, as an indication of his ascendancy within the Irish Party. Shortly after the publication of the telegram in the *Herald*, Devoy elaborated on the policy in an article in the same paper, entitled 'An Irish New Departure', and also through a series of interviews with prominent Clan men. Davitt was apparently 'impressed' by the formulation of the policy,[24] but he believed that it had been a precipitate move. Indeed, Parnell's election to the Home Rule Confederation of Great Britain had not signalled a split with the more moderate Butt. Nevertheless, leading figures in Clan na Gael were of the view that, despite their misreading of the situation, Parnell was unlikely to be 'much the worse in any way for the cable dispatch'.[25] This was a view which Davitt appears to have come to share.

In December, a few days before leaving for Ireland, he wrote in his diary, 'Am satisfied with my last spouting in America and glad it is ended'.[26] Indeed, he had had a hectic year since his discharge from Dartmoor. On the first anniversary of his release, he again wrote,

> Query: who or what is benefited by all this travel, speaking work etc ? [...] Difficult to answer [...] would twelve months of rest and attention to health and care of future life, have been more in conformity with wisdom and common sense?[27]

But, despite his private reflections on the benefits and attractions of a quieter life, his experiences in America had given him an even more pressing need to engage politically. Moreover, the land question in Ireland had gained greater urgency against the backdrop of an agricultural depression which began with poor harvests in 1877, and which was intensified by falling livestock prices and a prolonged period of abysmal weather. Small western farmers, notably in Mayo, were particularly badly affected, and many were unable to pay their rents or debts.[28] When Davitt returned to Ireland in December, a Mayo Tenants' Defence Association had already been formed, having been earlier proposed by the influential local political leader and editor of the *Connaught Telegraph*, James Daly, who had invited Davitt to Mayo at the beginning of 1878. Daly was appointed secretary of the tenants' association, and its chairman was J.J. Louden, a large farmer and barrister from Westport. Daly had

24 *DPB* (Carroll to Devoy, 8 Nov. 1878), vol. i, pp 372–3. 25 Ibid., pp 374–5. 26 Davitt's diary on US tour, 8 Dec. 1878, DP, TCD, MS 9528. 27 Davitt's diary, 19 Dec. 1878, DP, TCD, MS 9527. 28 See James S. Donnelly Jr, *The land and the people of nineteenth-century Cork: the rural economy and the land question* (London, 1975), pp 252–5; Jordan, *Land*, pp 200–1.

been actively involved in land politics in the west for several years, as had others, including the prominent Fenian, Matt Harris from Ballinasloe, who founded a tenants' defence association there in 1876, and who later gave evidence before the parliamentary committee, under G.J. Shawe-Lefevre, inquiring into the working of the 1870 land act.[29]

In the context of the mounting agrarian crisis, and especially with an already existing tradition of agrarian radicalism in the west, Davitt was anxious to win Fenian converts. He was particularly focused on a forthcoming meeting of the IRB supreme council which was due to take place in Paris in January 1879. It was around this time that he consulted Brennan and Egan to discuss the new strategy and to ascertain the prospect of support from Fenians in Ireland.[30] His claim that he met with Brennan and Egan on this issue one year earlier than he actually did reflects what seems to have been his genuinely held belief that he was the progenitor of the new policy. However, it is difficult to believe that after years of imprisonment, much of it spent in isolation, he had emerged from Dartmoor as politically advanced in his thinking as the leadership of Clan na Gael, which had been collectively exploring new ideas, and which must have had more of a sense of the state of the movement, on both sides of the Atlantic. Still, when Davitt attended the Paris meeting, both he and Devoy, who was present as a representative of Clan na Gael, were singing from the same hymn sheet. In fact, of eleven members present, only they and Matt Harris, who seems to have been one of four co-opted members, promoted the new strategy. The other members treated the proposal with a mixture of suspicion and derision. The exchanges between Davitt and the council's president, Charles Kickham, even became bitterly acrimonious.[31] During the early 1860s, Kickham had been a leader writer for the Fenian weekly paper, the *Irish People*, which at that time had argued that peasant proprietorship was necessary in order to deal with emigration.[32] However, it held the orthodox position that such land reform would only be possible after national independence. It was this orthodoxy which Davitt and Devoy in particular were trying to get the movement to depart from, while remaining committed to the ultimate Fenian objective of securing a republic. In the end, after a week of discussions, between 19 and 26 January, the supreme council rejected the 'new departure' proposals.

A few weeks after this setback in Paris, Davitt made his way back to Mayo, were the rural distress had not abated: the number of ejectment decrees sought by the county's landlords had increased sharply,[33] and small farmers and cottiers feared not only the threat of eviction but also the prospect of famine.

29 Samuel Clark, *Social origins of the Irish land war* (Princeton, 1979), pp 257, 272–3; Moody, *Davitt*, p. 210. **30** Moody, *Davitt*, p. 277. **31** Ibid., p. 279. **32** McGee, *The IRB*, p. 65. **33** Jordan, *Land*, p. 217.

Davitt claimed credit for initiating the mobilization of the tenantry from this point, and for suggesting the historic meeting in Irishtown in April which attracted an estimated crowd of around 10,000.[34] In fact, there is little doubt that the main organizer behind the meeting was James Daly.[35] Nevertheless, Davitt, although he did not attend the meeting,[36] was acutely aware of the opportunity which the rural crisis presented for the advancement of the 'new departure', and he took an active part in planning the event, especially through his contact with local Fenians. When the meeting was held, Daly presided over a line-up of speakers which comprised O'Connor Power, John Ferguson, Brennan, Louden, Harris and Malachy O'Sullivan of Ballinasloe, all of them agrarian radicals and all Fenians, with the exception of Ferguson and Louden. Two of the resolutions which were passed, both of them drafted by Davitt, embodied the spirit of the 'new departure': the first asserted Ireland's right to self-government; the second attacked the landlord system; and a third, formulated by local leaders, called for a reduction in rents.

Davitt and Devoy had had a meeting with Parnell in Dublin shortly before the Irishtown meeting as part of ongoing attempts to bring him into the ambit of agrarian radicalism, thereby widening the context of the evolving situation in the west. Parnell was clearly interested in the potential for a new political movement, but he was uneasy about the volatility of confrontational agrarian action and also had serious concerns about the radicalism of those like Davitt. Another meeting was nevertheless arranged for 1 June, and when it took place the situation had changed considerably: distress among smallholders had become more acute, not least because bad weather and poor harvests in Britain had left many Irish small farmers and labourers without the option of seasonal work; the Irishtown meeting had taken place, with great success, and had attracted the attention of politicians and journalists in Dublin; and the IRB had sanctioned the involvement of individual Fenians in agrarian agitation, provided that it did not undermine the movement.[37] When the next major land demonstration was held in Westport on 8 June, both Davitt and Parnell were in attendance. Held in the face of clerical opposition, it nevertheless attracted huge crowds. The demand for peasant proprietorship, which was stated here and first enunciated at the earlier meeting in Irishtown, was highly significant, for, as Philip Bull has noted, 'it appears to have been the first time that the demand [...] had been made within a popular movement in Ireland'.[38]

---

34 Davitt, *The fall*, p. 147. Davitt estimated that 7,000 people were present, but Lee, *The modernization*, p. 74, puts it closer to 10,000. **35** See Lee, *The modernization*, pp 73–4; Moody, *Davitt*, pp 284–5; Clark, *Social origins*, p. 273. **36** In his *Letters and leaders of my day*, vol. i (London, 1928), p. 74, T.M. Healy claimed that Davitt missed the train; but Moody, *Davitt*, p. 291, suggests that Davitt probably avoided the meeting as a way of explaining the omission of his name from the list of speakers. **37** Moody, *Davitt*, p. 288. **38** Philip Bull, *Land, politics and nationalism* (Dublin,

Despite his appearance at the Westport meeting, Parnell was still wary about becoming involved in the new movement. Over the summer months, however, Davitt invested his energies in consolidating the Mayo movement, in 'supplant[ing] the tenants' defence associations, which had provided a platform for Mr Butt';[39] and in an effort to bring Parnell on board, he drew up rules for a new National Land League of Mayo, which was established on 16 August. Given the fruits of Davitt's organizational labours, and especially the continuing discontent which resulted from the poor harvest of August–September, Parnell became convinced of the political wisdom of formally identifying with the agrarian agitation; on 21 October he assumed the position of president of the newly-founded Irish National Land League, which was then formed at the Imperial Hotel, Dublin. Moody has identified the formation of the League as the last of three Fenian new departures in the late nineteenth century: the first was the IRB's 'friendly neutrality' towards the home rule movement under Butt in the early 1870s (Davitt himself recognized this as the original departure);[40] the second was the conditional formula outlined by Devoy in 1878; and the 'new departure' represented by the Land League, which unconditionally placed Parnell at the head of a new radical movement, was, Moody argues, Davitt's own, as head of the League.[41] When the League was inaugurated, an executive of seven was appointed, comprising Parnell, Davitt, Egan, Brennan, William Henry Sullivan, and Andrew Kettle. Significantly, none, with the exception of Kettle – and even he was a recognized politician – was a farmer. Parnell himself took no active part in the administration of the organization;[42] this was managed by the radical triumvirate of Davitt, Egan and Brennan, operating out of offices in Middle Abbey Street, Dublin, and later in Upper Sackville Street.

From the launch of the League, Davitt immersed himself in the work of organizing the movement, and in rallying the tenantry behind the 'land for the people' slogan. It was through these frenetic activities, and due to the combative nature of the campaign, that the government was forced into a position of giving the League massive publicity, in Britain and in American, when it ordered the arrest of Davitt, James Daly and James Bryce Killen, a Belfast Presbyterian minister, on charges of sedition, following a number of speeches made at Gurteen, Co. Sligo on 2 November. When all three were remanded in Sligo jail, Parnell and other leaders took full advantage of what was clearly a counter-productive move on the part of the authorities. Davitt had been released from Dartmoor in 1877 on a ticket-of-leave basis, and this could have been revoked at any time, thereby condemning him to serve out the rest of

1996), p. 97.   **39** Davitt, *The fall*, p. 164.   **40** See Davitt's letter to R. Barry O'Brien, 6 Dec. 1893, DP, TCD, MS9377/1063.   **41** Moody, *Davitt*, pp 122–3, 249–53, 325–6.   **42** Ibid., pp 343–4.

his original sentence. However, given the political implications of such a move, the government was prudent enough to avoid it as a course of action, although obviously not prescient enough to realize that the arrest of Davitt under any circumstances would serve as propaganda material for the League. After a week in jail, Davitt and the others were released on bail. Later, in December, when they were indicted at the winter assizes in Carrick-on-Shannon, the attorney general intervened and had the indictments transferred by a writ of *certiorari* to the court of queen's bench.[43] Davitt's brief sojourn in a jail cell again had done little to deter him from the work of building the new League. Indeed, at the beginning of 1880, when arms were being supplied to Fenians in the west, and further purchases were being financed by Clan na Gael, he told Devoy that he himself had 'prompted' their use in a number of 'successful attacks made upon the opposition'.[44]

From the end of May 1880, the Land League organization began to expand beyond Connacht, facilitated, according to Paul Bew, by the tacit support given by Archbishop Thomas Croke of Cashel at this time. Priests in Mayo had begun to join the League in the autumn of 1879, but Croke's support attracted farmers in Tipperary.[45] During a speech in Loughrea, Co. Galway, in January 1880, Davitt had argued that the League must adopt 'a platform of compromise' that would appeal to all tenants and to the parliamentarians.[46] However, as the campaign progressed over subsequent months, Matt Harris, as a leading agrarian radical, became increasingly concerned about the effects which different class interests within the League would have on the overall dynamics of the movement. He ultimately came to believe, indeed, that the organization's original agenda had been sacrificed.[47]

Davitt at this time was entirely focused on building the broad movement into as formidable a force as possible, and it was with this in mind that he spent most of 1880 in America, consolidating support there and raising funds. On his arrival in May, he attended the Irish convention at Trenor Hall, New York, at which the constitution of the Irish National Land and Industrial League of the United States was framed, an organization to which he was elected secretary for the period of his visit. He was joined here by John Dillon, son of the Young Irelander, John Blake Dillon, with whom he would have an enduring friendship. Dillon had already toured with Parnell, and had remained on after the latter had returned to Ireland in March to take part in the general election (Dillon himself was returned in his absence as a member for Tipperary).[48] In America, Davitt had to contend with attacks on the Land League by Fenians such as John O'Leary and O'Donovan Rossa, and also now by Carroll; but he

43 Ibid., pp 352–3. 44 *DPB*, vol. i, p. 483. 45 Paul Bew, *Land and the national question in Ireland, 1858–82* (Dublin, 1978), pp 115–16. 46 McGee, *The IRB*, p. 67. 47 Bew, *Land*, pp 134–6. 48 F.S.L. Lyons, *John Dillon* (London, 1968), pp 35–6.

still had the support of Devoy and other important Irish republicans, including Harris, both of whom made their positions clear in their public statements
and in letters to the press.[49] This aided Davitt in gaining support as he committed himself to a demanding schedule. He saw very little of his mother, paying her only two brief visits in the first two months after his arrival.[50] This was
something which he later deeply regretted, for on 18 July, while in New York,
he received a telegram from Manayunk informing him that she was desperately ill. By the time he caught a late train, arriving at her home at 8.30 p.m.,
she was dead. This was a hard blow for him, given that he knew she had wished
to see Ireland again. Later that day he wrote in his diary,

> What a life of toil and trouble and suffering has been hers. And all this
> for me and through me. What a miserable life mine has been no one
> knows but myself. I banish my family from England in '70 in order that
> I should be unfettered in the cause – that is, I sent them to America out
> of my way. My father died broken-hearted after my imprisonment. My
> poor mother suffered for me the agony which a mother must undergo
> at the thought of her son's treatment in prison. On my release, instead
> of aiding her I spent my time and money for the same cause. I promised
> to take her back to Ireland and didn't and now she sleeps her last sleep
> beneath the same foreign soil that covers my father.[51]

Although Davitt was overwhelmed with grief, he was, as the consummate
political animal, still driven by the need to secure support, both moral and practical, for the campaign in Ireland, and to build morale among Clan na Gael
members. Having worked in the American League's offices in New York for
weeks, offices which he himself had rented and furnished, he organized a series
of lectures which took him on an extended tour across America to the Pacific
coast. Unlike his tour in 1878, he himself arranged the itinerary for this one,
without the direct involvement of Clan na Gael, although during his travels he
made sure to use his Clan connections to create new branches of the American
League and to rally support behind the cause of the Irish peasantry. He left in
August and did not return to New York until 18 October.[52] With a successful
tour behind him, and having secured substantial funds, he spared no time in
again throwing himself into a series of meeting and engagements. Significantly,
at one of the last meetings which he attended in New York before his departure for Ireland in November, a resolution in support of a radical scheme of
land nationalization was passed. Present at this gathering was an influential

49 Moody, *Davitt*, pp 383, 389. **50** Ibid., p. 396. **51** Davitt's diary, 18 July 1880, DP, TCD, MS
9533. **52** Moody, *Davitt*, pp 386–411.

American radical social reformer, Henry George, who had just written a widely acclaimed work, *Progress and poverty* (1879), in which he critiqued land monopoly and called for a form of land nationalization as the way of addressing social ills.[53] Davitt met George at the New York home of Patrick Ford, the editor of the Irish–American newspaper, the *Irish World*.[54] Davitt was very impressed by George and was influenced by his concepts. However, he had difficulties with the idea of land nationalization in Ireland under a British government; and, in any case, he was not ready to embrace such a policy at this stage, certainly not publicly. He had been radicalized during his first American tour, but his political ideas were still evolving, and with the mobilization of the tenantry underway in Ireland, he was preoccupied with the organizational work at hand. Nevertheless, the influence of George would prove instrumental in shaping the course which his political career would soon take.

Back in Ireland, he resumed his role as the principal organizer of the Land League. His close partners, Egan and Brennan, were in control of finances, and statistics and publication, respectively.[55] At the beginning of his tour in America in May, Davitt had told the *Irish World* that the land war was entering a more militant phase; and, indeed, by the end of August, the League, strengthened with the aid of American finances, had called on tenants to 'hold the harvest', to hold back from the payment of rents and arrears out of the sale of their produce. In September, the campaign was further intensified when, during a speech at Ennis, Parnell called for the social ostracization of 'land grabbers', those bidding for farms from which other tenants had been evicted. This had earlier been urged by Davitt and other agrarian leaders, but Parnell, only recently elected as the chairman of the Irish Party, gave the call a particularly authoritative and urgent quality.[56] By the end of 1880, the level of agitation and the robust condition of the movement had stirred Davitt. In December he wrote to Devoy,

> The income of the League is now about £100 a day [...] Our expenditure is enormous as we are sparing no money in the work of organization, boycotting, relief to evicted people, legal fights with landlords etc. Land League courts are being established everywhere in which the affairs of the district are adjudicated! The London Press declares that all the League has got to do now, in order to have the complete government of the country in its hands, is to issue League currency.[57]

Indeed, the League had brought the land question to an entirely new level. Its impact was immense. As Patrick Buckland has commented,

---

53 Bew, *Land*, 136. 54 Moody, *Davitt*, p. 414. 55 *DPB*, vol. ii, p. 23. 56 Moody, *Davitt*, pp 384, 418. 57 As above, fn. 55.

It is almost impossible to exaggerate the impact of the [...] crisis upon the ascendancy. Such concentrated class antagonism Ireland had scarcely ever known. Agrarian outrage had been lived with, but what was new with the advent of the Land League was that not only "bad" landlords but all landlords were the object of hatred.[58]

By the autumn of 1880, the chief secretary for Ireland, W.E. Forster, was putting considerable pressure on Gladstone's government to suspend *habeas corpus*. Forster had taken a particularly hard line against the agrarian disorder in Ireland, and, as Roy Jenkins has noted, had 'settled into an intransigent groove' on the matter. Gladstone himself was reluctant to adopt coercive measures, but Forster had secured significant support from other colleagues, and by the end of December the cabinet had approved his proposals for coercion. Gladstone did not take kindly to having his hand forced, and on new year's eve, the day after the cabinet approval, he revealed the details to John Morley, a friend and future Liberal MP, doing so 'much as a man might say (in confidence) that he found himself under the painful necessity of slaying his mother'.[59] On 24 January 1881, the Protection of Persons and Property bill was introduced in the house of commons, and for the land movement it became, as Davitt later wrote, 'necessary to prepare for the storm'. As a way of making a pre-emptive move against the suppression of the Land League and the arrest of its leadership, and thereby ensuring the continuation of its work, Davitt mooted the idea of a Ladies' Land League at a meeting of the League executive. Despite objections from Parnell, Dillon and Brennan, who all feared that such a tactic was 'a dangerous experiment', Davitt and Egan strongly supported the idea.[60] An American Ladies' League had already been established in New York by Parnell's sister, Fanny,[61] whom Davitt had met during his tour, and whom he had found 'one of the cleverest young ladies' he had met in America, a 'Thorough politician, able speaker, earnest manner'.[62] Following his suggestion to the executive, the plans for a Ladies' League in Ireland, with headquarters in Dublin, were quickly drawn up.

When Forster's bill was introduced, the Parnellites mounted a vigorous opposition in parliament and aggressively employed obstructionist tactics to frustrate the bill's passage. At this time, Davitt and Kettle had a meeting in London with Parnell and his parliamentary colleagues. They proposed that on the day on which coercion became law, the Irish Party should withdraw from parliament and cross to Ireland to initiate a general rent strike. According to Davitt's later account, Parnell was 'not averse to this extreme policy', but

58 P. Buckland, *Irish unionism*, i: *the Anglo Irish and the new Ireland, 1885–1922* (Dublin, 1972), p. 5. **59** Jenkins, *Gladstone*, p. 475. **60** Davitt, *The fall*, pp 298–9 **61** Moody, *Davitt*, p. 414. **62** Davitt's diary, 29 July 1880, TCD, MS 9533.

there was significant opposition to the idea among the other nationalist MPs present and the proposal was ultimately rejected. On the evening of 1 February, before travelling back to Ireland, Davitt spent two hours in the speaker's gallery in the house of commons. Seated not far from Disraeli, earl of Beaconsfield, he was spotted by the home secretary, Sir William Harcourt, who remarked to a colleague: 'do you see that scoundrel next to Beconsfield in the gallery? Well, I will have that fellow back in penal servitude tomorrow'.[63] His threat was not quite carried out the next day; but later on 3 February, Davitt was arrested as he crossed Carlisle (O'Connell) Bridge in Dublin, in the company of Brennan and Harris. His arrest proved the first move in the government's suppression of the Land League. He was eventually taken to London, and after a brief stay in Milbank penitentiary, he was finally brought to Portland jail in Dorset. Abruptly plucked from the maelstrom of the land war, he believed he had left behind a robust semi-revolutionary movement. In the weeks before his arrest, he had, however, shown an awareness of conflicting interests within the land movement; but so immersed had he been in the agrarian campaign, and so undeveloped were his own ideas, that he did not fully appreciate the nature or extent of these divisions. He would spend fifteen months in Portland, subjected to a news blackout, and it would only be after his release that the problems within the movement, and indeed the complexities of Irish politics, would become clear to him.

63 Davitt, *The fall*, p. 302.

2 / 'Preach ideas and not men': Davitt and Parnellism

O N THE EVENING OF Saturday, 6 May 1882, the newly appointed chief secretary for Ireland, Lord Frederick Cavendish, and his under-secretary, T.H. Burke, were murdered in the Phoenix Park, Dublin, by a secret society styling itself the Irish National Invincibles. The murders, occurring as they did only days after the 'Kilmainham treaty' agreed between Parnell and the Gladstone government, represented a major blow to the radical agenda which Davitt had hoped would develop out of the agitation of the Land League. Only weeks before his arrest and imprisonment he noted in a diary entry for 31 December 1880, 'Eventful year just dying out. 1879 Education; 1880 Organization; 1881 Result?'.[1] The result which eventually did transpire proved, in fact, to be a new political climate that was more conducive to the interests of Parnell and the conservative wing of the nationalist movement. Following his release from prison, Davitt considered it politically expedient to associate himself with the constitutional movement that was to succeed the Land League; but the post-Kilmainham years witnessed a growing antipathy between himself and Parnell and saw him assume an isolated position as a freelance radical, a role that was, indeed, to characterize the rest of his political career.

On the day of the Phoenix Park murders, Davitt, accompanied by Parnell, John Dillon and J.J. O'Kelly, was actually travelling by train to London after having just been released from Portland prison. Parnell, Dillon and O'Kelly, only recently freed from Kilmainham jail themselves, had gone to greet Davitt on his release. During his fifteen months' imprisonment, the latter, unlike his colleagues, had of course been subjected to a news blackout and was therefore ignorant of the exact circumstances of his release. He later noted that on the journey from Portland to London, Parnell seemed decidedly uneasy when asked about the negotiations between himself and the government. After receiving an 'imperfect outline' of the 'Kilmainham treaty', Davitt did not pursue the matter, given that 'we were all too full of "the triumph of the Land

---

1 Davitt's diary, 31 Dec. 1880, DP, TCD, MS 9534.

League" to give place to suspicion'.[2] All were, at this stage, unaware of the Phoenix Park incident, and were to remain so, even after being met at London station by a small welcoming party.[3] It was only later, after retiring to the Westminster Palace Hotel, where he and Dillon were to stay, that Davitt heard any news of the assassinations. Suspecting the machinations of sections of the press, he treated the news as a hoax. However, at 5.00 a.m. the following morning, his friend, Henry George, who had recently move to London, came to his room and reported otherwise.[4] Davitt was devastated, believing the murders to have undone much of the work already accomplished. Later that day he wrote in his diary, 'The blackest day that has perhaps ever dawned for Ireland [...]'[5]

Shaken by the news, Parnell, Justin McCarthy, and other leading nationalists made their way to Davitt's hotel. In their presence, Davitt drafted a manifesto condemning the killings, and after some revision by Parnell, it was signed and issued to press agencies in Britain. It was also cabled to John Boyle O'Reilly for publication in the United States, and to Alfred Webb in Dublin 'to be printed as a placard, and dispatched by Sunday night's last train to every city and town in Ireland, so as to be posted on the walls of the country on Monday morning'.[6] Webb duly stayed up all night and had 10,000 copies made ready for distribution.[7] Fearing anti-Irish reprisals in Britain, Davitt spent Sunday night at T.M. Healy's lodgings in London and was out by 6.00 a.m. the next morning, eager to peruse the newspapers.[8] The assassination of such prominent political figures as Cavendish and Burke was unprecedented in Britain and Ireland and caused what Davitt referred to as a 'cyclonic sensation'.[9] The wife of the murdered chief secretary, Lady Frederick Cavendish, warned against 'panic and vindictive vengeance',[10] a reaction which Davitt later singled out for praise.[11] However, the British political establishment was both alarmed and outraged, and in the face of public opinion the government introduced the Prevention of Crimes (Ireland) bill on 11 May, in which trial by three judges was, in certain cases, permitted instead of trial by jury; the lord lieutenant given the power to ban public meetings and suppress newspapers; and the police given greater powers of search. New coercive legislation for Ireland had previously been proposed and drafted by Forster, who had bitterly opposed

2 'Miscellaneous writings in Richmond jail, Dublin', 5 and 6 May 1883, DP, TCD, MS 9537. 3 The party present at Vauxhall Station, London, included Thomas Sexton, T.M. Healy, A.M. Sullivan, Frank Byrne, and Henry George; see Fintan Lane, *The origins of modern Irish socialism, 1881–1896* (Cork, 1997), p. 78. 4 Davitt, *The fall*, p. 357. 5 Davitt's diary, 7 May 1882, DP, TCD, MS 9535. 6 Davitt, *The fall*, p. 359. 7 Alfred Webb, *Alfred Webb, the autobiography of a Quaker nationalist*, ed. Marie-Louise Legg (Cork, 1999), p. 48. 8 Healy, *Letters*, vol. i, pp 159–60. 9 Davitt, *The fall*, p. 362. 10 Quoted in J.L. Hammond, *Gladstone and the Irish nation* (London, 1938), pp 283–4. 11 Davitt, *The Times-Parnell comm*, pp 350–1.

Parnell's release, or at least his release in advance of the introduction of the proposed legislation, and not without a public declaration by the latter condemning intimidation.[12] Forster had no support in Gladstone's cabinet and subsequently resigned on 2 May. However, the Phoenix Park murders altered the whole situation and forced the government to adopt its own particularly draconian measures.

Parnell, for his part, was deeply dismayed by the killings and even threatened resignation from public life, although he was dissuaded from taking such a course by his colleagues and by Gladstone. Owing to the hostility which coercion would naturally provoke in Ireland, he was compelled to oppose the crimes bill (which would become law on 12 July), but he maintained a line of communication with the Radical MPs, Joseph Chamberlain and Henry Labouchere, and with Gladstone through Mrs Katherine O'Shea. He was keen to moderate, as far as possible, the scope of the coercive measures; and, via Healy, he made it clear to Labouchere and Chamberlain that if the government would approach the matter in a conciliatory way, he and his party would conduct their opposition 'on honest Parliamentary lines'.[13] The Kilmainham settlement was certainly disrupted by the Phoenix Park murders but it was not altogether sabotaged. Only several days after the crimes bill, the arrears bill was introduced in the house of commons.

Besides the release of prisoners, Gladstone's essential undertaking in his 'treaty' with Parnell had been to extend the Land Law (Ireland) Act, 1881 to leaseholders, especially the fair rent clause, and to address the issue of tenants in arrears. As a *quid pro quo*, Parnell agreed to accept the Act and to use his influence to quell disorder. The historic importance of the Act was already apparent to him: in effect, it accepted the principle of dual ownership of the land by conceding the 'three fs'. Parnell was, however, also acutely aware of certain shortcomings in its provisions, namely the 150,000 leaseholders and the 130,000 tenants in arrears who were excluded from its workings.[14] He could not endorse a piece of legislation with such glaring flaws. Nevertheless, while the case of the leaseholders would not be dealt with until 1887,[15] the arrears bill was much in keeping with the Kilmainham arrangement.[16] It applied to holdings valued at £30 or under, and proposed that if the tenant could make the payment of one year's arrears, and proved, to the satisfaction

---

12 Hammond, *Gladstone*, p. 268. **13** Ibid., pp 294–7. **14** F.S.L. Lyons, *Ireland since the famine* (London, 1977), p. 172. **15** Land Law (Ireland) Act, 1887. **16** While the bill was in line with Parnell's proposal, Parnellites were concerned by the clause which made available a grant of £100,000 which could be used by Boards of Guardians to assist tenants wishing to emigrate. The Irish members effected an amendment which limited to £5 the amount of help to be given to a tenant. Around 20,000 emigrants ultimately left under this legislative mechanism; see Hammond, *Gladstone*, pp 304–5.

of the Land Commissioners, that the previous years' arrears could not be defrayed, the state would pay half the amount owed to the landlord and annul the balance.

On the same day that the arrears bill was introduced, the substance and far-reaching significance of the Kilmainham pact was made known in a debate in the house of commons which had been called for by the opposition. Parnell read from a letter of 28 April which he had written from Kilmainham to Captain William O'Shea who had been acting as an intermediary between the Irish leader and the government. When Parnell had finished reading his copy of the letter, it became clear that a crucial passage had been omitted. This was abruptly brought to the attention of the members by Forster who proceeded to produce a copy of his own, which had previously been supplied by O'Shea during negotiations. According to Healy, 'Parnell paled' at this point and 'Gladstone's face mantled with pious resignation'.[17] The former chief secretary then challenged O'Shea to read the letter in its entirety, and the latter was forced to oblige. The letter reflected Parnell's eagerness to have the government address the matter of the leaseholders and, particularly, the question of arrears, but the omitted sentence, which had so exercised Forster, significantly revealed that he would consider a resolution of these outstanding issues as a 'practical settlement of the Land Question', and that it would, moreover, enable the Irish Party 'to co-operate cordially for the future with the Liberal Party in forwarding Liberal principles and measures of general reform'.[18]

The precise nature of Parnell's undertaking caused disquiet among many of his parliamentary colleagues, not least because of the involvement of O'Shea who was widely disliked and viewed with suspicion. A.M. Sullivan, who '[m]ight be termed a conservative Nationalist',[19] actually wrote to Davitt towards the end of May 1882: 'Much depends on *you* just now. Would to God we had never heard of "Captain O'Shea MP" and his negotiations and intrigues. Alas! Alas!'.[20] The staunchly conservative Healy later remarked that he and other colleagues present in the commons had been 'filled […] with disgust' by the revelations of the O'Shea letter.[21] Yet, notwithstanding such sentiment, the Parliamentary Party still ultimately embraced the Kilmainham agreement and its concomitant rejection of revolutionary agitation. In fact, despite his initial opportunistic disavowal of 'compacts or compromises', Healy was essentially a stalwart of 'Kilmainham', referring to it as a 'sagacious' arrangement.[22] Even before the settlement was reached, he had distanced himself from the social radicalism of the Land League and, according to Frank Callanan, 'had difficulty concealing his contempt for the […] radicals'. In later months he

---

17 Healy, *Letters*, vol. i, p. 161. **18** Quoted in F.S.L. Lyons, *Charles Stewart Parnell* (Suffolk, 1977), p. 201. **19** Davitt, *Jottings*, p. 157. **20** Sullivan to Davitt, May 1882, DP, TCD, MS 9332/233. **21** Healy, *Letters*, vol. i, p. 162. **22** Callanan, *T.M. Healy* (Cork, 1996), pp 72, 74.

employed inflammatory language in criticizing the Land Act, but this was essentially rhetorical.[23]

Davitt, the leading figure on the agrarian left, regarded the 'treaty' as an abject surrender of the League's key demand for wholesale peasant proprietorship;[24] and despite Parnell's appeals that he not address public meetings, he made a speech in Manchester on 21 May 1882, in which he asserted that the Land League was not defunct and that the Arrears bill would not frustrate the League's primary goal of achieving the absolute end of landlordism.[25] He ultimately argued that 'the spirit and meaning' of the Land Act was tantamount to 'legal robbery' in exacting rents from land cultivated totally from the occupants' labour, and that the subsequent Arrears Act (August 1882) nullified the principle fought for in the Healy clause.[26] The negotiated settlement was, in his view, an ignominious debacle. From Parnell's perspective, however, the land reform legislation was sufficient to diffuse agrarian upheaval and, significantly, to facilitate progress on the constitutional question.

In a speech before the US House of Representatives in February 1880 Parnell had referred to landlordism in Ireland as an 'artificial and cruel system' which should be 'terminated'. In his address, he also deprecated a recent proposal by the English Radical, John Bright, which recommended a land purchase scheme based on the voluntary co-operation of landlords. He pointed out that such a proposal was inadequate and at odds with the Land League principle of compulsory expropriation of land.[27] However, despite this statement, he never actually held that compulsory purchase was fundamental to a settlement.[28] Shortly after his return from America he was a signatory to a League programme which called for compulsory sale on the basis of twenty years' purchase of the valuation of landlords' estates, but he only endorsed such a policy because to have done otherwise would have left him isolated. Davitt, who was on the committee charged with preparing the programme, noted that Parnell made no contribution, other than the 'extraordinary proposal' that the 'three fs', as reflected in Butt's 1876 bill, should be adopted.[29] While Parnell certainly sought the extirpation of landlordism as a social institution, he harboured essentially moderate views on the land question. He himself admitted that he would not have even 'taken off my coat and gone to this [Land League] work if I had not known that we were laying the foundation

---

23 Ibid., pp 68–9, 84. **24** Davitt, *The fall*, pp 363–4. **25** Moody, *Davitt*, p. 539. **26** Davitt, *The fall*, p. 364. The 'Healy Clause' stipulated that no rent should be paid in respect of improvements made by an occupant or his predecessor in title; see Callanan, *T.M. Healy*, pp 56–7. **27** 'Parnell's Speech to the House of Representatives of the United States, 2 February 1880' in Alan O'Day and John Stevenson (eds), *Irish historical documents since 1800* (Dublin, 1992), pp 94, 97–9. **28** F.S.L. Lyons, 'The economic ideas of Parnell' in Michael Roberts (ed.), *Historical Studies* 2 (1959), 65. **29** Davitt, *The fall*, p. 241.

in this movement for the regeneration of our legislative independence'.[30] Indeed, Gladstone was astonished by what Parnell was prepared to concede in reaching a political accommodation. He referred to the latter's Kilmainham letter as 'the most extraordinary I ever read'.[31]

Before his incarceration in Portland, Davitt had become mindful of the various interests within the Land League organization, especially as a result of its expansion. On 14 December 1880 he issued a communication to its officers and organizers in which he stated, 'Evidence is not wanting that numbers of men have formed and are joining the League who give but a half-hearted allegiance to the League programme [...] men who denounced the programme [...] but six months ago'.[32] Two days later, in a confidential letter to John Devoy, he warned of the potential for a 'Whig dodge', involving the new class of League members and the clergy collectively conspiring to subvert the *raison d'etre* of the League by ousting the 'advanced men'. Significantly, he stated his view that while the government's land bill would be inadequate, 'it will [be enough to] satisfy a great number inside the league and be accepted by the bishops and priests almost to a man. I anticipate a serious split [...] when the government measure comes out'. He informed Devoy, however, that he had taken precautions, and had already 'carried a neat constitution by a *coup de main* and on Tuesday next I intend to carry the election of an executive council of fifteen in whose hands the entire government will be placed'.[33] Remarkably, at this point, as Bew has noted, Davitt appears to have perceived the League's problem as mainly one of leadership.[34] More importantly, he apparently did not associate Parnell with any conservative threat. In an annotated list of Irish MPs and constituencies, which he jotted down during his subsequent solitary confinement in Portland, he referred to the Irish leader as 'sans peur et sans reproche'.[35] This would explain his inclination to forego suspicion on the day of his release when Parnell was reticent about political developments.

Davitt's imprisonment in Portland had served as a critical period of reflection, and it was during this time that he decided to adopt land nationalization as a policy. He committed to paper a new scheme for state ownership of the land which he would subsequently present as the solution to the land question. On his release he attempted to establish a line of continuity between this policy and the Land League charter-cry, 'The land for the people'. He had been heavily influenced in developing his ideas on land reform by Henry George's celebrated work, *Progress and poverty*, which argued that land monopoly was the source of social inequality and that the only solution to extremes

---

30 Quoted in Moody, *Davitt*, pp 332–3.   31 Hammond, *Gladstone*, p. 279.   32 Quoted in Bew, *Land*, p. 137.   33 *DPB*, vol. ii, pp 121–5.   34 Bew, *Land*, p. 138.   35 'fearless and beyond reproach', Davitt, *Jottings*, p. 152.

of poverty and wealth, in Ireland and elsewhere, was an end to private land ownership. George did make specific reference to Ireland in his work, primarily in order to disprove the Malthusian model in political economy. Focusing on the Famine of 1845-9, he argued that Ireland had not been the classic Malthusian country where population outstripped resources. Rather, the Famine was explicable in terms of the huge social inequalities in Irish society, and, critically, the monopoly which landlords had on the land. He wrote,

> Whether over-population ever did cause pauperism and starvation, may be open to question; but the pauperism and starvation of Ireland can no more be attributed to this cause than can the slave trade be attributed to the over-population of Africa, or the destruction of Jerusalem to the inability of subsistence to keep pace with reproduction. Had Ireland been by nature a grove of bananas and bread-fruit, had her coasts been lined by the guano-deposits of the Chinchas, and the sun of lower latitudes warmed into more abundant life her moist soil, the social conditions that have prevailed there would still have brought forth poverty and starvation. How could there fail to be pauperism and famine in a country where rack-rents wrested from the cultivator of the soil all the produce of his labour except just enough to maintain life in good seasons [...]?[36]

Ireland was, in fact, central to George's campaign of bringing about social reform at an international level. In March 1881 his pamphlet, *The Irish land question*, was published seven months in advance of his first visit to Ireland. In it, he applied the principles of his main work to the Irish agrarian situation, and asserted that the social problems in Ireland were not unique but were part of a much wider framework of injustice. He appealed to the leadership of the land movement to internationalize the land question by adopting a policy of land nationalization. 'Let them be Land Leaguers first, and Irishmen afterwards', he declared.[37]

Davitt retrospectively identified this more radical agrarian agenda with the aims of the Land League. It was typical of him in the post-Kilmainham years to reinterpret his past in order to demonstrate a certain consistency of purpose. In particular, he made considerable effort to preserve his image as an established social reformer. This was evident in his address to the *Times*-Parnell Commission in October 1889, in which he defended the Land League against allegations that the Irish movement was complicit in criminality. These claims

---

36 Henry George, *Progress and poverty* (London, 1881), p. 113.   **37** Henry George, *The Irish land question* (London, 1881), pp 1–2, 36.

were first made in *The Times* (London) in 1887 under a series of articles entitled 'Parnellism and Crime', the basis of which was a purported facsimile of a
letter apparently connecting Parnell to the Phoenix Park murders. It was in
his speech before the Commission that Davitt claimed, inaccurately, that the
Land League was largely 'the offspring of thoughts and resolutions' which he
had arrived at before his emergence from Dartmoor. In dealing with his Fenian
background he expressed no regrets about the activities for which he was originally imprisoned. Yet he was determined to vindicate the Land League, and
in its defence he made reference to the hostility which it faced from the IRB.
He also read from speeches of his own in which he denounced crime and agrarian violence.[38] However, he failed to disclose the extent to which he had still
been committed to physical force during the land war. The evidence suggests
that in his engagement with the land question up until his arrest in 1881, he
was, in fact, also involved in a specific separatist strategy.

In his letter to Devoy of 16 December 1880, he remarked, in rather conspiratorial terms, 'If we could carry on this movement for another year without
being interfered with we could do almost anything we pleased in this country.
The courage of the people is magnificent. All classes are purchasing arms openly'. He further recommended that if the government resorted to 'dragooning
the people after squelching the league', plans should be made to retaliate in
England.[39] Moody maintains that Davitt's position in these years was a decidedly ambivalent one, and that by the time of his letter to Devoy he was living
in a 'state of excessive mental stimulation and physical exertion'.[40] There is no
doubt that Davitt's involvement in politics and agitation after his imprisonment
in Dartmoor was sudden and dramatic, and undoubtedly overwhelming at times.
Still, his letter to Devoy is highly significant. The views expressed were consistent with the neo-Fenian position that a popular campaign for national independence would be precipitated by the certain failure of the government to concede peasant proprietorship. Two days before his communication with Devoy,
Davitt had disagreed with Thomas Sexton's view that the Land League was a
strictly 'social movement' and that it was therefore inappropriate to have green
flags carried at League demonstrations in Ulster.[41] If his correspondence with
Devoy during the land war had been made available to the *Times*-Parnell
Commission it would, as Moody acknowledges, have gravely undermined his
case, and his later written work based on his testimony, *Speech in defence of the
Land League* (1890), would certainly have been a different book altogether.[42]

Davitt never abandoned his republican ideals. It must be borne in mind,
however, that his involvement with land politics in the few years after his dis-

38 Davitt, *The Times-Parnell comm*, pp 2–3, 29, 363–4. **39** *DPB*, vol. ii, pp 24–5. **40** Moody,
Davitt, p. 442 **41** Bew, *Land*, pp 270–1, fn. 129. **42** Moody, *Davitt*, pp 440–1.

charge from Dartmoor was something of a political education. As was indicated in his letter to Devoy, he apparently believed that the general agrarian population in Ireland was naturally against a compromise on the land question. In fact, his opposition to the Kilmainham arrangement was based, in part, on his view that the Land League was still a formidable and unbroken force in the early months of 1882, and that seditious fervour in the country was still sufficiently strong. Of course, he was also now firmly committed to a policy of land nationalization. In a keynote speech in Liverpool on 6 June 1882, in which he enunciated his new programme, he said,

> The Arrears Bill, while being good in its way, and calculated to arrest crime and outrage to some extent, is a most convincing argument that the Land Act is a failure, and leaves the agrarian war almost where it has hitherto been [...] In my travels through the West and North last week I found everywhere a want of confidence in the Land Courts, and heard from all classes that the landlords, as in every other branch of Irish administration, had succeeded in turning the courts to their own purposes in all but a few instances.[43]

However, the reality was that the government's decision to address the issue of arrears seriously undermined agrarian militancy. While Davitt later referred to the Arrears Act as 'a curse',[44] he ignored the fact that the state paid £800,000 rent for 130,000 tenants who were now more concerned with having their claims heard in the land courts than, as Davitt envisaged it, acting as part of the vanguard of the movement. Of the 135,997 claims made, no less than 129,952 were allowed.[45] As J.J. Lee writes,

> Parnell has sometimes been criticized for diverting the social revolutionary train [...] [but] The only social revolutionary policy that commanded widespread support [...] was peasant proprietorship, and the Arrears Act, by increasing security of tenure, took a significant step in that direction. The Arrears Act was the small farmers' charter.[46]

Even Devoy accepted the Kilmainham 'treaty', and as early as the day of Davitt's release from Portland he wrote in the *Irish Nation*, 'To future generations it will mark a turning-point in the tide of adversity'.[47]

Parnell's opposition to the new wave of coercion strengthened his standing in Ireland, but there was still a leftist threat in the summer of 1882 which was very real to him. He needed to ensure that the crimes bill was not so dra-

43 *FJ*, 7 June 1882. **44** Davitt, *The fall*, p. 364. **45** Hammond, *Gladstone*, p. 304. **46** Lee, *The modernization*, p. 88. **47** Quoted in Bew, *Land*, p. 216.

conian as to make his position untenable. In particular, he sought a reduction in the duration of the proposed law from three to two years; the exclusion of treason and treason-felony from its terms; limitations on the right of search; and the appointment of county court judges instead of resident magistrates on tribunals. He communicated the urgency of such concessions to Labouchere. Indeed, he intimated that if progress was not made on these issues, his authority might be usurped by Patrick Egan, who, as the Land League treasurer, had set up the League's financial headquarters in Paris after Davitt's arrest. Egan was now in conflict with Parnell over an embargo which the latter had placed on League funds.[48] Parnell also had to deal with Dillon, who shared Davitt's views on the 1881 Land Act and who could not reconcile himself to the 'treaty'. It seems, indeed, that Parnell provoked both Davitt and Dillon by refusing to authorize further funds for the Ladies' Land League. In August 1882, he informed Katherine O'Shea that 'The two D's' had quarrelled with him over the matter. Yet he noted, with some satisfaction, that by refusing to allow any further expenditure by the ladies, he had frustrated the hopes harboured by Davitt and Dillon 'of creating a party against me in the country by distributing the funds among their own creatures'.[49] A few days later, Davitt wrote to Dillon, condemning Parnell's move against the ladies' organization as a 'mischievous blunder'.[50] Dillon's position on the Ladies' League was not, however, as unambiguous as Davitt's. According to Lyons, correspondence between Parnell and Dillon from early August showed that the latter had also had a hand in bringing the women's organization to an end.[51]

In his calculated suppression of the Ladies' League, Parnell also seriously damaged his future relations with his sister, Anna, the effective head of the organization and a radical figure in her own right who was intensely disillusioned with the scope of the land settlement. In her later account of the land war, *The tale of a great sham*, completed in 1907, she condemned the 1881 Land Act as a 'ridiculous mouse' and referred to the Arrears Act as a meaningless measure.[52] Her work was not only a retrospective attack on government legislation but a critique of the Land League leadership, without any differentiation made between the principal male figures. Following the eventual incarceration of the League leadership by October 1881, the Ladies' League assumed effective control of the organization. But even before this eventuality, Anna Parnell had had certain misgivings about the direction of the Land League itself, believing that there was a 'screw loose somewhere in the institution'. She noted that in actively pursuing a rent resistance strategy in the

48 Lyons, *Charles Stewart Parnell*, pp 221, 227. **49** Quoted in Katherine O'Shea, *The uncrowned king of Ireland, Charles Stewart Parnell: his love story and political life* (Gloucestershire, 2005), p. 180. **50** Davitt to Dillon, 24 Aug. 1882, DP, TCD, MS 9403/1556. **51** Lyons, *John Dillon*, p. 67. **52** Anna Parnell, *The tale of a great sham*, ed. Dana Hearne (Dublin, 1986), pp 99, 143.

course of 1881, she and her colleagues had incurred the hostility of their male counterparts. Given their experiences, the ladies believed that the subsequent releases of leading League figures in May 1882 was confirmation of a change in policy.[53] Anna bitterly rejected the new course signalled by the Kilmainham accord, and she wrote to Davitt several days after his discharge from Portland to make her position clear: 'I am glad you are out of prison – on that point at least I suppose we can agree'.[54] Her ill feeling was, no doubt, influenced by the recent manifesto condemning the killing of Cavendish and Burke, which she believed reflected the 'cringing attitudes of the Irish leaders'.

In her later analysis she argued that the loose screw in the Land League was the 'rent at the point of a bayonet' strategy which the League adopted in August 1880. The policy was basically one of brinkmanship, whereby a tenant would delay as long as possible the payment of an 'unjust' rent, despite the considerable legal costs incurred. Anna considered its adoption a critical development which thereafter rendered the Land League a 'fraud', essentially because legal fees were being met by the League itself.

> The effect of the decision that rent must be paid by those who were able to pay it, after all possible delays, accompanied generally by a great accumulation of costs, was [she argued] to nullify at once the solitary factor which held out a hope of success [...] The [...] League was now pitting its purse, not against the landlords' purses, but against the purses of the government, then the richest in the world.[55]

This point has been taken up in recent historiography. In his quasi-Marxian analysis of the land war, Bew contends that the 'rent at the point of a bayonet' strategy reflected the 'hegemony' of the larger farmers of Leinster and Munster within the Land League by the autumn of 1880, and highlighted the conflicting class interests within the land movement.[56] While acknowledging a general anti-landlord alliance among the peasantry, Bew advances his argument as the antithesis of the case made by Samuel Clark, who maintains that the there was no critical class conflict during the agrarian campaign.[57] There were early signs of conflict between grazier farmers and peasants in western areas of Galway and Mayo in the winter of 1879–80.[58] But, while Clark does

---

53 Anna Parnell, *Tale*, pp 89–91, 128. **54** Anna Parnell to Davitt, 12 May 1882, DP, TCD, MS 9378/1089. **55** Anna Parnell, *Tale*, pp 77, 96, 148. **56** Bew, *Land*, pp 122–3. **57** Clark's seminal treatment of the land war was his article, 'The social composition of the Land League', *IHS*, 17:68 (1971), 447–69. This was developed in his later work, *Social origins*. **58** David S. Jones, 'The Cleavage between graziers and peasants in the land struggle, 1890–1910' in Samuel Clark and James S. Donnelly Jr. (eds), *Irish peasants: violence and political unrest, 1870–1914* (Manchester, 1983), p. 381.

recognize that there were social differences between farmers in the land war, he asserts that they were never significant enough to weaken what he terms the 'challenging collectivity' of a peasantry pitted against a common adversary, landlordism. He points out that structural changes in post-Famine Ireland heralded a shared interest, or more precisely interdependence, between farmers and townsmen, and that, from a study of arrest sheets, it is clear that, unlike pre-Famine unrest, townsmen played a part in every area of League activity. Notably, he observes that while there was some hostility towards large grazier farmers, especially in the west, the paucity of resolutions denouncing graziers at League meetings was significant in itself.[59]

In Bew's analysis, class dynamic is central to understanding the nature of the Land League and the determinants of its policy, crucially the 'rent at the point of a bayonet' strategy. This was first proposed as a compromise resolution by Egan in August 1880, even though he himself said that he would rather have opted for a rent strike. Despite the unquestionable radicalism of Egan, Bew maintains that he 'implicitly adopted a policy which was to prove perfectly suited – with the low level of risks and easy martyrdoms – to the rural bourgeoisie of South Leinster.' In Bew's view, the League leadership was ultimately forced to sacrifice its militancy, and consequently the interests of the agricultural proletariat, by embracing a strategy designed to secure the allegiance of the rural bourgeoisie in the critical stage of the League's expansion in the latter part of 1880.[60] This argument is a compelling one, although it perhaps underestimates the level of solidarity within the land movement and, moreover, lacks clarity on class designation. As L.P. Curtis has noted, Bew fails to indicate where the lines should be drawn between the bourgeoisie and proletariat: 'How should historians classify the occupiers of farms between say, 15 or 30 acres, which numbered 135,793 in all of Ireland in 1881?'[61]

In her own account, Anna Parnell stated simply that it was impossible to say exactly what caused the Land League to adopt the 'rent at the point of a bayonet' plan. She nevertheless considered it a 'sham'. In her view, 'The programme of a permanent resistance until the aim of the League should be attained, was the only logical one'.[62] Davitt himself later wrote that February 1881 had been the critical point at which a no-rent campaign should have been launched, following the expulsion of the Irish Party from the house of commons in the wake of his own arrest.[63] Yet, despite his opposition to the Kilmainham 'treaty' after his release from Portland, and his vigorous efforts to revive the spirit of the Land League in the summer of 1882, he was not prepared to force the radical agen-

59 Clark, *Social origins*, pp 249–55, 300–2. 60 Bew, *Land*, pp 121–3. 61 L.P. Curtis, 'On class and class conflict in the land war', *IESH*, 3 (1981), 89–90. 62 Anna Parnell, *Tale*, pp 55, 78, 96. 63 Davitt, *The fall*, p. 309.

da to the point of a split. Anna Parnell did not, however, take the potential for a split, or indeed the internal divisions within the League leadership, into account. Moreover, writing in 1907, she must have learned from Davitt's last major work, *The fall of feudalism in Ireland* (1904), that he had recommended a rent strike in February 1881; but she failed to acknowledge the fact and instead viewed the League leadership as a homogeneous group. As Moody concludes, '[Her] strictures on the Land League leaders, though not without foundation, ignore completely the complex and critical field of forces, political, economic, and ecclesiastical, in which they had to work'.[64]

From Anna Parnell's perspective, only the Ladies' Land League surfaced with any integrity intact.[65] Indeed, after the publication of *The fall of feudalism*, she wrote to Davitt's publishers, Harper & Brothers, threatening litigation against 'libellous' statements made in the book.[66] Her allegation related to a passage in Davitt's work, where the 'author says a statement I made at a public meeting was a lie'.[67] Davitt had credited her with a part in the foundation of the Ladies' League. However, she considered this a challenge to the veracity of a speech which she made in 1881, in which she claimed that the idea of the ladies' organization had been decided upon before she consented to play a leading role in it.[68] Davitt mistakenly believed at first that the litigious threats were made by Mrs Parnell, formerly Katherine O'Shea.[69] A few days later, however, he wrote to H. Slater of Harper & Brothers and acknowledged, with some surprise, Anna Parnell as the complainant. He stated that he had read the said pages and could only say that he had intended his comments to be complementary. He insisted that 'there is absolutely no shade or shadow of any imputation against Miss Parnell's [claims]'.[70]

---

64 T.W. Moody, 'Anna Parnell and the land league', *Hermathena*, 117 (1974), 15–16. 65 Anna Parnell, *Tale*, p. 96. 66 Anna Parnell to H. Slater, Harper & Brothers Publishers, 7 May 1905, DP, TCD, MS 9511/5599. 67 Anna Parnell to Slater, 14 May 1905, DP, TCD, MS 9511/5601; see pp 299–300 of *The fall*. 68 On p. 300 of *The fall*, Davitt, in fn 1, cited a quotation from the *Report special commission* of a speech made by Anna Parnell on 2 Apr. 1881 in which she stated that while she welcomed the creation of the Ladies' Land League, it was Davitt, not she, who was responsible for its formation, and that her consent to play a leading role in it was not sought before Davitt announced his plan. In the passage on pp 299–300, of which this quotation is the footnote, Davitt wrote, 'Miss Anna Parnell had been consulted about this plan. She thoroughly approved of it […] Having been very much blamed on the one hand for suggesting the plan thus agreed upon, I am vain enough to covet the honour too generously given me on the other hand by Miss Parnell, in her own too modest account of the part she played in creating the force which pulled coercion down'. 69 Davitt to H. Slater, Harper & Brother Publishers, 10 May 1905, DP, TCD, MS 9511/5599. 70 Davitt to Slater, 15 May 1905, DP, TCD, MS 9511/5601. Davitt certainly contradicted Anna Parnell's reported statement. However, his assertion that there was no imputation against Miss Parnell was not necessarily disingenuous. In an interview which he gave to the *New York Daily World* in the summer of 1882, he said that he had talked with Parnell and some others about the idea of a ladies' organization, and that a meeting was subsequently called

Anna's threat to make the issue a matter of law (which, in fact, it never became) was clearly based on her determination to have herself and the Ladies' Land League accurately represented. Another contributing factor in her grievance might have been that she herself had recently been unsuccessful in requesting from Harper & Brothers a commission to write a history of the Land League. H. Slater informed Davitt that Anna 'claimed she was the only person who could do this work'.[71] In many respects, the manuscript which she did eventually produce was more incisive than Davitt's account, especially in detailing the workings and the policy of the League, particularly the 'rent at the point of a bayonet' strategy. But her work failed to consider the extent of disillusionment with the Kilmainham settlement, the complexities that shaped political developments, and the internal divisions within the leadership of the national movement in 1882, notably the animosity between Davitt and Parnell.

Davitt later wrote that Parnell had 'favoured' the coercion which followed the Phoenix Park murders,[72] in that it saved him from having to address 'the perils which lurked in the terms of the compact'.[73] Yet Davitt's strong disavowal of the course taken by Parnell was not enough to cause him to mount a public challenge. Indeed, the main opposition to Parnell began to dissipate by the autumn of 1882: Anna Parnell herself abruptly left public life after the dissolution of the Ladies' League, embittered by the political settlement and deeply affected by the sudden and untimely death of her sister, Fanny, in July;[74] Egan resigned as treasurer in October;[75] Brennan opted for Irish–American politics; and in September, Dillon, who had actually worked alongside Parnell in opposing the crimes bill during the summer, and who, like Davitt, was eager to avoid an open split, announced his plans to soon retire from parliament and from Irish politics owing to ill-health.[76] Davitt, for his part, stayed the course but effectively isolated himself by publicly proclaiming his commitment to land nationalization, a policy generally perceived as communistic and antinational. He was heavily criticized after enunciating his scheme in his Liverpool speech of 6 June. Even the *Roscommon Herald*, the most radical provincial paper in the country, which had previously been well disposed towards him, now argued that state ownership of the land would be tantamount to 'the dena-

---

to discuss it. He claimed that Anna Parnell travelled to the meeting in Dublin 'and the result was that the Ladies' Land League was organized'; see D.B. Cashman, *The life of Michael Davitt, founder of the national land league*, in King (ed.), *Michael Davitt*, vol. i, p. 230. In this account of events, Anna Parnell could be said to have interpreted Davitt's earlier meeting with Parnell and others as the genesis of the Ladies' League, while Davitt could be said to have considered the resolution passed at the meeting in Dublin as the beginning. **71** Slater to Davitt, 9 May 1905, DP, TCD, MS 9511/5601. **72** Quoted in Callanan, *T.M. Healy*, p. 74. **73** Davitt, *The fall*, p. 362. **74** R. Foster, *Charles Stewart Parnell: the man and his family* (Sussex, 1979), p. 280. **75** Lyons, *Charles Stewart Parnell*, p. 227. **76** Lyons, *John Dillon*, p. 68.

tionalization of Ireland'.[77] In response to Davitt's new position, Parnell told William O'Brien, the rising young Parnellite, 'If I were Davitt, I should never define. The moment he becomes intelligible, he is lost'.[78]

Following his speech in Liverpool, Davitt made preparations for a visit to the United States, where he was expected to attend a demonstration and meetings of various branches of the Land League in America. Plans had also been made for a conference in New York which was designed to resolve differences between two main factions of the League in the aftermath of Kilmainham.[79] It appears that Parnell had requested that Davitt make no speeches on land nationalization before leaving the country. Accompanied by William Redmond, Davitt stopped in Cork on 8 June on his way to Queenstown. Before his departure he addressed a large crowd, during which he said that he had no quarrel with Parnell and that he 'would not do or say anything to embarrass Mr Parnell's work or action in the house of commons. He has all the responsibility in the great movement upon his shoulders, and I am only a freelance by his side'. He said that his aim in travelling to the United States was to reassure audiences there that there was no split in the Land League movement. But, despite these declared intentions, he stated in his concluding peroration that 'what Ireland wants is the nationalization of the land administered in Dublin by an Irish Parliament (great cheering)'.[80] Part of his real agenda in travelling across the Atlantic was to internationalize the land question, to place it on a broad platform of social justice. It was in this context that he understood himself as a 'freelance'.

In an attempt to pre-empt Davitt's speeches in America, Parnell gave an interview to the *New York Herald* in which he argued that land nationalization would entail larger annual payments for tenant farmers than would be the case under 'our system'.[81] In America, Davitt was forced to defend his scheme. Speaking in New York, he argued that his plan was not a blueprint for communism, and he played down any differences between himself and Parnell.[82] Addressing a mass meeting of workingmen in the city two weeks later, he significantly attempted to situate the land question in an international labour context. He identified the plight of the Irish landed tenants not only with English democracy but also with the industrial workers of New York. His remarks were widely reported in the press (for example, the *New York Sun*, *Boston Herald* and the *Boston Globe*).[83] The *Brooklyn Daily Eagle* noted:

77 *Roscommon Herald*, 24 June 1882; cited in Bew, *Land*, pp 230–1. **78** William O'Brien, *Recollections* (London, 1905), p. 445. **79** Davitt, *The fall*, pp 366–7. **80** *FJ*, 9 June 1882. **81** Lane, *The origins*, p. 81. **82** *FJ*, 21 June 1882. **83** See Davitt's press cuttings book, 1881–2, DP, TCD, MS 9600.

Mr Davitt removed the Irish question from the Irish soil and made it a cosmopolitan issue. Just as the Freight Handlers' Union, the Carpenters' Union and so on insisted upon a readjustment of the relations between labour and capital, so, as Mr Davitt insisted, the Irishmen who would not pay rack-rents or any other excessive tax are striking against the tyranny of their employers. In other words, Irishmen in Ireland, he contended, are doing precisely what the strikers in New Jersey are doing; striking for higher wages; a large margin between the proceeds of their labour and the expense of living.[84]

The *New York Herald* acknowledged that Davitt had been well received at the mass meeting, but it questioned the benefit of his speech to the workingmen of New York, thousands of whom were on strike.[85]

By examining the land question in such a context, Davitt was leaving himself open to charges of communism. It was soon reported that there was rancour among the leaders of the Land League in America regarding the nature of the proposed land scheme.[86] In the Liverpool speech, Davitt had stated that there was 'not a particle more of difference' between the opinion which he held on the land question and that held by Parnell. In attempting to make this case he disingenuously said that there was no greater variance of outlook between himself and Parnell on this issue 'than there was when we first stood together on a public platform in Westport three years ago'. Ultimately, he based this on what he claimed to have been a firm belief that land nationalization would naturally follow on from peasant proprietorship. He continued, 'Believing this to be inevitable from the growing poverty of Irish agriculture, I am almost indifferent whether Mr. Parnell's plan or my own be adopted; but', he added, 'as I was the first to raise the cry of "The land for the people", I think the time has now come for giving a clear definition of what I mean and propose'.[87] This was an unconvincing statement, and Parnell was not the only figure in Ireland to reproach Davitt for adopting what was clearly a new land policy.

Matt Harris claimed that Davitt was attempting to destroy the movement which he himself had been instrumental in building.[88] And within days Harris was defended by James Daly who used the *Connaught Telegraph* to launch a personal attack on Davitt.[89] Daly's subsequent editorial was particularly vitriolic. In an attempt to divest Davitt of his status a leader of the Land League, he declared, 'The land for the people doctrine' had been proclaimed by Mayo nationalists some time before Davitt had 'by stealth possessed it'.[90] He hit a raw nerve with Davitt by further claiming that land nationalization was an invi-

---

84 *Brooklyn Daily Eagle*, 6 July 1882. **85** *New York Herald*, 6 July 1882. **86** Lane, *The origins*, p. 81. **87** *FJ*, 7 June 1882. **88** *FJ*, 21 June 1882. **89** *CT*, 24 June 1882. **90** Ibid., 1 July 1882.

tation to the British to rule Ireland, a point which Davitt had been particularly eager to refute in Liverpool. Davitt never, it must be stated, envisaged a final, definitive settlement of the land question under British rule. In Liverpool he had argued that the land nationalization policy was no more a recognition of England's right to rule Ireland 'than is involved in the payment of taxes or in calling upon its Government to advance the necessary funds for the carry out of a scheme of peasant proprietary'. He also tackled the argument that there would be resistance to the collection of a land tax. He stated that, 'given that such a tax would probably never exceed half the amount that is now paid in rent', people would willingly contribute; that security of the land and lack of fiscal obligation would ensure acceptance of the arrangement; and that people would be attracted by the potential for economic growth.[91] In this heated political climate, John Ferguson intervened in a damage limitation exercise, reiterating the feeble argument that there was no significant difference between Davitt and Parnell on agrarian policy.[92] But this intervention was futile. An extract from the *Irish Nation* featured in the *Connaught Telegraph* a week after Daly's stinging attack, in which Davitt was now castigated by Devoy.[93]

While in America, Davitt was supported by Patrick Ford, who was committed to land nationalization and vehemently opposed to the Kilmainham settlement. Ford worked closely with George during the latter's stay in Ireland in 1881–2.[94] But it is quite clear that Davitt was under pressure from the beginning of his tour. Shortly after his arrival there he wrote to Dillon telling him that he had been called upon by Devoy, who 'wore that conscious look of guilt which a knowledge of having wronged a friend engenders'.[95] Devoy had made it his business to disclose that, during the land war, Davitt had accepted a loan from a republican 'skirmishing fund'. Some weeks after his letter to Dillon, Davitt met Devoy in New York and paid back a \$735 balance from the fund, 'originally subscribed for "warfare" against England'.[96] Davitt paid the outstanding balance himself, and, although now 'almost without a cent', he was relieved to have 'that weight removed from me'.[97] An open rift between himself and Devoy emerged from this point, and, despite a later brief attempt at reconciliation,[98] they ultimately became bitter enemies, Davitt describing Devoy at one point as a 'satanic minded dog'.[99]

Davitt was unnerved by the intensity of the critical reaction to his land proposals. George wrote to Ford on 20 June recommending that he advise Davitt to remain steadfast.[1] It is obvious, however, that Davitt had not expected to

91 *FJ*, 7 June 1882. **92** *FJ*, 5 July 1882. **93** *CT*, 8 July 1882. **94** Lane, *The origins*, p. 69. **95** Davitt to John Dillon, 21 June 1882, DP, TCD, MS 9403/1555a. **96** Davitt, *The fall*, pp 169–70. **97** Quoted in Moody, *Davitt*, p. 537. **98** Terry Golway, *Irish rebel: John Devoy and America's fight for Ireland's freedom* (New York, 1998), pp 160–1. **99** Davitt to his sister, Sabina, 4 Jan. 1894, DP, TCD, MS 9325/97. **1** Lane, *The origins*, p. 84.

provoke such extreme hostility, and that he was particularly vexed by claims that he was being exploited by George. The *Connaught Telegraph* accused him of having become George's 'tool'.[2] The political fallout left Davitt uncharacteristically despondent. George's ideas did have some following in Ireland, principally among agricultural labourers and urban workers, and his land policy was to gain increasing support among Dublin radicals throughout the course of the 1880s.[3] Davitt, in fact, organized George's speaking engagements in the capital in 1884.[4] In 1883–4 land nationalization was also championed by members of the IRB, although generally for tactical reasons in undermining the Parnellite hold over the nationalist press.[5] Throughout the 1880s and 1890s there was some support for George and Davitt in Belfast, notably from the Revd J. Bruce Wallace, whose papers, *Brotherhood* and the *Belfast Weekly Star*, endorsed the alternative agrarian policy.[6] Davitt had, during his tour in the United States in 1882, secured Irish–American support for the continuation of a combative strategy on the land question;[7] but on leaving New York at the end of July he was in no doubt about the unpopularity of his own alternative agrarian scheme. He was, thereafter, much less willing to campaign publicly for land nationalization in Ireland, and instead concentrated his efforts more on promoting the policy in Britain.[8] Indeed, as late as 1890 Wallace's *Brotherhood* had to inform its readership that Davitt was committed to state ownership of the land, not peasant proprietorship.[9]

In a letter to Ford only days after Davitt's return to Ireland, George observed, in a somewhat critical manner, that the opposition had made Davitt 'morbidly afraid'.[10] Much of the hostility towards Davitt was truly visceral. Daly's editorial diatribe in the *Connaught Telegraph* denounced him in a very personal manner. Davitt was truly taken aback by the bitterness directed against him, but George's claim was something of an exaggeration. There is no doubt that the confidence with which Davitt had delivered his Liverpool speech was greatly diminished by the onslaught, but by proceeding gingerly he was also determined to avert a split in the nationalist movement. He had made this clear in an interview with the *Freeman's Journal* during his return journey from America: 'I will not fight the question of Nationalization against peasant proprietary if there is the slightest chance of creating dissension in the Land League'.[11]

In preaching land nationalization almost immediately after his release from Portland, Davitt had obviously hoped to re-build and maintain a radical momentum after Kilmainham. While reflecting on current controversies during a short period in Richmond jail, Dublin, between March and June 1883,

2 *CT*, 8 July 1882. 3 Lane, *The origins*, pp 89–90. 4 See Davitt's letter to George, 19 Mar. 1884, HGP, NYPL. 5 McGee, *The IRB*, p. 118. 6 Lane, *The origins*, pp 89–90. 7 Davitt, *The fall*, pp 366–7. 8 See Davitt's letter to Sabina, Nov. 1884, DP, TCD, MS 9325/84. 9 Lane, *The origins*, p. 90. 10 Quoted in ibid., pp 84–5. 11 *FJ*, 29 July 1882.

where he and Healy were imprisoned for having made seditious speeches several months earlier,[12] he remarked on the hopes he had had on his release from prison the previous year, one of which was to 'drive P[arnell] forward on nationalization'.[13] Indeed, Davitt's zeal for sustained radical activity was reflected in draft proposals which he had submitted to Parnell for a new 'National Land Reform and Industrial Union of Ireland'. Land nationalization had been included in the initial draft but, conscious of Parnell's aversion to the scheme, Davitt replaced it with the plain objective of 'the complete abolition of the landlord system'.[14] He had clearly hoped that Parnell might be persuaded to embrace a broad radical agenda. He therefore presented his proposals to the Irish leader on 3 August 1882, only a short period after his return from America. Although at this point his political influence had diminished, at least in the short-term, he made a concerted effort to sustain the radicalism of the Land League.

The draft proposals comprised quite an extensive social reform programme. Besides the complete abolition of landlordism, the social and economic objectives of the proposed organization included improvement of the social conditions of agricultural labourers, especially in the area of housing; improvement of agricultural methods; development of Irish fisheries; and the revival of Irish industries. In its educational provisions, it recommended improvement in scientific and technical education of the artisan and labouring classes; and the encouragement of national literature and the cultivation of the Irish language. In its political objectives, it sought the repeal of the Union; the abolition of the grand jury system of county government; improvement of representation on local boards and municipal bodies; and, pending independence, payment of national representatives and the extension of the franchise.[15] The formulation of the ideas embodied in these proposals was not a knee-jerk reaction to the post-Kilmainham political climate. During the land war, Davitt had hoped that the Land League would develop a broader social

12 Davitt had made his speech at Navan in November 1882, in which he warned that the peasantry in the west of Ireland would seize the land if the question of their dire poverty was not addressed in legislation; see Sheehy Skeffington, *Michael Davitt*, pp 115–16. Legal proceedings were brought against Davitt for this speech, and also against Healy for similar inflammatory remarks. In default of a recognizance of £1000 each, the condition of which was that they show good behaviour for a year, they and P.J. Quinn, a former secretary of the Land League, were imprisoned; see Callanan, *T.M. Healy*, pp 84–5. Davitt and Healy were arrested on the same day, 8 Feb. 1883, and were taken to Kilmainham jail and held in the cells which had been occupied by Parnell, Dillon and J.J. O'Kelly in 1881–2. Davitt and Healy had not spent a full day in Kilmainham before being removed to the Richmond Bridewell. It was suggested by the *Freeman's Journal* that even though the prisoners had first-class status, the governor was uncertain how to treat them; *FJ*, 9 Feb. 1883.   13 'Miscellaneous writings in Richmond prison, Dublin', 25 Mar. 1883, DP, TCD, MS 9537.   14 Moody, *Davitt*, p. 540.   15 DP, TCD, MS 9398.

function, 'independent of its special mission', with particular focus on the farming and labouring classes. In February 1880 he and Ferguson represented the League at the Land Law Reform League conference in London in an attempt to extend the Land League's influence in Britain.[16] It had, indeed, been Davitt's intention to effect a greater social function for the League after his return from America in November 1880, but his arrest a few months later thwarted such plans.[17]

The proposals which he presented to Parnell in August 1882 were, however, flatly rejected. Parnell's outright dismissal was consistent with his calculated move to supplant the radicalism within the national movement with a much more limited and conservative agenda. It must be remembered, of course, that the Land League had never been shaped or controlled by Parnell or any of his parliamentary colleagues; most of the League's leading figures were either Fenians or former Fenians.[18] In April 1882 Healy told the commons that he had 'as little to do with the political working of the Land League as any Gentleman of the Treasury Bench'.[19] Even at the height of the land war, Dillon himself had apparently complained that 'They all knew that if they wanted to decide on a land bill they must go up to Sackville Street, and ask the Land League before they could decide on a plan of action'.[20] But Parnell now saw the opportunity to consolidate control. His rejection of the proposed 'National Land Reform and Industrial Union' frustrated Davitt, quite literally so. Davitt was forced to write at the head of his draft paper, 'Submitted to and strongly disapproved of by Parnell, August '82'.[21] That day he noted in his diary, 'there is very little backbone in this man after all'.[22] The proposed body was never established, and instead the Irish National League (INL) was founded two months later as a replacement of the Land League. This followed negotiations between Thomas Brennan, Davitt, Dillon and Parnell at the latter's home, Avondale, in September. Parnell was averse to any suggestion of a revival of militant agrarian agitation, but he agreed to call a national conference to consider a programme for a new reform organization.[23] The 'Avondale treaty', as it came to be known, involved an understanding whereby Parnell would define land policy for the new body and Davitt would have the opportunity to shape other social and industrial proposals.

When the national conference to establish the new organization met at the Ancient Concert Rooms in Dublin on 17 October, the assembled delegates were presented with a proposed programme and constitution which had been drafted by Healy and Timothy Harrington, 'under Mr Parnell's direc-

16 E.W. McFarland, *John Ferguson, 1836–1900: Irish issues in Scottish politics* (East Lothian, 2003), p. 109. 17 Davitt, *Jottings*, p. 98. 18 Davitt, *The fall*, pp 163–4. 19 Quoted in Callanan, *T.M. Healy*, p. 69. 20 Quoted in Ibid., p. 641, fn. 128. 21 DP, TCD, MS 9398. 22 Quoted in Moody, *Davitt*, p. 541. 23 Davitt, *The fall*, pp 370–2.

tion'. The platform of the new body was principally national self-government. Its other objectives included local self-government; extension of the parliamentary and municipal franchises; and the advancement of Irish labour and industrial interests. Land reform was dealt with in Article 2, which resolved to effect not the complete abolition of landlordism, as proposed in Davitt's earlier draft, but an amendment to the purchase clause of the 1881 Land Act and the admission of tenants excluded from the terms of the Act, notably lease-holders.[24] Some of Davitt's proposals were included in the programme: improvement in the condition of agricultural labourers; the cultivation of Irish industries; national self-government; and reform of local government. However, it omitted his proposals on housing; fisheries; agricultural practices; education; national literature and the Irish language; and the payment of MPs. Ultimately, the adoption of the main programme before the conference was, as Moody notes, the effective ratification of the 'Kilmainham treaty'.[25] Moreover, the constitution of the new League gave the Irish Party a position of dominance in the organization's central council. Davitt later wrote,

> The outcome of the conference of October, 1882, was the complete eclipse, by a purely parliamentary substitute, of what had been a semi-revolutionary organization. It was, in a sense, the overthrow of a movement and the enthronement of a man; the replacing of nationalism by Parnellism; the investing of the fortunes and guidance of the agitation, both for national self-government and land reform, in a leader's nominal dictatorship.[26]

Davitt viewed the understanding which he had reached with Parnell at Avondale as the only viable way of avoiding a major split in the national movement at that time. Nonetheless, his disillusionment was obvious. During his speech at the conference he significantly alluded to his own plan for land reform, and stated that, notwithstanding his recent agreement with Parnell that he would not divide the conference on land nationalization, he 'reserved the right to advocate my own principles'. He let it be known that he could not conscientiously advocate the views which Parnell held on the land question. He then caustically stated what he considered to be the fundamental difference in their respective positions: 'I recognize that in any movement, no matter how advanced that movement may be, there must necessarily be a Conservative and a Radical element'. But, again resorting to tactical diplomacy, he continued, 'I can in connection with this movement as a representative of the Radical element take up towards Mr. Parnell […] a friendly Opposition'.[27]

24 Ibid., pp 374–5. 25 Moody, *Davitt*, p. 544. 26 Davitt, *The fall*, pp 377–8. 27 *FJ*, 18 Oct.

He later wrote that during the discussions at Avondale, it was he himself, not Parnell, who proposed that he should not raise the question of land nationalization during the conference.[28] However, the sharp differences between the two were apparent to all during the conference proceedings. The significance of Davitt's statement and his contribution to the conference was that it signalled the formal launch of his career as a freelance radical, even though it was a role in which he was, as yet, not completely comfortable.

Following what Lyons describes as 'the Thermidor of the land war',[29] Davitt began to turn his attention more to international social radicalism, campaigning on a Georgeite platform in promulgating the principle of land nationalization, and becoming involved in labour politics in Britain. Even though he largely avoided preaching land nationalization in Ireland, he still remained a somewhat isolated figure in the mainstream of nationalist politics throughout the 1880s. Most of his close radical associates left Ireland after the formation of the INL: after his resignation as treasurer of the Land League, Egan emigrated to the United States;[30] Brennan became an honorary secretary of the INL, but was so embittered following the meetings at Avondale that he, too, left for America;[31] and in the late spring of 1883 Dillon, having vacated his Tipperary seat, left to stay with his brother in Colorado, where he was to remain for over two years.[32] It must also be remembered that Davitt had no immediate family in Ireland; both his parents had, of course, died in America. He was quite close to Sabina, probably because she was his only literate sibling.[33] She travelled to Ireland in August 1882, and was later able to visit him during his imprisonment in Richmond jail. But it is apparent that he was not used to such supportive family attention: after only two weeks of incarceration he wrote to her, 'There is no necessity of you coming to see me oftener than twice a week [...] It is a waste of time to be coming every day'.[34]

Through political expediency Davitt hitched himself to the constitutional wagon, but it was an uncomfortable and, at times, lonely ride. He became a member of the organizing committee of the INL but did so reluctantly, engaging with it, as William O'Brien later noted, 'only in the domain of censure'.[35] The committee, consisting of thirty members, was initially intended as a provisional body, established pending the election of a central council. However, such a council was never elected and the committee itself remained the governing body of the INL. The new League was in stark contrast to the 'National Land Reform and Industrial Union' proposed by Davitt in his draft,

1882. **28** Davitt, *The fall*, p. 379. **29** Lyons, *Charles Stewart Parnell*, p. 237. **30** Egan was in Ireland in Dec. 1882, but by the end of Feb. 1883 he had left for the US; see DP, TCD, MS 9368/822. **31** Joan Haslip, *Parnell: a biography* (London, 1936), p. 244; see also Bew, *Land*, p. 238. **32** Lyons, *John Dillon*, pp 68–70. **33** Moody, *Davitt*, p. 490. **34** Davitt to Sabina, 21 Feb. 1883, DP, TCD, MS 9325/[103/7]. **35** William O'Brien, *Recollections*, p. 473.

which would have been democratically elected. In fact, the National League was ultimately designed to advance the electoral success of the Irish Party. Moreover, in consolidating the organization of the Party over the course of the next two years, Parnell aimed to simultaneously emasculate the left wing of nationalism. The role which Healy was to play in this project cannot be underestimated either.[36] The process of consolidation extended to Britain where the Irish National League of Great Britain (INLGB) displaced the Home Government Confederation.[37] As early as November 1882, Davitt informed Dillon that his new INL colleague, Joseph Biggar, and the executive of the Land and Labour League of Great Britain was doing its best to boycott his forthcoming lectures in the north of England.[38] Biggar was clearly determined to use his influence, wherever possible, to thwart Davitt. At the beginning of November 1882, he wrote to John Miskelly, a prominent figure in the Belfast branch of the INL, effectively upbraiding him for providing Davitt with a platform in the city.[39]

Parnell and his 'brilliant young lieutenants',[40] such as Healy and O'Brien, were very much central to what Davitt termed the parliamentary 'counter-revolution'.[41] Following Egan's resignation as treasurer of the Land League, the funds which had been held in Paris, totalling over £30,000, were not even transferred to the treasury of the INL but were controlled entirely by Parnell himself, with Biggar and Justin McCarthy acting as co-trustees.[42] The operation of the INL was crucial in financing the electoral campaigns of the Irish Party, most notably in preparation for the 1885 general election, the first since the Representation of the People Act (December 1884) which increased the Irish electorate by over two hundred per cent between 1884 and 1885.[43] By the time of the election, a special parliamentary fund, organized through the National League, had accumulated £17,950, most of which was expended on election expenses. The fund was also used to pay MPs after the election.[44] Moreover, to facilitate parliamentary success, Party discipline was consolidated. According to Callanan, Healy was the 'fiercest exponent of a disciplined party machine'. At the behest of Parnell, he drafted an election pledge in August 1884 which required a candidate to agree to 'sit, act and vote with the Irish party, and to resign one's seat if it should become impossible to carry out

36 See Callanan, *T.M. Healy*, p. 97. **37** C.C. O'Brien, *Parnell and his party* (Oxford, 1957), p. 132. In April 1883, the Land League in the United States was reconstituted the National League of America; see Davitt, *The fall*, pp 390–1. **38** Davitt to Dillon, 27 Nov., 1882, DP, TCD, MS 9403/1561. **39** Frank Thompson, *The end of Liberal Ulster: land agitation and land reform, 1868–1886* (Belfast, 2001), p. 283. **40** Davitt, *The fall*, p. 378. **41** Ibid., p. 377. **42** O'Brien, *Parnell*, pp 135–6, 140. **43** See B.M. Walker, 'The 1885 and 1886 general elections – a milestone in Irish history' in Peter Collins (ed.), *Nationalism and unionism, conflict in Ireland, 1885–1921* (Belfast, 1996), p. 3. **44** O'Brien, *Parnell*, pp 138–40.

such an undertaking', or if the Party deemed the member to be in breach of his commitment.[45] What distinguished this rule from other pledges was that it was compulsory and had to be undertaken before the candidate was elected; previously, home rule candidates in 1874 and 1880 had not been subject to such an obligation.[46]

The process of selecting parliamentary candidates also changed significantly. In what was his ultimate bid at this time to impede the march of Parnellism and to effect a resurgence in radicalism, Davitt recommended in January 1884 the nomination of former 'suspects' of 1881–2, the 'Irish representatives racy of the soil', for the forthcoming general election.[47] He reckoned on eight or nine hundred men dispersed throughout the country who could be selected. Accordingly, he called for the scheduling of conventions at this early stage to democratically select candidates. In response, Parnell advised counsel with the Party before any action was taken. Infuriated, Davitt wrote in his diary, '[Parnell] Asserts principle that no convention should be held without his consent!! Dictatorship with a vengeance this'.[48] The ruling which was eventually agreed by the organizing committee of the National League for the selection of candidates was framed to secure conservative control of the county conventions. Representation at the convention included four delegates from each National League branch in the county and three representatives of the Parliamentary Party. Of particular significance was the provision for the attendance of any of the Catholic clergy of the county. This was not an article of the National League constitution, and, according to Conor Cruise O'Brien, its adoption was probably, to some extent, aimed at thwarting Davitt and others who shared his politics.[49] Davitt described it as a 'clerical franchise', and complained bitterly to Richard McGhee, a radical Irish immigrant in Glasgow with whom he was to have a long friendship, that it meant that 'if the priests so choose they can run their own candidates'.[50] As it happens, only two days later, Archbishop Walsh of Dublin issued a private directive to his priests in Wicklow, where the first pre-election convention was held, instructing them to approach the convention with what was an essentially political agenda, part of which was the blocking of surprise candidates.[51]

Davitt's frustration in attempting to revive the left wing of nationalism was evident by the end of 1882.[52] The pressure was mounting by July 1883 when

45 Callanan, *T.M. Healy*, pp 99–100. **46** O'Brien, *Parnell*, pp 140–2. **47** *United Ireland*, 6 and 12 Jan. 1884; cited in Callanan, *T.M. Healy*, p. 97. **48** Davitt's diary, 25 July 1884, DP, TCD, MS 9541. **49** O'Brien, *Parnell*, pp 128–9. **50** Davitt's letter to McGhee, 23 Sept. 1885; cited in ibid., p. 129. McGhee was elected nationalist MP for South Louth in 1895 – Davitt introduced him in the house of commons on 10 Apr. 1896 (DP, TCD, MS 9567) – and MP for Mid–Tyrone in 1910; see N.C. Fleming and Alan O'Day, *The Longman handbook of modern Irish history since 1800* (Harlow, 2005), p. 157. **51** O'Brien, *Parnell*, p. 129. **52** See Davitt's letter to Dillon, 22

he told McGhee that the task was akin to 'twisting ropes of sand'.[53] O'Brien remarks that 'Despite the appearance of democracy, the National League remained throughout the period an autocratically controlled body, ruled by a committee it had not elected, and whose powers were undefined'.[54] The clerical factor was, as Davitt noted, also highly significant. This became apparent in the Bradlaugh case in 1884. The Radical, Charles Bradlaugh, had been elected to parliament for Northampton in 1880, but as an avowed atheist he was not permitted to take the oath of allegiance and was prevented from taking his seat until 1886. In a vote in May 1880 on the formation of a select committee to examine the legalities of the case, twelve out of twenty-seven Parnellites, including Parnell himself, supported him. However, by 1884 the situation had changed dramatically; in the vote in February that year, Bradlaugh did not receive the support of one home rule MP. Indeed, since Parnell's release from Kilmainham, Irish members consistently voted against Bradlaugh's admission to parliament, or at least abstained on the crucial divisions.[55] To some extent, this *volte-face* was indicative of a sense of grievance at the apparent failure of British radicalism to mount a credible opposition to coercion bills; but ultimately it reflected the Irish Party's eagerness to cement a political accommodation with the Catholic church in Ireland. Among prominent nationalists, Davitt alone consistently voiced support for the Radical member for Northampton, despite the moral sensibilities of the Irish hierarchy. At a meeting in Halifax in January 1883, at which he expressed his solidarity with Bradlaugh, he said wryly, 'I expect the calling of a Vatican Council after that, in order to pronounce on my conduct'.[56]

An historic understanding between the Irish Party and the Catholic church was, in fact, arrived at in October 1884. The bishops formally called on the Parliamentary Party to represent Catholic educational interests in the house of commons, namely grants for Catholic schools in Ireland. This marked a fundamental turning point. The political significance of this cannot have been lost on Davitt. O'Brien observes, 'Parnellism was now accepted; from now on in Catholic Ireland no one but a crank could condemn it as revolutionary'.[57] The basis of the 'clerical–nationalist alliance', as it is termed by Emmet Larkin, was, in effect, a recognition by the hierarchy of Parnell's leadership of Irish nationalism and of the legitimacy of his Party. In shaping a modern party, and in building a political base, Parnell did not depend on the Catholic clergy to the same extent that Daniel O'Connell had during the campaign for Catholic

Nov. 1882 in O'Day and Stevenson, *Irish historical documents*, p. 103. **53** Quoted in McFarland, *John Ferguson*, p. 145. **54** O'Brien, *Parnell*, p. 128. **55** Ibid., p. 50, 89. **56** Quoted in Walter L. Arnstein, *The Bradlaugh case, a study in late Victorian opinion and politics* (Oxford, 1965), p. 223. **57** O'Brien, *Parnell*, p. 90.

emancipation in the 1820s and the Repeal movement in the 1840s. In fact, the hierarchy was left in no doubt about its responsibilities under the clerical-nationalist accord in April–May 1888, when it had to withstand the dictates of Rome in order to preserve the alliance.[58]

By the mid-1880s Davitt was heavily involved in social activism in Britain. Only days after the national conference in Dublin which established the INL, he left on a tour of Scotland during which he preached land nationalization.[59] He particularly hoped to encourage a more co-ordinated anti-landlord protest in the Highlands. Fresh from the divisions in Ireland, he was heartened by his reception, although he was offended by the more unscrupulous side of local Irish politics in Glasgow, having been asked to address a regular gathering of the city's branch of the Land League, but instead finding himself forced to make an unprepared speech before a large meeting where admission had been charged.[60] During the Scottish campaign, he was joined by McGhee, Ferguson and Edward McHugh, all Irish immigrants who had lived in Scotland for years (McHugh since his childhood), and who, like him, were strongly influenced by the evangelical radicalism of Henry George.[61] Davitt considered the mobilization of British democracy crucial to Ireland's cause. He deemed the Irish constitutional leaders 'Political jackasses!' for failing to recognize the potential in identifying with the social and democratic movement in Britain, and he himself vowed to 'give it a helping hand [...]'[62]

McGhee, Ferguson and McHugh strongly supported Davitt's land reform policy and his involvement in British working-class politics. They themselves were influential figures in the labour and trade union movements. McGhee and Ferguson were particularly close to him and were among the few steadfast friends and allies that he had, especially in the post-Kilmainham years of isolation. Ferguson provided a secure platform in Glasgow where, according to E.W. McFarland, Davitt became 'the darling of Glasgow Irish audiences'.[63] Davitt even enjoyed something of a cult following among young Irish radicals in the city.[64] When Celtic's football ground was opened in the city in the early 1890s, he was given the honour of laying the first sod of grass.[65]

---

58 E. Larkin, *The Roman Catholic church and the plan of campaign in Ireland, 1886–1888* (Cork, 1978), pp xiii, 318–21. **59** See Davitt, *Land nationalization; or, National peasant proprietary. Michael Davitt's lectures in Scotland* (1885) in King (ed.), *Michael Davitt*, vol. i. **60** McFarland, *John Ferguson*, p. 155, note 54. **61** See Davitt, *Land nationalization*, p. 11; and McFarland, *John Ferguson*, pp 136–7, 163–4; see also Andrew G. Newby, *The life and times of Edward McHugh* (New York, 2005); Eric Taplin, 'Edward McHugh (1853–1915)', and 'Richard McGhee (1851–1930)', in J. Bellamy and J. Saville (eds), *Dictionary of labour biography*, vii (London, 1984), pp 152–9 **62** Davitt's diary, 31 Dec. 1883, DP, TCD, MS 9536. **63** McFarland, *John Ferguson*, p. 88. **64** Ibid., pp 165–6, 88, 138–9. **65** See Davitt diary, 4 Aug. 1894, DP, TCD, MS 9555. In this entry he writes, 'Attended football match at Celtic club grounds. Place looks well – much better than the day I laid the Donegal sod as a "foundation" for the grassy plot'.

During his arduous lecturing engagement in Scotland, he was a frequent visitor to Ferguson's home, 'Benburb', in Lenzie. Ferguson's publishing house, Cameron, Ferguson and Co. also produced Davitt's two pamphlets on land nationalization, containing the speech which he made in Manchester and his lectures in Scotland. Indeed, during the 1880s Davitt became a notable public speaker and journalist. His journalism was an important conduit through which to articulate his views, especially at a time when Parnellism was represented in the form of *United Ireland*, a partisan organ under the zealous editorship of William O'Brien who rounded on any expression of dissent. Given that Davitt was the principal dissenter, the paper was to the forefront in attacking his proposals for land nationalization.[66]

The marginalization of Davitt was not, however, a straightforward business. The problem for Parnell and his lieutenants was how to undermine that moral capital which Davitt possessed. O'Brien later acknowledged the essence of Davitt's appeal: 'Suffering is the most powerful of all arguments with the Irish people'.[67] Margaret O'Callaghan remarks, indeed, that, despite a youth and early manhood spent in Lancashire, Davitt 'imaginatively [...] still remained wedded to the image of a family on the roadside near Straide thirty years before'.[68] On a visit to Straide in January 1880, he made a speech on a platform erected over the ruins of the old homestead from which he and his family had been evicted. He lamented,

> How often in a strange land has my boyhood's ear drunk in the tale of outrage and wrong and infamy perpetuated here in the name of English laws and in the interest of territorial greed. In listening to the accounts of famine and sorrow, of deaths and landlordism, of coffinless graves, of scenes
>
> > On highway's side, where oft were seen
> > The wild dog and vulture keen
> > Tug for the limbs and gnaw the face
> > Of some starved child of our Irish race,
>
> what wonder that such laws should become hateful, and when felt by personal experience of their tyranny and injustice, that a life of irreconcilable enmity to them should follow, and that standing here on the

66 See James Loughlin, 'Constructing the political spectacle, Parnell, the press and national leadership, 1879–86', in D. George Boyce and Alan O'Day (eds), *Parnell in perspective* (London, 1991), pp 231–7. 67 William O'Brien, *Recollections*, p. 445. 68 Margaret O'Callaghan, 'Crime, nationality and the law: the politics of land in late Victorian Ireland' (1989); quoted in Bew, 'Parnell and Davitt' in Boyce and O'Day (eds), *Parnell in perspective* (Dublin, 1991), pp 38–9.

spot where I first drew breath, in sight of a levelled home, with memories of privation and tortures crowding upon my mind, I should swear
to devote the remainder of that life to the destruction of what has blast-
ed my early years, pursued me with a vengeance throughout manhood,
and leaves my family in exile today [...][69]

The difficulties faced in suppressing Davitt were shrewdly noted by the
London correspondent of the *Irish Times*, who wrote, 'The trouble [for Parnell]
is how to get rid of [Davitt], or [...] how to shake him from his rival height.
[They] are afraid as yet to attack Mr Davitt himself, so they attack him through
Mr George'[70]

Nevertheless, Davitt himself came under increasing pressure. Even George
expressed surprise at the ferocity of the attacks. In a telegram to Davitt in
January 1883, he had to exclaim, 'How bitter they are against you. You can
see it from their published letters'.[71] In July 1884 Davitt happened to meet
O'Brien in Dublin and was left in no doubt about his present position: 'Hot
discussion. If I won't join P. Party I am to be forced to the wall'.[72] O'Brien's
threat followed a speech which Parnell made several months earlier in
Drogheda in which he directly criticized the idea of an alliance between British
democracy and Irish nationalism and referred to Davitt's land policy as 'a will
o' the wisp [...] which may lead to serious disunion'.[73] This was a defining
speech in that it marked Parnell's first public rift with Davitt. In October, they
both accidentally crossed paths at Charing Cross Station, and, from Davitt's
diary entry, their mutual animosity was evident: '[Parnell] seemed surprised
[...] No politics talked. Cold formality on both sides'.[74] Significantly, as early
as July 1882, Fanny Parnell had informed her mother that, after conversing
with Davitt, she was convinced that he 'hates Charles!'.[75] Parnell's Drogheda
speech was important in his relations with Davitt, but, as C.C. O'Brien comments, it had a much wider significance, in that it was indicative of the new
confidence of the Parliamentary Party and of its hold over the nationalist
movement. It clearly reflected that the Party 'did not feel obliged to use its
old diplomacy towards the Land League's founder. At the same time it was a
solid piece of reassurance for any propertied nationalists who still feared revolutionary elements in Parnellism'.[76]

In the constitutional movement in Ireland, Davitt was an outsider. He was
on good terms with a small number of people, including John Redmond (at

69 Quoted in *Irish Bits*, 13 Aug. 1898, in King (ed.), *Michael Davitt*, vol. ii, p. 3. **70** Quoted in
Oban Times, 19 Jan. 1884. **71** George to Davitt, 9 Jan. 1883, DP, TCD, MS 9332/245. **72**
Davitt's diary, 23 July 1884, DP, TCD, MS 9541. **73** *FJ*, 16 Apr., 1884 (Parnell's speech was
made on 15 Apr.). **74** Davitt's diary, 14 Oct. 1884, DP, TCD, MS 9540. **75** Quoted in Foster,
Charles Stewart Parnell, p. 248. **76** O'Brien, *Parnell*, p. 88.

least during much of the 1880s)[77] and Archbishop Thomas Croke.[78] But, besides Dillon, the person whom he respected most in mainstream Irish politics was probably the Quaker, Alfred Webb, a man of 'the highest moral bravery'.[79] One of the books which Davitt was permitted to have in Portland was Webb's *Compendium of Irish biography* (1878), which the latter sent to him with the inscription, 'Michael Davitt, with the love and respect of the author, 10 August 1881'.[80] In later years they shared the same views on Indian nationalism, the Boer war and anti-Semitism;[81] and during Davitt's last days they worked together on the question of denominational education.[82] Davitt believed there were 'few, if any, men in Ireland […] more deserving […] of all the rewards of a blameless life and of a long unselfish service to the cause of Ireland'.[83] In her introduction to Webb's autobiography, Marie-Louise Legg points out that 'Alone of the leaders of Irish nationalism […] Davitt never failed Webb, and Webb admired Davitt in return'.[84] Webb was appointed the acting treasurer of the National League when it was founded in 1882, but, 'not being able to stand Parnell's autocratic arrangement about funds', he later resigned.[85] Parnell had attempted to dissuade him from taking such a course, informing him that his resignation would 'do incalculable damage to the movement'.[86] For over a year, he continued to appeal to Webb 'not to act hastily', but it was to no avail.[87] When Webb did eventually resign in June 1884, Davitt praised him for his 'dignified protest by way of resignation'.[88] Another close associate and friend of Davitt's in Ireland was James Collins of Dublin, who acted as a confidant and the manager of some of Davitt's affairs.[89] Collins appears to have had some responsibility in Ireland for distribution of Davitt's

---

77 Laura McNeil, 'Land, labor and liberation', p. 368.   **78** Mark Tierney, *Croke of Cashel, the life of Archbishop Thomas William Croke, 1832–1902* (Dublin, 1976), p. 148.   **79** Davitt, *The fall*, p. 715.   **80** Quoted in Moody, *Davitt*, p. 479.   **81** Webb, *Alfred Webb*, p. 73; see also Davitt's letter to Webb, 30 Oct. 1899, DP, TCD, MS 9490/4962; and 3 June 1903, DP, TCD, MS 9490/4970. **82** Webb, *Alfred Webb*, pp 74–5.   **83** Davitt to Webb, Christmas 1903, DP, TCD, MS 9490/4971. **84** Webb, *Alfred Webb*, p. 11.   **85** Ibid., pp 48–9.   **86** Parnell to Webb, 29 May 1883, RJP NLI, MS 33, 144/16.   **87** Parnell to Webb, 11 June 1884, RJP, NLI, MS 33, 144/19.   **88** Davitt to Webb, 17 June 1884, DP, TCD, MS 9490/4957.   **89** Collins's background is unclear. He seems to have been connected with the constitutional movement, and had an early association with Isaac Butt (Collins to Butt, 9 Sept. [?], DA, DMS, MS MD/1). In a letter dated 13 Apr. 1886, Davitt endorsed Collins's application for the position of superintendent of the cleansing department of Dublin corporation (DA, DMS, MS MD/3). The correspondence between Davitt and Collins shows that Davitt confided in Collins on political matters, and that the latter not only managed some of Davitt's affairs in Ireland, particularly during Davitt's bankruptcy in the early 1890s (see Davitt to Collins, 1892, DA, DMS, MS MD/9), but was also a friend of the Davitt family when they lived in Ballybrack, Co. Dublin (see, for instance, Davitt to Collins, 1895, DA, DMS, MS MD/16). In 1893 Davitt wrote to Dillon, requesting that he speak to the postmaster general in order to secure a position in the GPO, Dublin, for Collins's 18-year-old son (Davitt to Dillon, 29 Nov. 1893, DP, TCD, MS 9404/1617).

paper, the *Labour World*,[90] the editorship of which Davitt used as a platform to launch an attack on Parnell in 1890–1 during the O'Shea divorce scandal.

Following the national conference in Dublin in 1882, at which Davitt declared his intention to represent the radical element of the movement in a 'friendly opposition' to Parnell, the *Connaught Telegraph* commented, 'The position of Mr Davitt in the whole business in very suspicious [...] It is our firm belief that [he] would oppose Mr. Parnell if he dare do it; and if ever the time comes in which he thinks he can safely oppose [him] he will'.[91] From the early 1880s Davitt certainly felt at least inclined to seriously challenge Parnell and Parnellism, especially after the latter's Drogheda speech. Nevertheless, he eschewed such a course for a number of reasons. He believed that a formal opposition would precipitate deep disunion within the ranks of the movement. The evidence certainly indicates that the Castle authorities were eagerly anticipating a split in the summer of 1884.[92] Davitt was gravely worried about the impact which such a development would have on the political base in America. He apparently expressed his fears in a letter to the nationalist parliamentarian, F.H. O'Donnell, around this time. 'The Americans feel terribly sold', he wrote, 'but the admission that Parnellism is a failure would be the utter destruction of what is left of the Land League movement in the United States'.[93] For Davitt, unity was imperative. In 1903 he interestingly remarked to McGhee that he considered the Land League movement to have, 'in a sense', existed up until the Parnell split.[94] Moody maintains that Davitt's decision to avoid open confrontation after 1882 reflected his 'great moral courage' and lack of personal ambition.[95] It is true, Davitt did show considerable restraint, but his actions were based more on *realpolitik*.

Parnell's rebuke at Drogheda not only provoked Davitt but also McGhee and Ferguson, both of whom were prepared to retaliate. Davitt, however, cautioned against any retaliatory remarks.[96] In a letter to McGhee he elaborated on his reasons for avoiding a breach with the Irish leader. He explained, with some wishful thinking, that the Parliamentary Party was fearful of the possible support which 'nationalization candidates' would get from artisans and labourers after the extension of the franchise.[97] He believed, therefore, that the Party might make a pre-emptive move by opposing the suffrage bill which Gladstone had only just recently introduced to the house of commons in February 1884.[98] He considered extension of the franchise crucial to the

90 See Davitt to Collins, 17 Sept. 1890, DP, DMS, MS MD/6. 91 *CT*, 21 Oct. 1882. 92 McFarland, *John Ferguson*, p. 145. 93 F.H. O'Donnell, *The history of the Irish parliamentary party*, vol. i (London, 1910), p. 374. 94 Davitt to McGhee, 7 Aug. 1903, DP, TCD, MS 9328/[181/13]. 95 Moody, *Davitt*, pp 545–6. 96 McFarland, *John Ferguson*, p. 145. 97 Davitt to McGhee, Apr. 1884, DP, TCD, MS 9328/[180/5–9]. 98 H.C.G. Matthew, *Gladstone, 1875–1898* (Oxford, 1995), p. 176.

'propaganda of nationalization', for 'without the suffrage in the hands of the non-agricultural classes we can never hope to see our programme within measurable distance of the proverbial practical politics'. It was this which necessitated patience and diplomacy, at least 'for a time'. Yet he concluded with the reassurance, 'Of course, the time will come, when the Drogheda speech will and shall be answered'.[99] He imparted similar advice to Ferguson: 'There is great strength in a well regulated silence […] continue to preach *ideas and not men* and wait for the victory of the franchise'.[1]

It cannot be doubted that Davitt had a grudging appreciation for Parnell's attributes as a leader.[2] Ferguson definitely remained somewhat enamoured of Parnell's personality, notwithstanding the rancour of the 1880s.[3] But the rift between Parnell and Davitt was deep by the end of 1884 and there was much bitterness, despite the latter's later judgement that he had always found Healy, O'Brien and other lieutenants more Parnellite, 'in the anti-extreme sense', than the leader himself.[4] There is little to support Pauric Travers's suggestion that the dedication in Davitt's first major work, *Leaves from a prison diary, or, lectures to a 'solitary' audience* (1885),[5] may have been intended as a conciliatory gesture towards Parnell.[6] This work, based on Davitt's writings in Portland, was written in the form of a series of lectures given to 'Joe', a pet blackbird whose confidence Davitt had won during his solitary confinement in Portland, and to whom the book was dedicated. The wife of A.M. Sullivan, who visited Davitt in Portland, later described the bird as a thrush,[7] and from this Travers has suggested that the printed dedication to a blackbird may, in fact, have related to the 'blackbird of Avondale', as Parnell was known in popular song. However, this is highly unlikely, considering the extent of the divisions by this stage, and the fact that the text contained the first coherent formulation of Davitt's political ideas, ideas which underpinned his radicalism and set him apart from Parnell. Indeed, in a letter to Henry George shortly before its publication, he described it as having been 'designed for a kind of politico-socialist manifesto in Gt. Britain […] My object, of course, is to "get at" the democracies of England and Scotland in view of their coming enfranchisement so as to incline them towards justice to Ireland'.[8]

From the end of 1882 Davitt acted as the unofficial opposition in nationalist politics. Although he joined the organizing committee of the National League, he, as O'Brien later stated, rarely attended meetings, and when he addressed an audience as a member of the committee, his words were

99 As above, fn. 97.   **1** Davitt to Ferguson, 25 June 1884, DP, TCD, MS 9375/992.   **2** See Davitt to McGhee, 8 Oct. 1888, DP, TCD, MS 9328/[180/35].   **3** McFarland, *John Ferguson*, p. 138.   **4** Davitt, *The fall*, p. 378.   **5** The work was published in Dec. 1884 and dated as 1885.   **6** Travers made this suggestion in his 'Address to the Parnell Summer School', 12 Aug. 1997.   **7** Moody, *Davitt*, p. 491.   **8** Davitt to George, 8 Aug. 1884, HGP, NYPL.

'flavoured with a sub-acid criticism of whatever active policy happened to be for the moment in possession of the field'.[9] Davitt was certainly the bane of Parnellism, especially in its early years, but he was finding his role as a *frondeur* extremely taxing and his morale was suffering. In fact, it would be fair to say that he was largely unaccustomed to the cut and thrust of mainstream politics. His isolation was, no doubt, also compounded by the absence of Dillon who did not return until July 1885.[10] Indeed, it became clear in the spring of 1884 that Davitt himself was giving serious thought to leaving the country for a time. In May of that year, Ferguson wrote a letter to the *Freeman's Journal* in a somewhat emotional appeal to the Irish nation to call upon Davitt to forgo plans to move to Australia.[11] Ferguson had a propensity to act on impulse and Davitt was clearly irked by his 'well-meant' but politically damaging exuberance. Davitt replied to the *Freeman's Journal*, indicating that he had no plans to emigrate but was simply considering an extended lecturing tour in Australasia and North America.[12] He also angrily rejected Ferguson's proposition that he should enter parliament to represent Ireland's interests. The matter was not enough to damage their friendship, but Davitt believed that his radical associate had shown a singular lack of judgement. A parliamentary seat would, in Davitt's view, be the equivalent of a political gag. Moreover, he was at this stage determined that he would never sit in the British parliament.[13]

Towards the end of 1884, he made preparations for a tour of Europe, Egypt and Palestine which, he envisaged, would be followed by a series of lecturing engagements in Australia where he hoped to make some money. Commenting on the financial benefits experienced by Parnellite politicians, through increased business opportunities and lecturing appointments, Alan O'Day makes reference to Davitt's 'extended cruise in the Mediterranean' and concludes that while he was not involved in politics for personal gain, he 'was not loathe to accept lavish hospitality'.[14] However, the tour upon which Davitt embarked in early January 1885 was actually financed by the £400 which he received from his publisher in December for *Leaves from a prison diary*.[15] Moreover, the accusation that he accepted lavish hospitality is certainly not consistent with the position which he adopted in December 1885 when approached by a deputation from the Arran Quay ward, Dublin, requesting that he consider running as a candidate for the position of councillor in Dublin corporation. Davitt declared himself agreeable to the suggestion, but only on the condition that he could be sure of being excused from certain ceremonies connected with the corporation. He explained,

9 William O'Brien, *Recollection*, pp 470–1. 10 Lyons, *John Dillon*, p. 71. 11 *FJ*, 5 May 1884. 12 *FJ*, 6 May 1884. 13 See *Pilot* (Boston), 1 Aug. 1885. 14 Alan O'Day, *The English face of Irish nationalism, Parnellite involvement in British politics, 1880–86* (Dublin, 1977), p. 49. 15 James M. Cahalan, 'Michael Davitt: the "preacher of ideas", 1881–1906', *Éire-Ireland*, 9:1 (1976), p. 23.

There is banqueting and all that sort of thing in the Mansion House
that I have not as a rule taken part in [...] I do not think it is consistent
in a man who is constantly talking about an impoverished people [...]
to take part in junketing and banqueting [...][16]

According to Wilfred Scawen Blunt, Davitt did attend a function at the
Mansion House in September 1887, where he was received by the lord mayor
of Dublin, T.D. Sullivan. Nevertheless, it is acknowledged by Blunt that Davitt
was not normally in the habit of attending such social gatherings.[17]

Few things enthused Davitt like travel, and as he journeyed through France
(under police surveillance at times),[18] Italy and across the Mediterranean to
Egypt and Palestine, he filled his travel diary with copious notes on social,
political and cultural life in the respective countries, even making references
to the aesthetic attributes of men and women of different nationalities.[19] While
visiting different towns and cities he was conscious of disparities of poverty
and wealth, and while he would often make it his business to observe conditions in the poorer quarters,[20] he also found time to visit historical, architec-
tural and literary landmarks. In the course of his tour he visited the house of
Dante and of Michelangelo, and pondered the 'puzzle' of the tower of Pisa.[21]
In Rome, he marvelled at the interior of St Peter's and '[h]eard the pope [Leo
XIII] at the Cistine Chapel'.[22] In later entries of his travel diary, he commented
on the land system in Palestine, and a few days later recorded having
'Witnessed "Wailing of Jews" at Wall of Jerusalem'.[23] His distance from Ireland
in these months had given him time to think and to lick his political wounds.
He told Webb that he was glad to be away from speech making.[24] Webb had,
in fact, appealed for his support in a controversy surrounding an impending
visit to Ireland by the Prince of Wales.[25] The Parnellites, as represented by
United Ireland, had initially intended to simply boycott the visit. However,

---

16 *Glasgow Observer*, 26 Dec. 1885. **17** W.S. Blunt, *The land war in Ireland* (London, 1912), p.
312. **18** Davitt's diary, 5 and 6 January 1885, DP, TCD, MS 9543; 'From Ballybrack to Jerico',
MS 9643/70, 9643/102; Davitt's letter to Sabina from Monte Carlo, undated (sometime between
13 and 21 Jan. 1885), DP, TCD, MS 9325/87. **19** See Davitt's diary, 26 and 27 Jan., and 26 and
29 Mar. 1885, DP, TCD, MS 9543. During visits abroad in later years, Davitt also made observations on the physical attributes of indigenous peoples. Visiting Western Australia in 1895, he
found Aboriginal men 'strongly built but weak in the legs', and the women 'hideously ugly in the
face'; Davitt, *Life and progress in Australasia* (London, 1898), p. 37. In Samoa, which he visited
in Dec. 1895, he encountered a 'bright looking [...] courteous and agreeable people', whose men
were the 'finest built' and whose women the handsomest he had seen among native peoples; DP,
TCD, MS 9644. **20** For example, see Davitt's diary, 1 Jan., 26 Mar. and 29 Mar. 1885, DP, TCD,
MS 9543. **21** Ibid., 30 and 31 Jan. 1885. **22** Ibid., 1 and 2 Feb. 1885. **23** Ibid., 5 and 10 Apr.
1885. **24** Davitt to Webb, 5 Mar. 1885, DP, TCD, MS 9490/4954. **25** James Loughlin,
'Nationality and loyalty: Parnellism, monarchy and the construction of Irish identity, 1880–5' in
Boyce and O'Day, *Ireland in transition, 1867–1921* (London, 2004), pp 48–9.

to avoid unionist domination of the coverage, the nationalist press eventually adopted a critical, and even abusive, stance on the prince's visit. Webb opposed the Parnellite line and argued that a courteous reception of the royal visitors could affirm Irish rights and highlight opposition to coercion. In articulating these views – which were, in any case, ultimately based on his understanding that under home rule the monarch would be head of state – he incurred the wrath of nationalist opinion in Dublin. Davitt was determined to avoid further conflict with Parnell and his close associates and therefore declined to back Webb. But his response to Webb also reflected their respective identification with different traditions of nationalism, the latter informed more by the nationalism of Grattan, O'Connell and O'Neill Daunt rather than a nationalism based on historicist claims.

In the early weeks of Davitt's tour, after his arrival in Turin in the last week of January, he had a meeting with the veteran Hungarian leader, Louis Kossuth, whom he approached, furnished with a letter of introduction from Joseph Cowen, the Radical MP for Newcastle.[26] Cowen was sympathetic to Davitt and had earlier offered to pay his bail to save him from imprisonment in Richmond in 1883.[27] Davitt's encounter with Kossuth seemed to reinforce his sense of his own political purpose and its integrity. In his notes on this meeting he wrote that on parting, the old man said, 'no matter what happens my friend you and I will do our duty'. 'Duty', Davitt noted, 'seemed to be his highest idea of man's mission in society'.[28] This principle occurred to him later during his trip, when he reflected on returning home.[29] Indeed, it was difficult for him to completely escape Ireland. A week after his meeting with Kossuth, he found that his reputation had preceded him when a group of English residents in the hotel where he was staying in Rome boycotted the dining area of the establishment and prevailed on the innkeeper to request that Davitt take his meals in his room.[30] Yet this was the least of his worries. Though later enjoying the splendours of Naples, he was still troubled and depressed by the state of affairs in Ireland. His diary entry for 17 March indicated the degree to which he was affected by the 'practical capture' of the movement by Parnellism. He reflected,

> I wish I were there today and no cause for this tour. Have thought many-time since leaving that I was acting wrong to national cause to leave cause entirely in hands of P[arnell] caucus. No one has the courage to view critically their doings, and this encourages the few who are 'bossing' the

26 Davitt's diary, 24 Jan. 1885, DP, TCD, MS 9544. 27 William Duncan, *Life of Joseph Cowen (MP for Newcastle, 1874–86)* (New York, 1904), p. 184. 28 As above, fn. 26. 29 Davitt's diary, 24 Apr. 1885, DP, TCD, MS 9543. 30 *Pall Mall Gazette*, 14 Feb. 1885; see also Davitt's diary, 2 Feb. 1885, DP, TCD, MS 9543.

movement to do what they please – But on the other hand what could I do, even if I remained. To fight these men would be to fight P[arnell] who allows them to do what they please, in his name, and a contest of this kind is exactly what I have struggled to avoid during the last two years [...] It is better after all to be away, though it is hard to have to compel oneself to go away on account of the actions of a few men whom one has helped to lift out of obscurity and who only seek their own ambitions [...] However, they will or I am very much deceived, show themselves in their true light yet, and, perhaps, it may not be too late to lift the movement up to the level and strength of true democracy.[31]

By the end of April 1885, after having visited Egypt and Palestine, Davitt had already decided that on his return to Ireland he would postpone his trip to Australia, believing that it was his 'duty to return and try my best to push the popular movement in a more aggressive attitude'.[32] His eagerness to return to the political fray was heightened further when he learned in Geneva of the 'central board' scheme proposed by Joseph Chamberlain, then president of the Board of Trade in the Liberal administration.[33] After travelling to Switzerland and Germany from Italy on his return trip, he arrived back in Ireland sometime in late May or early June and familiarized himself with the political developments that had occurred during his five months' absence. His first public pronouncement in Ireland was made in Athy, Co. Kildare, in July, and his renewed sense of purpose was evident in the gusto with which he addressed his audience. Even the *Freeman's Journal* observed that he had not delivered a more cogent or forceful speech since the days of the Land League.[34] Wisely avoiding any reference to land nationalization, he called for a revival of the campaign to abolish landlordism, 'root and branch'; and in a thinly veiled attack on the INL, he preached the necessity of cultivating the country's industrial interests and native trade, and urged the full implementation of the National League's industrial charter, which 'has been allowed to remain a dead letter'.[35] Shortly after his Athy speech, he wrote to McGhee, 'I am rousing the country again for another Land League fight and it is hard to determine whether the landlords or the T.P. O'C[onnor] clique are more afraid'.[36] Moody has noted that Davitt's unique role from 1882 onwards was that of a freelance – 'nationalist, labour leader, democratic reformer, humanitarian, and internationalist' – and a critic and educator of the national movement.[37] But it was only from the summer of 1885 that Davitt really began to feel comfortable in this role.

31 Davitt's diary, 17 Mar. 1885, DP, TCD, MS 9543. 32 Ibid., 24 Apr. 1885. 33 Ibid., 9 May 1885; on Chamberlain, see Hammond, *Gladstone*, pp 367–9. 34 *FJ*, 6 July 1885 (Davitt speech was made on 5 July). 35 Ibid. 36 Davitt to McGhee, 14 July 1885, DP, TCD, MS 9521/5933. 37 Moody, *Davitt*, pp 547–8.

On the same day that Davitt read of Chamberlain's 'central board' idea in a newspaper in Geneva, the proposal was narrowly rejected by the Liberal cabinet. The scheme had emerged from negotiations between Chamberlain and Parnell, via Captain O'Shea, between November 1884 and January 1885. As presented to the cabinet by Chamberlain, it involved the restructuring of local government in Ireland into democratic 'county boards' which would, in turn, elect a 'central board'. This main administrative body would have control over education and communications. Chamberlain had indicated his willingness to give the 'central board' control over the land question, but, at Parnell's insistence, it was ultimately excluded from the final draft.[38] The scheme was far removed from legislative independence; but, then, Parnell had not considered it a substitute for an Irish parliament. O'Shea was meant to communicate this to Chamberlain but failed to do so.[39] When Davitt first read of the proposal, it certainly stirred his interest, although he was concerned about the extent of the 'central board's' powers. Nonetheless, it made him 'glad I resolved to come back'.[40] He believed that it possibly represented a move towards Irish self-government and, perhaps, heralded fresh thinking within the British government.

On 9 June 1885 the Liberal government fell after a budgetary defeat on the issue of whiskey duty.[41] Chamberlain had already resigned in late May after the rejection of his plan, along with his Radical colleague, Charles Dilke, who shared in the conception of the 'central board' scheme. Both, however, were eager to explore the possibilities in reaching an Irish settlement. They announced their intentions to visit Ireland to gain an understanding of conditions and feelings, as Chamberlain later described it to Davitt.[42] Davitt apparently recognized the 'sincerity' of their aims, but his view was not shared by other nationalists. From the end of June, *United Ireland* adopted a particularly virulent line in opposing the visit.[43] It recommended that Chamberlain, with his 'bastard out-of-date sympathy', remain in England along with Dilke.[44] The articles were the work of O'Brien and Healy, probably more so the latter. Parnell had not instigated the offensive, but, intent on avoiding conflict in the Irish Party, he refused to publicly distance him from his colleagues' comments.[45] Davitt was depressed by the diatribe, fearing the potential impact it would have on Radical voters in Britain when they read of it in the English press.[46] He himself praised the efforts of Dilke and Chamberlain in a speech in Hyde Park, for which the latter wrote to him expressing gratitude.[47] In fact, almost twenty years later Davitt communicated to Chamberlain his view that the 'unprovoked

38 Hammond, *Gladstone*, pp 366–9. **39** Lyons, *Charles Stewart Parnell*, p. 271. **40** Davitt's diary, 9 May 1885, DP, TCD, MS 9543. **41** Matthew, *Gladstone*, p. 168. **42** Chamberlain's letter to Davitt, 1 July 1885, DP, TCD, MS 9374/983. **43** Lyons, *Charles Stewart Parnell*, p. 289. **44** Quoted in Callanan, *T.M. Healy*, p. 119. **45** Lyons, *Charles Stewart Parnell*, p. 289. **46** See Davitt, *The fall*, p. 476. **47** Chamberlain's letter to Davitt, 1 July 1885, DP, TCD, MS 9374/983.

and unjustifiable' attacks were the reason, or at least a major reason, for the latter's subsequent antagonism to Gladstone's first home rule bill.[48]

In his speech in Athy, Davitt had indicated that he did not distinguish one English politician from another. He definitely distrusted middle-class Liberalism, but he referred to the Tories as the 'landlord party' and could not help 'den[ying] the possibility of [their] being naturally capable of passing good laws'.[49] He singled out the recent 'ostensible friendliness' of the Conservatives as a particularly worrying political development. The Conservatives had been making overtures to the Parnellites for some weeks; the combined vote of the Irish Party and the opposition on the budget had actually been instrumental in the government's defeat and subsequent resignation. When the Conservative government came to office in June, the Crimes Act was not renewed, and the new lord lieutenant of Ireland, Lord Carnarvon, strongly indicated a conciliatory approach. Little time was wasted. On the day of Davitt's speech, Carnarvon held discussions with the Irish Party's vice-chairman, Justin McCarthy. This paved the way for a further private meeting with Parnell on 1 August, during which the lord lieutenant found him 'singularly moderate'.[50] During their talks, Parnell underscored the necessity of an Irish settlement based on a legislative body with authority over purely Irish matters, including the power to cultivate Irish industries by means of protective tariffs. On the question of Irish representation at Westminster after a settlement, he apparently expressed the view that Irish members should be retained, although he indicated that he was agreeable to their exclusion as part of a deal. Carnarvon found himself well disposed to the Irish leader, who 'indicated plainly his fear of the extreme party', and of Davitt in particular.[51]

Despite his *tête-à-tête* with the lord lieutenant, Parnell also made advances during the autumn of 1885 to extract a commitment from Gladstone on home rule. In October Mrs O'Shea sent the Liberal leader a paper drafted by Parnell which outlined a proposed constitution for Ireland. In response to this overture, Gladstone declared his position in a speech in Edinburgh a few weeks later. This was welcomed by Parnell; but while he was encouraged by the statement, he believed a more explicit declaration on Irish self-government was required. This was not forthcoming, and on 21 November he issued a manifesto to Irish voters in Britain, advising them to vote against the Liberal Party in the general election.[52] Davitt was appalled by the decision, considering it a sheer affront to the principle of uniting Irish nationalism and British democracy. On the first day of polling, he wrote despondently to McGhee, 'Parnell

---

48 Davitt to Chamberlain, 6 Aug. 1903, DP, TCD, MS 9374/985. Chamberlain replied to Davitt on 8 Aug. 1903 stating that before Gladstone's bill, he had only ever understood home rule as a 'large scheme for local government', ibid. 49 *FJ*, 6 July 1885. 50 Quoted in Lyons, *Charles Stewart Parnell*, p. 286. 51 Ibid., pp 285–8, 103. 52 Hammond, *Gladstone*, pp 421–5.

and his crowd are going in for a new form of toryism. They fear the democracy. Priests, parsons, Parnellites and peers appear to be on the one platform now, and the programme is: keep the democracy out of Westminster'.[53] In an attempt to advance the democratic agenda, Davitt himself campaigned for radical candidates in the north of England and on Clydeside during the election,[54] for which he was 'duly excommunicated, as usual,' by some of Parnell's 'choleric young lieutenants'.[55]

Davitt had written an article for the *Dublin University Review* in September, in which he expounded his views on 'Irish Conservatism and its Outlooks'. This piece was in response to an earlier article by Standish James O'Grady which championed a social reform programme under the patronage of the 'territorial proprietors' of Ireland.[56] Davitt attacked the notion as a 'plan of conservative social salvation', a desperate attempt to secure for the landlord class a refuge from the rising tide of democracy. O'Grady felt an affinity with aristocratic culture and firmly held that society would function better under aristocratic rule. In an exchange with Davitt, he made clear his aversion to this 'rising tide of democracy'. 'The bare possibility that Ireland will be justly ruled is', he wrote, 'taken away when the lowest and most dependent class becomes sovereign'. And in response to the suggestion that democracy would produce 'premiers, statesmen, secretaries, &c.', he retorted, 'Yes; as the boiler sends up scum'.[57]

Significantly, in depicting the ideological alignment in a prospective Irish parliament, Davitt designated Parnell the leader of the main 'Nationalist Conservative' party in office, which would represent the interests of the churches and the commercial and propertied classes. A 'Socialist Left' would represent democratic and social reform interests, while the 'territorial proprietors' would form a 'Right Centre' party. He remarked, however, that the latter 'would be sure of the protection of the ruling intermediate Parnellite party, once they [had] acquiesced in national self-government'.[58] Shortly after the publication of his article, Davitt wrote to Labouchere on the subject of Toryism within Irish nationalism.[59] He explained that such a conservative element would be more amenable to negotiating with a Conservative government, especially following the Ashbourne Act in August in which Salisbury's government recognized the principle of peasant proprietorship, and out of

53 Davitt to Richard McGhee, 23 Nov. 1885; quoted in T.W. Moody, 'Michael Davitt and the British labour movement', *RHST*, 5th series, 3 (1953), 64. **54** O'Brien, *Parnell*, p. 105. **55** Davitt, *The fall*, p. 481. **56** Davitt, 'Irish conservatism and its outlooks' (1885) in King (ed.), *Michael Davitt*, vol. i, p. 96. **57** Quoted in Patrick Maume, 'Standish James O'Grady: between imperial romance and Irish revival', *Éire-Ireland*, 39:1 & 2 (2004), 17. **58** Davitt, 'Irish Conservatism', pp 101–2. **59** Davitt to Labouchere, 9 Oct.,1885; cited in Lyons, *Charles Stewart Parnell*, p. 303.

which landlords were guaranteed agreeable prices.[60] He also stated that priests and bishops would be more willing to do business with the Conservative Party, given its support for denominational education.[61]

Parnell certainly envisaged a cultural, intellectual and political role for the Anglo-Irish in a self-governing Ireland, and there is no doubt that he believed that a comprehensive land purchase scheme had the potential to remove the aversion which landlords had towards the concept of home rule.[62] However, according to Bew, Parnell did not just aspire to the inclusion of the Anglo-Irish in a post-feudal Ireland but to the ultimate hegemony of that class in such a political context. In fact, Bew maintains that Parnell engaged with the land question in 1879–80 in order to bring about the 'conditions in which the Irish landlords could take their proper place as leaders of the Home Rule movement'. He maintains that the 'nascent domestic Irish Catholic bourgeoisie or its literary or legal representatives was decidedly not Parnell's *first* choice. He did not wish it to be the exclusively dominating force within the new dispensation of power'. Bew's ultimate contention is that Parnell was essentially a Tory, and that, although the Parnellites fought the election on a 'perfectly legitimate' programme, the Irish leader's dealings with the Tories from the summer of 1885 revealed his innate class conservatism.[63] This argument tends to ignore the extent to which Parnell, a political pragmatist, had alienated his own class during the land war, especially as a result of his public attacks on landlordism. Moreover, there is no firm evidence that his dealings with Conservative minister like Carvarnon were predicated on a fixed plan to establish an Anglo-Irish regime in Ireland.

Davitt's ideas on Parnell's ideological position were broadly outlined in his *Dublin University Review* article. He did not, however, appear to understand the latter's conservatism in the narrow terms of aristocratic hegemony. This, of course, did not assuage his exasperation with the Irish Party's pre-election manifesto. In his attachment to the idea of an Irish alliance with British democracy, he could not bring himself to accept the sound basis of Parnell's strategy of playing the parliamentary arithmetic card against the two main British parties, neither of which had by the general election embraced home rule. In fact, there was no basis for believing, as Davitt did,[64] that an overwhelming Liberal victory in the election would have led Gladstone to introduce a home rule bill in any case. The election result left the Irish Party with the balance of power: Liberals 335; Tories 249; Parnellites 86. Parnell must surely have appre-

---

60 The Purchase of Land (Ireland) Act, 1885 ('Ashbourne Act'), enabled tenants to borrow the entire purchase money, to be repaid by four per cent annuities over forty-nine years. **61** O'Brien, *Parnell*, p. 106. **62** Liam Kennedy, *Colonialism, religion and nationalism in Ireland* (Belfast, 1996), p. 79. **63** Bew, *Charles Stewart Parnell* (Dublin, 1991), pp 28, 138, 74. **64** See Davitt's diary, 1 Jan. 1886, DP, TCD, MS 9545; also, Davitt, *The fall*, p. 481.

ciated the miscalculation made in alienating Chamberlain in the course of 1885, but it is difficult to credit Davitt's later claim that the Irish leader confessed 'more than once' that the policy behind the manifesto had been a mistake.[65]

Davitt had a natural, visceral aversion to the Conservatives and was ultimately more amenable to the Liberals and their politics. For Gladstone, he had high regard. On hearing the Liberal leader speak in the house of commons a good year even before the 'Hawarden Kite' was flown, he remarked, 'Truly marvellous old man'.[66] He was, therefore, greatly encouraged by the subsequent Gladstonian endorsement of home rule and the formation of a Liberal government in February 1886, the main plank of which was self-government for Ireland. Given the historic nature of the development, Davitt was stirred by the potential for a new era in Anglo-Irish relations. Following the 'Hawarden Kite', he delivered a series of speeches in defence of the concept of home rule, two of which were published as pamphlets. In *Reasons why home rule should be granted to Ireland* (1886), he listed eight arguments to support his case. He specifically asserted that Ireland would prosper under self-government and that this would eventually benefit the British labour market by significantly reducing the numbers of emigrant Irish labourers who 'overcrowd your large towns with unskilled labour'.[67] Given his own background in Haslingden, he himself was, of course, well aware that anti-Irish prejudice was engendered, at least in part, by the influx of Irish workers into the English labour market.[68] In his pamphlet he argued, moreover, that once the Irish question had been resolved, British democracy would be free to invest all its energies in the democratic and social reform agenda in Britain.[69]

His other speech, delivered in Glasgow less than two weeks after Gladstone's first home rule bill, was a salute to the 'heroism' of the Liberal leader and an attempt to counteract unionist objections to home rule, especially in regards to the 'Ulster protest'.[70] Davitt was probably asked to put in an appearance in Glasgow by Ferguson who was gradually finding that the city was becoming a base for a nascent Liberal Unionist organization in Scotland.[71] Irish unionism had become an organized movement by the mid-1880s in response to the development of Parnellism, its *bête-noir*, and its arguments, Davitt noted, were being articulated 'over here'.[72] The Irish Loyal and Patriotic Union, founded in May 1885, was distributing pamphlets, booklets, and leaflets throughout Britain, promulgating the points of the unionist case.[73]

65 Davitt, *The fall*, p. 481. 66 Davitt's diary, 23 Oct. 1884, DP, TCD, MS 9541. 67 Davitt, *Reasons why home rule should be granted to Ireland* (1886) in King (ed.), *Michael Davitt*, vol. i, p. 6. 68 Davitt, *Jottings*, p. 12. 69 Davitt, *Reasons why home rule should be granted to Ireland*, p. 6. 70 Davitt, 'Home rule: speech at Glasgow' (1886) in King (ed.), *Michael Davitt*, vol. i p. 25. 71 McFarland, *John Ferguson*, p. 179. 72 Davitt, 'Home rule: speech at Glasgow', p. 25; see also Davitt, *The fall*, pp 500–1. 73 Patrick Buckland, *Irish unionism: The Anglo-Irish*, pp 24–5.

Its sister organization, the Ulster Loyalist Anti-Repeal Union, was formed in January 1886, and it mobilized unionist opposition to home rule in the north of Ireland.[74]

Healy's success in a Monaghan by-election in the autumn of 1883, and subsequent efforts to organize nationalism in Ulster, had led to what Alvin Jackson terms 'a renaissance of loyalism' throughout Ireland, mainly in the northeast.[75] In his speech, Davitt was determined to refute the idea that Ulster was unified in opposition to home rule. He pointed out that over half of the parliamentary seats in the province were occupied by nationalist members (Parnellites won in seventeen of the thirty-three Ulster constituencies in the 1885 general election). He also addressed the question of the civil and religious liberties of the Protestant minority in Ireland by referring to the 'legislative safeguards' against sectarianism in the government's measure. Webb, now a prominent figure in the Irish Protestant Home Rule Association, also attempted to assuage Protestant fears in his pamphlet, *The opinions of some Protestants regarding their Catholic fellow-countrymen* (1886).[76] Ultimately, Davitt reiterated Gladstone's comments that the Irish people had spoken in the election and that 'the Protestants of Ulster or elsewhere' could not exercise a veto on the matter of legislative independence.[77]

In his peroration, Davitt presciently noted that Scottish opinion would be crucial on the question of home rule. 'Scotland is now the arbiter', he said, 'not only of Mr. Gladstone's fate, but of the fate of Home Rule'.[78] Indeed, when the bill was defeated in the common in June 1886, it was revealed that thirty-seven per cent of Scottish Liberal MPs, as against nineteen per cent of English members, failed to support Gladstone.[79] The consequent fall of the Liberal government in July spurred the nationalist movement to concentrate its energies and resources on placing home rule at the centre of British politics again, and to collaborate with the Liberal Party in achieving that end. Davitt was seriously committed to this constitutional project. The underlying tensions between himself and Parnell remained, however. During the crisis around the home rule bill, Parnell had informed Davitt that in the event of securing an Irish parliament, the land question ought to be abandoned. When Davitt incredulously asked what Parnell would do to justify such a policy, in light of his record of attacking the landlord system, the Irish leader sardonically replied, 'The first thing I should do would be to lock you up'.[80]

---

74 Buckland, *Irish unionism: Ulster unionism and the origins of Northern Ireland, 1886 to 1922* (Dublin, 1973), pp 8–10. 75 Alvin Jackson, *Colonel Edward Saunderson, land and loyalty in Victorian Ireland* (Oxford, 1995), p. 51. 76 James Loughlin, 'The Irish Protestant Home Rule Association and nationalist politics, 1886–93', *IHS*, 24:95 (1985). 77 Davitt, 'Home rule: speech at Glasgow', p. 27. 78 Ibid., p. 30. 79 Jenkins, *Gladstone*, p. 555. 80 Quoted in Lyons, *Charles Stewart Parnell*, p. 357.

Parnell was fully conscious of the growing threat of Davitt as a radical figure, given that the latter was, around this time, heavily involved in agrarian agitation in Scotland and Wales, labour activism throughout Britain, and was building an important profile through his journalism. Despite the fundamental differences which their exchange highlighted, Davitt entered into a closer working relationship with the Irish Party in order to advance the national cause. On an invitation from Egan, he even travelled to Chicago in August with a Party delegation to attend the convention of the Irish National League of America where support for the constitutional strategy was still undetermined.

The Irish delegation comprised O'Brien, John Redmond and John Deasy as representatives of the Party. Davitt accompanied them, largely because of his influence with Irish-America and his close connections with Alexander Sullivan, former president of Clan na Gael and an influential figure in American politics. Yet Davitt's influence in America was not as great as it had once been, owing to his rejection of the use of physical force in the early 1880s. During the Fenian bombing campaign in Britain in 1883, he wrote to Ferguson condemning the 'few men who now call themselves the "dynamite party"'.[81] Two explosions had gone off in Ferguson's adopted city, Glasgow, in January, the first in a series of attacks on British cities that year.[82] In his letter, Davitt noted regretfully that Patrick Ford, the 'man who has been so strenuous a supporter of the moral force doctrine', was apparently now loyal to O'Donovan Rossa, the intriguer behind the first wave of bombings.[83] For Davitt, this kind of violence was counter-productive. He told Ferguson that even Forster had conceded that if the murders of Cavendish and Burke had not occurred in 1882, 'Ireland would have speedily become almost ungovernable. The people of Ireland would have thought that in fact the honourable member [Parnell] was governing Ireland'.[84] Ferguson was equally scathing of 'the dagger and dynamite'. At the St Patrick's day celebrations in Glasgow after the bombing in the city, he argued that violent tactics only served to retard the growing interest between the British and Irish working classes.[85] Even the local IRB in Glasgow had a major difficulty with the militancy of the dynamiters. They believed that the direct campaign of the dissidents would lead to a volatile political situation and provoke reprisals on Irish communities. Significantly,

---

81 Davitt to Ferguson, 25 Mar. 1883, DP, TCD, MS 9399/1501. **82** K.R.M. Short, *The dynamite war, Irish–American bombers in Victorian Britain* (Dublin, 1979), 104. **83** Davitt to Ferguson, 25 Mar. 1883, DP, TCD, MS 9399–1501. In 1894 Davitt told Dillon that he believed that 'the wretched old fool', Rossa, had, for over ten years, been used as a 'decoy-duck' by agents of the British government in New York 'who have tracked many a man to his doom through the idiotic "policy" of 'this half-demented creature'; Davitt to Dillon, 28 May 1894, DP, TCD, MS 9405/1674. **84** Davitt to Ferguson, 25 Mar. 1883, DP, TCD, MS 9399/1501. **85** McFarland, *John Ferguson*, pp 140–1.

as Máirtín Ó Catháin has pointed out, the IRB and the dynamiters not only differed on tactics but also, crucially, in social background, the latter drawn from an Irish immigrant underclass which had less of a stake in society.[86]

Notwithstanding Davitt's rejection of the use of political violence from the early 1880s, he himself was no pacifist, and he certainly appreciated the power of the implied threat of violence, the whiff of cordite. For instance, in January 1886 he had a meeting in Dublin with the Radical MP for Sheffield, A.J. Mundella, which was particularly revealing. He ascertained that the Liberal member's visit to Dublin was a party mission on behalf of Gladstone to fully assess the expectations of the Irish in regard to home rule. Mundella informed Davitt that Gladstone was, indeed, ready to commit himself to such a policy.[87] However, Davitt disliked the pomp of this declaration, especially as it was 'reinforced with a thoroughly John Bullish threat' of coercion if unrest started up again in Ireland. In reply, Davitt asserted, much to Mundella's astonishment, that coercion had been tried in 1881 with inevitable consequences, and that if it were attempted again he himself would freely join in any retaliation that would ensue.

Davitt was known to make militant statements on occasion. During the evictions in Bodyke, Co. Clare, in June 1887, he stated angrily that he wished he had never encouraged tenants to refrain from violence and illegality.[88] The following month he used the same language in response to evictions in Co. Wexford, and in the process criticized the 'moderate' attitude of the organizing committee of the National League.[89] And when he later resigned from the house of commons in October 1899, in protest against the Boer war, he said that no cause would ever have redress in that parliament unless backed by force.[90] In making such statements, he was effectively firing a shot across the bows of both the Tories and the Liberals, and in doing so he was indicating that many in Ireland had only adopted constitutional methods in the expectation of significant results. In his calm recollection of his interview with Mundella, it is significant that, by his own admission, he was not entirely bluffing in his threat of retaliation.[91] Certainly, he disavowed bombing campaigns and such tactics, but the position on political violence which he adopted, at least from the time of the Phoenix Park murders, and to which he subsequently adhered, had more to do with his belief in the efficacy of constitutional action

86 M. Ó Catháin, 'Fenian dynamite: dissident Irish republicans in late nineteenth-century Scotland', in Oonagh Walsh (ed.), *Ireland abroad: politics and professions in the nineteenth century* (Dublin, 2003), pp 166–71. 87 DP, TCD, MS 9399/1502. 88 *FJ*, 3 June 1887. Several days later, he stated publicly that his pronouncement at Bodyke was not made in haste; see *FJ*, 6 June 1887. 89 L.M. Geary, *The plan of campaign, 1886–91* (Cork, 1986), p. 75. 90 'Davitt's Speech of resignation from the House of Commons, 25 Oct. 1899' in King (ed.), *Michael Davitt*, vol. i. 91 DP, TCD, MS 9399/1502.

rather than a principled opposition to insurrection. As he stated it to Ferguson in 1883,

> Principles of reform, intelligently and fearlessly propagated, are far more destructive to unjust or worn out systems than dynamite bombs which only kill individuals or knock down buildings, but do no injury to oppressive institutions; and that man must be politically blind who cannot see that the firing of ideas of ameliorative social reform into the heads of England's toiling millions is infinitely more likely to hasten the solution to our own national and social problems than will be the blowing down of houses and the killing of innocent persons among these very millions.[92]

This was the substance of his speech before the Chicago convention in 1886.

When he arrived in the United States for the convention, the vital question of constitutionalism was debated at a pre-convention public meeting on 14 August. Brennan and Egan were present, the latter having become president of the National League of America in 1884.[93] At the opening of the meeting, Congressman John Finerty effectively defended the dynamite campaign. Although Davitt thought well of Finerty, he could not, as he later told McGhee, permit him to dominate the proceedings with 'warlike speeches'.[94] In response, Davitt addressed the issue directly. He remarked that it was one thing 'to set up an Irish Republic by patriotic speeches delivered three thousand miles away, but they could not do it on the hills and plains of Ireland – hence they had to accept the best measure it was possible to obtain'.[95] He then underscored the 'brilliant prospects' of home rule following the Gladstonian endorsement, and clarified the nature of the Irish Party's *rapprochement* with the Liberals. Later, at a private meeting before the main convention sessions, he, O'Brien and Redmond discussed the issue with Sullivan, Egan and Patrick Ford. Sullivan emphasized the efficacy of tactical violence, but eventually, with the help of what C.C. O'Brien calls 'a certain element of ambiguity',[96] Davitt and O'Brien managed to persuade the Irish–American delegates to back the constitutional agenda. When the question was ultimately put before the convention it was almost unanimously endorsed, and a motion was passed expressing gratitude to 'the democracy' of England, Scotland and Wales for its support.[97] The movement was solidly behind Parnell.

---

92 Davitt to Ferguson, 25 Mar. 1883, DP, TCD, MS 9399/1501. 93 Short, *Dynamite*, p. 190. 94 Davitt to McGhee, 1 Sept. 1886, DP, TCD, MS 9521/5952. 95 *FJ*, 16 Aug. 1886; see also Davitt, *The Times-Parnell comm*, pp 165–9. 96 O'Brien, *Parnell*, p. 196. 97 Lyons, *Charles Stewart Parnell*, p. 356; Short, *Dynamite*, p. 230.

Davitt did not return to Ireland immediately after the convention. Over the next few months he travelled across the United States, spending much of November in Canada.[98] Part of his interest in remaining was to undertake market research for a woollen company which he was intending to launch in Ireland. For most of the preceding nine years since his release from Dartmoor, he had been engaged in frenetic political activity and had not had much time for a personal life. However, in December he was married in Oakland, California, to Mary Yore, a young Irish–American, whom he had first met there during his second visit to America six years earlier.[99] He was now forty years old, and craved the stability which married life afforded.[1] In the years after his initial release from prison he spent much of his time in lodgings *en route* to meetings; he was essentially of no fixed abode for most of his adult life until after his marriage when he and his wife were presented with a house, 'Land League Cottage', in Ballybrack, Co. Dublin, a testimonial which he accepted as the people's tribune. His matrimony did not, however, keep him away from Irish politics for long. He returned home in February 1887 with his new bride and again threw himself into the political fray.

A fresh agrarian campaign was afoot in Ireland, precipitated by an agricultural depression in 1885. Davitt himself had observed the effects of this during a visit to Achill Island, Co. Mayo, in January 1886. He was struck by the 'Awful picture of want', and noted that things were worse than in 1879: 'Cattle, sheep, pigs could be sold then, but not now'.[2] Parnell drafted a Tenants' Relief bill in an attempt to address the problem before the onset of winter in 1886, but, despite the backing of his new Liberal allies, it was defeated in September.[3] In response to the growing crisis, the Plan of Campaign was launched in October 1886 by Harrington, Dillon, and O'Brien, following the latter's return from the Chicago convention. The Plan was designed to secure reductions in rent, and where a landlord proved unyielding, rents on his estate would be withheld and placed in an 'estate fund' as a source of financial support for evicted tenants and those who expected eviction. The architects of the Plan emphasized its continuity with the land war, but there were significant differences. Unlike the Land League, it was not supported or financed by Irish-America; and although it was connected with the National League, it was not officially backed by the Parliamentary Party. Most significant of all, Parnell remained detached from the agitation and finally, in May 1888, openly expressed his disapproval of it before a Liberal audience at the Eighty Club in London. By this stage, O'Brien was already disheartened by the aloofness of many Parnellite MPs and by Davitt's 'sneers'.[4]

---

98 For a list of newspaper reports mapping Davitt's itinerary, see his press cutting book, DP, TCD, MS 9611. **99** Moody, *Davitt*, p. 407, p. 551. **1** See Davitt's diary, 21 Mar. 1885, DP, TCD, MS 9543; Davitt's diary, 30 Dec. 1886, DP, TCD, MS 9545. **2** Davitt's notebook, Achil, Jan. 1886, DP, TCD, MS 9546. **3** Lyons, *Charles Stewart Parnell*, pp 359–60. **4** Quoted in Sally

In May 1886 Davitt had informed W.S. Blunt of his concern at the Irish Party's neglect of the land question. But, while he worked to raise relief funds for tenants as the economic crisis deteriorated in the course of 1887, and even incurred criticism from Liberal quarters for his remarks at Bodyke, he had serious misgivings about the Plan. According to Blunt, Dillon asserted that Davitt's problem with the land campaign was rooted in the fact that it had not been his own idea.[5] Davitt himself, however, later claimed that shortly after his return to Ireland, Parnell had requested that he avoid involvement with the agitation.[6] Davitt happened to concur with the Irish leader's line of reasoning at this time. He shared the latter's belief that it would damage the prospects of home rule by alienating British opinion. Parnell told him that 'the conversion of about one hundred thousand out of some four million English voters' was all that was required to secure a Liberal victory at the next general election.[7] He stated that it was therefore imperative that Gladstone was not handicapped in any way. Gladstone had already privately criticized a speech made by Dillon in December 1886 in which he (Dillon) implied future retaliation against policemen under home rule.[8] Tensions were running high. Davitt's own inflammatory outburst at Bodyke reflected not only his anger at evictions, but his own bitter sense that the Liberals were not doing enough to end them. Still, he fully appreciated the political implications of an agrarian war, and he was certainly not prepared to jeopardize the prospects of home rule for a campaign based on rent reductions. He did, however, join with a number of other high-profile nationalists in condemning the conduct of the police who were acting under the direction of the new Conservative administration, which would introduce a coercion act in March 1887. It was, indeed, around this time that the Gaelic Athletic Association (GAA), of which Davitt, Croke and Parnell were patrons, introduced a rule banning members of the Royal Irish Constabulary (RIC) from joining the organization.[9] In January 1888 Davitt wrote to the leading British journalist, W.T. Stead,

> The Castle crowd assert that the Gaelic Athletic Association is largely *Fenian*; yet the Castle instructs its police to encourage the Gaels to smash the National League! The tables are now turned on the Castle, for, at the Gaelic Athletic Convention which was held in Thurles, last Friday, a resolution was passed, unanimously, against allowing any member of the RIC from competing in Gaelic sports.[10]

Warwick-Haller, *William O'Brien and the Irish land war* (Dublin, 1990), p. 103. **5** Blunt, *The land war*, pp 92, 291. **6** Davitt, *The fall*, 518. Davitt's reason for avoiding involvement with the Plan was challenged by Blunt, *The land war*, pp 291–2, who claimed that before the spring of 1888 he had never heard from Dillon, O'Brien or Davitt any word of Parnell's disapproval of the Plan of Campaign. **7** Davitt, *The fall*, p. 518. **8** Lyons, *John Dillon*, pp 86–7. **9** McGee, *The IRB*, pp 167–8. **10** Davitt to Stead, 8 Jan. 1888, SP, CAC, MS 1/19.

Despite Davitt's opposition to the Plan, he reacted angrily to the condemnation of the agitation in a papal circular to Irish bishops in April 1888. This followed a fact-finding mission to Ireland by Mgr Ignatius Persico in the summer of 1887. A few days after the publication of the circular in the *Freeman's Journal*, Davitt wrote to the *Pall Mall Gazette* describing the development as an indication of the convergence of conservative forces, by which he meant the papacy and the Conservative Party. He referred to Persico as Lord Salisbury's *aide-de-camp*.[11] Shortly after the rescript, Catholic members of the Irish Party announced plans to call a meeting on the matter at the Mansion House, Dublin. Davitt expressed grave doubts about that decision. At a demonstration in Liverpool a few days before the meeting was due to be held, he stated that the division of the Party along such lines would be perceived in Ulster and elsewhere as having sectarian overtones. He argued, moreover, that the subject was simply getting too much attention. 'The organs of public opinion in Ireland had', he said, 'already dealt with the issue, and the best thing they could do was to let it drop'.[12] However, Parnell did not object to the meeting of the Catholic members, and his address at the Eighty Club was billed as 'one of the most important pronouncements the leader of the Irish Parliamentary Party and the Irish people has ever addressed to his sympathizers and followers'.[13] In his speech Parnell said that the papal decree would be a 'disastrous failure', although, as a Protestant, he registered his satisfaction at leaving the matter to his Catholic colleagues.[14]

At the Mansion House meeting on 17 May, those Catholic colleagues present passed a resolution accepting the moral jurisdiction of the church but not its interference in the realm of Irish politics. The Irish hierarchy found itself under mounting pressure in these months, given its endorsement of Parnell as leader of Irish nationalism in 1884 and its alliance with the Irish Party. 'The responsibility [...] for seeing that [Rome] did back down rested with the Irish bishops', observes Larkin.[15] This was all the more pressing, now that home rule seemed a very real prospect. Ultimately, less than two weeks after the Mansion House conference, the hierarchy declared that it interpreted the circular as a judgement pertaining only to the province of morals.[16] According to Larkin, the Irish bishops' response to the papal decree was crucial both to the maintenance and to the refinement of the clerical-nationalist alliance. In fact, in his conceptually audacious, albeit fatalistic,[17] proto-state thesis, Larkin maintains that the effective management of local political control and main-

---

11 *FJ*, 30 Apr. 1888.   12 *FJ*, 14 May 1888.   13 *FJ*, 4 May 1888; cited in O'Brien, *Parnell*, p. 218.
14 O'Brien, *Parnell*, p. 218.   15 Larkin, *The Roman*, p. 321.   16 O'Brien, *Parnell*, p. 223.   17 For a critical assessment of the Larkin thesis, see J.J. Lee, 'On the birth of the modern Irish state: the Larkin thesis', in Stewart J. Brown and David W. Miller (eds), *Piety and power in Ireland, 1760–1960, essays in honour of Emmet Larkin* (Belfast and Notre Dame, 2000), pp 130–57.

tenance of order by Parnell's National League, together with the solid alliance with the Church by 1888, represented the Irish state in embryonic form, a state in waiting since the *de facto* recognition of its executive, legislative and judicial functions in the detail of Gladstone's first home rule bill. The outcome of the papal rescript controversy was, in Larkin's view, 'a compromise in which the new State was neither religiously pluralistic nor purely clerical. What actually evolved was a Catholic State in which Catholic values and interests predominated [...]'[18]

In his public pronouncements during the controversy, Davitt specifically attacked the papal intervention. However, as he had indicated in his earlier *Dublin University Review* article, he identified the Irish Catholic church and Parnellism as the conservatives within. In a speech at Portumna, Co. Galway, in June 1888, he castigated Rome for condemning the Plan. He also took the opportunity to allude to his own radicalism. 'Make no mistake about it', he declared, 'it is the Land League, and not landlordism, that will ultimately triumph in this fight [...] The land of Ireland is the people's inalienable inheritance, and the people's right is certain to be vindicated'.[19] During a speech in Limerick in November 1887 he reiterated his views on Irish conservatism. Again, Parnell would lead a constituent assembly with a majority 'Conservative Nationalist Party'. Davitt clearly did not envisage a confessional Irish Catholic state, considering that he imagined the alignment of both Catholic *and* Protestant Churches with Parnell, along with the state's bourgeoisie. The left would be represented by a 'Democratic' or 'Radical Nationalist Party' which would have a republican and a strong social reform agenda, including free and technical education, better housing for the poor, development of industries, and improvement in the social conditions of the labouring masses. It would get its support from small farmers, agricultural labourers, and the urban artisans and mechanics. A 'Minority Party' would represent the interests of that 'pro-English' element, those formerly associated with the ascendancy class.[20] Some months before his Limerick speech, Davitt had actually made reference to the ideological alignment within nationalism in a letter to the editor of *North and South*, the organ of Protestant home rulers, after the paper declared that the Plan of Campaign would be tantamount to 'organize[d] fraud' if it were extended beyond oppressive landlords.[21] In the context of a debate on the nature of Irish nationalism, Davitt wrote that *North and South* was part of the conservative element of nationalism.

Davitt seemed to believe that as long as a strong radical voice was articulated within the Irish movement, the Land League would continue to exist,

---

18 Larkin, *The Roman*, p. 318. **19** *FJ*, 4 June 1888. **20** *FJ*, 17 Nov. 1887. **21** James Loughlin, 'The Irish Protestant', p. 354.

albeit subliminally. However, there was no doubt that Parnellism was in the ascendant. Davitt was forced to recognize this in the later years of the 1880s. By the autumn of 1888, the Plan of Campaign was experiencing serious financial difficulties with costs running at around £20,000 a year. The situation was made worse by the formation of a landlord syndicate. Parnell agreed to become associated with the agrarian agitation, but on his own terms. In October 1889 the Tenants' Defence Association was launched, its aim being to raise funds to financially assist evicted tenants. Unlike the earlier days when the Land League had been independent of parliamentarians, Parnell and the Irish Party were now in a position to shape and control the agrarian organization. Davitt was elected to the council of the Tenants' Defence Association, but, as C.C. O'Brien remarks, the fact that he accepted election to such a body, 'stresses rather than mitigates the dictatorship of the party. The founder of the Land League was accepting a necessarily subordinate position within a movement entirely controlled by the parliamentarians whom he had long distrusted and disliked'.[22]

In February 1888, Davitt confided in his diary that he firmly believed that Parnell had an ulterior motive in urging him to become a member of parliament. He surmised that the Irish leader was acting at the behest of the Liberals who '[want] me muzzled' on the social question.[23] A few days later he wrote to McGhee, expressing the same opinion, and adding that Parnell's other motive was to 'use me to balance the Dillon and O'Brien faction'.[24] Less than a year earlier, Davitt had told McGhee that Parnell 'is practically part of the Liberal party'.[25] Indeed, Davitt and others on the left were expressing grave concerns about the nature of the liberal–nationalist alliance. Even the *Irish Times* repeatedly made references to the 'absorption' of the Irish Party.[26] Davitt and Ferguson stressed that the alliance must be based on a democratic partnership rather than a merger. Speaking in Glasgow in the summer of 1887, the latter cautioned his Irish audience to 'act with the Liberal party as loyal allies, but not in any sense as their inferiors [...] Not until the Irish Parliament opens in Dublin can we afford to lose our identity in the Liberal organization'.[27] Davitt later voiced his own concerns publicly at a meeting at Knocknaroo, Queen's County, in which he blamed the alliance for 'the evils inflicted upon us by tory rule since 1886'. He castigated prominent Liberals who, as 'doctrinaires of the old school of political economy', had an ideological affinity with the Tories on economic questions and consequently acqui-

22 O'Brien, *Parnell*, pp 228–9, 232. **23** Davitt's diary, 17 Feb. 1888, DP, TCD, MS 9548. **24** Davitt to McGhee, 22 Feb. 1888, DP, TCD, MS 9521/5960. **25** Davitt to McGhee, 13 Apr. 1887; quoted in O'Brien, *Parnell*, p. 227. **26** *Irish Times*, 7 May 1888; cited in O'Brien, *Parnell*, p. 227. **27** McFarland, *John Ferguson*, p. 197.

esced in the 'exterminating policy of Lord Salisbury [who viewed eviction] as a means of thinning the population of Ireland'.[28] A few days later in a letter to the Liberal *Daily News*, he challenged claims that he had referred to Gladstone in disparaging terms in his Knockaroo speech. Nevertheless, he reiterated his view that in nationalist Ireland 'the glorification of Gladstone was carried to a ridiculous extent'.[29] The alliance, he insisted, must be an equal partnership.

Davitt was committed to the constitutional project, but of course he also had a social reform agenda. Later, in 1890–1, his own paper, the *Labour World*, supported the Liberals, but it was not an unqualified support. The editorial in the second issue actually sought clarification on the nature of lib-labism itself: 'Will they [Liberals] aid and encourage them [labour candidates] whenever possible? Will they submit their superior claims in many constituencies?'.[30] Furthermore, it queried the reticence of Liberal leaders on labour issues, especially the eight-hour day for miners. In his editorial, Davitt suggested that the working class was being treated as it had been fifty years previously, after the 1832 Reform Act had satisfied middle-class Liberalism. He therefore presented what he considered a salutary historical lesson for the latter day Liberals by warning, albeit in a 'friendly spirit', that 'our Chartists of today have votes and will use them'. Anthony Taylor has shown that although the Liberal Party erected monuments to former Chartist leaders such as Samuel Bamford and Ernest Jones, and appeared to have successfully embraced the Chartist tradition, there were considerable difficulties in assimilating that tradition into Liberalism. He states that from 'the early 1880s onwards inconsistencies between the Chartist past and Liberalism are more apparent as Lib/Labs became steadily disillusioned with Liberalism in power [...]'[31]

In his address to the *Times*-Parnell Commission, Davitt himself expressed his indebtedness to Ernest Jones and declared that 'the first lesson I ever learned in the doctrine of liberty was from English and not from Irish history'.[32] However, part of Davitt's reason for appearing before the Commission was to preserve the Liberal–nationalist alliance which, given the nature of the inquiry, was in doubt, as well as the future of Parnell and the Irish movement. The pressure was eased in February 1889 after the revelation, uncovered by Davitt and Egan some months earlier,[33] that the disreputable Irish journalist, Richard Pigott, had forged the letter purporting to implicate Parnell in the

28 *FJ*, 10 Sept. 1888. 29 Cited in *FJ*, 13 Sept. 1888. 30 *LW*, 27 Sept. 1890. 31 Anthony Taylor, 'Commemoration, memorialization and political memory in post-Chartist radicalism: the 1885 Halifax Chartist reunion in context' in Owen Ashton, Robert Fyson and Stephen Roberts (eds), *The Chartist legacy* (Suffolk, 1999), pp 255–85. 32 Davitt, *The Times-Parnell comm*, p. 30. 33 McGee, *The IRB*, p. 187.

Phoenix Park murders. But the charge of the movement's association with criminality had to be challenged. In May Egan wrote to Davitt, informing him of the high level of interest in *The Times* case among Americans generally. It had 'so far [...] advanced the Irish cause half a century' in America, and Egan looked forward 'with *great interest*' to Davitt's submission.[34] It was to this that Davitt turned his undivided attention. Two weeks after receiving Egan's letter, he told Sabina that his submission would 'be the best effort of my life'.[35] This was in stark contrast to the nonchalant attitude of Parnell who did not even regularly attend the court.[36] A week before Davitt was due to make his speech, Parnell actually informed him that he was in favour of not recognizing or appearing before the Commission.[37] But, after meticulously collating the relevant information in his defence, Davitt presented his evidence in a speech which continued over the course of a week, between 24 and 31 October. In early December he wrote to Parnell, complaining that he had not been reimbursed for money expended during the inquiry.[38] This was soon rectified, for in January he noted having received from Parnell the sum of £500 for money 'expended by me, out of pocket, in connection with the Special Commission'.[39] This was followed a few months later by £225 which had been outstanding.[40] The Irish Party had raised £40,000 specifically for the purpose of meeting the costs of the inquiry.[41]

The Commission ultimately exonerated Parnell and the other nationalist figures named in the serious charges, including involvement in the Phoenix Park murders. However, Davitt's robust defence of the movement – and by implication, Parnell – did not represent a final *rapprochement* between himself and the Parnellites, despite his acceptance of party funds. Only a few weeks before his speech, he appealed to McGhee to check Ferguson's enthusiasm over the seemingly improved relations with the parliamentary leaders. 'For heaven's sake', he implored, 'tell Ferguson not to write to *any* of these men. He can expect nothing from the *best* of them, but sneers and ingratitude'. He explained to McGhee his own reasons for supporting Parnell at the Commission, which again amounted to a grudging respect for Parnell's leadership qualities and a determination to maintain unity:

> Parnell is cold, and if you will, ungrateful. But what about his possible successors! Better from my point of view to stick to a sick lion though

34 Egan to Davitt, 4 May 1889, DP, TCD, MS 9368/840. 35 Davitt to Sabina, 18 May 1889, DP, TCD, MS 9325/95. 36 Davitt, *The fall*, p. 597. 37 Parnell to Davitt, 16 Oct. 1889, DP, TCD, MS 9378/1080. 38 Davitt to Parnell, 10 Dec. 1899, DP, TCD, MS 9378/1081. 39 DP, TCD, MS 9378/1084. 40 Parnell to Davitt, 4 Mar. 1890, DP, TCD, MS 9378/1086. 41 Lyons, *Charles Stewart Parnell*, p. 405.

he has given you a paw now and then, than to have for masters a crowd of ambitious jackals who want to play the part of a lion, without possessing a single attribute of the nobler animal'.[42]

The restraint which Davitt counselled both McGhee and Ferguson to exercise in 1884 would, nevertheless, soon give way in the O'Shea divorce scandal, and it was at this juncture that the bitterness of the 1880s would surface.

42 Davitt to McGhee, 8 Oct. 1888, DP, TCD, MS 9328 [180/35].

3 / Crusading journalism and the *Labour World*

FROM THE MID-NINETEENTH CENTURY, since the repeal of the stamp duty on papers in 1855, the newspaper increasingly became part of political life, and indeed party political alignment, in Britain. The rise of the political press in the latter part of the century was notable for its partisanship, and the role of the successful journalist was elevated to an unprecedented level, epitomized in W.T. Stead's remarks that his journalistic position rendered him 'more useful, more powerful than half-a-dozen ordinary MPs'.[1] Despite its appearance as late as 1890, Davitt's labour journal, the *Labour World*, was one of the earliest of its kind. Its importance was acknowledged by Moody over half a century ago when he observed that it had yet to be properly assessed in the history of working-class journalism.[2] Indeed, of the areas of Davitt's later career which have been neglected, his journalism is among the most important. The *Labour World* is, moreover, an invaluable source, not only in appraising the nature of his political thought and the extent of his radicalism but also in assessing his relationship with the British labour movement and his accomplishments as a journalist. A proper study of the paper in the context of labour history is clearly now long overdue.

Davitt was, after all, a well-recognized freelance journalist by the 1890s,[3] and his articles for Irish, British and international papers were, together with his lecturing programmes and book sales, his financial mainstay over the last twenty-five years of his life. It was his established profile that led the *New York American*, one of the papers of William Randolph Hearst, to commission him for the task of reporting on the Anglo–Boer war in 1900. He was also commissioned to investigate atrocities against Jews in Kishinev, Russia, in 1903. Yet he was not a career journalist. As H.M. Hyndman noted, he was generally poorly paid for his work.[4] His journalism did, however, serve an important

---

1 Quoted in Stephen Koss, *The rise of the political press in Britain* (London, 1981), p. 210. 2 Moody, 'Davitt and British labour', p. 69. 3 Journalism was cited as his profession when he entered parliament in 1895. See Michael Stenton and Stephen Lees (eds), *Who's who of British members of parliament*, vol. ii, 1886–1918 (Sussex, 1976), p. 92. 4 H.M. Hyndman, *Further reminiscences* (London, 1912), p. 40.

political function during key stages of his later political life, and it was primarily for this reason that he adopted the profession. This was especially so in the post-Kilmainham political climate of the 1880s when he became a self-styled freelance activist. Within a fortnight of his release from Richmond prison in June 1883, he recorded in a notebook that he had written to the managing editors of a number of press agencies in the United States, 'offering a weekly letter on Irish affairs'.[5] Besides American papers, he also contributed to Irish and British papers and periodicals from the early 1880s,[6] and was a regular writer for the *Melbourne Advocate* from 1883, establishing a lasting friendship with its proprietor and manager, Joseph Winter,[7] a leading figure connected with the Irish political community in Melbourne.[8] Journalism was, then, an important outlet for Davitt, given that he could not articulate his eclectic ideas through a party political machine and was without a political faction of his own. His ultimate platform was the *Labour World*. As editor he was the first among home rulers to call for Parnell's resignation during the divorce scandal in 1890. Ironically, the strong anti-Parnellite stance which was taken incurred the censure of leading figures in the Irish and British labour movements and, in the end, critically weakened the paper's standing as a labour organ, cutting short Davitt's editorial ambitions.

Two years before the launch of the *Labour World*, Davitt had actually applied for the post of manager and editor of the *Freeman's Journal*, following the sudden death of its owner, Edmund Dwyer Gray, in March 1888. According to Archbishop Thomas Croke, the position was sought after by Davitt, Harrington, Sexton and, apparently, T.P. O'Connor.[9] The post was a prestigious one, although O'Connor had already launched his own paper, *The Star*. Over the course of the previous year O'Connor had put considerable effort into securing financial backing for this paper, a liberal-radical organ with particular emphasis on home rule and 'progressive' politics. *The Star* was founded in January 1888, and while O'Connor, as a professional journalist, appreciated the potential financial gains in such a venture, he was driven more by the opportunity to advance political ends through his journalism[10]. This was especially important in popularizing home rule. As Ian Sheehy has noted, *The Star* gave O'Connor the chance to become 'the first Irish Nationalist on the

---

5 16 June 1883, 'Notes after release from Richmond prison', DP, TCD, MS 9538. The newspapers in question were the *NY Daily News, Philadelphia Times, Cincinnate Commercial* [*Gazette*], *Chicago Tribune, St Louis Republican, New Orleans Times, Denvir Herald, St Paul's Daily Globe, San Francisco Chronicle*, and *Montreal Post*.   6 See Davitt's series of articles, 'About our artisans and industries', in *Evening Telegraph* (Dublin), 14, 21 Nov. and 5, 12 and 19 Dec. 1885; and 9 Jan. 1886. See also King (ed.), *Michael Davitt: collected writings*, vols. i and ii.   7 See correspondence with J. Winter, DP, TCD, MS 9324/72–82.   8 Patrick O'Farrell, *The Irish in Australia, 1788 to the present* (Cork, 2001), p. 223.   9 See Larkin, *The Roman*, p. 191.   10 L.W. Brady, *T.P. O'Connor and the Liverpool Irish* (London), 1983, p. 103.

London press to be able to express his highest aspirations'.[11] It also gave him the chance to re-state his call for 'a union of the two democracies' of Britain and Ireland, an idea which he had first promoted in 1881 and the theme for which Davitt distinguished himself in the 1880s.

With regard to the *Freeman's Journal* post, it transpired that the directors decided to hold the job for the son of Gray, who was aged just 18 years, and who would, it was hoped, assume the position at a later date.[12] The matter of the vacancy was, however, also important because of a tactical intervention by Parnell. On learning of Gray's death, the Irish leader had written to the principal director of the paper, Alderman Kernan, setting out what he considered to be the best criteria for judging candidates. The candidate suitable for the post would, in Parnell's view, enjoy the support of the Irish people as a whole, should 'commend himself to the class from whom the shareholders are largely taken and to the shareholders themselves', and should possess sufficient journalistic experience. Larkin remarks that this intervention was a clever political move. By insisting that the new managing director ought to have the 'confidence of the Irish people as a whole', Parnell was effectively indicating that he had a veto on the selection, given that as the leader of nationalist Ireland he already commanded that confidence.[13] Davitt, who was actually the only formal applicant, certainly did not stand a chance under these circumstances.

The idea of a paper of his own had been on his mind since the late 1870s. At the height of the land war he encountered Francis William Soutter, an 'advanced' radical from London, who had established a weekly workingman's paper in December 1880. Shortly after the launch of the paper, the *Radical*, Soutter visited Ireland where he met leading members of the Irish movement, including Davitt and Egan.[14] The *Radical* strongly supported the anti-coercion campaign, and featured articles on women's suffrage and land nationalization. The main piece in its first edition lamented the lack of labour representation in parliament.[15] It lasted only until July 1882, but the venture was highly praised by Henry George, who remarked that it represented 'real Radicalism'.[16] Davitt naturally felt a more pressing need to undertake a similar venture as the 1880s progressed. In the opening pages of his diary for 1884 he spoke of the need for a weekly paper, 'a national and social reform organ conducted by me'.[17] The *Labour World* was eventually launched in London in

---

11 Ian Sheehy, 'T.P. O'Connor and *The Star*, 1886–90' in Boyce and O'Day (eds), *Ireland in transition*, p. 84. 12 Gray's son, who was also called Edmund Dwyer Gray, did not return until early 1891, from an extended trip to Australia; see Felix M. Larkin, '"A great daily organ": the *Freeman's Journal*, 1763–1924', *History Ireland* 14:3 (2006), 44–9. 13 Larkin, *The Roman*, p. 193. 14 F.W. Soutter, *Recollections of a labour pioneer* (London, 1923), p. 108. 15 Henry Pelling, *Origins of the Labour Party, 1880–1900* (Oxford, 1965), p. 15. 16 Soutter, *Recollections*, pp 110–11. 17 Davitt's diary, 1884 (opening notes), DP, TCD, MS 9541.

September 1890. Davitt was joined by McGhee as a shareholder in the venture.[18] The paper was established against the advice of George, who believed, with some justification, that Davitt might have been taking on too much at this time. At the very least George hoped it would not be called '*The Labour World*', or anything of that sort'.[19] But the title was quite a deliberate choice on Davitt's part.[20] The paper was a penny weekly, consisting of a substantial sixteen pages. With Davitt as editor and managing director, it promised to engage with political, social and reform issues in 'these islands' and beyond, and to unite in 'the bonds of human brotherhood', the workers of all nations. It also promised to report on literary, scientific and sporting matters 'of special interest to workingmen and women'.[21] It reflected Davitt's own distinctive politics, as was implied in the connotations of internationalism in its title. It had been a 'long planned project', and, as Davitt indicated in a letter to Sabina, he was excited to have it under his 'sole direction'.[22]

Moody has stated that part of the historical value of the paper resides in its having had 'no rival' in its own particular field.[23] He is incorrect, however, in claiming that it appeared before Keir Hardie's *Labour Leader*. The latter had, in fact, been launched as a monthly in January 1889, although it folded within a year only to be revived again in February 1893.[24] Nevertheless, as a publication of its kind, the *Labour World* was a truly pioneering journalistic project. Keir Hardie conceded as much by claiming, albeit inaccurately in the case of the *Labour Leader*, that the only other labour papers in existence at the time were his own monthly and the miners' organ, the *Labour Tribune*.[25] Davitt was fully conscious of the extent to which he was breaking new ground. He recognized the aversion of advertisers towards the word 'labour' in newspaper titles, and he acknowledged that several previous 'labour' papers had had a transient existence,[26] an ironic observation considering that his own paper lasted only eight months. The *Labour World* declared itself 'independent of political matters', but it was clearly well disposed to lib-labism, being as it was supportive of 'the Liberal Party in policy or legislation that shall have as its object the social and industrial improvement of the working classes'.[27] It had been almost a decade since Davitt penned ideas on independent parliamentary labour rep-

18 The initial shareholders and signatories of the Labour World News Company's memorandum of association were Davitt, McGhee, Mr D'Arcy Reeves, Mr Sherlock, Mr William Saunders, Mr Bennet Burlagh and James Rourke; see *FJ*, 17 May 1892. **19** George to Davitt, 9 May 1890, DP, TCD, MS 9332/252. **20** The Labour World News Company also ran a Sunday edition called the *Sunday World*. **21** DP, TCD, MS 9422/2270. **22** Davitt to Sabina, 9 Apr. 1890, DP, TCD, MS 9325/[103/12]. **23** Moody, 'Davitt and British labour', p. 68. **24** Fred Reid, 'Keir Hardie and the *Labour Leader*, 1893–1903' in Jay Winter (ed.), *The working class in modern British history, essays in honour of Henry Pelling* (Cambridge, 1983), p. 20. **25** James Keir Hardie, 'Michael Davitt: the democrat', *Socialist Review* (Aug. 1908), 413. **26** See *Pall Mall Gazette* interview as quoted in the *FJ*, 11 Sept. 1890. **27** DP, TCD, MS 9422/2270.

resentation while in Portland jail.[28] But in 1890 he was wedded to a lib-lab position and was to broadly adhere to this up until at least 1895. Despite his reservations about the nature of the Liberal–nationalist alliance by the end of the 1880s, he still recognized the 'union of hearts' as critical to the interests of the Irish nationalist cause. The alliance was crucial to Irish nationalists and had a significant impact on the Irish in Britain. As Ó Tuathaigh points out, the Liberals thereafter enjoyed a level of support from the immigrant Irish, at least until the Great War, which was 'strong enough to withstand both the enticing carrot of Conservative education policies, and the more natural political claims of a nascent Labour party on a largely working-class community'.[29]

The alliance was certainly a major turning point. O'Connor noted that from June 1886 the branches of the INLGB, of which he was president, were organizing the Irish vote for the Liberal Party, when only six months previously they had been acting as 'committee rooms' for Tory candidates.[30] When O'Connor founded *The Star* he viewed it as an opportunity to galvanize support for the alliance and also to promote home rule. His journalistic role was all the more vital because the considerable hold over much of the London press which the Liberals had enjoyed for thirty years was seriously weakened by the Party's defeat in the 1886 general election. It was in this climate that O'Connor secured the political backing of John Morley and the financial backing of prominent Liberal figures such as J.J. Coleman, the mustard magnate and Liberal MP. O'Connor put considerable personal effort into the paper and was most likely responsible for the greater part of the features and reports on Ireland and home rule. Based in London, the halfpenny evening paper sold around 160,000 copies daily, and was the only radical organ of its kind in the city.[31] It had an impressive staff complement, which included H.W. Massingham as assistant editor, and the young Sidney Webb and George Bernard Shaw. However, problems were to arise later, especially between Massingham and O'Connor on the labour question.

O'Connor, like Davitt, had observed significant developments in labour politics, especially in the latter years of the 1880s. *The Star* was, indeed, launched around the same time as the 'Bloody Sunday' demonstration in Trafalgar Square. O'Connor was open to supporting the development of 'new unionism', and *The Star* covered in detail the match girls' strike in July 1888.[32] It also reported on the London dock strike in August of the following year. In its first issue, the paper's political programme not only included home rule but also a social agenda which had as its objectives improvements in the housing of the working class, land reform and progressive taxation. Sheehy argues

28 Davitt, *Leaves*, vol. ii, p. 161.   29 Ó Tuathaigh, 'The Irish in nineteenth-century Britain', p. 172.   30 O'Brien, *Parnell*, p. 193.   31 Sheehy, 'T.P. O'Connor', pp 79–83.   32 Brady, 'T.P. O'Connor', p. 114.

that such a broad programme significantly reflected O'Connor's attempts to re-define the Liberal–nationalist alliance.[33] But over the course of 1890 O'Connor found himself under increasing pressure from Shaw and, particularly, Massingham to adopt a more radical line. Massingham, who came to have some involvement with the business side of the Labour World News Company,[34] and who would demonstrate alongside Davitt in 1898 in support of striking quarrymen in Wales,[35] wanted the paper to give more support to the labour cause. O'Connor did not exercise tight editorial control over the paper, and Massingham proceeded to promote the miners' eight-hour day, a provocative stand at a time when the Liberals were voicing their opposition to the Miner's bill in the commons. Conscious of Liberal sensibilities, especially those of capitalist Liberals such as Coleman, O'Connor dropped the policy of support for the miners.

He was prepared to address the labour question but only in the context of progressive liberalism. In September 1890, *The Star* joined with the Liberals in castigating Jim Connell, the author of the labour anthem, *The Red Flag*, who stood as a labour candidate in Finsbury.[36] Tensions among the paper's staff eventually led to its demise in 1891. Later, when O'Connor established his next journalistic venture, *The Sun*, in 1893, he revisited the question of labour representation, arguing that the Liberal Party should put forward workingmen in predominantly working-class constituencies. But, as L.W. Brady had noted, he ultimately maintained the same position on labour: in *The Sun* he acknowledged the importance of the 'social question', but he remarked that it stood 'to some extent beyond and outside the conflicts of the two great parties'.[37]

The *Labour World* was certainly inclined towards radical liberalism, but its socialist tendencies were also unmistakable. Unlike *The Star*, it was an avowedly labour publication which vigorously championed the cause of the progressive labour movement and 'new unionism'. Its editorial of 21 September 1890 set out the demands of the 'progressive labour movement'. It demanded a more democratic organization of labour; the end of landed monopoly and landlord appropriation of that 'immense annual increment which is due to the general industry and enterprise'; and, significantly, 'the extension of state and municipal control and ownership of such monopolies as can be best managed by public bodies in the public interest'. Implicit in these demands were the points of the 'workers' charter', which included shorter hours, healthier working conditions, better housing, and political and social equality.

The paper was a platform for Davitt's Irish Democratic Trade and Labour Federation (IDTLF) which he had founded in January 1890 to renew the

33 Sheehy, 'T.P. O'Connor', p. 78, 85. 34 DP, TCD, MS 9422/2271. 35 DRD, NLW, MS 954. 36 C. Desmond Greaves, *The life and times of James Connolly* (London, 1961), p. 40. 37 Quoted in Brady, 'T.P. O'Connor', p. 130.

demands of labour within the nationalist movement. The Federation was essentially a trade union for agricultural and town labourers in the south of Ireland. Its stated objective was to 'defend the right of the working classes of Ireland'.[38] In its first edition, the *Labour World* outlined the programme of the Federation. Besides an independent Irish parliament, it demanded universal adult suffrage and the abolition of all property qualifications in municipal and poor law board election, land nationalization, free education for children, a reduction of working hours to a 'reasonable' limit, and adequate dwelling for labourers. To achieve these ends, it proposed a 'cordial' co-operation with British democracy.[39] Parnell's attitude towards the Federation was adversarial. When Davitt approached him at the time of the adultery scandal in 1890 to ask about the veracity of the Captain O'Shea's allegations, he evaded the question and instead attacked the Federation. Calmly, but with an implied threat, he informed Davitt,

> I don't approve of your labor organization in the South of Ireland; it will lead to mischief and can do no good. What do the labourers and artisans want that we cannot obtain for them by the efforts of the National League as well if not better than through those of this new combination? I though you were opposed to 'class movement'? What is trade-unionism but a landlordism of labor? I would not tolerate, if I were head of a government, such bodies as trade unions [...] You are [moreover] overlooking Mr Gladstone's position and difficulties. Any agitation in Ireland, except one making directly for Home Rule, increases the obstacles he has to contend with over here. It diverts attention from the main issues of our movement, and your new labor organization in Cork will frighten the capitalist Liberals, and lead them to believe that a Parliament in Dublin might be used for the purpose of furthering some kind of Irish socialism.

Davitt was undaunted by Parnell's censure and later described it as a 'superb piece of bluff', designed to avert attention from the adultery charges.[40] The Federation would, however, come to be affected by the political repercussions of the O'Shea divorce case. At its height, it had around thirty branches in the south of Ireland,[41] but it collapsed during the Irish Party split in 1891. Even so, it played a significant part in the rise of trade unionism in Ireland, and its policies proved influential in rural protest up to 1917.[42]

With the *Labour World*, Davitt was at the forefront in advancing the cause of labour. The organ declared itself 'a journal of progress for the masses'.[43] Its

38 *LW,* 21 Sept. 1890. **39** Ibid. **40** Davitt, *The fall,* p. 636. **41** Emmet O'Connor, *A labour history of Ireland* (Dublin, 1992), p. 53. **42** Emmet O'Connor, *A labour history of Waterford* (Waterford, 1989), p. 93. **43** DP, TCD, MS 9422/2270.

strong labour agenda was evident from its concentration on trade unionism and issues relating to workers. A weekly column featured a biographical sketch of particular labour leaders, such as Tom Mann, the president of the Dockers' Union, and it also contained a column entitled 'Half-hours with Labour Poets'. The treatment of women's working issues was ably dealt with by 'Edith' in her weekly feature, 'Among Women Workers', where she provided a forum for discussion on areas such as women's unionization and pay issues.[44] In one article she interviewed Keir Hardie on the degree of unionization among working girls in Scottish towns; in another she called for a bill to regulate wages and fix hours for barmaids.[45] As V.E. Kunina has observed, the paper was ahead of its time in promoting the rights of women workers, and in highlighting the level of trade unionism among them.[46] It also featured notices of meetings and an informative full-page section on labour developments and disputes internationally, including reports on the condition of agricultural labourers in Ireland and England. On Labour Day, 1891, the full programme of speeches was carried, and a listing of both the speakers and the members of the Demonstration Committee.[47] The focus of Labour Day was the eight-hour day. The editorial included a quote from Marx, which seemed to allude to the notion of alienated labour. It is unlikely, however, that this was the work of Davitt, for the Labour Day edition of the paper featured a letter from him (dated 29 April), in which he announced his decision to step down as editor, although he made it clear that he would remain a director of the Labour World News Company.

It would seem that he did not insist on keeping the paper under his own personal control in the same manner that Hardie insisted on being central to the *Labour Leader*. The *Labour World* was a ready forum for Davitt's political views, but his editorship was not as conspicuous as that of Hardie. Although he had considerable regard for the journalism of Stead, describing his *Review of Reviews* as 'a *vade-mecum* to all students of contemporary politics',[48] he did not embrace the 'new journalism' of the 1880s and 1890s to the same degree as Hardie, and especially not in the fashion of Stead, or Blatchford, editor of the *Clarion*. During public speeches, Davitt often made reference to his family's eviction in Mayo and his years of imprisonment, but autobiographical detail did not feature in the *Labour World*, and personal comment was largely confined to the editorial commentary. Hardie's *Labour Leader* was, in contrast, quite characteristic of 'new journalism', in that Hardie's personality was always to

---

44 'Edith' may have been Edith Lupton, Secretary of the Laundry-Women's Co-Operative Association. The name was signed to a letter by the Association published in the letters page of the *Labour World* on 19 Nov. 1890. **45** *LW*, 1 Nov. 1890. **46** V.E. Kunina, *Maikl Devitt, sun irlandskogo naroda: stranitsy zhizni I borby, 1846–1906* (Moscow, 1973), p. 132. **47** *LW*, 2 May 1891. **48** Davitt to Stead, *c.*1890, SP, CAC, MS 1/19.

the fore. His name appeared in practically every page,[49] and through a personal column, 'Between Ourselves', the readership became acquainted not only with the editor's political ideas but with quite personal accounts of the austerity of his working-class boyhood. The readership was also treated to thumbnail sketches of family members and their severe hardships. And although the *Labour World* gave full coverage to the programme of the IDTLF and the issues with which Davitt was concerned and involved, it did not routinely parade his political deeds. It was quite unlike the *Labour Leader*, which kept Hardie's exploits before the public eye and often illustrated the point in cartoon form. Davitt's paper hardly featured political cartoons at all, certainly none depicting him. Nor did he properly utilize, as Hardie did, the typographical innovation of 'new journalism' by making the format of the paper more attractive with subheadings to articles and features and front-page illustrations. While the *Labour World* was, for instance, somewhat easier on the eye than the *Freeman's Journal* or *The Times*, it was by no means audacious in its typeface.

But, as Fred Reid has pointed out, 'new journalism' was much more than typographical innovation: 'What was to ensure the commercial viability of newspaper publishing in the 1890s and beyond was the combination of political and apolitical features'. He notes that the *Clarion* was founded on this basis, and included columns featuring topics such as sports and leisure, as well as political comment.[50] The *Clarion* and the *Labour Leader* were actually rivals in the later 1890s, both hoping to appeal to the membership of the Independent Labour Party (ILP), yet they were very different papers which reflected the personalities of the respective editors. Blatchford considered that the socialist movement was too strait-laced, and he attributed this to the 'lily-livered Methodists' who led the ILP. Hardie, conversely, feared that the movement was being compromised by 'irresponsible levity'.[51] Associated with the temperance movement since his early twenties, he viewed the drinking habits of Blatchford and other socialists with utter distaste. The *Clarion* was a much more adventurous paper, whereas the *Labour Leader*, rejecting the commercialism of 'new journalism', was intended as a strictly edifying organ. Nevertheless, the contents of the *Clarion* were not in any way designed to be lewd or unscrupulous; Blatchford's political commentary was as serious as Hardie's. The personality factor was ultimately important. Reid's view is that Hardie simply 'could not admit gratuitous fun in his paper'. Jokes only ever appeared when they facilitated a political or moral point; similarly with book reviews and short stories.[52] He featured a women's column and a children's page, but their contents were didactic and sententious; and

---

49 Reid, 'Keir Hardie and the *Labour Leader*', p. 20. 50 Ibid., p. 30. 51 Quoted in Pelling, *Origins*, pp 173–4. 52 Reid, 'Keir Hardie and the *Labour Leader*', p. 30.

as articles on sport were not consistent with his edifying agenda, the topic was banned from the paper.

Davitt was of a similar disposition; word and deed had to be purposive. For instance, the 'New Books and Magazines' column in the *Labour World* looked at a recently published work on *The conquest of the Sioux Indians*, as well as a reprint of Mary Wollstonecraft's classic, *A vindication of the rights of women*. But Davitt's thinking was not infused with the same evangelical fervour that characterized Hardie's work and journalism. The ambit of the *Labour World* also allowed for more apolitical content than the *Labour Leader*. On occasion 'Edith's column' on women found space to touch on fashion, and there was a 'Cream of Comics' section which included two-to-four-line gags, poor in quality but apolitical nonetheless. Beginning in March 1891 a novel, *Blood love; or, The lily of Leman Street*, started to run as a serial. Davitt also ran a sporting section that gave a listing of soccer and rugby results, as well as a brief section on the GAA. The paper was not hibernicized; its appeal was international. Indeed, it is telling that Davitt gave so little space to Gaelic sporting fixtures and results, considering his role as one of the GAA's early patrons. To some extent, it illustrates that he was not a cultural nativist.

In its early editions, the *Labour World* featured horseracing tips in a column entitled 'Silk and Satin', but a decision was taken to discontinue the item. In his 'Answers to Correspondents', Davitt responded to the query of one reader regarding the editorial decision to end the feature: '[…] we are opposed on principle to betting and gambling of all kinds, and resolve not to give them any encouragement in The Labour World'.[53] Such an editorial policy was also held by the liberal *Leeds Mercury* and other sections of the nonconformist press. Working-class betting was carried out in public houses and other venues, despite an Act in 1853 that forbade off-course gambling. Although Davitt was conscious of commercial demands on newspaper publishing in the 1890s, the issue for him was that he could not promote an activity which averted the attention of the labouring classes from the real issues pertaining to their lives. In the 1880s and 1890s the working class was largely digesting the contents of the likes of *Lloyd's Weekly Newspaper*, with its tabloid features, and the ephemera of Alfred Harmsworth's *Answers to Correspondents*. By the late 1890s the latter had a weekly circulation of up to 600,000.[54]

Although the *Labour World* featured reports on suicides, it did not run the human-interest stories featuring lurid crimes that were the hallmark of the mainstream popular press. On a political level, however, it was launched with a lead story that was publicized in fairly dramatic terms. In the first edition, Davitt announced a 'Sensational Disclosure' for the following week's edition,

---

53 *LW*, 1 Nov. 1890. 54 Royle, *Modern Britain*, p. 271.

27 September 1890, and promised 'our readers as startling a chapter of secret history as was ever written'. The piece was entitled 'Pigott and his Patrons; or Unionism and Crime' and was designed to expose the *agents provocateurs* behind the 1883–4 dynamite plots and the Pigott forgery. In the 27 September issue the editor explained, evidently in response to some queries presented to the paper concerning such a 'hideous business', that the leading feature was not motivated by sensationalism, or indeed Irish self-interests, but by the pursuit of truth and justice. In defence of the lead serial, the editorial presented an interesting twist. It was argued that *agents provocateurs* would ultimately be used against the burgeoning labour movement, as 'has happened already in Belgium, Germany, France and America in connection with labour organizations in these countries'. The exposure of agents in the Irish political scene was, therefore, relevant to the wider political struggle. Most editorial reviews greatly anticipated the unfolding of these revelations.

Davitt was already quite an accomplished investigative journalist. His articles in the Dublin *Evening Telegraph* in December 1885, on rack renting in Dublin slums were superlative pieces, described indeed by James M. Cahalan as 'of top-notch muckraking' quality.[55] In the first of his articles, he investigated the living conditions of fifty-eight labourers, of both sexes, in Dublin.[56] The men comprised ordinary day labourers and some mechanics, while the women were seamstresses, dressmakers, washerwomen, and charwomen. The total weekly earnings of these labourers amounted to £35 10s. 6d., while the weekly rent paid by them was almost one-sixth of the total, that is, £6 6s. 10d. Davitt stated that his findings revealed 'a system of grinding exaction in comparison to which the rack-renting of impoverished western cottiers will scarcely compete in vindicating'. His next piece concentrated not only on the very low paid, but on 'the next class', those who earn from seven to fifteen shillings a week. In a study of fifty-two persons this time, he found their total weekly earning to be £47 10s. 10d. and their total weekly rent to be £6 12s. 9d. In investigating these conditions, Davitt sought to address the very serious problem of slum housing in Dublin at that time. He made use of government statistics, quoting from 'The report of her majesty's commissioners for inquiring into the housing of the working classes', which recorded that 'in Dublin out of about 54,000 families 32,000 live in single rooms'.[57]

Despite its main 'Sensational Disclosure', the *Labour World* did not run any stories comparable to Stead's 'The Maiden Tribute of modern Babylon' or Hardie's later 'West End Scandal', which were major exposure pieces on social injustice and debauchery. Stead's piece had famously represented a significant development in journalistic convention. Brady argues, however, that there has

55 J.M. Cahalan, 'Michael Davitt', p. 25.   56 *ET*, 12 Dec. 1885.   57 *ET*, 19 Dec. 1885.

been too much focus on Stead in the study of the development of 'new journalism'. He maintains that while Stead has rightly been viewed as an innovator, O'Connor may have done more to transform the practice of journalism.[58] It was only a year after Stead's keynote article, 'Government by Journalism',[59] that O'Connor was busy organizing the foundation of *The Star*, in which he combined existing journalistic techniques, such as human interest stories, gossip and sports news. Brady points out that O'Connor was 'more completely a working journalist', and while *The Star* was characteristic of 'new journalism', O'Connor 'let the new style speak for itself for the most part'.[60] Davitt's venture was also a practical undertaking. In fact, the *Labour World* resembled more a labour bulletin, albeit a substantial and lively one, which contained an impressive array of information and a call to solidarity.

The exposure campaign was one aspect of 'new journalism' which Hardie embraced wholeheartedly. As with Stead, his campaigns were part of a moral crusade permeated with Christian righteousness (although it is difficult to ascertain whether he was consciously indebted to Stead). In early 1896 the *Labour Leader* ran a series entitled 'The West End Scandal', which picked up on the judgement by Glasgow magistrates' court in the case of a Mrs Pollock who was charged with running a brothel. Several factory girls who had been introduced to prostitution through the brothel gave evidence against her. Their names and evidence were published in the press, but the names of the 'old gentlemen' clients involved were withheld from publication. Hardie was intent on exposing the double standards in the newspapers, and over the course of five weeks he produced a series of articles in which the names of the gentlemen in question were promised. Yet despite hints and insinuations in the *Labour Leader* each week, the names were never fully revealed. Reid remarks that the 'revelation' degenerated into sensationalism and the story was ultimately terminated. Stead's 'Maiden Tribute' in the *Pall Mall Gazette* in 1885 was also sensationalist, but with the qualification that at least his articles were intended to shock in order to precipitate legal reform. Reid claims that Hardie was really intent on exposing evangelical workers in Glasgow who were linked to Scottish liberalism, and who were, in his view, self-serving and hypocritical in their work among the poor and destitute. 'The West End Scandal' was Hardie's first leading exposure piece, and, according to Reid, it was primarily designed to illustrate that established Christianity 'was failing the people while socialists fought for righteousness'.[61]

Davitt's *Labour World* was professionally produced and well written. Its initial attraction was such that demand exceeded output. The editorial of 27

---

58 Brady, 'T.P. O'Connor', p. 106.   **59** Stead, 'Government by Journalism', *Contemporary Review*, 49, May 1886; cited in ibid., p. 106.   **60** Ibid., p. 107.   **61** Reid, 'Keir Hardie and the *Labour Leader*', pp 23–4.

September 1890 began by apologizing for the initial shortage in circulation. Davitt naturally hoped to see the widest possible circulation. Taking on the concerns of Dublin newsagents, he wrote to James Collins on 17 September 1890, adamant that he had no intention of letting Eason have a monopoly in Ireland. In the same letter he wrote excitedly of an order from the American News Agency of New York for 5,000 copies weekly.[62] More than 60,000 copies of the second edition were ordered.[63] The paper did not rely too heavily on advertising, but, advertising space taken together, it did run about one full page out of a total of sixteen in each edition, Lipton's Teas taking up the largest spaces.[64] However, it was ultimately to encounter financial difficulties. Some capital was raised by a number of supporters in England,[65] but it proved unavailing, and by the end of May 1891 the *Labour World* had run its course. By the time of his resignation, Davitt had, in any case, lost heart in the project. On 2 June, an extraordinary meeting was held to wind up the company, and Davitt's business partners and fellow shareholders, Gavin Clarke and Mr D'Arcy Reeves, were appointed liquidators.[66] In August they made a call of £1 per share.[67]

The paper had provided a ready platform for Davitt's views following the O'Shea divorce verdict in November 1890, and it was his stance at this political juncture which was largely responsible for the paper's demise. In the leadership crisis it became a manifestly partisan organ. Davitt's call for Parnell's retirement from leadership was issued on 20 November, before the Catholic Church in Ireland had made its position clear. As soon as the verdict was announced he strongly urged Archbishop Croke to speak out. Croke shared Davitt's view of the situation. On the day of the verdict he wrote to Davitt acknowledging the seriousness of the matter. He expressed the view that Parnell's resignation, 'at least for a while, would seem to be a matter of course'. He actually went further, no doubt alluding to the fact that Parnell had not made a single public speech in Ireland since 1886: 'A leader is one who leads', he stated, 'and Parnell has not led for the last half dozen years. Besides, leaders die or get discredited [...]'[68] But at this point Croke was unwilling to make a public declaration on the scandal. He was clearly apprehensive about the unfolding situation. Writing to Stead several days after his letter to Davitt he remarked, 'For the immediate present, at least, silence is for me the better part of valour'.[69] He explained in another letter to Davitt that his reticence was due

62 DA, DMS, MS MD/6. 63 Moody, 'Davitt and British labour', p. 68. 64 Besides Lipton's Teas, the paper featured advertisements for Tower Tea, Eadie's Pills, Jameson's Whiskey, Guinness, Pearl Life Assurance, Arnott's costumes. There were also advertisements for hotels, and items such as stitching machines, and stockings and socks. 65 Moody, 'Davitt and British labour', p. 69. 66 See *FJ*, 17 May 1891. 67 DP, TCD, MS 9422/2274. 68 Archbishop Croke to Davitt, 17 Nov. 1890, DP, TCD, MS 9334/280 69 Croke to W.T. Stead, 21 Nov. 1890, quoted in

to a fear of splitting the Irish Party, given that Party members had endorsed Parnell's continued leadership at a meeting in Leinster Hall as late as 20 November, where they had 'apparently nailed their colours to the mast'.[70] However, Davitt was impatient, and on 27 November the *Labour World* castigated the Irish clergy for its procrastination. An unequivocal condemnation of Parnell's leadership was not forthcoming from the hierarchy until 3 December 1890.

On the divorce crisis itself it is difficult to accept Davitt's later indignation regarding the true nature of the scandal. After all, members of the Irish Parliamentary Party were aware of the affair between Parnell and Mrs O'Shea as early as February 1881;[71] the Liberal government learned of it as early as May 1882; and it was alluded to publicly during the Galway election campaign in 1886.[72] Blunt suggested, in fact, that Davitt was aware of the situation in June 1886. Blunt recalled that after Parnell had failed to speak at a home rule meeting at which he was expected, Davitt remarked angrily,

> [...] it makes one's blood boil at moments like this when every man of us ought to be working night and day, that he should be away idling at Captain O'Shea's [...] It is a disgrace. We say nothing about it; but we all know it, and it will go hard with him some day, for we are all getting very tired.[73]

That day did arrive when Captain O'Shea filed his petition; and in the following weeks and months Davitt was in no doubt that the political implications were potentially explosive. In a diary entry for early January 1890 he noted, 'The Parnell-O'Shea business still talk of town. Most people spoken to seem to think it won't do Parnell much harm anyway. This huge mistake'. Yet, this sharp observation sits incongruously alongside the next line in the diary entry which expresses doubt about the veracity of the allegations of adultery: 'O'[Shea]'s being cuckold does not lessen much (if any) the crime (*if even committed*) of adultery with another man's wife [...] Hope sincerely [Parnell] will come out all right' [my italics].[74] Indeed, after approaching Parnell about the matter some time around February, Davitt was given an assurance that 'he [Parnell] would emerge from the whole trouble without a stain on his name or reputation'. Davitt seems to have taken this as an unequivocal denial of the charge of adultery itself. This is certainly the impression given in his account in *The fall of feudalism*.[75] Other than this account we are unable to know more

Tierney, *Croke*, p. 235. **70** Croke to Davitt, some time between 20 and 25 Nov. 1890; quoted in O'Brien, *Parnell*, pp 291–2. **71** Davitt, *The fall*, p. 306. **72** O'Brien, *Parnell*, pp 167–8. **73** Blunt, *The land war*, pp 152–3. **74** Davitt's diary, 1 Jan. 1890, DP, TCD, MS 9553. **75** Davitt, *The fall*, p. 637.

about his actual meeting with Parnell. The existing manuscript of his diary for 1890, which might have recorded some significant entries, contains only loose fragments for January.[76]

Parnell, it must be said, had assured other colleagues that his honour would survive the divorce proceedings intact. During their meeting, he even urged Davitt to reassure 'friends who might be anxious on the matter'.[77] Davitt was apparently confident of the integrity of the assurances he had received because he accordingly informed Stead that Parnell had 'never deceived me in his life'.[78] Writing fourteen years later, he suggested:

> What was possibly working in [Parnell's] mind [in the course of their conversation] was a firm belief that the person who instituted the suit would be induced to withdraw it from the courts, and that in this manner Mr Parnell's assurances of innocence would be negatively confirmed should the case not come to trial.[79]

It is true that Parnell had also told William O'Brien that it was 'exceedingly doubtful' that the case would stand up beyond the early stages of the proceedings.[80] But it is quite remarkable that, given the history of the affair, Davitt should have accepted such 'assurances of innocence' at all. One is tempted to suggest that his outrage over the adultery was merely feigned. However, given the private doubts which he consigned to his diary in January 1890 regarding the veracity of the allegations, one is ultimately led to conclude that what must have been working in *his* own mind was what Frank Callanan calls an 'almost wilful naiveté'.[81]

While Davitt was to be the first in nationalist Ireland to make a public call for the leader's retirement when the verdict was announced, he was not alone in thinking the option the only judicious move. Even the steadfast Parnellite, Harrington, privately felt 'that his [Parnell's] giving way voluntarily would on the whole be the best way out of the difficulty'.[82] Davitt felt he had to take account of the potential strains on the Liberal–nationalist alliance and, significantly, the weight of English nonconformist morality. Indeed, Stead expressed his moral outrage to Gladstone on 20 November and advised him that he had begun a campaign against Parnell, warning, 'I know my Nonconformists well, and no power on earth will induce them to follow that man to the poll or you either, if you are arm in arm in [*sic*] him'.[83] The *Pall Mall Gazette* led a scathing attack on Parnell immediately after the announcement. Stead was no longer

76 Davitt's diary, 1890, DP, TCD, MS 9553. **77** Davitt, *The fall*, p. 637. **78** Quoted in Callanan, *T.M. Healy*, p. 244. **79** Davitt, *The fall*, p. 637. **80** Quoted in Lyons, *Charles Stewart Parnell*, p. 463. **81** Callanan, *T.M. Healy*, p. 244. **82** Quoted in O'Brien, *Parnell*, p. 310. **83** Quoted in Frank Callanan, *The Parnell split, 1890–91* (Cork, 1992) pp 17–18.

editor of the paper, but his successor, E.T. Cook, adopted the same morally indignant and inflexible stance.[84] Other nonconformist organs, such as the *Leeds Mercury* and the *Sheffield Independent*, came out against Parnell.[85] The *Methodist Times* put its view bluntly: 'Mr. Parnell's trial is over; the trial of the Irish people has begun'.[86] And the Baptist leader, Dr John Clifford, was categorical in a letter to *The Star*, in which he bluntly demanded, 'HE MUST GO [...] Men legally convicted of immorality will not be permitted to lead in the legislation of the kingdom'.[87] As John Glasier has observed, 'Ministers such as Clifford [...] had accepted home rule as a moral issue'.[88]

It so happened that a meeting of the National Liberal Federation was due to be held in Sheffield only days after the court's decree. Before the meeting, John Morley contacted Gladstone (who was not due to attend) and requested his views on the official Party line. The Liberal leader had been resisting calls for him to round on Parnell, and his response to Morley was 'that we must be passive, must wait and watch'.[89] Gladstone was determined to adopt such a position, despite the protestations of Stead and even Cardinal Manning. Pressure was growing, however, and this became apparent at the Sheffield meeting, which was held on 20 and 21 November. Morley, in attendance with Sir William Harcourt, was left in absolutely no doubt about the tide of opinion. Harcourt himself reported to Gladstone on 22 November that the opposition to Parnell's continued leadership was not confined to 'screamers' such as Stead, but was *absolutely unanimous and extremely strong*.[90] Morley later reflected, 'Men, in whose hearts religion and morals held the first place, were strongly joined by men accustomed to settle political action by political considerations. Platform-men united with pulpit-men in swelling the whirlwind'.[91] This was the political maelstrom into which Davitt thrust himself and his new paper.

In his dealings with the Irish leader over recent years, Gladstone had been much impressed. He referred to Parnell as 'very clever' in April 1886 following a meeting in Morley's house of commons study where all three were negotiating the financial details of the first home rule bill;[92] and when Parnell visited Hawarden in December 1889 his host found him 'one of the very best people to deal with that I have every known [...] He seems to notice and appreciate everything'.[93] But even before he had received Harcourt's report,

84 *Pall Mall Gazette*, 18 Nov. 1890; quoted in Trevor Fisher, *Scandal, the sexual politics of late Victorian Britain* (Gloucestershire, 1995), p. 130. **85** John F. Glasier, 'Parnell's fall and the nonconformist conscience', *IHS*, 12 (1960–61), 122. **86** Quoted in Tierney, *Croke*, p. 235. **87** *The Star*, 19 Nov. 1890; cited in Fisher, *Scandal*, p. 130. **88** Glasier, 'Parnell's fall', p. 132. **89** Quoted in John Morley, *The life of William Ewart Gladstone*, iii (London, 1904), p. 431. **90** Quoted in Lyons, *Charles Stewart Parnell*, p. 490. **91** Morley, *The life of Gladstone*, vol. iii, p. 433. **92** Alvin Jackson, *Home rule: an Irish history, 1800–2000* (London, 2003), p. 38. **93** Quoted in Jenkins, *Gladstone*, p.569.

Gladstone was feeling the full weight of the crisis. In gathering his thoughts on the case, he noted the position taken by Davitt in the *Labour World*.[94] In his editorial comments, Davitt had argued that Parnell was 'under a moral cloud which he has brought upon himself' and that he should stand down in the interest of the national cause.[95] Gladstone agreed; but, believing that any decision should ultimately rest with the home rule party and the Irish people, he reasoned he had 'no right spontaneously to pronounce [his own] opinion'.[96] Yet only a few days after the Sheffield meeting, he finally felt that he had no option but to make clear his view that Parnell's continuance in the leadership of the Irish Party would be detrimental to the Liberal Party and to the cause of Ireland. J.J. Coleman had warned that if Parnell did not resign, the Liberals would lose five seats in puritan East Anglia.[97] According to Katherine O'Shea, Parnell perfectly understood the political pressures which Gladstone was under, although he still considered it significant that the 'old Spider', as he called Gladstone, had 'always loathed me'.[98]

Nonconformist sentiment and its potential political ramifications spurred Davitt into action from the outset. Other factors also naturally provoked him to take such a strong stand. Parnell's frequent absences from meetings and political business over the previous number of years had left Davitt resentful, sometimes bitterly so. This resentment had been compounded by Parnell's firm belief that he was 'above the human weakness of apology', as he explained it privately to Katherine O'Shea.[99] During Davitt's outburst which, according to Blunt, occurred in 1886, he apparently referred to Parnell as 'a mere *laissez faire* leader'.[1] In one of the early editions of the *Labour World*, he wrote, 'One man with a conviction is worth a hundred with only interest'.[2] Davitt was undoubtedly a man of passionate conviction and this was evident in the frenetic schedules to which he committed himself. His appetite for politics was insatiable. As Moody states, 'he could never disengage himself from the dust and heat and unending pressures of political life'.[3] When travelling to undertake his long-anticipated lecturing tour in Australia in 1895, he learned that his six-year-old daughter, Kathleen, had died suddenly. He received a telegram from his wife once he had reached Colombo, Ceylon.[4] She urged him to continue on with his 'mission'. On that basis, he travelled on to Australia, and over the next seven months kept a copious amount of notes on every aspect of life in the colonies. He was deeply affected by his daughter's death,[5] but from his published work, *Life and progress in Australasia* (1898), it

94 Matthew, *Gladstone*, pp 313–14. **95** *LW*, 22 Nov. 1890. **96** Matthew, *Gladstone*, p. 314. **97** Stephen Koss, *Nonconformity in modern British politics* (London, 1975), p. 27. **98** Katherine O'Shea, *The uncrowned king*, p. 236. **99** Quoted in ibid., p. 111. **1** Blunt, *The land war*, p. 153. **2** *LW*, 21 Sept. 1890. **3** Moody, *Davitt*, p. 551. **4** Telegram to Davitt, 25 Apr. 1895, DP, TCD, MS 9477/4425. **5** See, for example, Davitt's diary, 22 Mar. 1896, DP, TCD, MS 9567. Years later,

is clear that he was enthralled by his experiences in the Antipodes. The times in which he lived were, of course, harder and much less sentimental than our own; but it was to some extent an indication of the intensity of Davitt's political nature that he did not return to Ireland on receiving the telegram, or at least did not return sooner than he eventually did.

He was obsessive in the pursuit of his political objectives, which sometimes inclined him to bouts of moroseness. He could, according to Moody, laugh at himself.[6] But, while there is no doubt that he could indeed be witty, there is no indication that he had a sense of self-irony. Sophie O'Brien remarked that he was prone to irritability but that his marriage had had a salutary effect on him. In her memoirs, she wrote, '[Mary] cured him of his depression by laughing at it'.[7] Indeed, Davitt seemed to find life in their new 'Land League Cottage' home in Ballybrack, Co. Dublin, quite agreeable. In a diary entry in 1888 he noted,

> How I could enjoy an existence that would divide itself into – gardening in the morning – attending to correspondence and doing some bread-and-butter work in the afternoon and then indulging in 'mine own fireside' in the evening listening to Verdi and Rossini [...] as rendered by a most loving and thoroughly devoted little wife!.[8]

He lamented, however, that, despite its attraction, such a life would not be possible 'so long as the Social Vampire exists in Ireland'. He lived by a code of duty, and he was given to priggishness when others did not adhere to that code. He viewed Parnell's absences, especially when in the company of Mrs O'Shea, as a gross dereliction of duty. In the *Labour World* of 13 December 1890 he referred to Parnell as the 'Pretender', criticizing him for neglecting the cause of Ireland for eight years. He was appalled by what he considered Parnell's wanton disregard for that cause, and, moreover, by his leaving the home rule movement open to such ridicule, some of it extremely virulent. For instance, in the *Methodist Times* the Revd Price Hughes remarked bitterly that,

> [...] if the Irish race deliberately select as their recognized representative an adulterer of Mr Parnell's type they are as incapable of self-government as their bitterest enemies have asserted. So obscene a race

and on quite a sinister note, he told Alfred Webb, 30 Mar. 1906 (DP, TCD, MS 9490/4975) that Land League cottage in Ballybrack had sad memories 'as our little girl Kathleen – our first born – died there largely owing to the brutality of a woman we had in our employment'. **6** Moody, *Davitt*, p. 552. **7** Mrs. William O'Brien, *My Irish friends* (Paris, 1937), p. 32; quoted in King, *Michael Davitt*, p. 51. **8** Davitt's diary, 15 Jan. 1888, DP, TCD, MS 9548.

as in those circumstances they would prove themselves to be would obviously be unfit for anything except a military despotism.[9]

C.C. O'Brien makes the point that Davitt's attack on Parnell was political-ly motivated rather than morally so.[10] There is no doubt that politics were the overriding factor. Still, Davitt's moral references cannot be discounted entire-ly. In an outburst in the *Labour World* he condemned the Irish hierarchy for stalling on the 'moral issue', asserting, 'The bishops and priests of Ireland have left it to the sturdy dissenters of Great Britain to make their protest'.[11] Keir Hardie suspected the influence of Catholic publicist and business manager of the *Labour World*, Charles Diamond, on Davitt's truculent anti-Parnellite posi-tion.[12] Diamond, originally from Ulster, was one of the main organizers of the Irish nationalist movement in Britain. He established his own paper, the *Irish Tribune*, in Newcastle in 1884, and before long created the Catholic Press Company.[13] The Company published the *Catholic Educator* and the *Catholic Home Journal*, together with more than thirty weekly papers which had a local readership in most of the areas of Catholic population in Britain.[14]

It may very well have been a suspicion of Diamond that led McGhee to question the influences upon Davitt's position in the split (although the nam-ing of Diamond as a direct anti-Parnellite influence on Davitt does not seem to appear anywhere other than in Hardie's article). To McGhee's concerns, Davitt retorted sharply,

> [...] you are wrong in assuming that I have been influenced by anybody in the stand I have taken in the *Labour World* [...] I am [...] astounded that you and Ferguson should find my action inconsistent, while you, yourselves, are acting, in my belief, even more inconsistently than Tim Healy, who in season, and out of season, has been denouncing Parnell, for the last five years.[15]

---

9 *Methodist Times*, 20 Nov. 1890; quoted in Fisher, *Scandal*, p. 130.   **10** O'Brien, *Parnell*, p. 287.
11 *LW*, 27 Nov. 1890, quoted in ibid., p. 304.   **12** Keir Hardie, 'Michael Davitt', p. 413.   **13**
E.P.M. Wollaston, 'The Irish nationalist movement in Great Britain' (MA thesis, London University, 1958), pp 244–7.   **14** The papers of The Catholic Press Company included: the *Catholic Herald*, London, costing 1d. every Friday; the *Manchester Catholic Herald*, 1d. every Friday; the *Birmingham Catholic News*, *Bristol Catholic News*, *Catholic News* (Preston); the *Blackburn Catholic News*, the *Tyneside Catholic News*, each 1d. every Saturday; the *Glasgow Observer*, 1d. every Saturday; the *Catholic Pulpit*, 2d. monthly; the *Cumberland Catholic Herald*; *Liverpool Catholic Herald*; *Bradford Catholic Herald*; *Dundee Catholic Herald*; *Clydeside Catholic Herald*; *Lanarkshire Catholic Herald*; *Leeds Catholic Herald*; *Hull Catholic Herald*; *Bolton Catholic Herald*; *Aberdeen Catholic Herald*, each 1d. every Friday. These papers were listed on the headed paper of The Catholic Press Company. See such headed paper in the correspondence between Davitt and Diamond, DP, TCD, MS 9478/4469–4492.   **15** Davitt to McGhee, 24 Nov. 1890, DP, TCD, MS 9521/5972.

Davitt had a point in his assessment of Ferguson's behaviour. The latter had been acting inconsistently during the crisis, although this is probably explicable in terms of his determination to avoid identification with any particular faction. In any case, his stance was enough to have him labelled a Parnellite by the *Glasgow Observer* in the late 1890s when he ran foul of Diamond who had taken control of the paper in 1894.[16] It was a measure of Davitt's frustration during the split, and probably even his hubris, that he attacked McGhee who had been his close confidant for years. McGhee was, after all, his *'Awocato del Diavolo'*.[17] But, then, Davitt's passions were obviously running too high for even friendly criticism. He tersely assured McGhee, 'It is not Parnell's adultery with Mrs O'Shea in itself which causes me to side with those who say that he ought for a time to bury his head in oblivion'.[18]

The political repercussions were Davitt's chief concern, but he must also have found the long-running liaison between Parnell and Mrs O'Shea morally objectionable. Although he only called for Parnell to resign for 'the brief space of a few months',[19] his reaction to the scandal was nonetheless visceral. Davitt could, indeed, be quite prudish at times. During his tour in Europe in 1885 he came across a young German couple on honeymoon at the hotel where he was staying in Monte Carlo. He noted peevishly in his diary that during dinner, and in the presence of 'thirty other people of both sexes', they 'billed and cooed in a most "provoking" manner. How the other ladies at the table looked! especially those whose honeymoon period had not occurred in *late* years!'.[20] He may also have been bemoaning his own unmarried state at that time. Some weeks later as he was about to leave Naples he received a birthday present from 'a girl'. He confided in his diary,

> Wonder – but no! I am too old. Fifteen years ago I might have had a chance [...] but I can no longer boast of these attributes which take the eyes of young girls [...] my youth is [...] buried in the stone-yards and iron cells of Dartmoor.[21]

In considering Davitt's moral indignation it is important to remember that he was steeped in the tradition of the Fenian movement, which saw no contradiction in its members incurring the condemnation of the clergy while at

---

16 McFarland, *John Ferguson*, pp 220, 275–6. **17** Davitt to McGhee, 20 May 1890, DP, TCD, MS 9328 [180/39]. In Davitt's handwriting in this letter, the translated version of 'devil's advocate' could be taken as 'Advocato del Diabolo', but it could also be taken for, and is more likely to be, the Italian translation, 'Awocato del Diavolo'; 'Advocato del Diabolo' has no meaning in Italian, Spanish or Latin. **18** Davitt to McGhee, 24 Nov. 1890, DP, TCD, MS 9521/5972. **19** *LW*, 22 Nov. 1890. **20** Davitt's diary, 13 Jan. 1885, DP, TCD, MS 9543. **21** Ibid., 21 Mar. 1885.

the same time embracing Catholicism and practising the faith fervently. In January 1870 the church designated the Fenian Brotherhood a condemned and proscribed society.[22] This was only months before Davitt's own arrest for trafficking in weapons. The reality, particularly from the early 1860s, was that young men such as Davitt swelled the ranks of the IRB, prepared to defy the censures of the hierarchy while at the same time remaining devoutly Catholic. Davitt's attitude to the church and politics was characteristically Fenian: acting independently in the sphere of political life while accepting the remit of the church in the realm of morality. Accordingly, he did not eschew confrontation with the hierarchy. This was apparent in his response to Rome's censure of the Plan of Campaign in 1888 when he stated, 'Catholic as Ireland is she is not going to take her politics from Rome [...] The question of faith does not come in at all'.[23]

Despite his often outspoken criticism of the clergy, however, Davitt attended Mass throughout the course of his life and, as Moody puts it, 'held firmly to the Catholic piety in which he had been reared'.[24] He believed that religion was an integral part of civilized society, and he valued the moral contribution of the Catholic church in Ireland. In his prison jottings he wrote despairingly of the spread of atheism, noting that at least 'Ireland is probably the only country in the world where the Christian faith is sincerely and earnestly practiced [*sic*] by the whole people'.[25] On the day that he attacked the church for its tardy response to the O'Shea verdict, he told the *New York Sun* that the 'Catholic people [... of Ireland] are jealous of the moral reputation of our race; we should have been before the Nonconformists in expressing our condemnation'.[26] Given his traditional Catholic roots and his Fenian background, it is clear, then, that his moral sensibilities were probably offended by Parnell's adulterous behaviour. Yet, for all that, he was no Catholic purist. This was evident in his support for Charles Bradlaugh in 1883–4. Despite his demand that the church address the 'moral issue' in the divorce scandal, the *Labour World*, it must be stated, did not reflect the evangelical zeal that was characteristic of Hardie's journal. The first issue of the *Labour Leader* was led by a Tennyson poem on the risen Christ.[27] This would not have featured in Davitt's paper which was rather more in line with the humanistic tone of the *Clarion*.

Davitt distinguished specific 'heads or divisions into which [morality] resolves itself'. Social morality, he argued, was predicated on the 'subservience

22 See Donal A. Kerr, 'Priests, pikes and patriots: the Irish catholic church and political violence from the whiteboys to the fenians' in Stewart J. Brown and David W. Millar (eds), *Piety and power in Ireland, 1760–1960: essays in honour of Emmet Larkin* (Belfast, 2000) p. 38. 23 *FJ*, 30 Apr. 1888. 24 Moody, *Davitt*, p. 181. 25 Davitt, *Jottings*, p. 126. 26 Interview with Davitt, *New York Sun*, 27 Nov. 1890; quoted in Travers, 'Davitt after the Land League', pp 90–1. 27 Kenneth O. Morgan, *Kier Hardie, radical and socialist* (London, 1997), p. 42.

of private to public wellbeing'.²⁸ In his initial attack on Parnell he called for an 'act of self-denial in the best interests of the Irish people'.²⁹ Of course, the vehemence of his assault reflected the repressed animus which he had felt towards Parnell since at least the end of 1882. In *The fall of feudalism* he singled out T.M. Healy, T.P. O'Connor and other nationalist MPs as the architects of Parnellism, arguing that they were more dictatorial and reactionary than the Party leader himself.³⁰ But there can be no doubt that Davitt's antipathy towards Parnell had not lessened with the passage of time. During the land war, the latter had been the patrician figure who, in spite of his own class background, had become pro-active on the land and social justice question. Yet later, with the consolidation of the Irish Party machine and the development of 'Parnellism', Parnell, the man, started 'play[ing] the dictator', as Davitt put it during the height of the crisis in 1890–1.³¹ Parnell's rule throughout the 1880s was, for Davitt, the antithesis of democratic integrity. Of the former's autocratic control, Davitt wrote prophetically in 1884, 'How will it end? How all dictatorships have ended'.³²

Davitt was both dismayed and incensed by what he perceived as Parnell's hubris. There were two aspects to his antipathy, not altogether unconnected. He viewed Parnell as a Tory nationalist, and ultimately, he tended to equate personal virtue with political integrity, the mark of the latter being self-abnegation before one's political cause. If, therefore, self-abnegation was the cardinal political virtue, egotism was the corresponding vice. In reflecting on the nature of Parnell's ultimate demise, Davitt later commented,

> [Parnell] frequently quoted two lines of Shakespeare which inculcated fidelity to one's self as the rule of existence. Herein lay the secret of his pride, and the vulnerable spot in his Achilles's heel. A fanatical cult of one's own *ego* in a public man [...] is very apt to beget infidelity to the nobler duties and obligations of life [...]³³

But Davitt, too, had a penchant for quoting 'grand old Will Shakespere [*sic*]', and on his thirty-sixth birthday, as a prisoner in Portland, he quoted from *Macbeth*: 'I have done no harm! – but I remember now, / I am in this earthly world, where to do harm / Is often laudable; to do good, sometimes, / Accounted dangerous folly'. For Davitt, the choice was simple: 'Laudable harm or dangerous folly [...] I vote for the latter even with its consequences [...]'³⁴ *Macbeth* is a play of stark contrasts, principally between virtue and treachery, and it appealed to Davitt. In his diaries he sometimes made references to his

---

28 Davitt, *Jottings*, p. 123. **29** *LW*, 22 Nov. 1890. **30** Davitt, *The fall*, p. 378. **31** *LW*, 31 Jan. 1891. **32** Davitt's diary, 25 July 1884, DP, TCD, MS 9541. **33** Davitt, *The fall*, p. 658. **34** *Macbeth*, Act iv, scene ii, lines 75–78; quoted in Davitt, *Jottings*, p. 236.

own personal sacrifices for the political cause in quite quixotic terms. In language itself reminiscent of a tragic Shakespearian soliloquy, he wrote in a diary entry a week before his forty-eighth birthday, 'Don't know why anyone should be brought into this world in order to undergo the misfortunes, trials, sufferings, losses, ingratitudes, treacheries, insults, infamies, worries comprised within the 48 years of my stormy life'.[35]

Moody writes that Davitt tended to be critical of his own shortcomings.[36] It is true, Davitt did berate himself over matters such as his poor handling of his financial affairs, especially after he had started a family. He admitted that he was 'always in money matters a damned fool'.[37] On the political stage, however, he was not given to such self-criticism at all. He had had a hard life and did work tirelessly and selflessly for his cause; but he was not accustomed to entertaining doubts about his own political judgements. This helps to explain much of the sheer ill-will he felt towards Keir Hardie from the early 1890s, when Hardie and his independent labour associates repeatedly challenged the Liberals on their social policy and even attempted to split the Liberal vote in certain constituencies during the 1892 general election. For Davitt, Hardie's personal integrity was brought into question when he failed to appreciate the importance of the Liberal–nationalist alliance to the prospect of home rule. Davitt had reason to embrace the alliance, but his arbitrary conclusions on Hardie were simply untenable. Political cussedness notwithstanding, it must be stated that Davitt would not have envisaged himself as leader of the nationalist movement. According to Gladstone's secretary, E.W. Hamilton, Gladstone considered him a possible successor to Parnell in March 1890 as the divorce crisis heightened.[38] But, while Davitt would no doubt have been flattered, it is unlikely that he would have treated the suggestion with much seriousness. He did not even envisage Dillon in a leadership role. In January 1890 he confided in his diary, 'If P. falls Heaven save us from a Dillon leadership'.[39] This may have been because he anticipated faction fighting, particularly between Dillon and Healy, or he may have felt, as C.C. O'Brien has remarked, that 'Dillon's melancholy, scrupulous, introspective temperament' disqualified him from leadership.[40] It is also true, of course, that for some considerable time Davitt had viewed Parnell as the only possible leader.

Nevertheless, when the divorce verdict became known he was resolute in his call for the leader's retirement, and was embittered by the latter's immediate announcement that he had no intention of doing so, 'either permanently or temporarily'.[41] The *Labour World* was strident in its anti-Parnellism during the Irish Party split. There were a few letters in its letter page in support of

35 Davitt's diary, 18 Mar. 1894, DP, TCD, MS 9555.   36 Moody, *Davitt*, p. 552.   37 Davitt's diary, 31 Dec. 1893, DP, TCD, MS 9554.   38 Callanan, *T.M. Healy*, p. 245.   39 Davitt diary, 1 Jan. 1890, DP, TCD, MS 9533.   40 O'Brien, *Parnell*, p. 252.   41 Quoted in ibid., p. 295.

Parnell after the scandal broke, but the paper did not maintain a fair balance of views. While thanking those who wrote disparagingly 'witty letters and poems on Parnell', Davitt did explain in his 'Answers to Correspondents' column that such letters were not published 'because they would not help the national cause'.[42] However, this intervention did not reflect a balanced editorial policy and the correspondence that was printed was, with the exception of but a few letters, critical of Parnell. Davitt himself excoriated Parnell in the most vituperative editorials. He declared that the latter had neither conceived nor founded the Land League but had simply 'obtained control of funds'.[43] The editorial of 3 January 1891 traduced Parnell and welcomed 'the death of one-man power in Irish politics'. Davitt justified his position by arguing that Parnell's failure to stand down for a period confirmed his hubris and egregiously wanton abuse of the national interest. The *Labour World* soon became the leading paper in the campaign against Parnell, serving the anti-Parnellites in the North Kilkenny by-election in December 1890. The anti-Parnellite invective was to become more pronounced in the final months of the paper. Even Healy, whom C.C. O'Brien has described as the 'vindictive public man, the political scald-crow with his terrible beak',[44] later acknowledged that after the disappearance of the *Insuppressible*, Davitt's paper was 'the only support we had in the Press [...] His attacks on Parnell were fiercer than anything we had said or written'.[45]

In attacking 'Parnellism' Davitt was, however, implicitly referring to its 'young lieutenant' adherents, of whom he had been privately critical since the early 1880s. In dissecting 'Parnellism' he significantly noted that 'Tim Healy was the first to apply the term'.[46] Davitt prided himself on having 'never been a Parnellite', as he told McGhee.[47] With that self-conceit to which he was sometimes given, he considered the ultimate demise of the Parnellite myth a testimony to his own integrity as a democrat. Within a week of the Irish Party split, he again wrote to McGhee, 'They had slobbered so much individually and collectively over Parnell that they seem inclined to embrace him again. I cannot help admiring the splendid audacity of the man'.[48] It is ironic, indeed, that Davitt should have developed in the columns of the *Labour World* much of the idiom of anti-Parnellism that Healy was to employ in the coming months and years. 'Parnellism' was understood by Healy to mean the excesses of one man's leadership, whereas Davitt understood it to mean the excesses of one man and the self-aggrandizement of his lieutenants. In fact, Davitt essentailly viewed himself as a straightforward home ruler, not an anti-

---

42 *LW*, 17 Jan. 1891. 43 *LW*, 13 Dec. 1890. 44 C.C. O'Brien, 'Timothy Michael Healy' in O'Brien (ed.), *The shaping of modern Ireland* (London, 1960), p. 173. 45 Healy, *Letters*, vol. i, p. 354. 46 *LW*, 13 Dec. 1890. 47 Davitt to McGhee, 24 Nov. 1890, D, TCD, MS 9521/5972. 48 Davitt to McGhee, 12 Dec. 1890; quoted in Callanan, *T.M. Healy*, p. 391.

Parnellite as such. But ultimately, in the climate of the split, his interpretation gave way to the exigencies of the anti-Parnellite campaign. In an editorial which targeted Parnell's landlord origins, he moved to dismantle the mystique of Parnellism:

> [Parnell] was lauded to the skies for having 'stepped down' from his 'social elevation' to head a movement against his own order [...] But it was not the man who was praised for his labour. It was the landlord, the 'superior' being, the member of the 'upper tier' who had espoused the cause of the people. To him all praise was given. Power followed praise, and in a short time Parnellism became a substitute for Nationalism, and the movement which began upon a principle and pop-ular right became the political property of Charles Stewart Parnell.[49]

Although Davitt's editorial was directed at those 'young lieutenants' as much as '*the man*', the theme of Parnell's social origins was something that was to be developed by Healy.

The suppressed antagonism which Davitt felt towards Parnell had erupt-ed. Others, such as Ferguson, also had grievances against Parnell, but Davitt was unreserved in his condemnation. As stated, he did, to a certain extent, view the split as a vindication of his own 'democratic' agenda. However, as Callanan observes,

> In his tendency to assimilate the split to his forecast of an irresistible democratic tide, he was wistfully oblivious to the more complex eddies of the course of Irish nationalism. In regarding the anti-Parnellite vic-tory in the split as in some way a belated endorsement of his own posi-tion in the 1880s he permitted his *amour propre* as a radical spurned to outweigh his political judgement.[50]

While Davitt could clearly identify the influence of the conservative section of the national movement in his dissection of the Parnellite construct, he seems to have failed to appreciate the potential of the burgeoning Catholic right of the Party in the split. E.W. McFarland has noted that Ferguson also failed to recognize this. But, she argues, he more than Davitt 'sensed the ideological complexities of the split'. He also keenly realized that the cause of home rule and the radical agenda to which he and Davitt had been committed for years would be fatally injured by the internecine conflict. McFarland contends, in fact, that Ferguson became the voice of home rule radicalism during the cri-

---

49 *LW*, 31 Jan. 1891. 50 Callanan, *T.M. Healy*, p. 391.

sis. He concentrated on maintaining local unity, 'protecting the infrastructure of nationalist politics [...] and lifting his colleagues' eyes to the "revolt of labour"'.[51]

Davitt, on the other hand, was totally immersed in the anti-Parnellite campaign. He consequently incurred heavy criticism from the left for adopting such a position, and the charge of clerical interference was levelled against him. James Connolly later concluded that Davitt had 'misjudged the whole situation', and, having failed to seize the opportunity to bring Parnell into the democratic ranks, he instead 'fought with all his force and aggressiveness to establish the priesthood in full control of secular affairs in Ireland'.[52] Davitt, of course, did not see Parnell within 'democratic ranks' and felt particularly provoked by the labour programme which the latter adopted from March 1891, a programme which included land nationalization.[53] Davitt's view was that it was a disgraceful attempt by Parnell to ingratiate himself not only with the Irish working class but also the British labouring masses, and he warned that the workingmen of England remembered the 'Parnell of old [...] and his insulting manifesto of 1885'.[54] He argued, moreover, that Parnell's programme was taken straight from the *Labour World*.[55] Actually, Parnell had spoken out on labour issues even before he became ascendant within the Parliamentary Party. When the debates on the Factories and Workshops bill were taking place in 1878 he supported state regulation of the working hours of married women and children.[56] And in the winter of that year he raised the matter of relief for agricultural labourers. Even later, during the land war, he drew attention to the question of adequate housing for labourers, and when the Labourers' Housing Act became law in 1883, he appealed to farmers to respect its provisions. He had considerable support among the working class in Dublin and Cork, and although his strong pronouncements on labour issues in Dublin in 1890–1 cannot be viewed in isolation from the split, his concerns cannot be seen as entirely opportunistic. Ultimately, however, Parnell believed that the social question was less important than the issue of national independence. As leader of a broad movement, he favoured what Liam Kennedy has referred to as 'an Irish version of "one-nation" toryism'.[57]

Despite Davitt's more convincing radical credentials, the editorials in the later editions of the *Labour World* were nevertheless dominated by the Irish Party split, not the cause of labour. From December 1890, and into the early part of 1891, he was busy organizing the campaigns of anti-Parnellite candi-

51 McFarland, *John Ferguson*, pp 220–1, 230. 52 James Connolly, editorial in the *Harp*, Aug. 1908, quoted in O.D. Edwards and Bernard Ransom (eds), *James Connolly, selected political writings* (London, 1973) p. 211. 53 *National Press*, 18 Mar. 1891; cited in Lyons, 'The economic ideas of Parnell', p. 74. 54 *LW*, 7 Mar. 1891. 55 As above, fn. 53. 56 Kennedy, *Colonialism*, p. 96. 57 Ibid., pp 96–101.

dates in a series of by-elections in Ireland. He fiercely defended his campaigns against the accusation of clerical interference, and in the editorial of 3 January 1891 he argued that Parnell and Tim Harrington were using this charge to alarm nonconformists in England. Given Davitt's concern for the Liberal alliance and the role of nonconformist sentiment, it is ironic that while the Irish movement was divided, the crisis did, as Glasier points out, ultimately reinforce 'both nonconformist adulation of Gladstone and the awareness of nonconformist strength by the liberal leadership'.[58]

Sheehy Skeffington claimed that Davitt's paper ceased to exist mainly because 'it was before its time. It was a pioneer paper, the herald and prophet of the advanced labour movement [...]'[59] Sheehy Skeffington's own adulation for Davitt is clearly evident in this statement. Hardie's verdict, however, was that Davitt's 'anti-Parnellism killed the *Labour World*'.[60] Davitt himself later noted in a diary entry that the split had indeed dealt a 'death-blow' to the journal.[61] In the early months of the paper, the Federated Trades and Labour Union (FTLU) in Waterford voted to take it into the Trades Hall reading room. Yet the situation had dramatically changed over a year later in December 1891 when Davitt was locked in a contest with John Redmond in the Waterford by-election. 'Now', remarks Emmet O'Connor, 'the trade societies published long lists of "splendid subscriptions" to Parnellite funds'.[62] A few days after the contest, Davitt wrote to McGhee: 'The labourers voted almost to a man against me!'[63] The Irish Party split had a dramatic affect on labour organization in Ireland. In the Cork Trades Association, the anti-Parnellites, Eugene Crean and Michael Austin, who would later be recommended by Davitt as labour-nationalist candidates for the 1892 general election, were summarily discharged from their offices of president and secretary respectively.[64]

The *Labour World* had Davitt's own personal mark on it, his fundamental commitment to land nationalization and labour, and his view that home rule for Ireland was in the interests of the British working class. His adherence to lib-labism in the paper did, nevertheless, bring criticism into the letters page. In November and December 1890, the paper featured a number of letters to the editor in 'Our discussion Forum' which were critical of what their authors saw as Davitt's identification of the workingman with the Liberal cause. The author of one of the letters, George Copsey, secretary of the Legal Eight Hours and International Labour League, wrote on 20 December 1890, questioning whether the editor had actually grasped the point of the labour movement or

58 Glasier, 'Parnell's fall', p. 137.   **59** Sheehy Skeffington, *Michael Davitt*, p. 148.   **60** Hardie, 'Michael Davitt', p. 413.   **61** Davitt's diary, 25 Dec. 1894, DP, TCD, MS 9556.   **62** O'Connor, *A labour history of Waterford*, pp 95–6.   **63** Davitt to McGhee, 27 Dec. 1891, DP, TCD, MS 9521/5975.   **64** Maura Murphy, 'Fenianism, Parnellism and the Cork trades, 1860–1900', *Saothar*, 5 (May 1979) 33.

the wider economic context of the labour struggle. He pointed out that Davitt was singularly mistaken in thinking that working-class support would be enlisted for the Liberals when the Liberal Party and the Radicals identified with the call for the nationalization of the land. 'Surely the most immediate question', Copsey insisted, 'is that of the legal eight-hour working day'. For Davitt, Irish self-government, land nationalization and the international labour cause were indispensable parts of an ideological framework that had as its foundation egalitarianism and a universal democratic imperative. This was reflected in the *Labour World*. And while he was undoubtedly constrained by his support for the Liberals, his paper still represented an important landmark in labour journalism. It actually exceeded Hardie's paper in circulation. Over a decade after its launch as a weekly, the circulation of the *Labour Leader* was 24,000,[65] whereas 60,000 copies of the second edition of the *Labour World* were ordered.[66] Of course, sustaining such an output was another matter.

In considering Davitt's abilities as a newspaper editor, Moody comments simply that he was 'temperamentally unfitted to the grind of a newspaper office'.[67] There is no doubt that Davitt found the work a major burden. Even in the early stages the pressure was evident. Indeed, a few years after the paper had folded, he informed Dillon that he would 'not again have my name associated with an "organ" – especially in Dublin – for any earthly consideration'.[68] This letter, written in 1894, was an obvious allusion to the pressure brought about by the split, and his particular objection to working a paper in Dublin was probably due to the strength of the Parnellites in the city. It is odd that Moody does not see fit to give adequate consideration to the effects of the split in the context of the collapse of the *Labour World*. He does, however, mention other factors that played a part. For instance, the company had 'staff difficulties' from the beginning.[69] On a more personal level, Davitt suffered poor health, a recurring theme in his diaries, which was usually attributed to overwork. In particular, his efforts in gathering evidence to present to the *Times*-Parnell Commission proved a tremendous strain upon him. After his submission he told McGhee that his health was 'more run down' than at any time since his release from Dartmoor.[70] When the Commission's report was made public early in 1890 he was still suffering the effects of his labours; his intellectual faculties were fatigued and his memory affected 'more than I ever found it'.[71] Given that he went on to establish a paper that year and to then have daily stresses compounded by the unfolding divorce scandal, it is not surprising that he expressed a certain fatigue in his letter to Dillon.

65 Morgan, *Keir Hardie*, pp 141–2. 66 Moody, 'Davitt and British labour', p. 68. 67 Ibid., pp 68–9. 68 Davitt to Dillon, 13 July 1894, DP, TCD, MS 9405/1674. 69 Moody, 'Davitt and British labour', p. 69. 70 Davitt to McGhee, 28 Nov. 1889, DP, TCD, MS 9328 [181/7]. 71 Davitt's diary, 11 Jan. 1890, DP, TCD, MS 9553.

His despondency notwithstanding, he continued to write for various papers and to appreciate the importance of the press on the political stage. When he was elected to parliament in 1893, he became 'Home Rule correspondent' for the *New York Sun*, a post which he believed would give him the 'opportunity of giving [a ...] summary from nationalist standpoint of progress of Home Rule course'.[72] Despite his claim to Dillon that his editorial ambitions had ended with the *Labour World*, he still harboured hopes of starting another radical paper. As late as March 1906, only two months before his death, he was talking with 'feverish energy' of such an undertaking.[73] He intended to launch an organ in Ireland called the *Irish Democrat*, and he had approached T.M. Kettle and Sheehy Skeffington about the prospect of their working with him on the project. They had established a paper of their own in 1905 entitled the *Nationist*,[74] an organ for which Davitt had considerable regard, as his correspondence with Sheehy Skeffington indicates.[75] It supported home rule, women's suffrage, and focused on social issues such as the conditions of workers in Dublin. However, it was beset by financial difficulties and proved short-lived. The idea of the *Irish Democrat* was clearly something to which Davitt had given some thought. He had asked many others, besides Kettle and Sheehy Skeffington, to write for the paper.[76] But, of course, the idea was never realized owing to his death in 1906. Sheehy Skeffington did go on to produce another paper of his own in 1907, the *National Democrat*, a penny monthly, which was in itself something of a tribute to Davitt and his politics. The title was taken from an article written by Davitt in 1905 in which he imagined the political alignment in a future Irish national assembly in 1910, with a 'National Democratic Party' representing democratic and socially progressive politics.[77] The first issue of the *National Democrat* made reference to the vision charted by Davitt in this article. Sheehy Skeffington stated in its editorial,

> If, then, this paper is to be true to its name, it must inevitably follow closely the lines marked out by Michael Davitt for the progress of the Irish nation, must continue, in some fashion, the work on which he was engaged on the very eve of his death.[78]

Despite its ambitious beginnings, the *National Democrat* was also short-lived. Sheehy Skeffington understood the importance of the *Labour World* to Davitt. He wrote,

72 See Davitt's diary, 28 Apr. 1893, DP, TCD, MS 9554. **73** T.M. Kettle, 'Michael Davitt – the nationalist', *Socialist Review* (Aug. 1908), 418. **74** Roger McHugh, 'Thomas Kettle and Francis Sheehy-Skeffington' in O'Brien (ed.), *The shaping*, p. 29. **75** See Davitt to Sheehy Skeffington, 3 Feb. 1904, SSP, NLI, MS 40,470/5. **76** Kettle, 'Michael Davitt', p. 418. **77** Davitt, 'The Irish national assembly (session 1910)', *Independent Review* 5 (Apr. 1905), 284–5. **78** *National Democrat*, Feb. 1907.

[T]he man who writes primarily to express the ideas that are in him, and only in a secondary degree to make a living, must always feel the craving for an organ of his own wherein he can say precisely what comes to mind, unhampered by any restrictions.[79]

It is in this respect that the *Labour World* is of vital importance. Davitt was a freelance, crusading journalist. His paper had a clear political agenda in its declared aim of uniting the labouring masses, everywhere. He was, of course, conscious of commercial pressures. But, while the paper did feature serialized fiction and pieces on fashion, it was intended as an edifying organ and a rallying point for labour organization. As a source, it is invaluable in understanding the nature of Davitt's radicalism, from his ideas on labour representation in parliament, for example, to his treatment of social and economic questions. The tone of the paper was, indeed, socialist; it had a more radical edge than O'Connor's paper, *The Star*. Yet, in order to fully understand Davitt's politics, an exposition of his economic ideas is required. For, as we shall see, while he was unbending in his commitment to land nationalization, his position on state control and ownership of other monopolies and core utilities was much more qualified.

---

79 Sheehy Skeffington, *Michael Davitt*, p. 148.

4 / Davitt and Irish economic development: ideas and interventions

A DEARTH OF WRITTEN MATERIAL has proved the bane of those attempting to reconstruct the economic ideas of Parnell. This is apparent in F.S.L.
Lyons's obvious frustration in noting that the Irish leader's preferred mode of
literary communication was the telegram, a medium clearly not amenable to
the delineation of ideas.[1] With Davitt, however, we are much more fortunate
in this respect. Owing to his career as a writer and working journalist, an extensive amount of material is available. Indeed, compared to Parnell, he was, as
Bew observes, the more intellectual of the two.[2] It was during his imprisonment in Portland that he formulated the key aspects of his later political
thought, including his ideas on the organization of labour and the role of the
state in the regulation of labour and industry. His radical proposals for land
nationalization were also outlined in his 'jottings in solitary', a miscellany of
essays, notes and personal reflections.[3] These various ideas were later presented in a coherent form with the publication of *Leaves from a prison diary*.
His third book, *Life and progress in Australasia*, based on the notes kept during
his Antipodean tour, is also hugely important. It is not simply a travel narrative but, rather, an invaluable source on his socio-economic thinking. In it he
offers a commentary on the social, economic and political developments in
the respective Australasian colonies, on areas such as land taxation, protectionism and labour politics.

This work on Australia, together with *Leaves from a prison diary*, must be
central to any assessment of Davitt's economic ideas. Of primary importance
also, of course, are the articles and pamphlets that he wrote over the course
of at least twenty years, and naturally the *Labour World*. Indeed, in considering his ideas, it will be necessary to do so discursively, given that his writings
spanned such an extensive period. The importance which he attached to the
principle of land nationalization in explaining society's social and economic

---

1 Lyons, 'The economic ideas of Parnell', p. 61; see also Kennedy, *Colonialism*, p. 75. 2 Bew,
'Parnell and Davitt' in Boyce and O'Day (eds), *Parnell in perspective*, p. 50. 3 'Jottings in solitary', DP, TCD, MS 9639. King's edited publication of this manuscript is an abridged version.

ills requires that we begin with a closer look at his land reform scheme and also the influence of Henry George on his thinking, before moving on to more specific economic and ideological questions, including the significance of his own practical involvement in the world of business.

Notable among his early journalistic contributions are the engaging series of articles which he wrote for the Dublin *Evening Telegraph* between November 1885 and January 1886 on the cultivation of native industries. Entitled 'About our Artisans and Industries', these pioneering articles advanced practical proposals on industrial rejuvenation at a time when Dublin industries were moribund. Davitt had spoken of the need for Irish industrial development after his release from Dartmoor.[4] However, the *Telegraph* articles reflected a maturity in his thinking. They were, moreover, no mere academic exercise. In the years that followed these early pieces of writing, he undertook a number of industrial ventures, incurring considerable financial costs. His practical interventions met with little success, but the ideas which he expounded were nevertheless significant. In its obituary on him in 1906 the *Freeman's Journal* singled out these particular writings as 'the most practical and far-reaching survey of the industries and industrial possibilities of [Dublin] that has ever been written'.[5]

With the notable exception of Guinness brewery, and a number of other smaller industries such as printing and tobacco, industries in Dublin were indeed in a poor state in the later decades of the nineteenth century.[6] In addressing the issue, Davitt stressed that the need for industrial regeneration could not be considered in isolation from the rest of what was essentially an agricultural country. In the first of his articles, he argued that the problems of town and country were inextricably linked, and that in order to fully understand the drain on Irish capital one must fundamentally address the land question.[7] For his part, he was convinced that land nationalization was ultimately fundamental to social and economic progress. During the land war he had, in fact, made efforts to involve urban workers in the popular movement. In March 1880, the Land League organized a huge rally in the Phoenix Park in collaboration with around fifteen trades organizations to highlight the common interests between urban labourers and farmers. The rally was a huge success, attracting crowds of between 30,000 and 70,000, although later suggestions by Davitt that the League should be organized in Dublin were rejected by some Leaguers, including Ferguson, who feared that the aims of the agrarian campaign might be lost in such expansion.[8]

Davitt declared himself a champion of land nationalization on his release from Portland in 1882, but it is difficult to say at what point exactly he first

4 Moody, *Davitt*, p. 237. **5** *FJ*, 31 May 1906. **6** Cormac Ó Gráda, *Ireland: a new economic history, 1780–1939* (Oxford, 1995), pp 304–6. **7** *ET*, 14 Nov. 1885. **8** Moody, *Davitt*, pp 368–9, 433.

embraced the principle. It is generally held that he was ultimately inspired to adopt it as policy after a systematic study of George's work, *Progress and poverty*, during the period of imprisonment in Portland. According to Lyons, however, Davitt had come to believe in land nationalization after his first meeting with George in 1880.[9] He also apparently promised the support of the Land League for *Progress and poverty* during this visit.[10] And during a public meeting in 1884, he himself stated 'with considerable pride' that during his American visit he had encouraged George to bring out a copy of the work in England.[11] Davitt claimed, in fact, that he had been a 'land nationalizer' before he even met George.[12] This was also stated by George, who maintained that from the inception of the Land League, Davitt, together with Thomas Brennan and John Ferguson, had aimed to make land nationalization part of the League's policy.[13]

There were earlier radical influences on Davitt which could explain an early commitment to this land policy. After all, as Lane points out, 'land nationalization as a policy had been a touchstone of British advanced Radicalism from at least the early 1870s'.[14] Indeed, in 1851 when Chartism was a spent popular movement, Ernest Jones was instrumental in drawing up a new radical programme which contained demands that exceeded the points laid out in the original Charter. Among these was the demand for land nationalization, a principle which Jones promulgated more than any other aspect of the new programme.[15] Davitt was, it will be remembered, exposed to Jones's influence at an early stage. However, according to Bew, it was during the latter part of the land war that Davitt seriously considered a land nationalization scheme, although his views were probably in a state of flux at this time and he had by no means arrived at any definitive solution to the land question.[16] Bew's assessment is probably the most accurate, yet, whatever the precise moment may have been at which Davitt embraced the more radical land policy, the essential point is that until the summer of 1882 he gave his support to the Land League policy of peasant proprietorship and never publicly declared himself in favour of land nationalization.

There is no doubt that his time in Portland was crucial in shaping his thinking. Any uncertainties he may have experienced prior to his arrest in 1881 were to dissipate during this period of incarceration. Conditions here were considerably more relaxed than those which he had had to endure in Dartmoor. In his prison writings, he even had time to reflect on the influence of Buddhism on Japanese society.[17] He later described his cell in Portland as a 'palace' com-

9 Lyons, *Charles Stewart Parnell*, pp 230–1.   **10** E.P. Lawrence, *Henry George in the British isles* (East Lansag, MA 1957), p. 8.   **11** *FJ*, 10 Apr. 1884.   **12** Moody, *Davitt*, p. 523.   **13** Lane, *The origins*, p. 78.   **14** Ibid., p. 68.   **15** Miles Taylor, *Ernest Jones, chartism, and the romance of politics, 1819–69* (Oxford, 2003), pp 144–5.   **16** Bew, *Land*, p. 136.   **17** 'Jottings in solitary', DP, TCD,

pared with the living conditions he had endured in prison in the 1870s.[18] In arresting him during the land war and revoking the terms of his earlier release, the authorities had hoped to isolate him. It was owing to the fact that he was prohibited from reading any material deemed 'current affairs' during his time in Portland that he was probably unable to read the recently published pamphlet by George which specifically dealt with the Irish land question. Davitt had read *Progress and poverty* on two occasions before his imprisonment, but he was now able to peruse and digest its arguments and proposals in relative leisure. He re-read it twice, in fact.[19] Alfred Russel Wallace had written an article on land nationalization in November 1880 and was the first president of the English Land Nationalization Society,[20] but George's work was acknowledged as the most cogent treatise on the subject and Davitt was very much affected by it. The scheme which it proposed appealed directly to his egalitarian sentiments.

Actually, Davitt was to remain wedded to land nationalization in principle from this point onwards. He observed in 1898 that 'the advent of Henry George to the [Australasian] colonies six or seven years ago imparted a powerful impetus to the cause' of land reform.[21] George had, it is true, made a considerable impact during his tour of the region in 1890.[22] Since the publication of *Progress and poverty* in the United States in 1879 and in Britain in 1880 the influence of his ideas was immense. During the 1880s the book sold around 100,000 copies in Britain.[23] Its highly controversial message reverberated across the Atlantic. The ideas which it presented had originated in the late 1860s when George was making certain observations on social conditions in America;[24] but the culmination of these ideas, *Progress and poverty*, was to be the definitive statement of his ultimate view on the principal causes of poverty and inequality, not just in America, but world-wide. It proposed a highly radical solution. George drew attention to the correlation between wealth and social poverty in modern industrial society, and argued that this was a universal phenomenon. In his view, land was the source of all wealth. It therefore followed that a monopoly on this finite resource was the underlying cause of poverty. He wrote,

> The recognition of individual proprietorship of land is the denial of the natural rights of other individuals – it is a wrong that *must* show itself in the inequitable division of wealth. For as labour cannot produce with-

MS 9639/317–9. **18** Davitt's diary/notes on prison visits, 1898, Easter Sunday 1898, DP, TCD, MS 9571. **19** Moody, *Davitt*, p. 504. **20** Russel Wallace, 'How to nationalise the land: a radical solution to the Irish problem' in *Contemporary Review* 38 (Nov. 1880, pp 716–36). **21** Davitt, *Life and progress*, p. 56. **22** C.A. Barker, *Henry George* (New York, 1955), pp 547–8. **23** McFarland, *John Ferguson*, p. 110. **24** Lawrence, *Henry George*, pp 4–5.

out the use of land, the denial of the equal right to the use of land is necessarily the denial of the right of labour to its own produce. If one man can command the land upon which others must labour, he can appropriate the produce of the labour as the price of his permission to labour.[25]

In this analysis, land monopoly was tantamount to robbery because the revenue derived from land ownership was not from the land itself but from the labour carried out on it. George argued that the increase in the value of land had the demographic effect of forcing people into the cities to compete for low-paid work. At a meeting in Dublin in 1884 he remarked on how in the squalid quarters of Belfast he had come across a family who had been evicted from an estate in Donegal and who were compelled to compete for employment in the city.[26] The ultimate argument of *Progress and poverty* was that common title to the land was an inalienable right. This right, argued George, should be reasserted through the abolition of private ownership and the imposition of a tax equal to the total value of the land.

Although *Progress and poverty* directly informed Davitt's thinking in Portland, he did differ from George on the question of landlord indemnity. In the section of his prison jottings entitled 'Random thoughts on the Irish Land War', he conceded, unlike George,[27] that landlords should receive compensation for their interest in the land. He started with the proposition that in accordance with 'strict justice' they should not even 'obtain their fares from Kingstown to Holyhead', but he acknowledged that compensation was consistent with conventional political justice. The important point was that landlordism would be abolished, and he proposed substituting it with a land tax on all land values, to the extent of ten per cent of estimated annual produce. Although he would later adjust his figures,[28] he stated, by way of presenting his compensation package, that landlords were due half the total annual rental of the land. In his estimation, the landlords' entitlement was an annual sum of £7,000,000. He considered that the full compensation should amount to a twenty-year purchase based on this annual figure, or £140,000,000. This would come from a public loan at three per cent interest per annum which would be chargeable to the imperial revenue then collected in Ireland by means of the

25 George, *Progress and poverty*, p. 306. 26 *FJ*, 10 Apr. 1884. 27 George simply dismissed the idea of landlord compensation; see *Progress and poverty*, pp 328–30. 28 In his keynote speech in Liverpool on 6 June 1882, he adhered to the figures he had outlined in 'Jottings in solitary' (*FJ*, 7 June 1882). However, during his visit to the US in June–July that year he had modified his calculations; the compensation package for landlords was now estimated at £150,000,000. See Cashman, *The life of Michael Davitt*, p. 245. This was also the figure contained in his 1902 pamphlet, *Some suggestions towards a final settlement of the land question* (see chapter 7).

land tax. After the liquidation of the debt, all civil and local government taxes and rates could be abolished, given that the land tax 'would produce all that would be required to carry on the government of the country as well as what would meet the charges for maintaining the poor and keeping the country in "repair"'.[29]

Within weeks of his release from prison, he offered this as the ultimate solution to the land question.[30] Later, in *Leaves from a prison diary*, he outlined the benefits to the farmer under land nationalization, stating that the land tax would amount to only half of what was currently paid in rent. The state would, of course, lay down certain conditions: there would be restrictions on the subdivision of land beyond certain limits; the land would have to be cultivated; and the farm should not be larger in size than could be personally managed by the farmer. The state would also reserve the right to work mines or minerals on the land, for which the farmer would be compensated.[31] But, subject to the observance of these conditions and, of course, payment of the land tax, the farmer would enjoy practical control of the farm and its produce. In a later article in 1890, 'Retiring the landlord garrison', Davitt further argued that the security provided by state ownership of the land would also enable Irish agriculture to 'weather the storm of external competition', which he saw looming at that time. He drew particular attention to the expanding agricultural competition of the United States, and to the potential of the resources of South America, Canada, and Australia. He presented the US as an example, where 'over a hundred million acres have been added to its cultivated land', and where increasing developments in infrastructure were set to add more.[32] Considering the advances made by international competitors, and indeed other factors such as the relative cheapness of transit costs which he identified, he argued that Irish agriculture would only be able to meet the new challenges if the land of Ireland and its rental were given to a representative national authority in Ireland. Internally, too, social problems such as congested districts could only properly be dealt with through state ownership of the land.

Davitt did not view public ownership of the land as a panacea for all Ireland's problems,[33] but he was convinced that it was the key to fundamental social change and greater economic stability. In April 1884, he wrote an article for the British socialist monthly, *Today*, in which he addressed 'The Irish Social Problem'. He condemned the 1881 Land Act in principle, and drew attention to the shortcomings in its workings, notably the issue of 'fair rents' fixed by the Land Courts. The Act certainly did not work as well as Gladstone had hoped, given that agricultural prices were still falling and this meant that

---

29 'Jottings in solitary', DP, TCD, MS 9639/316. 30 See *FJ*, 7 June 1882. 31 Davitt, *Leaves*, vol. ii, pp 80–1. 32 Davitt, 'Retiring the landlord garrison', *Nineteenth Century* 27 (May 1890) p. 794. 33 Davitt, *Leaves*, vol. ii, p. 66.

the reduction in rent did not significantly improve the small farmers' position. Davitt criticized peasant proprietorship because, he argued, it did not deal with the basic questions of housing, advances in agricultural industry, or land availability. He contended that arguments about over-population were absurd when one considered that there 'are 10,000 square miles of Irish land under grass'. He referred to the availability of such land in the face of such want as 'the curse of Tantalus'. 'Why', he asked, 'should this land be allowed to starve for labour while thousands of labourers and cottiers' families are being emigrated or left starving for the want of its use?' Rather than dealing with social ills, he vigorously asserted, peasant proprietorship 'will only extend the absolute ownership of land: *an ownership which will always be in the market for purchase and re-consolidation into large estates*'. He claimed that in accepting this scheme 'the landlord party is showing consummate judgement'.[34]

It was because of Davitt's belief in the centrality of the land question to social reform that land nationalization was so vigorously championed by the *Labour World*. Although short-lived, the radical labour journal crucially served as a platform for the promotion of that political philosophy which was embodied in the ideas outlined in *Leaves from a prison diary*. In identifying the causes of poverty in the second volume of this work, entitled 'Social evils and suggested remedies', Davitt pointed to the conflict between 'labour and monopoly', or more precisely, the conflicting economic interests between landlords and employers on the one hand, and on the other, labourers and wage-earners. He contested the suggestion that poverty was a product of thriftlessness and intemperance, arguing that there was no correlation between these virtues and higher wages.[35] The same point was made in a *Labour World* editorial, in which he critiqued the Victorian virtue of 'self-help' and, specifically, the claim that improvements in the lives of workingmen were the result of *laissez faire*.[36] In his treatment of the causes of poverty, he also attacked the Malthusian population theory, and in doing so argued that 'it is clearly not population pressing on subsistence which compels men to work for a bare living, but a privileged class, for its own advantage, limiting the subsistence available to workers'.[37]

He advanced a number of 'remedial proposals' in addressing the social question. Primarily he singled out the abolition of land monopoly as a prerequisite to a more democratic organization of labour, because 'so long as land is private property, the landed can and will appropriate the wealth produced by labour'. He proposed a tax on all land, 'exclusive of improvement', up to its total value. The full revenue from this, inclusive of mines and minerals,

---

34 Davitt, 'The Irish social problem', *Today* 1:4 (Apr. 1884) p. 252. **35** Davitt, *Leaves*, vol. ii, pp 58–60. **36** *LW*, 1 Nov. 1890. **37** Davitt, *Leaves*, vol. ii, p. 64.

would be 'enormous', and should fall to the national exchequer 'for the general good of the entire community'. Under this arrangement a chancellor of the exchequer would remit what was raised in local and general taxation and pay the cost of civil administration by the revenue from the land and minerals. The results of national ownership of land would, Davitt argued, be far-reaching: wages would increase because wage-earners would not have to pay indirect taxation out of their incomes; speculative land values would end; and with the reclamation of the land and exploitation of mineral resources, there would be a demand for labour in the country and an incentive to the agricultural population to avoid migrating to the towns.[38]

In further developing his solution to the social question, he proposed a co-operative form of production. In true Georgeite form, he contended that the utilization of freed land would have a favourable affect on labour relations in the towns. Less competition for employment in towns would, it was argued, consequently result in a rise in wages above the minimum of a bare living, and out of this situation workers themselves would be in a position to accumulate a capital fund which would enable them to enter upon 'a co-operative enterprise in which they would be their own employers, and their wages exactly equivalent to their earnings'. Davitt did not have a problem with free trade. He envisaged, rather, a form of co-operation that would eliminate 'cut-throat' competition. Indeed, he proposed 'industrial partnerships' between workers' co-operatives and capitalists, and asserted that while the community had a moral right to appropriate land, there was 'no such justification for boldly appropriating existing accumulations of capital'. He declared that 'a common ownership of the land and the means of production' would represent the nearest approach to social justice.[39] He did not reveal how 'the complete organization of industry on the joint ownership of capital' would be made practicable. J.S. Mill, whose ideas greatly influenced Davitt, reasoned that with the success of co-operative and industrial enterprises, owners of capital would be encouraged to 'lend their capital' to associations of workers, or 'even to exchange their capital for terminable annuities'.[40] Davitt, however, did not venture a position on the matter, and the principle of profit-sharing was never quite elaborated upon.

Davitt considered Smith's *Wealth of nations* (1776) an important contribution to industrial progress, and although he discerned crucial errors in this work with regard to the law of wages and relations between capital and labour, he noted the importance of the 'advent of Political Economy writers from [...] Smith to our own day'.[41] He was familiar with the writings of Leonard Simonde de Sismondi, Leonce de Lavergne, Emile de Laveleye, Herbert

38 Ibid., pp, 66–76, 103. **39** Ibid., p. 110. **40** Ibid., pp 109–15. **41** Davitt, *Jottings*, pp 120–1.

Spencer, and during his time in Portland he made a study of Joseph Kay's *Free trade in land* (1878).[42] In setting out his remedial proposals in *Leaves from a prison diary* he relied heavily on Mill's *Principles of political economy* (1848-65), which, like Kay's work, proposed peasant proprietorship. Davitt quoted liberally from Mill's book in order to support his theory on co-operative production and industrial partnership, ideas which Mill himself had advanced on the question of social justice.[43] It is noteworthy, however, that in developing his thesis, Davitt did not make reference to the co-operative movement in Ireland, specifically the Owenite experiment on John Scott Vandeleur's estate at Ralahine, Co. Clare, which existed between 1831 and 1833. At a time when the post-Waterloo agricultural economy in Ireland was adversely affecting smallholders and cottage industries, the Ralahine project was extremely pioneering. No mention is made, either, of the leading advocate in the co-operative movement, William Thompson who was, indeed, described by Mill as 'a very estimable man'.[44] Of course, unlike Thompson and the Owenite associations, Davitt did not renounce competition. While Mill himself had embraced the concept of co-operation from the early 1850s, 'he wished neither to eliminate competition nor consolidate class difference'.[45]

Principles of political economy was clearly a determining influence on Davitt's ideas. It certainly played a formative role in the thinking of both Devoy[46] and Ferguson. Ferguson's pamphlet, *The land for the people* (1881), was not only heavily influenced by the social gospel of George, but also clearly owed a debt to the ideas of Kay, T.E. Cliffe Leslie, and Mill.[47] Given that the Land League itself cited Mill's radical views on land reform as a moral basis for its campaign,[48] Davitt must undoubtedly have read and made reference to the later, highly controversial pamphlet by Mill, *Ireland and England* (1868), in which the celebrated economist argued that English property ideology simply could not be applied to Ireland, and that native customary ideas on land tenure should prevail. Speaking before the *Times*-Parnell Commission, Davitt remarked that the leadership of the Land League had 'educated the Irish people upon the principles of Mill's political economy'.[49]

Ireland and England was Mill's most significant contribution to the issue of land tenure in Ireland. The historicist case which it made led to his being labelled the 'most recent and most thoroughgoing apostle of communism'.[50] He had contributed to the Irish land question since the first publication of

42 Ibid., p. 32.   **43** Davitt, *Leaves*, vol. ii, pp 106–10.   **44** Quoted in Lane, *The origins*, p. 15.
45 Pedro Schwartz, *The new political economy of J.S. Mill* (London, 1972), p. 225.   **46** Moody, *Davitt*, p. 238.   **47** McFarland, *John Ferguson*, pp 116–17.   **48** Moody, *Davitt*, pp 319–20.   **49** Davitt, *The Times-Parnell comm*, p. 191.   **50** Quoted in E.D. Steele, 'J.S. Mill and the Irish question: reform and the integrity of the empire, 1865–1870', *Historical Journal* 13 (1970), p. 440.

Principles of political economy in 1848 and in its successive editions up to 1865. E.D. Steele claims, however, that Mill did not establish a consistent line of argument throughout. On the contrary, it is argued, he positively contradicted himself, demanding fixity of tenure in one passage and withdrawing the demand in another. Even though *Ireland and England* represented a definitive statement on the land question, Steele further contends that, in his writings on Ireland, Mill was more concerned with maintaining the integrity of the empire, and was ultimately 'less radical than is often supposed'; indeed, he was a 'convinced imperialist'.[51] It has been suggested by Bull, however, that Mill did demonstrate a 'consistency of intent', and that the real significance of his work, especially the post-Famine editions, was its introduction of a 'moral imperative' to the land question.[52] Mill's analytical, social scientific approach to the question was certainly intellectually appealing to Davitt. Situating the Irish question in an international context, the prominent economist argued that India 'was now governed with a full perception and recognition of the differences from England'. He therefore concluded, 'What had been done for India has now to be done for Ireland'.[53]

The 'moral imperative' was fundamentally important to Davitt, both as an Irish nationalist and a social reformer. Addressing a meeting in Manchester shortly after his release from Portland, he reminded his audience, 'Never has landlordism succeeded in obtaining a moral recognition from the Irish people'.[54] He argued that the people had an inalienable right to the benefits of the soil. This echoed James Fintan Lalor who had proclaimed,

> The soil of Ireland for the people of Ireland, to have and to hold from God alone who gave it – to have and to hold to them and their heirs for ever, without suit or service, faith or fealty, rent or render, to any power under Heaven.[55]

Although Lalor was not an advocate of land nationalization (despite Davitt's claim that they shared the same purpose), he and Davitt did concentrate on the 'philosophic foundations' of the land question, unlike others who focused on what David Buckley has referred to as the 'legal superstructure'.[56] Davitt believed that Mill had been moving 'steadily' towards a position of declaring land monopoly the source of social ills.[57] This position was of course, in Davitt's view, the starting point for fundamental social and political reform. In many of his speeches in Britain after 1882, he connected the land question with the

51 Ibid., pp 419, 450 **52** Bull, *Land*, pp 32–3. **53** T.A. Boylan and T.P. Foley (eds), *Political economy and colonial Ireland* (London, 1992), p. 156. **54** Davitt, *The Land League proposal: a statement for honest and thoughtful men* (1882) in King (ed.), *Michael Davitt*, vol. i, p. 9. **55** Quoted in Buckley, *James Fintan Lalor*, p. 36. **56** Ibid., pp 37, 42, 91. **57** Davitt, *Leaves*, vol. ii, pp 107–8.

cause of labour. He stated the case plainly in a letter to the editor of the *Daily Chronicle* in 1886, reprinted in pamphlet form by the English Land Restoration League under the title *Landlordism, low wages and strikes*, in which he argued that the royalties claimed by the landocracy represented a deduction from profit and a reduction of wages. He explained that 'from the banker in the City, to the pedlar of pencils in the Strand, every man, woman and child in London, and in the United Kingdom as well, pays a tax to some landlord', directly or indirectly. He remarked that in their 'outcry against "Capital"', advanced advocates of labour had tended to ignore this as the underlying cause of exploitation.[58] However, the Marxist, Hyndman, believed that Davitt was too preoccupied with land monopoly and that he had underestimated the dynamics of capitalism. In his memoirs, Hyndman recalled attending a meeting at which Davitt spoke on land reform, and being struck by the fact that the latter appeared to give little thought, if any at all, to the prospect of continued capitalist competition after public ownership of the land had been achieved.[59] This was essentially Hyndman's problem with George, even though he had been inspired by Georgeite ideas in the early 1880s.[60] Interestingly, in outlining the contents of *Leaves from a prison diary* shortly before its publication, Davitt told Henry George that he had dealt with the question of capital 'in a tentative way'.[61]

Davitt did not share Hyndman's extreme left-wing convictions. He felt that Proudhon's aphorism 'Property is theft' was 'much abused'.[62] He firmly believed, indeed, that 'the small capitalist' had a role in the functioning of any healthy society,[63] which in itself perhaps partly explains his motivation in undertaking numerous industrial ventures in the late 1880s. Ferguson, too, believed that labour and capital were, as McFarland notes, 'natural allies'.[64] However, while acknowledging fears concerning 'restraint in trade', Davitt nevertheless declared his support for state legislation for the regulation of the relations between labour and capital: the state should make employers liable for workers' injuries; and, similarly, with regard to hours of labour, employment of women and children, and sanitary inspection, state regulation should be extended. Yet he dismissed any suggestion of the state becoming 'a universal employer'. He insisted, somewhat vaguely, 'The common sense of the community will dictate the conditions under which industry should be pursued, and the further interference of the State will be rendered unnecessary'. Ultimately he argued that with regard to the function of the state, especially

58 Davitt, *Landlordism, low wages and strikes* (1886) in King (ed.), *Michael Davitt*, vol. i, p. 2. 59 Hyndman, *Further reminiscences*, pp 41–2. 60 Chushichi Tsuzuki, *H.M. Hyndman and British socialism* (Oxford, 1961), pp 45–6. 61 Davitt to George, 8 Aug. 1884, HGP, NYPL. 62 *ET*, 12 Dec. 1885. 63 Davitt, 'Impressions of the Canadian north-west', *Nineteenth Century* 31 (Apr. 1892), 633. 64 McFarland, *John Ferguson*, p. 119.

in reference to the regulation of industry or ownership of enterprises, 'it is impossible to lay down any hard and fast line'.[65] In *Life and progress* he remarked that he had always favoured the nationalization of railways and canals.[66] And while in Portland, he wrote that the government ought to control and '*steward for the community*' the nation's land, water, mines, railways, telegraphs, roads and harbours.[67] But he did not hold that the state had a moral right to claim ownership of *all* industries and resources.

Davitt's approach to the question of the state's control and ownership of industry and resources was, naturally, much more limited than the position adopted by Hyndman's Social Democratic Federation (SDF), which proposed the nationalization of all the means of production, distribution and exchange.[68] Although Davitt called for the organization of an independent labour party to represent working-class interests,[69] it is significant that he did not understand the state or class in Marxist terms. For Marx, the state did not transcend class. In *The German ideology* he wrote, 'The conditions under which definite productive forces can be applied are the conditions of the rule of a definite class of society, whose social power, deriving from its property, has its *practical*-idealistic expression in each case in the form of the State'.[70] Davitt could not countenance the Marxist principle of collectivism. In his Australian work he remarked that a programme for an unmixed economy could not be applied to land and labour in a modern, property-owning society where individualistic sentiment was prevalent.[71] He viewed communism as impracticable, although there is no evidence that his judgement was based on a thoroughgoing reading of Marx. In advocating what he referred to as 'state socialism', he stated that a doctrinaire position could not be adopted in regard to 'State regulation of industry, or supervision or ownership of enterprises that either approximate to or are complete monopolies'.[72] This was reflected in his outline of the labour agenda in the early days of the *Labour World* when he called for 'the extension of State and municipal control and ownership of *such monopolies* as can best be managed by public bodies in the public interest' (my italics).[73] As W.P. Ryan observed, it was a demand without 'essence or accent of revolution'.[74]

In the internal programme of the Labour World News Company, which was for the viewing of shareholders, it was stated that the paper would engage with new reform movements and agitation outside Britain and Ireland, especially in the United States, Canada and Australia.[75] While the *Labour World*

65 Davitt, *Leaves*, vol. ii, pp 118–25. 66 Davitt, *Life and progress*, p. 64. 67 Davitt, *Jottings*, p. 119. 68 Pelling, *Origins*, pp 25–6. 69 Davitt, *Leaves*, vol. ii, p. 161. 70 Marx and Engels, *The German ideology*, part one, ed. C.J. Arthur (London, 1985), p. 194. 71 Davitt, *Life and progress*, p. 84. 72 Davitt, *Leaves*, vol. ii, p. 128. 73 *LW*, 21 Sept. 1890. 74 W.P. Ryan, *The Irish labour movement* (Dublin, 1919), p. 136. 75 DP, TCD, MS 9422/2270.

did not survive the O'Shea divorce scandal, Davitt himself took a personal interest in developments in these countries, particularly Canada and Australia. Within months of the *Labour World*'s demise, he was touring north-western Canada; and, of course, several years later he embarked on his visit to the Australasian colonies. He was attracted to the radical and imaginative ideas which he believed were being generated, out of necessity, in these new societies. He was fascinated by the challenges facing 'embryo communities' in the Canadian provinces, although his main focus was on Australasia. Many of the impressions which he formed during these trips also reinforced his own socio-economic ideas, particularly with regard to the land question and the concomitant social question. In both regions he was intrigued by the potential of large tracts of land, and his experience of Canada in particular forced him to consider the benefits of emigration, albeit in a qualified manner.[76]

He had frequently stated his opposition to the concept of emigration as a remedy for social ills. Given his own position as a member of the Irish diaspora, it is understandable that he more than most nationalist leaders would have lamented the interminable depletion of Ireland's population. The issue had been hotly debated during the land war. Addressing the US House of Representatives in 1880, Parnell had attempted to refute suggestions that emigration could serve as a solution to acute distress in Ireland. He adopted the same stance on his return to Ireland when he opposed emigration proposals, such as those of the Quaker philanthropist, James Hack Tuke, which were being welcomed by the government.[77] Parnell's answer to the problem of congestion and rural poverty was internal migration, from places such as Mayo to the more fertile plains of Meath, Kildare, Limerick and Tipperary.[78] Bew observes that his call for such a scheme would seem to have been 'the high point of his "leftism"'.[79] Parnell later qualified his recommendations in 1881 by suggesting more localized population movements. To that end, he established a migration company, the Irish Land Purchase and Settlement company, although it soon folded. Ultimately, his estimate of the potential of land utilization was, according to Kennedy, exaggerated.[80]

Davitt himself directly challenged Tuke's emigration scheme in his 1890 article, 'Remedies for Irish distress'.[81] He recommended, as an alternative to Tuke's proposition, the migration of peasants to the 'enormous' areas of grazing and waste land in the western counties, where larger land holdings would enable poor farmers to expand their crops. He argued that migration would be

76 Davitt, 'Impressions', pp 635, 637   77 Kennedy, *Colonialism*, pp 88–9.   78 Parnell's speech to House of Representative of the United States, 2 Feb. 1880, in O'Day and Stevenson (eds), *Irish historical documents*, pp 92–100.   79 Bew, *Charles Stewart Parnell*, p. 48.   80 Kennedy, *Colonialism*, p. 88.   81 Davitt, 'Remedies for Irish distress', *Contemporary Review* 58 (Nov. 1890) in King (ed.), *Michael* Davitt, vol. ii, pp 2–3.

facilitated by the establishment of agricultural schools where the peasantry would receive training in improved agricultural methods. On the question of financing such a scheme, he referred to the evidence of the economist, Robert Giffen, who found that Ireland was being overtaxed by the imperial exchequer by almost £3,500,000. This excess would, in Davitt's assessment, fund a migration programme. He significantly argued that such a scheme would encourage a state of social self-dependence among poor rural communities, much like the bold peasantry envisioned by de Valera forty years later, although without the isolationist premise. Emigration for Davitt, then, was not a viable solution to Irish rural distress. He condemned it as 'the one sovereign remedy for Irish social ills which the philanthropists of England have always held to'.[82]

However, as pointed out by Kennedy, emigration was an established economic strategy adopted by generations of Irish families, and while redistribution of the land could, for example, contribute to the issue of crowded households, it could not 'address the problem of surplus sons and daughters within households right across rural Ireland'.[83] Davitt did not deal with the broader issues surrounding emigration, although it must be borne in mind that his article was a polemical piece. He warned that 'The sending of twenty or thirty thousand families from Ireland to Canada should be, and would be, resisted all round'. The issue of Irish emigration was a sensitive one, clearly associated in Davitt's mind with the wider, outstanding political question of Ireland's relationship with Britain. Of the 'anomalies' in Ireland's economic condition, he wrote, 'Again, food in enormous quantities – in cattle, sheep, pigs, butter, bacon, eggs, &c. &c. – will be shipped every week during the winter, as was the case in 1879–80, while relief will be coming in the opposite direction'.[84] Ireland's anomalous position kept it out of Davitt's considerations of emigration during his visit to Canada in the autumn of 1891. But, remarking on the rich, expansive lands in the north-west of the Dominion, he suggested that large numbers of agricultural labourers from Britain could be induced to settle there. This would, he suggested, take the pressure off British cities, and would be viewed with less hostility by labour leaders. He stated that he was not an advocate of emigration, but that his proposal was made 'homoeopathically'.[85] No mention, of course, was made of the possibility of Irish labourers settling in these areas.

The primacy of land utilization was a recurring theme in Davitt's writings on his international experiences. During his visit to Russia in 1903 he noted the 'enlightened' enterprise of rural manufacturing villages as a response to overcrowded cities.[86] And in one particular observation made in *Life and progress* he remarked upon the extent of unemployment in Sydney. It struck him as

82 Davitt, 'Remedies', pp 3, 7.   **83** Kennedy, *Colonialism*, p. 89.   **84** Davitt, 'Remedies', pp 8–11. **85** Davitt, 'Impressions', pp 638–41.   **86** Davitt, *Within the pale, the true story of anti-Semitic persecutions in Russia* (New York, 1903; repr., New York, 1975), pp 75–8.

'sadly disappointing and [...] so horribly out of place in countries containing beyond question resources enough in its soil alone to feed half the world if workers could be put upon the land'. However, he also witnessed a number of pioneering programmes during his visit to the region, and his experiences of the labour settlements of Southern Australia, two hundred miles from Adelaide along the Murray River, were very much in contrast to the situation he witnessed in Sydney. The Murray River labour villages had originated out of unemployment agitation in Adelaide in the winter of 1893. To deal with the large numbers of artisans and labourers out of work, the trades council of the city facilitated the organization of labour settlements. In the initial set-tlement, a grant of 16,000 acres was made under the Crown Lands Act 1893 to one hundred families who volunteered to resettle, while a loan of £200 was made available for the purchase of tools and horses. Davitt visited the settle-ments, which had been in existence for sixteen months, and was fascinated by the venture. He believed that, should it prove successful, it would be 'a great object lesson in social reform [...] not alone to the sister colonies but to older countries too, in which tens of thousands of idle hands are an every-day com-ment upon the evil of millions of land also idle and economically useless, for want of necessary labour'[87]. Yet, while impressed by the communities which he visited, he questioned the long-term feasibility of 'communistic' settle-ments. What really made an impact on him was the innovative utilization of land. He was particularly energized to see that South Australia, like the other colonies, had its Henry Georgeites who were working for the radical fiscal reform advocated in *Progress and poverty*.

George's work had, indeed, proved inspirational to many radical social reformers. His following among socialists in Britain in the early and mid 1880s was immense. Lawrence points out that it was he, not Marx, who was 'the cat-alyst of Britain's insurgent proletariat'.[88] But George's stature in British social-ist politics was something of a paradox, for although his theories on the land question were far-reaching, he was by no means a socialist. In fact, his repu-tation in Britain was damaged in August 1887 when he rejected American socialist ideas, and later in October that same year when he refused to con-demn the imposition of the death penalty on eight anarchists charged with the murder of a policeman in Chicago, despite a lack of evidence.[89] Davitt was concerned by any development that would compromise George's influence in radical British politics, but the latter's expressed ideas on socialism would not have seriously affected their relationship. There were, after all, socialists who continued to hold George in high esteem, despite fundamental differences. Davitt's ultimate concern, of course, was the popularization of a radical land solution, but even in this George had a tendency to be ambiguous.

87 Davitt, *Life and progress*, pp 88–9. **88** Lawrence, *Henry George*, p. 3. **89** Ibid., pp 82–3.

George's understanding of land nationalization differed significantly from that of Davitt. More precisely, George was an advocate of the single-tax theory. He did not explicitly remark upon this element of his scheme until 1884. He had previously only made vague references to the principle of taxation, and newspaper coverage had not made note of it, with the curious exception of the Scottish press.[90] But, at a meeting in Dublin in 1884, at which Davitt was in attendance, he did state that 'Nationalization of the land [...] did not mean making the land the property of the Government, it meant making it the property of the people of the community'.[91] For Davitt, the tax on the land, in the case of Ireland, was based on the functioning of a self-governing state. From the mid-1880s, George clarified his ideas on taxation. Essentially, he proposed the abolition of all taxes for revenue and the imposition of a single tax upon the value of the land. He stressed that the tax would be on the value of the land alone and not upon the value of improvements, which belonged to the individual. Although George often spoke as if he were an advocate of land nationalization, his scheme ultimately proposed that the state would take the rent, but not the land. This distinction was almost imperceptible to audiences in Ireland and Britain in the early and mid-1880s when he was speaking on land nationalization platforms. Actually, in his comments on the land laws of New Zealand, where 'land-value taxation has made considerable progress', Davitt pointed out that the 'Single Tax' programme shared a common purpose with land nationalization – that of the industrial independence of the land worker and the economic welfare of the whole community – 'but by an indirect way'.[92] Davitt was certainly not inclined to labour the point. He was, after all, in general agreement with George and, moreover, considered him an essential asset to the cause of radical social reform and to the education of the labouring masses.

In a section of his *Jottings in solitary*, Davitt commented, 'The people of any country will never really be the sovereign power of such country until "the ignorant masses" thereof become the "educated" masses'.[93] He viewed education as crucial to the advancement of both social and political progress. Of course, his own education had, in part, been facilitated by his attendance at the Mechanics' Institute in Haslingden. Quite a number of his contemporaries were also driven by the same philosophy of self-improvement through education. While an apprentice to a stationary company in Belfast in the 1850s, Ferguson attended evening classes on economics and literature at the Queen's College in the city, where he came across the ideas of Cliffe Leslie, whose historicist ideas on land reform were to have an enduring influence on him. As

90 Ibid., p. 53. **91** *FJ*, 10 Apr. 1884. **92** Davitt, *Life and progress*, p. 392. **93** Davitt, *Jottings*, p. 99.

well as literature, Ferguson also studied history and French and German.[94] Davitt, too, was familiar with the writings of leading historians such as Macauley, Froude, Lecky, Thiers, Guizot, and had a working knowledge of Spanish and French.[95] He had an insatiable appetite for learning; his commitment to the self-improvement ethic probably explains, to some extent, his renowned aversion to alcohol. According to Devoy, he had an 'almost morbid' prejudice against alcohol, and it was only during their visit to Paris in 1879, that Devoy managed to persuade him to take a glass of wine with his meal. While in Dartmoor prison, Davitt looked back fondly to his early days in Haslingden where he remembered people being able to celebrate St Patrick's day without turning it into a 'drunken festival and tap-room saturnalia'.[96] Celebrations of St Patrick's day in immigrant Irish communities in Britain in the decade after the Famine were, according to Mike Cronin and Daryl Adair, 'muted affairs [...] surrounded by the air of the genteel'. Irish societies, such as the Hibernians, were influenced by the Catholic church in organizing events which focused more on a celebration of Irish culture rather than 'drunken revelry'.[97] In Lancashire in the early 1860s, the Irish nationalist organization, the National Brotherhood of St Patrick, had a strong presence, and, in celebrating Irish culture and identity, it emphasized the 'virtue' of sobriety.[98]

Davitt was indebted to the educational opportunities made available to him in Lancashire. However, he lamented the lack of such provisions in Ireland. Writing on 'The education of the Irish citizen' in his prison jottings, he therefore advocated a 'People's institute' with centres in the three hundred or so baronial districts of Ireland. The building of the institutes in each locality would, he proposed, fall to volunteer labour, and management would be devolved upon a baronial committee which would ultimately have responsibility for maintenance. The cost of the enterprise would come from a local tax of two pence per head from each of the local inhabitants. When functional, the institute would hold evening classes in 'the rudimentary branches of learning', and with a permanent staff of lecturers on agriculture, improved methods in agricultural cultivation and machinery would be taught. Conscious of the need for improvements in dwellings, he further recommended instruction on household management. In continuing with his treatment of the education of the Irish citizen under the general heading of branches of civilization, he also pointed to the importance of the industrial art of commerce. He held that the inculcation of such learning would be instrumental in achieving indus-

94 McFarland, *John Ferguson*, pp 11–13. 95 Moody, *Davitt*, p. 504. 96 Ibid., p. 173, 269, 278. 97 M. Cronin and D. Adair, *The wearing of the green: a history of St Patrick's Day* (London, 2002), pp 33–4. 98 See Gerard Moran, 'Nationalists in exile: the National Brotherhood of St Patrick in Lancashire, 1861–5', in Roger Swift and Sheridan Gilley (eds), *The Irish in Victorian Britain: the local dimension* (Dublin, 1999), pp 212–35.

trial independence among the poorer farmers and labourers. Developing these ideas in Portland, he clearly had designs for the Land League on his release. He remarked that the League had an obligation to 'attend to collateral work [...] outside the scope of [its] immediate programme'.[99] A proposal for a mechanics' institute was, indeed, part of the detail presented to Parnell in the draft for the new 'National Land Reform and Industrial Union of Ireland'.

Davitt's views on the social question were, as we shall now see, clearly inextricably linked to his ideas on industrial reform and Irish economic development. Parnell's primary concern after the land war had been the advancement of the national question and progress on the already certain areas of land purchase. He was not, however, indifferent in the matter of industrial development. There is evidence to suggest that at this time he considered the agricultural and industrial sectors linked.[1] His interest in industrial development actually preceded his election in 1875,[2] but his pronouncements on such matters were mainly notable from 1881. In May of that year, he stated that there was a wealth of industrial resources in Ireland, although he would later have to reconsider this. He stressed, moreover, that there was sufficient capital and entrepreneurship in Ireland to nurture native industries. These views were important to his argument for national self-government because he traced the source of Ireland's underdevelopment to the Union. An end to the Union would, he maintained, revive the Irish economy. The view that the constitutional link with Britain was detrimental to Irish economic performance had been part of the Irish nationalist critique of the Union since the 1830s. A variety of economic arguments were formulated, often tendentiously, to illustrate the point.[3]

In the 1830s and 1840s Repealers argued that a growth in exports since the Union could actually indicate economic weakness. M.J. Barry dubiously contended that there was no necessary correlation between an increase in exports and imports and economic growth.[4] Kennedy states that this was a theoretically unsound position to take. He points out, moreover, that although industrial exports rose by around 50 per cent between 1800 and 1826, their share of total exports dropped from 45 per cent in the mid-1790s to 32 per cent by the mid 1820s, and to 24 per cent by 1834. In the same period agricultural exports increased from 47 per cent of the total in the 1790s, to 62 per cent in the mid-1820s, and further to 73 per cent in 1835.[5] Another argument in the critique of the Union, one that was adopted in the latter part of the nineteenth century, was that Ireland was being overtaxed. Gladstone had, in fact, imposed income tax on Ireland for the first time in the 1850s, and despite

99 Davitt, *Jottings*, pp 88, 91–5, 111. **1** Kennedy, *Colonialism*, pp 93–5. **2** Lyons, 'The economic ideas of Parnell', p. 70. **3** Kennedy, *Colonialism*, p. 90. **4** 'First repeal prize essay: Ireland as she was, as she is, and as she shall be' (Dublin, 1945), cited ibid., p. 41. **5** Ibid., pp 41–2.

the decrease in population over the course of this decade, Irish tax yields increased by almost 60 per cent in the course of the 1850s.[6]

The issue of taxation became an important one to home rulers. It was, of course, central to the case made by Davitt in 1890 for the financing of a migration scheme to relieve Irish social distress. Following the drafting of the second home rule bill in 1893, Gladstone, in response to Irish concerns over certain financial clauses, declared that he would establish a Royal Commission to enquire into the financial relations between Britain and Ireland. Such a commission was appointed in May 1894, and in September 1896 its final report was published. The report contained statistical data which supported the case that Ireland was, indeed, being overtaxed. It proved a focal point of mass meetings in Ireland, and united some unionists and nationalists in protest.[7] The matter of overtaxation had been raised by Ferguson in 1892. Following the Royal Commission's report, he drew heavily from the new, rich statistical evidence to back up his own work, *Three centuries of Irish history* (1897). Excessive taxation, McFarland points out, was now a 'favourite obsession' among Irish nationalists.[8] Kennedy maintains, however, that although certain nationalist arguments had merit, it is difficult to believe that, had Ireland's tax burden been reduced, it would have made a major economic difference.[9] It would have made some difference if savings were judiciously invested, but Kennedy believes that in practice this was unlikely to have happened.

In the decades preceding the Famine, Ireland experienced a period of industrial decline, and, as Ó Tuathaigh has remarked, the seeming coincidence between this and the abolition of protective tariffs by 1824 encouraged the view that there was a connection between the two. Ó Tuathaigh points out that Ireland's 'economic situation' in the Industrial Revolution, notably its lack of coal and iron resources with which to produce the steam power necessary for fuelling the Revolution, makes the cycle of decline more explicable.[10] Many, however, believed that they had identified an indubitable causal link. According to Kennedy, Repealers did not concentrate on protectionist arguments, despite the nature of their analysis of the Union. Yet Young Irelanders were more open to such arguments. Thomas Davis argued that Ireland should follow the example of Germany in adopting protective tariffs.[11]

On the subject of Ireland's industrial sector and its potential, Robert Kane's 1840s survey of the country's natural resources was a frequently cited reference.[12] The state of Irish industrial and natural assets was also highlighted in 1853 by the staging of Ireland's first international industrial exhibition. The event was the result of a post-Famine drive to stimulate the revival of Irish

6 Ibid., p. 48. 7 Lyons, *John Dillon*, pp 176–7. 8 McFarland, *John Ferguson*, p. 237. 9 Kennedy, *Colonialism*, p. 53. 10 Ó Tuathaigh, *Ireland before the Famine, 1798–1848* (Dublin, 1990), p. 119. 11 Kennedy, *Colonialism*, pp 42–3. 12 Kane, *The industrial resources of Ireland* (Dublin, 1845).

rural-based industries. In a wider context, it was also inspired by the Great Exhibition at Crystal Palace in 1851, which had encouraged exhibitions in numerous other countries, the underlying belief being that international fairs could generate economic growth. The exhibitions in Dublin and Crystal Palace were, of course, very different in their scope and nature, the latter being a testimony to Britain's imperial hegemony. In its own right, the Irish exhibition represented a significant development; but as an event, it was less than successful. It did not attract popular support; it did not cover its costs; and, as Alun Davies has noted, it 'probably hastened the decline of some rural industries by exposing their vulnerability to competition from imports'.[13] Although it encouraged some business, it also tended to highlight the impoverishment of Irish industrial resources. The categories titled 'machinery' and 'manufacturing' illustrated the disparities in levels of industrialization between Ireland and Britain. The only exhibits in this category that managed to impress were those from the northeast of the country. In the category of 'raw materials', incompetent planning meant that mineral resources were compiled indiscriminately instead of systematically as a collection comprising lead, iron, copper, sulphur, coal, silver, gold and granulated charcoal.[14]

Among Young Irelanders, Davis attached considerable importance to Ireland's raw materials. His ideas actually played a significant role in the formulation of Arthur Griffith's economic doctrine over half a century later. Griffith was influenced by Davis's view that the exploitation of Ireland's natural resources, the endowments of which they both overstated, would lead to industrial regeneration. Griffith also argued, in line with Davis, that the cultivation of quality Irish industries would depend on protective tariffs as a defence against the competition of the mature British industry. Griffith was mainly influenced by the work of the German economist, Frederich List, author of *The national system of political economy* (1841). List had advocated a protectionist policy for Germany. There was much in List's work, translated into English and published in 1885, that was specifically incompatible with the ambitions of Griffith's Sinn Féin. According to List, a protectionist state policy could not succeed in a small state. Despite these incongruities, however, Griffith used List's ideas to 'prove' that the cosmopolitan economics of Adam Smith were fallacious, and to assert that economic nationalism was desirable and that a nation must develop both agriculture and industry.[15] Griffith's ideas were based on the convergence of a number of influences. *The resurrection of Hungary* contained among its proposals the recommendation that 'A System of Protection

13 Alun C. Davies, 'Ireland's Crystal Palace, 1853', in J.M. Goldstrom and L.A. Clarkson (eds), *Irish population, economy and society* (Oxford, 1981), p. 269. 14 Ibid., pp 256–9. 15 Richard Davis, *Arthur Griffith and non-violent Sinn Féin* (Kerry, 1974), p. 128.

for Irish Manufacturers – example – like the Hungarian Vedegylet Association – should be set up'. The Vedegylet (Hungarian Protective Association) was promoted in the mid-1840s by Louis Kossuth. Its objective was the protection of Hungarian manufacture. Griffith was impressed by the enterprise but, as Thomas Kabdebo has pointed out, 'It was not nearly as successful in economic terms as in political terms. Griffith might not have known as the Kossuth literature accessible to him described it as an unqualified success'.[16] Davitt, of course, met Kossuth in 1885, but their discussion was confined to European politics, with no mention, it seems, of economic theories.

There was a renewed interest in protectionist arguments in Ireland in the later nineteenth century, as indeed there was throughout Europe. Isaac Butt was critical of English-style free trade for Ireland. In 1846 he had published *Protection to home industry*, in which he argued for a political economy for Ireland. At that time, classical political economy was in the ascendant in Ireland, its most notable proponents being Nassau Senior and Archbishop Richard Whately. Both viewed *laissez faire* economics as sacrosanct, and their influence upon political economists was huge. For instance, The Dublin Statistical Society, established in 1847, ostensibly as a response to the Famine crisis, simply bolstered the classical economic theory. It claimed that its finding were based on scientific research, but, as R.D. Collinson Black makes clear, its transactions of 1847–9 'include [practically no table] which could reasonably be considered to deserve the adjective "statistical"'.[17]

Nonetheless, there were those, such as Butt, who contested the prevailing orthodoxy. Butt's *Land tenure and Ireland: a plea for the Celtic race* (1866) and *The Irish people and the Irish land* (1867) advanced a strong case for security of tenure and proposed land agitation as a means of securing that end. Davitt later paid tribute to Butt, describing his works as

> text-books for Land-League speakers and writers [...] storehouses of historic facts, of the doctrines of political economy, of the conclusions and findings of commissions [...] while the views and opinions of the author were instinct with Celtic feeling and indignation at the wrongs and injustices of the tillers of the soil.[18]

These works on land reform had a considerable influence on the early thought of Ferguson.[19] Butt's ideas were certainly influential. But in critiquing the prevailing orthodoxy in the post-Famine period, Mill and the influential econo-

---

16 Quoted in Thomas Kabdebo, *Ireland and Hungary, a study in parallels with an Arthur Griffith bibliography* (Dublin, 2001), p. 41. **17** R.D. Collinson Black, *The statistical and social inquiry society of Ireland* (Dublin, 1947), p. 5. **18** Davitt, *The fall*, p. 81. **19** McFarland, *John Ferguson*, pp 46–7.

mist, John Elliot Cairns, came in for particular criticism for proposing ways of adapting political economy to the conditions peculiar to Ireland. It was only some decades later, around 1870, that their ideas were being integrated into policy in a limited form.[20] As T.A. Boylan and T.P. Foley have stated, 'The decline in prestige of political economy was concomitant with the increased emphasis on Ireland's difference from England'.[21]

This was the context within which protectionist arguments gained greater currency in the later nineteenth century. In September 1881, at the height of the land war, Parnell actually declared that a home rule government would adopt protective tariffs.[22] At a subsequent meeting in Cork, he bemoaned the fact that 'we cannot yet have our own Parliament to protect Irish manufacturers'.[23] Later, shortly before the general election in November 1885, he again raised the protectionist argument, which generated 'quite a sensation' in Britain.[24] He believed, however, that protection could only really be applied to a small number of industries, and for only a few years at that. According to Kennedy, it is unlikely that in an independent Ireland Parnell would have presided over 'a strongly interventionist Irish parliament'. His economic policies would probably have been similar to the free market approach adopted by Cumann na nGaedheal in the 1920s.[25]

But the articulation of protectionist language in Parnell's speeches was significant, particularly during the moves towards home rule in 1885, when he declared that his expectations for self-government included tariff-imposing powers. It was to this 'protectionist war-cry' that Erich Strauss has ascribed the motivation of Joseph Chamberlain in definitively opposing home rule.[26] C.C. O'Brien correctly points out, however, that Chamberlain's discord with the Irish preceded the contentious issue of protection.[27] Davitt, of course, also believed that Chamberlain's position developed after he and Dilke had been snubbed by Irish nationalists in 1885.[28] On the matter of Parnell's protectionist expectations, which were eventually dropped, Davitt remarked tersely to Labouchere in October 1885, 'Parnell's attitude on Protection is absurd. If we had a national assembly in Dublin tomorrow he could not carry a measure in favour of Protection'.[29] This view was accurately reflected in the findings of the 1884 Select Committee on Irish industry, which suggested that nearly half

20 R.D. Collinson Black, *Economic thought and the Irish question, 1817–1870* (Cambridge, 1978), p. 63. 21 Boylan and Foley, *Political economy*, p. 160. 22 Lyons, 'The economic ideas of Parnell', p. 70. 23 Quoted in Kennedy, *Colonialism*, p. 91. 24 *Glasgow Observer*, 17 Oct. 1885. 25 Kennedy, *Colonialism*, pp 54, 101. Cumann na nGaedheal's policies in the 1920s were contrary to the protectionism of Griffith, one of its founding fathers. See T.K. Daniel, 'Griffith on his noble head: the determinants of Cumann na nGaedheal economic policy, 1922–32', *IESH*, 3 (1976). 26 E. Strauss, *Irish nationalism and British democracy* (London, p. 177). 27 O'Brien, *Parnell*, p. 111. 28 Davitt to Chamberlain, 6 Aug. 1903, DP, TCD, MS 9374/985. 29 Quoted in O'Brien, *Parnell*, p. 113; see also Davitt's remarks in *The fall*, pp 478–9.

(twenty-eight) of the fifty-nine companies giving evidence attributed their economic problems to foreign competition; but, significantly, only fourteen considered protectionism a solution to their difficulties.[30] Later, during a tour of the Scottish Highlands in the spring of 1887, Davitt directly challenged Chamberlain's argument that an Irish parliament would result in the imposition of protective duties on English and Scottish manufacturers. Addressing a demonstration at Wick, he declared that if ever he obtained a seat in an Irish parliament he 'would oppose any measure which would tend to interfere in any way with the Irish people buying the necessaries of life in the cheapest possible markets'.[31]

It is in the context of the broad nationalist critique of the economic consequences of the Union that Davitt's position on Irish economic development must be examined. He was a theoretical free trader, who believed, moreover, that arguments for protectionist measures were often specious and unconsidered. In 1888, during a public meeting of the North City Milling Company, of which he was a director, he responded to a call for 'protection' by saying that 'we were all protectionists when it means large dividends, but practical free traders when it meant buying cheap articles'.[32] During the Canadian cattle question in 1906, he similarly argued that calls for protectionism were impulsive and unrealistic. The indications at the time were that the Liberal government would allow the free importation of Canadian cattle, not least because of the overwhelming demand for cheap food for the British masses. Davitt acknowledged that the increase in competition resulting from the removal of trading restrictions would affect Irish agricultural production, but he maintained that protectionism was not the solution. He suggested that, if anything, the problem pointed to the shortcomings in Irish agricultural production itself, namely the inefficiency of Irish farming practice. He recommended that the process of fattening cattle should be carried out in Ireland, instead of livestock being shipped off 'half finished', and that breeders should use the land to cultivate the necessary root and crops necessary for fattening the livestock. The import of his pronouncements on the issue was that Irish farmers should be thinking innovatively instead of claiming a divine right to a traditional market.[33]

Davitt encountered protectionist arguments during his Australian tour, especially in Victoria which was the leading protectionist colony. His expressed views on protectionism in that colony are interesting, because he commented that the best argument put forward for protection by the state was that it was strong evidence of colonial independence. 'In the face of this reasoning', he

30 Kennedy, *Colonialism*, p. 54. **31** *Glasgow Observer*, 30 Apr. 1887. **32** Davitt's diary, 13 Feb. 1888, DP, TCD, MS 9548. **33** Bew, *Conflict and conciliation in Ireland, 1890–1910* (Oxford, 1987), pp 124–30.

remarked, 'I always surrender my arms as a theoretical free trader'. He noted that the argument that such measures were necessary for the protection of infant industries was a reasonable position for 'new countries' to take. He observed, moreover, that the policy in Victoria had led to some far-reaching labour legislation in the form of a minimum-wage bill, 'which is intended to be a kind of Labour complement to the tariff-fed manufacturing capitalists'.[34] One of the results of the cultivation of factory manufacturing under high tariffs had been low wages and poor working conditions. This forced the Labour Party in the colony to press for corrective measures from the legislature. It was argued that the wage earners should get some of the profits secured to the manufacturers by the tariffs. But, although Davitt accepted Victoria's right to adopt a protectionist strategy for economic growth, he still held that,

> a feeding-bottle diet, no matter how excellent in its way, is not necessarily the best kind of food for an adult. New South Wales [...] has shown that it can walk, and run, and work, in an industrial and producing sense, without the patent infants' food kind of nourishment which Victoria still demands for its trade and commercial sustenance.[35]

Davitt was not opposed to protectionism in principle, then. His attitude was that it was primarily a matter for each individual state to determine in its own right. But, ultimately, he was not ideologically predisposed to favour protectionist arguments. Before his arrival in New South Wales he received a letter from a John D. Fitzgerald of Sydney who asked him 'not to touch on fiscal subject [because] not only were most of our Australian Home Rulers Protectionists, but our bitterest radical foes were of those who belonged at any rate in the state of NSW, to the free trade Party'.[36] Davitt did not heed Fitzgerald. He replied in a letter of 20 June 1895, that he could not please everyone, continuing, 'I am a Free Trader because I believe in freedom – freedom political, racial, and economic for all. Perhaps that has arisen from my frequent imprisonments'.[37] One of his concerns during the controversy on the Canadian cattle question was, indeed, the political implications of the Irish Party's opposition to the removal of trading restrictions. He believed that such a stance would entail alignment with the 'pro-landlord section of the House of Commons'. As Bew has observed, his natural allies in the debate were 'the Free Trade and Labour feelings and interests'.[38] Only weeks before his inter-

---

34 Davitt, *Life and progress*, pp 146–7.   **35** Ibid., pp 145–6.   **36** See John D. Fitzgerald letter to Mrs Davitt, 24 Nov. 1907, DP, TCD, MS 9375/1003. Fitzgerald gives an account of his correspondence with Davitt in response to an appeal Mrs Davitt had made in the Sydney *Freeman's Journal* for material for a biography she was preparing of her late husband.   **37** Davitt to Fitzgerald, 20 June 1895, DP, TCD, MS 9375/1002.   **38** Quoted in Bew, *Conflict*, p. 125.

vention in the Canadian cattle issue, Davitt had, in fact, made a very explicit statement on protectionism in a letter to the editor of the *Nationist* on the subject of Irish-Ireland.[39] He was responding specifically to an earlier criticism that he was working 'for English democracy' and that he advocated trade with Britain.[40] After referring to his own record of trying to cultivate native Irish industries, he stated,

> The corollary of an Irish-Ireland, in your sense, is an English-England, French-France, and American-America all economically secluded from each other's markets, and living an existence of racial and commercial isolation [...] My idea of an Irish-Ireland is [...] with all her people [...] cultivating every available acre of Irish soil, and exporting millions of what we can spare from our own needs to England, or any other country, and receiving in economic exchange all the useful and needful articles we require [...] I would want to see our harbours crowded with ships; English or any nation's ships; filled with whatever would tend to make our people and country more prosperous and preserving; knowing that this wealth could not come to our shores except in exchange for its commercial equivalent exported out of the surplus products of Irish labour and skill .[41]

At the time when Parnell was pushing for tariff-imposing powers in a prospective home rule bill, Davitt was writing his series of articles in the *Evening Telegraph* on the revival of Irish industries. He identified the lack of manufacturing industry with the history of landlordism in Ireland.[42] He had made this point when he received the freedom of Limerick city in April 1884. He commented that the decay of cities like Limerick 'was owing to the paralysing system and influence of landlordism which had hitherto prevailed in the country'.[43] On the question of the industrial successes in Ulster, he argued that manufacturing in that part of the country had been facilitated by the prevalence of the 'Ulster custom' prior to the Land Act of 1881. He claimed that by limiting the influence of the landlord, the tenant-right custom had 'proved beneficial to trade and commerce'. This argument was current among some economic historians in the twentieth century.[44] However, it has been contested more recently, especially with regard to the view that rents were lower in the north and that tenants were inclined to invest more of the profits than would have been the case with the landlords. Cormac Ó Gráda

39 *Nationist*, 8 Feb. 1906. **40** *Nationist*, 1 Feb. 1906. **41** As above, fn. 39. **42** *ET*, 5 Dec. 1885. **43** Quoted in *Oban Times*, 19 Apr. 1884. **44** See George O'Brien, *The economic history of Ireland from the Union to the Famine* (London, 1921), p. 442; cited in Ó Gráda, *Ireland*, p. 315.

argues, for example, that there is some merit in the contention that tenant right, 'instead of reducing the landlord's share of the Ricardian rent, was a means of ensuring that stipulated rents were paid'.[45]

It is, of course, important to point out that industrial growth in Ulster was concentrated in a relatively small area around Lagan Valley. Davitt, for his part, was concerned with fostering industrial regeneration throughout the whole country. He became particularly vocal on the issue on his return from Europe and Palestine in 1885, especially in challenging the Parnellites on the neglect of the INL's 'industrial charter'. The ideas which he subsequently articulated in his *Evening Telegraph* pieces illustrate his difference with Parnell on a number of important points relating to industrial development. He argued that, while it was understandable to attribute the poor state of Irish industry and commercial interests to English competition and misrule, it was not possible to throw upon 'the brutal Saxon' the responsibility for all but the total absence of national self-independence in industrial enterprise.[46] He maintained that there were a number of Irish industries which could be fostered without an injection of foreign capital and without protection. His argument was similar to the views which he later expressed on the cattle question: he contended that there was a lack of ingenuity and imagination in certain areas of industrial production; he stressed, moreover, that an increase in independent industrial development would require the exploitation of certain natural resources and investment in scientific and technical education. His discussion did not deal with the industries of the northeast but, rather, the moribund industries in the rest of the country.

In the second of his *Evening Telegraph* articles he examined the bottle-making industry which, he claimed, could be exploited by indigenous business.[47] He identified it as an industry which had the potential for hundreds of jobs, up to £50,000 a year in wages in addition to existing salaries. He estimated demand for bottles in Ireland to be around 140,000 in total. The annual production of bottles, however, was only about 60,000. Davitt claimed that the problem was due to the fact that there were only three 'bottle manufactories' in Ireland, all in Dublin – Ringsend Company, the Dublin Company, and the Irish Glass Bottle Company – and that they confined their production to black bottles. The difference between production and consumption was supplied by importations from England, Germany, Scotland, Sweden and France. The south of Ireland was largely supplied by Bristol and Liverpool; and the Scottish manufacturers of whiskey bottles had Belfast as their main Irish market. Davitt explained the problem in Ireland, and the disparity in production and supply, by pointing out that Ireland was not only limited to several companies but, more importantly, that its production methods were dated. The Dublin man-

45 Ó Gráda, *Ireland*, p. 128. 46 *ET*, 21 Nov. 1885. 47 Ibid.

ufacturers used what he described as the 'old "coal tank" system', which was being replaced by the 'Siemens' gas system. He pointed out that with the older system, the impurities produced by the coal during combustion affected the colour and quality of the glass; in the latter, however, the impurities were separated from the gas during combustion, thereby producing a clearer and more malleable article. There was also, he claimed, a saving of 40–50 per cent in coal by the adoption of the Siemens system. In particular, he highlighted the obvious benefits in Irish glass production on a larger scale. The freightage charges on the importation of goods from England, Scotland and Europe was 'not less than from 1s. to 2s. per gross', with an average loss of four per cent in breakage incurred as a result of transit. Moreover, 'the package of the bottles in mats and crates is an additional charge upon profits'.

He insisted that the manufacture of bottles in Dublin would be entirely exempt from such deductions, and that the charges that would be involved in supplying the rest of Ireland would be relatively small. Of the actual materials for bottle production, he wrote,

> The sand, lime, and blue clay used in the manufacture of black bottles are found in the county Dublin, while the rock salt which is necessary as a flux comes from Carrickfergus by boat. The sand necessary for the manufacture of clear glass bottles can be had in almost unlimited quantity at the Muckish mountain in Donegal.

The exploitation of this resource, he argued, would generate employment for the people of that area. He proposed that when the sand was extracted from this region it should be brought from Dunfanaghy to Dublin by boat. The costs would, in his view, be negligible. In fact, he argued that the mode of transportation could enable any company manufacturing these bottles to compete in Liverpool and Glasgow for contracts with the manufacturers of Lancashire and Scotland who get their existing supply of sand from Antwerp and the Wash. There is no doubt that he had consulted Kane's work, *The industrial resources of Ireland*. Under a section entitled, 'Varieties of clay, and sand', Kane wrote,

> The weathering of the quartz rock of the Muckish mountain in Donegal, has given origin to a species of sand of singular character. It is perfectly white, in rather large grains, and is chemically pure. If the approaches to the mountain were more easy, and that this kind of sand were brought into the market upon fair terms, there is no doubt but that it would be preferred to the sands of the south of England, none of which can at all compete with it in purity of colour and composition.

Kane had actually connected this raw material with the potential for industrial development. He claimed confidently that,

> [while] The quality of fuel consumed in the burning of porcelain and
> earthen-ware, and in the melting of the materials in which glass con-
> sists, might appear to many to present a serious obstacle to the intro-
> duction of such occupations among us, [s]uch is in reality not the case.[48]

Davitt had apparently done his research, then, and probably with some
informed understanding of the industries in Scotland and the north of England,
felt that the conditions for a successful bottle-making industry in Ireland were
very promising. But he was not content with simply writing about industrial
revival. He understood the issue in the context of the wider social question,
and this, together with his instincts for hands-on involvement, induced him
to become proactive on the matter. In the latter half of the 1880s he became
heavily involved in practical industrial projects, to which he invested a considerable amount of personal time and finances. He had been concerned with
the issue of industrial regeneration for some time. In 1882 he was involved
with the Dublin Industrial Exhibition.[49] Around this time he also founded the
West of Ireland Cottage Industries, an enterprise based in Carraroe, Co.
Galway, which was essentially designed to counter the flow of emigration from
the area and to provide relief through the channel of light employment.[50]
Using approximately £600 or £800 of National League money between 1882
and 1883, he attempted similar ventures in County Louth, Donegal and elsewhere.[51] In 1884 he gave a lecture at the Mechanics' Institute, Galway, on the
subject of 'Irish manufacturers and cottage industries. How to revise and promote them'.[52] But it was really during the later years of the 1880s that he fever-
ishly threw himself into a series of industrial ventures, among them a bottle-
making factory. He undertook this project in 1888, but the enterprise proved
unsuccessful. This may have been principally due a lack of investment, and
the fact that he bore all the legal costs himself.[53]

He also established a woollen company, The Irish Woollen Manufacturing
& Export Company, in the spring of 1887. It was clear that he had carried out
some market research during his visit to the United States between August
1886 and February 1887. After his return to Ireland, he was interviewed by
the *Freeman's Journal* about the initiative.[54] He explained that the chief purpose of the company was the export of Irish woollens, a viable venture, he

---

48 Kane, *The industrial resources*, p. 238. 49 See Davitt's letter to the editor of the *Nationist*, 8
Feb. 1906. 50 See DP, TCD, MS 9370/871. 51 See above, fn. 49. 52 Davitt, 'Notes for lec-
tures', 26 Sept. 1884, DP, TCD, MS 9541. 53 See *FJ* obituary to Davitt, 31 May 1906; and
Sheehy Skeffington, *Michael Davitt*, p. 132. 54 *FJ*, 18 Apr. 1887.

argued, given that seventy per cent of woollens worn in America were import-
ed. In response to the reporter's query about import duties, he said that the
Irish product would be on an equal footing with English and Scottish ship-
ping houses, and that he was confident that the Irish article would be of better quality. He noted that as an export business, the company would not have
mills of its own but would aim to 'stimulate the work of the existing mills by
widening as far as possible the market for Irish woollens'. It would particularly endeavour to aid the small millowners: 'We propose to buy from [small
manufacturers] on the principle of payment at delivery of orders, and in that
way increase their confidence and help them to extend their works, improve
the workmanship of their goods, and gradually multiply their hands'. He indicated that if the project was successful, the Company would market other articles of Irish manufacture, such as Belleek pottery and Irish lace and candles.

The Company was to begin with a capital of £10,000.[55] Shares were put at
£5 each.[56] The managing directors included Davitt, Thomas Mayne (Parnellite
MP for Tipperary from 1883 and an ally of Archbishop Croke),[57] John
McQuaid, T.C. Francis Callaghan, Peter White, and J.G. Mooney.[58] The principal financial backers of the enterprise were described by Davitt as 'about
twenty business men in [Dublin]'.[59] Mooney was probably significant in this
respect, in that he may have belonged to the prominent Dublin business family of the same name.[60] Croke and Archbishop Walsh of Dublin were, together with Parnell, named as strong supporters of the venture,[61] although Croke,
who had stakes in other similar ventures, asked Davitt, 'Would it be shabby
to take only 20 [shares]?'.[62]

The company, with its offices at Usher's quay, Dublin, established links
throughout Britain and North America, and had agencies in Hamburg and
Paris.[63] Plans were also made to extend its operations into Australia.[64] Davitt
put a considerable amount of personal effort into the business, especially in
generating international interest. The company's prospectus was largely aimed
at an American audience. Despite Davitt's earlier assertion that all could not
be blamed on the 'brutal Saxon', the prospectus gave a brief history of 'How
England endeavoured to destroy Irish manufacture'.[65] The company had a
propitious beginning, and at its first half-yearly meeting a dividend of seven
per cent was declared.[66] Yet, while welcoming this promising return, Davitt,
who presided at the meeting, warned that the international market was a high-

---

55 See *Nationist*, 8 Feb. 1906. **56** *FJ*, 18 Apr. 1887. **57** Tierney, *Croke*, p. 183. **58** See the
prospectus of the woollen company, written by Davitt, *Revival of the Irish woollen industry*, in King
(ed.), *Michael Davitt*, vol. ii, p. 15. **59** *FJ*, 18 Apr. 1887. **60** See Patrick Maume, *The long gestation: Irish nationalist life, 1891–1918* (Dublin, 1999), p. 236. **61** *FJ*, 18 Apr. 1887. **62** Croke
to Davitt, 22 Aug. 1887, DP, TCD, MS 9334/288. **63** See *Nationist*, 8 Feb. 1906. **64** Davitt,
Revival, p. 15. **65** Ibid. **66** *FJ*, 5 May 1888.

ly competitive one. Indeed, by February 1888 he was forced to note in his diary that although business was doing 'fairly well in America, order[s were] not as large as expected'.[67] In May, Peter White was consequently dispatched to the United States on his third business trip with a collection of woollen samples.[68] As the *Freeman's Journal* observed at this time, the venture represented a pioneering and professional marketing undertaking in foreign markets.[69] However, Davitt was to incur considerable financial losses in his personal commitment to it. In early 1896 the company was liquidated.[70] He later stated that the enterprise had contributed to the prosperity of the woollen industry in Ireland,[71] although the industry was, in any case, going through a period of recovery in the latter half of the nineteenth century. The number of mills rose from 11 in 1850 to 61 in 1870 and 82 in 1899. Martin Mahony & Co. of Blarney was weaving tweed with looms powered by three 145–horse-power turbines and two steam engines. By the 1890s this company was employing over 700 workers. However, most of the mills that emerged were small, water-powered operations.[72]

Davitt was involved in a number of other business ventures from the later part of the 1880s, including of course the North City Milling Company. In the late 1890s he had investment interests in South African mining and in other companies. But he himself admitted that he was not suited to financial affairs.[73] He remarked jokingly to Sophie O'Brien that if he were given a share in the Bank of England the country's credit would fall.[74] His involvement with the woollen company ultimately cost him £500.[75] It must also be said that he involved himself in too many business ventures. In January 1888 he was asked to become a director of a flax company in Belfast, but he acknowledged in his diary, 'Am too much of a director already. Too many irons in fire altogether. Must stop short or will soon become demoralized with projects, companies, etc, etc. Better stick to my pen if I do not want to find myself bankrupt'.[76] While he possessed no business acumen, his pen did make an important contribution to the subject of Irish industrial rejuvenation. Several months after the launch of the woollen company he told an audience in Limerick that it would be incumbent on a prospective national parliament to undertake the revival of Irish industries and investment in technical education. He specifically concentrated on the woollen industry, stating, 'I am satisfied that Ireland under Home Rule could soon become the most flourishing woollen manu-

67 Davitt's diary, 14 Feb. 1888, DP, TCD, MS 9548. **68** *FJ*, 24 May 1888. **69** *FJ*, 8 May 1888. **70** Davitt informed Sabina of the 'smash up' of the company in a letter dated 28 Mar. 1896, DP, TCD, MS 9325/[104/6]. **71** *Nationist*, 8 Feb. 1906. **72** Ó Gráda, *Ireland*, p. 294. **73** Davitt's diary, 31 Dec. 1893, DP, TCD, MS 9554. **74** Sophie O'Brien, *My Irish friends* (Paris, 1937) p. 36, cited in King (ed.), *Michael* Davitt, vol. i, p. xviii. **75** *FJ*, 31 May 1906. **76** Davitt's diary, 25 Jan. 1888, DP, TCD, MS 9548.

facturer in Europe'. He also gave some consideration to the northeast, arguing that land nationalization could boost Ulster's linen industry.[77] The industry was actually experiencing a period of stagnation in the 1880s, resulting
from changing fashions and protectionism in Europe. By the middle of the
decade, it was acknowledged that four of the twelve joint-stock spinning-mills
in Belfast had 'been unable to declare a dividend for some time, and that the
share values of several had fallen drastically'.[78] Davitt argued, however, that
the low rents that would exist under state ownership would induce the south
of Ireland to cultivate all the flax fibre necessary for northern mills. He understood that the cultivation of flax had diminished precisely because of heavy
rents and the extension of grazing; but he argued that under state ownership,
the Irish parliament, in order to beat foreign competition, could offer premi-
ums for the growth of all flax by remission of rent on farms devoted to this
produce until the industry had recovered.[79]

In his address in Limerick, Davitt focused on the responsibilities of a
prospective Irish parliament, but he was critical of the view that self-government was a prerequisite for industrial revival. In his *Evening Telegraph* article
of 5 December 1885, he insisted that Ireland could produce most of its own
manufactured articles, despite English competition; all that was required was
the investment of some of the money already in the country in industrial projects. In Limerick he stated, significantly, that the woollen and linen industries could be resuscitated without the 'interference' of tariffs. In his article,
he also denounced dependence on protectionist arguments: 'If we only wait
until we obtain Protection', he wrote, 'we will not have a long wait until there
is nothing left to Protect'.[80] It is true, as a matter of historical fact, that in the
early nineteenth century the woollen industry deteriorated despite protection.[81] In 1881 Parnell had suggested that, pending independence, the Irish
could only address the question of Irish industries by adopting a strategy of
purchasing home goods, or what he called 'indirect protection'.[82] In a speech
in Longford in 1885 Davitt himself urged the Irish people to support Irish
manufacturing industry by purchasing goods manufactured in Ireland.[83]
However, he disliked what he considered the fatalism of 'indirect protection' as a strategy. He later noted,

> *Support Irish manufacturers!* While I am trying to help in the revival of
> some industries, [I] have to pay 120% more for the paper I write let-
> ters upon than similar English paper would cost! Not very encouraging.
> How fearfully stupid it is to put such a tax upon home produce. One

77 *FJ*, 17 Nov. 1887.   **78** Ó Gráda, *Ireland*, p. 290.   **79** As above, fn. 77.   **80** *ET*, 5 Dec. 1885.
81 Kennedy, *Colonialism*, p. 43.   **82** Quoted in Lyons, 'The economic ideas of Parnell', p. 70.
83 *Glasgow Observer*, 22 Aug. 1885.

would almost feel inclined to think that these Irish makers were in league with English makers for the total crushing out of Irish manufacture.[84]

According to Kennedy, one of the principal reasons for the decline of the woollen industry was poor workmanship.[85] Davitt himself put great emphasis on improved quality in workmanship in Irish manufacturing and stressed the need for advanced practices in production. Education, he argued, was central to technical proficiency. He attributed the demise of Irish engineering firms to the lack of such industrial aptitude. The decline of The Royal Phoenix Works and Mallets of Ryder's Row might, he noted, be primarily due to the want of technical or scientific education in Ireland compared with England or Scotland.[86] He suggested that this might also explain why preference was given to foreigners over natives in the work of superintendence and direction. When he was elected to Dublin Corporation in January 1886 he became very active on this issue. On 5 January he was one of the main figures at a meeting organized to prepare a scheme for a technical school in the city.[87] The *Freeman's Journal* recorded the progress of the project the following week.[88] Its editorial pointed out that the movement was 'purely industrial and educational' and had no political agenda. It expressed optimism about the prospects for the technical school programme, particularly with Davitt as one of the principal promoters.

Another flagging Irish industry to which Davitt turned his attention was the leather trade.[89] He stated that, unlike some other industries, the decline of the leather trade could not, in the immediate term, be attributed to the Act of Union. Tanning had been a very productive industry in the early nineteenth century. In the 1830s Bandon had seventeen tanneries and Cork had forty-six. But during the Industrial Exhibition of 1853 the industry was represented by only a few tanners of Dublin. By 1892 there was only one tannery left in Bandon, and in 1907 Ireland's share of UK leather production was only £87,000 out of a total of £18 million.[90] In his *Evening Telegraph* article of 9 January 1886, Davitt advocated an entrepreneurial drive to raise the industry. He claimed that the amount of leather used in Ireland amounted to five pounds weight per head of population. In money terms this was, he estimated, 1s. 4d. per pound, or in total £300,000. He assumed – 'and I think I will not be far wrong' – that the Irish manufactured only one-thirtieth of this themselves, thus incurring 'an annual loss of labour and profit to something like £290,000!' He ultimately argued that if all the leather was manufactured in Ireland, this

84 Davitt's diary, 25 Jan. 1894, DP, TCD, MS 9555. **85** Kennedy, *Colonialism*, p. 43. **86** *ET*, 5 Dec. 1885. **87** Davitt's diary, 5 Jan. 1886, DP, TCD, MS 9545. **88** *FJ*, 11 Jan. 1886. **89** *ET*, 9 Jan. 1886. **90** Ó Gráda, *Ireland*, p. 325.

1 Stellfoxe's Victoria Mill, Baxenden, near Haslingden,
where Davitt, aged 11, lost his right arm on 8 May 1857.

2 Davitt in Haslingden, following his release from Dartmoor prison in 1877.

3 Davitt and William Redmond in New York, June–July 1882,
shortly after Davitt's release from Portland prison.

4 Davitt (fourth from right) with a party of visitors at the
Mount of Olives in Jerusalem on 11 April 1885.

5 Davitt, Freemantle, Western Australia in 1895.

6 Davitt with reception committee, Freemantle, Western Australia, 1895.

7 (*above*) Davitt, MP, outside house of commons.
8 (*left*) Davitt in Russian hat, Moscow, 1905.

9 Davitt, aged 58.

sum, after a fair profit, could be divided into wages which would provide constant employment for over 3,000 more artisans. His argument implicitly called on Irish manufacturers to adapt to the vicissitudes in market forces and to face the demands on the leather industry, especially technological demands. This is consistent with L.M. Cullen's view that the industry declined in Ireland because of a failure to adopt new technology. He claims that the adherence to a traditional method that produced a better quality article contrasted with the commercial appeal of rapid-tanned leather.[91] Ó Gráda argues, however, that Irish tanners cannot be entirely blamed for the decline. He points out that the change to exporting Irish cattle on the hoof reduced the supply of hides, and, moreover, that there was a decline in the Irish boot and shoe industry which may have adversely affected the industry.[92]

Davitt's *Evening Telegraph* articles on Irish industries were, as the *Freeman's Journal* stated, practical and far-reaching.[93] His industrial activities from the later 1880s clearly illustrate that he believed his own ideas to be practicable. But, as he himself remarked, he had 'too many irons in the fire'. Although he was not, by his own admission, adept at business, an examination of his industrial projects is nonetheless important, not only in understanding his ideas on economic development, but also is considering his sometimes fraught role as both an entrepreneur and a labour activist. This was very apparent in one particular business interest in which he incurred more than financial costs. The case involved a bitter dispute in 1890 with the Dublin branch of the Millers' National Union. As a director of the North City Milling company, Davitt was held responsible for wage cuts and for having men discharged from employment and replaced with boys.[94] He had been a director of the company since February 1886, having become associated with it through Egan, who himself was a director in the late 1860s and early 1870s.[95] The dispute troubled Davitt enough to cause him to consider resignation from the company, but he was dissuaded from taking this course by the board of directors, not least because it was felt that such a move would probably prove prejudicial to the interests of the company.[96] If the dispute was a cause of concern among the members of the board, then one can easily appreciate how problematical it must have been for Davitt, given that the *Labour World* was established at this time, a paper specifically committed to addressing labour interests.

The dispute flared up in June 1890, and as late as December 1891 Davitt received a letter from J.M. Mooney, a fellow director, who was 'indeed sorry to learn you are still persecuted in your connection here'.[97] It was R.B.

91 Cited in ibid., p. 325. **92** Ibid., p. 325. **93** *FJ*, 31 May 1906. **94** DP, TCD, MS 9322/48–60. **95** Bew, *Land*, p. 239; see *Irish World*, 6 Apr. 1889 for background on Egan's early working life in the offices of the milling company. **96** J.M. Mooney to Davitt, 4 Aug. 1890, DP, TCD, MS 9322/59. **97** Mooney to Davitt, 31 Dec. 1891, DP, TCD, MS 9322/60.

Cunninghame Graham, with whom Davitt had shared a labour platform in the May Day demonstration in Hyde Park only weeks earlier, who received a letter from Henry Russell, general secretary of the Millers' National Union, explaining that the secretary of the Dublin branch, J.J. Casey, had written to the executive council of the union accusing Davitt himself of being 'the cause' of the wage cuts. As a director, Davitt would have had no actual part in hiring and firing or knowledge thereof. He contacted Cunninghame Graham, stating this fact as his defence. The Dublin branch secretary acknowledged that this was technically the norm for a director. However, Casey had done his home-work, and from studying the pay sheets and time lists of the various mills, he discovered that,

> Your men work 3 hours longer in the week than any other mill men in the city and your men get two and three and four shillings per week less for their long hours than is paid for in the short hours in Mooneys, Customs House or Bolands or Browns.[98]

In short, Casey considered Davitt's ignorance to be indefensible in itself.

Against these charges of hypocrisy, Davitt appeared disingenuous in his utter indignation. Casey did, of course, reduce the issue to one of personal integrity, both in his tone and in the manner in which the allegation was made. He had referred to Davitt as the actual cause of the wage cuts in his letter to Henry Russell. Moreover, had he approached Davitt directly, the onus would have been more firmly on Davitt's explaining himself and taking action accordingly. Yet while Casey's approach was very personal, Davitt did not address the issue, one way or another. He was clearly averse to admitting that workers were being exploited in a company of which he was a director. Such equivocation was, at times, typical of Davitt. As Moody comments, his 'habit of reinterpreting his past actions and attitudes in accordance with altered conditions was partly the outcome of a longing for integrity in his political conduct, partly of his quickness of response to the appeal or challenge of a new situation'.[99] In the dispute with the millers' union, he focused on the issue of the perceived affront to his personal integrity, and not once in the course of the correspondence did he contest Casey's statement on the rate of pay at the company. Instead, he retorted that he would forfeit his interest in the company and have the actual value of the same divided between the workmen and the Dublin branch of the millers' union if the charges against him were proven.[1] Ultimately, he wrote to Casey in July 1890, ironically on *Labour World*

---

98 J.J. Casey to Davitt, 21 June 1890, DP, TCD, MS 9322/51. 99 Moody, *Davitt*, p. 552. 1 Davitt to Casey, 2 July, 1890, DP, TCD, MS 9322/54.

stationery, calling him 'a disgrace both to the Irish name and to Trade Unionism'. He stated further,

> You, in the name of members of your branch could stoop to this mean and dastardly device of libelling me, secretly, in letters to Englishmen, and, when your acts of falsehoods are found out [...] you sneak away like a paltry coward from your charges [...][2]

Davitt's behaviour in the dispute, especially the knee-jerk reaction, certainly suggests that he was being less than forthright. Hubris undoubtedly played a part as well. As a champion of the common worker, he would, no doubt, have been eager to put the matter behind him. It was definitely inconsistent with the position he occupied some years later when, as an MP, he sat on a Select Committee inquiring into complaints by Irish workers regarding the government's alleged non-observance of the 1891 Fair Wages Resolution of the house of commons.[3] But the charges levelled against him by Casey continued to be used by his political enemies for some time, at least in the Irish context, and particularly during the internecine political warfare of the Irish Party split. Mooney's reference to Davitt's continued persecution in December 1891 must surely have been an allusion to an attack on Davitt a week earlier in the *Irish Independent*, then a Parnellite organ, in which he was accused of having exploited the mill workers. This followed a similar attack, published a day earlier in the *Evening Herald*, one of the papers of the 'Independent' group, which claimed that Davitt had acted unscrupulously in launching the *Labour World*. Knowing that the venture was liable to be a failure, he had, it was claimed, sold his own shares after attracting financial backers, who were ultimately left to take the loss when the company folded.[4] Davitt sued the 'Independent' company for the libellous allegations. During the court hearing in May 1892, he argued, in his defence against the charge that he had acted 'like a level-headed speculator', that he had not sold one share, and that he had in fact suffered losses of £1,200. He also flatly denied the suggestion that he had lowered workers' wages while a director at the milling company, a charge which was brought up in the course of the cross-examination. In the end, the judge found in his favour and he was awarded damages of £20.[5]

Davitt established himself as a campaigner for labour rights in his activism from the mid-1880s. There is no convincing reason to believe that he began the *Labour World* as anything other than a serious political and business venture; and the accusations levelled against him by the 'Independent' in

---

2 Davitt to Casey, 10 July 1890, DP, TCD, MS 9322/58.   3 See DP, TCD, MS 9375/1006–10. 4 The claims in the *Evening Herald* were made on 22 Dec. 1891, and the allegations in the *Irish Independent* were on 23 Dec.; see *FJ*, 17 May 1892.   5 *FJ*, 17 May 1892.

December 1891 must be viewed in the context of the split. In considering his entrepreneurial enterprises generally, however, it must be borne in mind that he firmly believed in the rights of the what he would have termed the 'scrupulous' capitalist. He did not, of course, consider the interests of labour and capital to be mutually exclusive, but his commitment to the idea of a community of shareholders must be taken into account in considering his role in the North City Milling Company. If anything, the dispute with the millers' union illustrates the disparity that sometimes existed between his declaration of principles and their application. Even while editing the *Labour World* he had problems with his 'infernal printers' who, as he informed McGhee, taught him 'something of the tyranny of trade unionism'.[6] However, despite his inconsistencies, he still played a significant role in the advancement of the cause of labour, particularly in Britain.

6 Davitt to McGhee, 4 Oct. 1890, DP, TCD, MS 9328, 181/11.

5 / The union of democracies: Davitt and British labour

GIVEN THE INFLUENCE OF Henry George on the development of the British labour movement, and the existence of an agrarian dimension to British advanced radicalism even before the advent of George's reform gospel, it was natural that Davitt should have turned his attention to social activism in Britain from the early 1880s. Addressing an audience in Strabane, Co. Tyrone, in 1888, he proclaimed, 'I start with the proposition that the land question is essentially a labour question'.[1] He had, of course, attempted to situate the Irish land question in an international labour context as early as the summer of 1882; and as an early advocate of independent labour representation in parliament, he argued that the monopoly which the privileged and wealthy had on political power in Britain was responsible for imperialist policy.[2] Yet he had a fraught relationship with Hardie and those who did vigorously pursue an independent labour line in British politics from the early 1890s. Moreover, he incurred the censure of notable figures within the Irish labour movement who criticized him for failing to fully engage with the interests of the Irish proletariat. Indeed, Davitt's political thought does not easily conform to an ideological paradigm, which perhaps explains his neglect in Irish and British labour historiography. Rather, his apparent contradictions reflect, to some extent, the nature of his own peculiar radicalism.

George first visited Ireland in the autumn of 1881, during Davitt's imprisonment in Portland. Acting officially as a correspondent for Patrick Ford's *Irish World*, his visit was really intended as a political tour designed to advance his radical social agenda. Shortly after his arrival he reported on the level of 'whiggery', or conservatism, within the Land League, and on the failure of the Irish land movement to identify with the cause of the British working class. He pointed out that the Land League was, after all, 'largely analogous to trade union movements for shorter time and higher wages'.[3] After delivering a lecture in Belfast in January 1882, he met Ferguson and was invited to speak at the forthcoming St Patrick's Day Irish National Demonstration in Glasgow.[4]

1 *FJ*, 11 June 1888.   2 Davitt, *Leaves*, vol. ii, p. 152–60.   3 Quoted in Lane, *The origins*, pp 73–4. 4 McFarland, *John Ferguson*, pp 132–3.

During his stay in Glasgow in March, he had the opportunity to address the inaugural meeting of the local branch of the Democratic Federation (later, from 1884, the Social Democratic Federation under H.M. Hyndman), a recently established organization which appealed to the interests of the working class. Significantly, the Federation actively opposed the government's coercion policy in Ireland; and, in the context of agrarian upheaval in Ireland, distress among Scottish Highland crofters, and a widespread agricultural depression, it advocated land nationalization.[5] George's writings had, of course, already been well received in Britain, and his personal appearance on the political stage in both Britain and Ireland increasingly popularized his straightforward economic arguments on social inequality. Richard McGhee remarked that *Progress and poverty* ultimately appealed to 'the senses, the feelings and the intellect'.[6]

In Glasgow, George was honoured by Ferguson and McGhee, and drew strong support from the Scottish radical, John Shaw Maxwell, and the future crofter MP, Angus Sutherland.[7] He also shared a platform with Hyndman and Helen Taylor, the stepdaughter of Mill.[8] The propagation of his ideas was particularly significant at this time, for, as J.D. Young points out, the Democratic Federation was essentially 'a sort of staging post for men who had not yet found a place in radical or socialist politics'.[9] Following his release from Portland, Davitt was immensely encouraged by the growing popularity of *Progress and poverty*, 'that powerfully reasoned work', and had high expectations of the influence now enjoyed by its celebrated author, especially in Britain.[10] Having relocated to London in late January 1882 for the beginning of the new parliamentary term, George met quite a number of the Irish nationalist parliamentarians, of whom he was able to make a political assessment. However, as he informed Ford shortly afterwards, he was not sanguine about the prospects of a radical impulse from within the Irish Party, and he consequently underscored the vital importance of Davitt as a radical figure.[11] Before his eventual return to the United States in October 1882, he was fêted at a farewell dinner at the Gresham Hotel, Dublin, at which Davitt, Ferguson, T.D. Sullivan and a number other personal friends were present.[12]

When Davitt started on a tour of Scotland several weeks after George's departure – addressing meetings in Glasgow, Greenock, Aberdeen, Edinburgh, Dundee, Inverness and Coatbridge – he reinforced the Georgeite message and restated what he considered to be the essential doctrine of the Land League.[13]

5 Pelling, *Origins*, p. 18. 6 Quoted in McFarland, *John Ferguson*, p. 110. 7 J.D. Young, 'Working class and radical movements in Scotland and the revolt from Liberalism, 1866–1900' (PhD thesis, University of Stirling, 1974), p. 132. 8 McFarland, *John Ferguson*, p. 133. 9 Young, 'Working class and radical movements', p. 133. 10 Davitt, *Jottings*, p. 43. 11 Lane, *The origins*, pp 75–6. 12 *FJ*, 2 Oct. 1882. 13 Davitt's first Scottish tour took place between 24–5 Oct. and 4 Nov. 1882.

The gospel of 'The Land for the People' [he told his Glasgow audi-ence], is a universal gospel [...] The poorest child that lives to-day in the poorest quarter of Glasgow has as much right, in the intentions of its Maker, to live by labour on the natural agencies which are creat-ed for the sustenance of the Scotch people as the Duke of Sutherland.[14]

He was particularly uplifted by his reception in the Highlands where he found 'very much better specimens of people than lowland Scotch. Can understand their Gaelic and have been understood in return when speaking Irish'.[15] He also noted that the more educated Highlanders had read George and had 'promise[d] to keep the ball rolling in the Highlands'.[16] At the end of his visit, he reflected, 'Believe I have done good work – certainly I have broken down a great deal of Scottish prejudice against the Irish land movement, and car-ried the banner [...] into the Highlands. Will it remain there!'[17]

The timing of Davitt's first Scottish tour was especially propitious. Edward McHugh, himself a Gaelic speaker and 'an ideal propagandist'[18] had already pre-pared some of the groundwork, having visited the island of Skye and other Highland districts in the spring of 1882 following the opening disturbance of the crofters' war. During his speaking engagements, he preached Davitt's radical 'social gospel', not the official Land League policy of peasant proprietorship,[19] and he made good use of George's writings in emphasizing the international dimen-sion to the land issue.[20] He was joined on his tour by John Murdoch, editor of the *Highlander* and leading campaigner for crofter rights.[21] Murdoch had lived in Dublin in the 1850s and was strongly influenced by the ideas of Fintan Lalor.[22] Davitt later wrote that McHugh's early mission had been a 'marked success',[23] although local intelligence and police reports in some areas indicated that the Irish agitator had not, in fact, attracted much support from crofters and was referred to as 'trusdair' (a 'filthy fellow').[24] According to Andrew Newby, McHugh did not seem to face any significant opposition from the Presbyterian inhabitants of Skye, despite his being an Irish Catholic.[25] Indeed, by August, McHugh him-self was confident enough to inform the National Land League of Great Britain that the Highlands 'were ripe for the cry of "The Land for the People"'.[26]

The proactive agitation which distinguished the Highland land war from earlier periods of agrarian disorder in the region began on Lord MacDonald's

---

14 See Davitt, *Land nationalization*, p. 10. 15 Davitt's diary, 4 Nov. 1882, DP, TCD, MS 9535. 16 McFarland, *John Ferguson*, p. 138. 17 Davitt's diary, 9 Nov. 1882, DP, TCD, MS 9535. 18 Davitt, *The fall*, p. 228. 19 McFarland, *John Ferguson*, p. 128. 20 Newby, *The life and times*, p. 49. 21 Davitt, *The fall*, pp 228–9. Ferguson claimed that £200 was set aside for this campaign; see McFarland, *John Ferguson*, p. 152, note 20. 22 James Hunter, 'The politics of highland land reform, 1873–1895', *SHR*, 53 (Apr. 1974), 47. 23 Davitt, *The fall*, p. 228. 24 McFarland, *John Ferguson*, p. 137; Hunter, 'The politics of highland land reform', p. 49. 25 Newby, *The life and times*, p. 49. 26 Quoted in McFarland, *John Ferguson*, p. 137.

estate on the east coast of Skye, near Portree, in April 1882. Tenants in the Braes district of the estate embarked on a rent strike when they were denied the restoration of their customary grazing rights on Ben Lee mountain. The landlord responded by trying to have summonses of removal served on tenants whose rents were in arrears, but on 7 April the process server was confronted by a group of tenants who seized his papers and burned them. When the police subsequently proceeded to make arrests they were attacked by a large crowd, which included men, women and children.[27] The incident, which the press quickly labelled the 'Battle of the Braes', was followed later in the year by similar disturbances at Glendale, thirty miles from Portree. Davitt's arrival actually coincided with the latter outbreak of protest.[28] The situation was also exacerbated by an economic crisis: the fishing industry on the east coast of Skye suffered a major setback after the destruction of boats and fishing equipment in a severe storm in October; and a particularly bad winter in 1882–3 resulted in a poor potato crop.[29]

The historic significance of the agrarian unrest at the Braes and other areas of Skye was that it was the first time since the Jacobite rebellion of 1745 that a military force had been dispatched to the island. Although the agitation was localized in 1882, Davitt and other activists like Ferguson and McHugh were intent on instigating a co-ordinated crofter campaign as a means of advancing their radical social agenda. Ferguson's Glasgow base was important in itself, for by 1871 more than 20,000 of the city's population were originally from the Highlands, and there was a sizeable number of second- and third-generation Gaels, not only in Glasgow but also in other western Lowland towns.[30] One of the young radicals closely associated with Ferguson, John Bruce Glasier – who would later eulogise Davitt in poetry[31] – was of Highland stock. His parents had been evicted in the most recent clearances.[32] The mid-nineteenth-century famine clearances were, as T.M. Devine has stated, the 'last in the cycle of great evictions which transformed Gaelic society from the last quarter of the eighteenth century', and their place in popular memory and pamphlet literature actually played an important role in the upsurge of the later agrarian resistance.[33]

Economic conditions undoubtedly played some part in precipitating the upsurge of crofter rebellion in the early 1880s. But, given that there had previously been periods of serious economic depression, social distress alone does not satisfactorily account for the nature of the crofters' war. The agitation demonstrated many of the features of earlier Highland protests, notably the

27 T.M. Devine, *Clanship to crofters' war, the social transformation of the Scottish highlands* (Manchester, 1994), p. 218. 28 McFarland, *John Ferguson*, p. 138. 29 Devine, *Clanship*, pp 221–2. 30 Ibid., pp 219, 242. 31 McFarland, *John Ferguson*, pp 165–6. 32 Young, 'Working class and radical movements', p. 133. 33 Devine, *Clanship*, p. 61.

key involvement of women, the use of crude weapons, and the confinement of the disturbances to specific localities. However, there is evidence of an attitudinal change which facilitated a more aggressive form of protest. Murdoch had remarked on a passive disposition among many crofters in the 1870s. Yet by the 1880s there was a greater sense of defiance, as reflected in the Gaelic poetry of that decade. In accounting for the change in Highland temperament, Devine suggests that the younger generation, accustomed to the relative prosperity of the 1860s and 1870s, and unfamiliar with the hardships of the famine years, was not subject to the fatalism which characterized earlier attitudes and was therefore more confident and assertive.[34] The generational factor has also been advanced in explaining the Irish land war.[35] In fact, the development of land politics in Ireland was a determinant in the crofters' war, notably the legalization of the '3fs' in the Land Law (Ireland) Act, 1881. The Irish agrarian campaign, and the legislation which it precipitated, was indeed detailed in the Highland press, particularly the *Highlander*. According to Devine, many Skye men had also become familiar with the situation in Ireland while working as labourers on Scottish fishing boats during seasonal work in Irish waters.[36]

During his tour in Scotland, Davitt acknowledged the moral basis of the new spirit of resistance in the Highlands. At Inverness he declared, '[...] this rebellion of sentiment is the inevitable herald of a moral force onslaught by public opinion upon the institution of landlordism in this country'.[37] Writing in the *New York Daily News* the day before this speech, he even referred to Skye as 'the Scotch Irishtown'.[38] He reported on the level of distress in the crofting community and noted that the audiences which he addressed in the various Scottish Lowland towns contained Highlanders who had been driven from their homes. Murdoch himself had drawn a parallel between the peasantry of Ireland and north-west Scotland during a visit to the United States in 1879–80 when he was attempting to raise funds for his paper which was in financial straits. Addressing a meeting at the Academy of Music, Philadelphia, in January 1880, he remarked on the analogous living conditions of Irish and Scottish

---

34 Ibid., pp 217–23. **35** J.S. Donnelly, *The land and the people*. Donnelly contends that tenants in the 1870s were determined to avoid suffering the fate of the Famine generation, and that the agrarian war was precipitated by an economic depression which frustrated a 'revolution in rising expectations', pp 249–52. The 'revolution of rising expectations' thesis has, however, been challenged in Irish historiography; see Clark, *Social origins*, pp 11–12; and Bew, *Land*, pp 30–1. Indeed, Devine also cautions against an overstatement of economic factors in the case of the Scottish Highland land war. **36** Devine, *Clanship*, p. 223. Devine's assertion has been challenged by Dr Andrew Newby, who has argued that there is no evidence of Scottish fishing labourers having become knowledgeable of the Irish agrarian situation during their time as maritime seasonal workers (Newby stated this case in a paper delivered at the Michael Davitt Centenary Conference, St Patrick's college, Dublin, 28 May 2006). **37** Davitt, *Land nationalization*, p. 24. **38** *New York Daily News*, 3 Nov. 1882, DP, TCD, MS 9602.

Highland tenants and alluded to a pan-Celtic dimension to their common struggle.[39] As Clive Dewey has shown, a cultural revival in the Celtic periphery from the mid-nineteenth century informed the thinking within agrarian movements in Ireland and Scotland in the 1870s and 1880s. It established the view that 'from time immemorial the whole Celtic race had enjoyed tenant rights such as those contemporary Irish and Scottish tenant leagues were demanding'.[40] At the Philadelphia venue, Murdoch shared the platform with Parnell and Dillon who were then touring American cities, mobilizing support for the Land League. At the request of Dr William Carroll of Clan na Gael, Murdoch had joined the Irish politicians as an auxiliary speaker in their series of public engagements. He was, however, later eliminated from the schedule due to Parnell's apparent concerns over additional expenses, much to the chagrin of Carroll.[41] Davitt did not cross paths with Murdoch during this tour,[42] but it was he who would ultimately come to work closely with Murdoch and identify with his pan-Celticism. Indeed, the tone of Davitt's language of resistance which he articulated in his speeches resonated with an older Irish tradition of counter-hegemony which has been treated in recent historiography by scholars investigating a rich and unusual variety of social documentation.[43]

Mounting support for the crofters, not least from certain Scottish Liberal MPs[44] and sections of the provincial press,[45] forced the government to establish a Royal Commission to inquire into crofters' grievances. The commission was convened in May 1883 at the Braes in Skye, under the chairmanship of Lord Napier. Davitt learned of the development while in Richmond jail, and was subsequently kept abreast of the proceedings by reports in Glasgow papers which were regularly sent to him by McGhee. In a prison letter to McGhee he expressed his dissatisfaction with the composition of the commission. Nevertheless, he was confident that it would focus widespread attention on landlordism and have a 'beneficial effect in moulding opinion upon the social problem'.[46] The establishment of a commission represented a change

---

39 James Hunter, 'The Gaelic connection: the highlands, Ireland and nationalism, 1873–1922', *SHR*, 54 (Oct. 1975), 179–80. **40** Clive Dewey, 'Gaelic agrarian legislation and the Celtic revival: historicist implications of Gladstone's Irish and Scottish Land Acts, 1870–1886', *Past & Present*, 64 (Aug. 1974), 43. **41** Hunter, 'The Gaelic connection', p. 180; see also Moody, *Davitt*, pp 358–59. **42** P. Harding, 'John Murdoch, Michael Davitt and the land question: a study in comparative Irish and Scottish history' (MLitt thesis, University of Aberdeen, 1994), p. 63. **43** See Breandán Ó Buachalla, 'From Jacobite to Jacobin' in Thomas Bartlett, et al. (eds), *1798: a bicentenary perspective* (Dublin, 2003). **44** Hunter, 'The politics of highland land reform', p. 49. **45** Devine, *Clanship*, p. 225. **46** Davitt to McGhee, 22 May, 1883, DP, TCD, MS 9328/178. Many of those who supported the crofters' cause were of the opinion that the Commission's composition favoured landlordism. Lord Napier himself was a landowner; Cameron of Locheil and Sir Kenneth MacKenzie of Gairloch both owned estates in the highlands; Charles Fraser-MacIntosh

in government policy on the crofting question and was an indication of the growing strength of a burgeoning crofter movement. In the Highlands, Davitt had declared,

> Whether it be agreeable to the landocracy of Scotland or not, there is, beyond question of doubt, a Scotch land movement in existence. It may not be organized [...] but there is in the popular mind of Scotland a revolt against the idea that the land of this country can continue to be administered in [*sic*] behalf of a privileged class, to the detriment of the Scotch nation.[47]

It was in his capacity as a freelance radical that he hoped to harness this popular sentiment. In fact, when he spoke in Aberdeen during his tour, he presented himself not as an Irish land agitator or even a Celt, but as an international social reformer.[48]

While Davitt strongly endorsed the campaign in the Highlands and contributed £150 to the crofters' cause, he did not spend any significant amount of time among the crofting community.[49] Most of his political activism in Scotland over the next few years was concentrated in southern towns and in mining districts in the west where there were significant numbers of Irish immigrants.[50] Some Scottish activists had been concerned by the degree to which Highland grievances were being represented by the Irish;[51] but, as James Hunter has observed, the crofters' movement that did emerge was 'a distinctively Highland creation'.[52] In March 1883 the Highland Land Law Reform Association (HLLRA) was founded in London. Its programme was broadly based on that of the Irish Land League in calling for 'fair rents, durability of tenure, and compensation for improvements', although it further demanded 'such an apportionment of the land as will promote the welfare of the people throughout the Highlands and Islands'. Its president was Donald H. MacFarlane, Parnellite MP for Co. Carlow, but a Higlander by birth. The Association's various vice-presidents included J.S. Blackie, an ardent Celticist and professor of Greek at the University of Edinburgh; Dr Roderick

---

had called for the inquiry and would himself be elected as a crofter MP in the 1885 general election, but he was a landlord in any case; and of the two Gaelic scholars on the Commission, Alexander Nicolson was sheriff of Kirkcudbright and the son of a Skye landowner, and Donald MacKinnon was a professor of Celtic at Edinburgh and a Conservative. See Hunter, 'The politics of highland land reform', p. 50, fn. 1.   **47** Davitt, *Land Nationalization*, pp 23–4.   **48** Ibid., p. 13.   **49** McFarland, *John Ferguson*, p. 157, note 82.   **50** J.D. Young, 'Changing images of American democracy and the Scottish labour movement', *International Review of Social History* 16:1 (1973), 81–2; J.D. Young, 'The Irish immigrants' contribution to Scottish socialism, 1888–1926', *Saothar*, 13 (1988), 90, 93.   **51** Hunter, 'The politics of highland land reform', pp 48–9.   **52** James Hunter, *The making of the crofting community* (Edinburgh, 1988), p. 160.

MacDonald and John McKay, both crofters' sons and leading figures in the Gaelic Society of London; Charles Fraser-MacIntosh, Liberal MP for Inverness and a notable Gaelic scholar; and the land reformer, Dr. G.B. Clark.[53]

Although the leading figures of the HLLRA were not crofters themselves, they were instrumental in establishing an effective popular agrarian movement in the Highlands which was representative of the crofting community. By the summer of 1884 the Association had a membership of around 5,000 crofters.[54] It has been argued that the organization constituted the first mass political party in Britain, 'a precursor of the British Labour Party'.[55] There is a certain validity in identifying the HLLRA as a forerunner of the Labour Party. However, a rich pedigree of working-class organization can be identified as far back as the London Corresponding Society in the 1790s.[56] It is important to note, moreover, that the HLLRA was not a leftist organization; among its leadership, only Clark had any socialist tendencies. It was, according to Hunter, 'more akin to the Irish parliamentary party of the 1880s and 1890s than to the early Labour party'.[57] In fact, almost a year after its formation, Davitt considered it appropriate to advise McGhee to 'Build up a Scotch Land League by all means – to be run by Scotchmen, of course'. He himself had already met a deputation of Welshmen in Chester to counsel them on a similar movement in Wales.[58]

The idea of a radical agrarian organization in Scotland resulted in the establishment of the Scottish Land Restoration League (SLRL) at the end of February 1884, a Georgeite body, with McGhee and McHugh as founding members, and Shaw Maxwell, Glasier and Murdoch in its executive. It proposed state ownership of the land, and George's visit to Glasgow was the occasion of its inauguration.[59] According to E.P. Thompson, the League 'at once became a more formidable force than its English associate'.[60] George had shown a keen interest in conditions in the Highlands during his first visit to Britain, and he continued to express the same level of interest in the crofting question when he returned in 1884.[61] Yet the radical Georgeite solution to the land problem was not embraced by the crofters' movement,[62] and land nationalization was rejected by the HLLRA as 'a delusion, an impossibility'.[63]

53 Hunter, 'The politics of highland land reform', pp 50–1. Despite MacFarlane's presidency, it has been claimed that the HLLRA was actually led by Clark, 'the natural chairman of the executive committee'; H.J. Hanham, 'The problem of highland discontent, 1880–1885', *RHST*, 5th series, 19 (1969), 42. 54 Hunter, 'The politics of highland land reform', p. 52. 55 D.W. Crowley, 'The crofters' party, 1885–1892', *SHR*, 35 (1956), 110. 56 E.P. Thompson, *The making of the English working class* (London, 1980), pp 22–3. 57 Hunter, 'The politics of highland land reform', p. 67. 58 Davitt to McGhee, Feb. 1884, DP, TCD, MS 9328 [180/11]. 59 Quoted in McFarland, *John Ferguson*, p. 168. 60 E.P. Thompson, *William Morris, romantic to revolutionary* (London, 1977), p. 351. 61 Hanham, 'The problem of highland discontent', p. 41. 62 Hunter, *The making*, p. 160. 63 Quoted in Hunter, 'The politics of highland land reform', p. 67.

Relations between the HLLRA and the SLRL were actually quite strained, the latter claiming that the policy of the Highland Association was 'a miserable, unscientific compromise' with landlordism.[64]

Davitt fully supported the SLRL, and when it fielded five candidates in western Scotland in the 1885 general election, he campaigned on its behalf.[65] Speaking at a land reform demonstration in Glasgow, along with Shaw Maxwell (SLRL candidate for the Hutchenstown and Blackfriars division of Glasgow) and William Forsyth (SLRL president and candidate for the Bridgeton division), he expressed a hope that his fellow countrymen in the city would vote for 'Land Restorers'.[66] And conscious of the opportunity provided by the recent extension of the franchise, he told an audience in Greenock two days later that it was preposterous to have a working-class constituency represented by 'a lord or a baronet or a bloated capitalist'.[67] He trusted that a democratic party would emerge in the next parliament. Given the connection made between land monopoly and industrial capitalism, the campaigns of the 'land restorationist' candidates whom Davitt endorsed were, indeed, highly significant in the early development of independent labour politics in Britain. By 1884 there was evidence of the influence of the SLRL on young trades council delegates in Glasgow, Aberdeen and Edinburgh, where resolutions advocating land nationalization were put forward, albeit unsuccessfully.[68] Davitt certainly recognized the extent of George's appeal. He noted in a diary entry in April 1884, 'Saw George off from Kingstown to America. Hope he comes back soon. English can only be revolutionized on social question and George is now a power in Gt. Britain by which the revolution can be helped along'.[69]

Georgeite propaganda had a particularly significant impact on militant miners' leaders in the west of Scotland. A key figure in the region was William Small, a former draper who assumed the position of general secretary of the Lanarkshire miners in 1882. Small distinguished himself as something of an authority on mining matters after spending much of his time in the British Museum researching old Scottish mining Acts.[70] In September 1884 he convened a meeting in Hamilton, which was attended by Shaw Maxwell, Glasier, Murdoch and young trade unionists such as the Belfast-born Robert Smillie, the future president of the Miners' Federation of Great Britain. Small had been in contact with Davitt, probably through the 'Scots-Irish' miners' leader, Andrew McCowie, and at the meeting he produced a letter from Davitt which

64 Quoted in Ibid., p. 67. **65** Moody, 'Davitt and British labour', p. 64. **66** *Glasgow Observer*, 24 Oct. 1885. In 1881, 13.7 per cent of the population of Blackfriars was Irish born, and in Bridgeton the figure was 13.9 per cent; see McFarland, *John Ferguson*, p. 187, note 40. **67** *Glasgow Observer*, 24 Oct. 1885. **68** Young, 'Working class and radical movements', p. 141. **69** Davitt's diary, 12 Apr. 1884, DP, TCD, MS 9541. **70** Robert Smillie, *My life for labour* (London, 1924), pp 41–2.

proposed the formation of a Miners' National Labour League in Scotland, to agitate for the nationalization of mineral royalties and for state insurance for miners.[71] Shaw Maxwell and Glasier attempted to have a branch of the SLRL set up at the meeting, but miners' representatives were determined to remain independent. Nevertheless, a decision was taken to form a Scottish Miners' Anti-Royalty and Labour League. This development, according to Young, 'signalled the beginning of the [Scottish] labour movement's revolt from the values of *laissez-faire* Liberalism'.[72]

Following the Hamilton meeting, Small appealed to other miners' leaders to join the anti-royalties campaign. He was supported by John Weir, the secretary of the Fife and Clackmannan Miners' Association.[73] The Fifeshire miners were particularly well organized in Scottish mining trade unionism and Weir was an influential figure.[74] He was not, however, able to secure the backing of his own executive committee. Yet Small's efforts were significantly aided by the fact that the campaign was endorsed by the Catholic clergy in Lanarkshire. Over the course of the next year he, Davitt and various Catholic priests toured the county's mining districts establishing branches of the Anti-Royalty and Labour League.[75] Small was a staunch socialist and a notable figure in Hyndman's SDF. In June 1885 he was instrumental in securing the passage of a resolution endorsing independent labour politics at a mass meeting of Lanarkshire miners.[76] But the majority of Scottish miners were not yet open to the idea of endorsing such a position. Keir Hardie, who was promoting the demands of the Scottish miners' unions through his journalism in the *Ardossan and Saltcoats Herald*, was vehemently opposed to Small's criticism of the Liberals and refused to back the anti-royalties agitation.[77] At this stage he was still firmly committed to advanced Liberalism and was largely unimpressed by Georgeite propaganda or by George's visits to Britain, even though he later dubiously claimed that *Progress and poverty* had led him 'into communism'.[78]

Small himself considered standing as an independent miners' candidate in Mid-Lanark in the 1885 general election.[79] Branches of the Irish National League in Scotland were becoming increasingly identified with radical and labour politics,[80] and Small addressed League meetings in the constituency, during which he referred to 'the sufferings of the working class in Ireland and

71 Young, 'Working class and radical movements', pp 137–40; see also Fred Reid, *Keir Hardie, the making of a socialist* (London, 1978), p. 80. 72 Young, 'Changing images', p. 82. 73 Ibid., p. 82. 74 Morgan, *Keir Hardie*, p. 16. 75 Young, 'The Irish immigrants' contribution', p. 93. 76 Young, 'Working class and radical movements', pp 143–50. 77 Reid, *Keir Hardie*, pp 82–3. 78 Quoted in Young, 'Changing images', p. 81. Morgan, *Kier Hardie*, p. 14, observes that nothing in Hardie's later career supports the assertion that he was strongly influenced by George at an early stage. 79 Reid, *Keir Hardie*, pp 81–2. 80 Keith Harding, 'The Irish issue in the British labour movement, 1900–1922' (PhD thesis, University of Sussex, 1983), p. 18.

Scotland at the hands of landlords'.[81] However, matters were complicated after Parnell's manifesto in November, in which he called on the Irish in Britain to vote against the Liberals. Small eventually decided against standing, but he gave his full backing to SLRL candidates.[82] Davitt himself was desperate to see electoral gains for 'land restorationists' in the general election. Amidst talk of a growing split between himself and Parnell, it was even reported that he was intending to field men of his own against Parnellites in at least twenty constituencies.[83] Parnell's manifesto certainly frustrated Davitt's radical policy and his hopes for the SLRL. Shaw Maxwell polled 1,158 votes,[84] but only about a dozen of those were from Irish electors.[85] In the wake of the election, the INL branch in Slamannan, near Falkirk, passed a resolution in which it 'deeply regret[ted] the action of the Executive in withdrawing the Irish vote from [...] Maxwell, the candidate for the Blackfriars division of Glasgow'. In the other constituencies in which SLRL men ran, Forsyth secured 978 votes; Morrison Davidson (Greenock) polled 65 votes; Wallace Greaves (Tradeston) polled 74 votes; and John Murdoch (Patrick) polled 74 votes.[86]

The 1885 general election was also contested by the HLLRA, with considerably greater success. Five 'crofter candidates' were fielded: D.H. MacFarlane (Argyll); Fraser-MacIntosh (Inverness-shire); Roderick MacDonald (Ross and Cromarty); G.B. Clark (Caithness); and Angus Sutherland (Sutherland).[87] All were successful, with the exception of Sutherland, although he later secured the seat in the 1886 general election.[88] The appearance of a 'crofters' party' in the house of commons in the new year firmly placed the Highland question on the political agenda, especially as the crofters were supported by Irish nationalist MPs. The Napier Commission had already produced its report in April 1884. It rejected demands for customary occupancy rights, arguing that there was no concrete historical basis upon which such concessions could be made. Instead it proposed as a solution the restoration of the traditional crofting township, to which control over a designated area of land would be transferred. The communal townships would also have the power to compulsorily purchase neighbouring private land. Napier's report was in marked contrast to that produced by the Bessborough Commission three years earlier which identified the Landlord and Tenant (Ireland) Act, 1870, as inadequate, and which recognized the entitlement of Irish tenants to full occupancy rights. As Dewey remarks, the Napier Commission deemed that the concession of tenant rights 'would be too violent a disruption of existing property rights'

81 Quoted in Young, 'Working class and radical movements', p. 155. **82** Reid, *Keir Hardie*, pp 81–2. **83** *Glasgow Observer*, 22 Aug. 1885. **84** Young, 'Working class and radical movements', p. 157. **85** Moody, 'Davitt and British labour', p. 64. **86** Young, 'Working class and radical movements', p. 157. **87** Hunter, 'The politics of highland land reform', p. 54. **88** Crowley, 'The crofters' party', pp 120–1.

because the Highlands 'had not yet reached an individualistic stage of development'.[89] G.B. Clark acknowledged that the report was more favourable to the crofters' cause than had been expected, but the crofting community in general found its recommendations unsatisfactory.[90]

Crofter delegates at the Napier Commission had argued in their submissions that there was an historic precedent for occupancy rights in the Highlands under an ancient Gaelic clan system. It was no coincidence, then, that Scottish Gaelic revivalists were involved in the Highland tenant agitation. In 1880 Professor Blackie, whom Davitt labelled 'a thorough Celt',[91] urged members of Gaelic societies in Scotland to engage in the 'well-marked sphere of action'.[92] Irish nationalist arguments for land reform were also reinforced by idealized references to an early communal clan society in Ireland under ancient laws. Ultimately, given what Dewey terms the 'historicist reaction' in the methodology of the social sciences from the 1870s,[93] together with the formidable character of the crofters' movement by 1886, Gladstone rejected Napier's proposals, and the Liberal government consequently introduced a bill which resulted in the Crofters Act in June 1886. This legislation, modelled on the Land Law (Ireland) Act, 1881, conceded the 'three fs' to virtually all crofters in north-west Scotland. This, of course, met most of the central demands of the HLLRA, but not all. In its passage through parliament, the bill had been opposed by the crofters' MPs. They argued that a fundamental shortcoming in the legislation was the failure to address the issue of land availability. There was also the matter of relief for the cottar class to which the legislative provisions hardly applied. Even before the bill had become law, a HLLRA meeting at Tiree passed a resolution advocating land seizures by cottars. The widespread dissatisfaction with the legislation and the reconstitution of the HLLRA as the Highland Land League in September, dedicated to restoring to the Highland people 'their inherent rights in their native soil',[94] opened up a new phase of the crofters' war.

Davitt must have been keenly observing the reaction to the Crofters Act. He had already turned his attention to agrarian agitation in Wales. In a diary entry in January 1886 he noted, 'Reports from Wales satisfactory. Movement for formation of land league going ahead'.[95] He had begun corresponding with W.J. Parry, champion of the Welsh quarrymen, by this stage.[96] The impact of the agricultural depression of the late 1870s had made the land question a significant factor in Wales during the 1880 general election, and the issue gained

---

89 Dewey, 'Gaelic agrarian legislation', pp 66–7. 90 Hunter, *The making*, p. 146. 91 Davitt, *The fall*, p. 229. 92 Quoted in Dewey, 'Gaelic agrarian legislation', p. 55. 93 Ibid., pp 48–9, 69–70. 94 Hunter, *The making*, pp 163–4. 95 Davitt's diary, 13 Jan. 1886, DP, TCD, MS 9545. 96 J. Graham Jones, 'Michael Davitt, David Lloyd George and T.E. Ellis: the Welsh experience, 1886', *WHR*, 18 (1996–7), 457–8.

even greater political currency in the subsequent years.[97] The land war in Ireland and the precedent set by the consequent Land Act (1881) naturally focused attention on the issue even further. Davitt himself was invited to address a meeting in Blaenau Ffestiniog in February 1886 where he spoke alongside David Lloyd George and the radical Welsh proponent of land nationalization, Michael Daniel Jones. During his short visit, Davitt also addressed audiences at Flint and Llandudno, during which he attacked land-lordism and proclaimed the universal benefits of land nationalization.[98] His intervention was generally resented in the Welsh press;[99] and older Welsh radical leaders, such as Thomas Gee, whose views were typical of the anti-Irish sentiment which was prevalent in Wales, opposed the visit. However, from the early 1880s the apparent similarities between social and political issues in Wales and Ireland gradually informed an attitudinal change, particularly among the younger generation of radicals. Indeed, the early students at the University College at Aberystwyth expressed a cultural affinity with the Irish and identified with the Young Ireland tradition in Irish nationalism.[1]

The invitation extended to Davitt to speak at Ffestiniog was, in itself, an indication of the new thinking within Welsh political circles. As Kenneth Morgan has noted, Davitt was invited because, unlike Parnell, he was the 'very personification of "widening the area of agitation" beyond Ireland'.[2] A leading figure in the emergent Welsh nationalist movement was the young radical, Tom Ellis, who was heavily influenced by the cultural nationalism of the Young Irelander, Thomas Davis. Ellis himself had been prominent among the students at Aberystwyth, whose ideas ultimately inspired the formation of *Cymru Fydd* ('Young Wales') in 1886. For Ellis, the emergence of a new Wales was dependent on a transformation of the existing agrarian system. In his view, the national question and the land question were inextricably linked.[3] Following the Ffestiniog meeting he made contact with Davitt, and in reply Davitt wrote, 'I have read your comments upon the Welsh land movement with great interest, and you appear to me to have grasped the real meaning of our Irish agitations of the last twenty five years'.[4] Ellis was a close associate of the young Lloyd George. Both were of the same generation of radicals, although there were significant differences in their political outlooks. Ellis's nationalism contained a more cultural, even spiritual, strain; and on the question of Irish home

97 Kenneth O. Morgan, *Wales in British politics, 1868–1922* (Cardiff, 1970), pp 57–8. **98** Davitt spoke at Flint on 11 Feb. at Blaenau Ffestiniog on 12, and at Llandudno on 13; see Morgan, *Wales*, p. 70; also Jones, 'Michael Davitt', pp 460, 470. **99** Jones, 'Michael Davitt', p. 459.**1** Morgan, *Wales*, pp 69–70. **2** Ibid., pp 70, 104–5. **3** Kenneth O. Morgan, 'Tom Ellis versus Lloyd George: the fractured consciousness of *fin-de-siècle* Wales', in Geraint H. Jenkins and J. Beverley Smith (eds), *Politics and society in Wales, 1840–1922: essays in honour of Ieuan Gwynedd Jones* (Cardiff, 1988), p. 103. **4** Davitt to Tom Ellis, 1 Mar. 1886, DRD, NLW, MS 63.

rule, Ellis was a staunch advocate of the Irish demand, whereas Lloyd George came close to aligning himself with Chamberlain in the Liberal Party split in 1886. Nevertheless, the young Lloyd George considered Davitt his 'most admired character in real life'.[5] On the platform at Ffestiniog he did not commit himself to land nationalization,[6] but, according to Morgan, he was more amenable to Georgeite thinking 'than Ellis could ever be'.[7]

The intensification of the agricultural crisis in Wales led to an upsurge in rural protest. In northern counties, grievances such as high rents became associated with the much older issue of tithes. In June 1886 Gee, who established a land league and who was the leading figure in the anti-tithe movement, drew together a meeting of tenant farmers at Rhyl in North Wales. At this meeting a policy was drawn up which included proposals for a land court based on the Irish example and a compulsory reduction of rental by fifty per cent. At another meeting at Denbigh several months later, at which Gee and Ellis spoke, a land bill was drafted along the lines of the Irish Land Act (1881). A tithe war had by now flared up. 'Anti-tithe leagues' were formed throughout Wales, and in 1887 they combined with Gee's land league in demanding a tithe reduction of up to twenty-five per cent. The Liberal MP, Stuart Rendel, who had been elected to Montgomeryshire in 1880, had always distanced himself from agrarian agitation. He had serious misgivings about the anti-tithe campaign and was determined to negate any comparison with Ireland. Ellis, however, revelled in the analogy. He and other combative young radicals viewed the unrest in Wales as 'a form of awakening'. As the situation grew worse in May 1887, Lloyd George inquired of Ellis, 'Do not you think this tithe business is an excellent lever wherewith to raise the spirit of the people?'[8]

At this point, the ubiquitous Davitt had embarked on his second Scottish tour, during which he spent a fortnight in the Highlands.[9] This expedition owed a great deal to Ferguson's efforts to build upon the opposition to the Crofters Act and, through a series of campaigns, to draw a parallel between Scottish and Irish issues.[10] Gladstone's endorsement of Irish home rule, and the Irish nationalist parliamentarians' solidarity with the crofter MPs, had already led the HLLRA to openly back self-government for Ireland during the home rule crisis in the summer of 1886.[11] Demands for home rule for Scotland had also begun to emanate from some crofters' meetings, and before

5 Morgan, 'Tom Ellis versus Lloyd George', pp 102, 104, fn. 35. As MPs, Davitt and Lloyd George both sat on a Select Committee on pensions in 1899; see DP, TCD, MS 9417/1958. 6 John Grigg, *The young Lloyd George* (London, 1973), pp 51–2. 7 Morgan, 'Tom Ellis versus Lloyd George', p. 104. 8 Quoted in Morgan, *Wales*, pp 85–6, 94–5. 9 Davitt's second Highland tour took place between 23 Apr. and 9 May 1887. He attended meetings at Wick, Helmsdale, Dornoch, Bonar Bridge, Invergordon, Dingwall, Stromeferry, Portree and Uig on the island of Skye, and Stornoway on the island of Lewis. 10 McFarland, *John Ferguson*, pp 194–5. 11 Hunter, 'The politics of highland land reform', p. 57.

the end of the year a Scottish Home Rule Association was formed.[12] As Davitt proceeded through the Highlands at the end of April 1887, Ferguson wrote a letter to the *Irish World* in which he celebrated 'how side by side Scotland and Ireland are now in the fight for Home Rule and land reform'. This, he declared, 'is the touch of democratic nature which I so often told them in the old times would one day make the British and Irish democracy kin [*sic*]'. Referring to Highland land agitation and resistance to coercion in Ireland in the same context, he appealed to 'the Irish, Scotch and German reformers of America' for financial contributions to the Crofter's Aid Committee. This body had originally been formed in Glasgow as a crofters' support organization, but it was now being adapted to serve an electoral function. Ferguson presented 'Davitt's idea' that, sufficiently funded, such an organization could be used to 'clear Scotland of her "Unionist" members' in the next election.[13]

The home rule crisis, as John Morley noted, heralded 'the withdrawal from the liberal party of the aristocratic element'[*sic*].[14] In the few years after the crisis, the crofters' movement, formerly independent of mainstream party politics, gradually became more closely aligned with Gladstonian Liberalism.[15] Davitt's formal invitation to the Highlands came, indeed, from several branches of the Highland Land League which passed resolutions inviting him 'with a view to checkmating Mr [Joseph] Chamberlain', who was then also touring the region, accompanied by his close friend and Liberal Unionist colleague, Jesse Collings.[16] Land reform had been a central plank of Chamberlain's 'unauthorized programme', and while propagating his Radical agenda in the autumn of 1885 – during which he spent a week in Scotland in September – he advocated peasant ownership on the basis of small landholdings, a policy summed up under the slogan 'Three acres and a cow'.[17] He had shown a keen interest in the crofting question. Yet, by 1887 the political landscape had changed significantly, and, given that the new Conservative administration had adopted a policy of coercion in the Highlands,[18] Davitt was determined to capitalize on Chamberlain's association with 'Tory coercionists'.[19]

Davitt was accompanied on his tour by Angus Sutherland, and on each leg of the journey he took the opportunity to attack the Chamberlain mission. Addressing a meeting at Helmsdale, he remarked, 'When Mr. Chamberlain visited the Highlands in 1885, he brought with him his unauthorized programme of "three acres and a cow" [...] On the occasion of his present tour, he has not even offered you a cow'.[20] Actually, during a visit to the township

12 Hunter, 'The Gaelic connection', p. 188. 13 *Glasgow Observer*, 14 May 1887. 14 Morley, *The life of Gladstone*, p. 293. 15 Hunter, 'The politics of highland land reform', pp 58–9. 16 *Oban Times*, 16 Apr. 1887. 17 Peter T. Marsh, *Joseph Chamberlain: entrepreneur in politics* (London, 1994), pp 203, 211–13. 18 Hunter, *The making*, pp 160–5. 19 *Oban Times*, 7 May 1887. 20 *Glasgow Observer*, 30 Apr. 1887.

of Babyle in Lewis, Chamberlain did express himself in favour of amending the Crofters Act to make more land available to the crofters.[21] However, Davitt, in the course of his own series of speaking engagements, ably exploited his rival's support for the Conservative government, making reference to coercion and to the Tory 'exterminating doctrine of emigration as a solution to the crofter difficulty'.[22] Davitt had significant appeal. Crofters in the Uists, Barra and areas of Skye even appealed to him to run as their candidate in the next general election. The sitting MP for Inverness-shire, Fraser-MacIntosh, had declared himself a Liberal Unionist during the 1886 general election, and it consequently became clear that he had no future in the Highland Land League, despite his protests that 'political bias' contravened the founding constitution of the HLLRA.[23]

Davitt, for his part, declined the invitation to stand as a candidate. Such a prospect was simply not feasible: it would have compromised his freedom as a freelance activist; and, in any case, there is no indication that he had, as yet, reconciled himself to the idea of taking a seat in the British parliament, and certainly not one representing a constituency outside Ireland. Moreover, as he told McGhee, he believed that the crofters in the west had 'neither the pluck nor the intelligence of the Crofters on the east coast'. They were, he noted, prepared to compromise at any cost and would 'take any one or any party up from whom they may get something'.[24] In his opinion, they had already been lost to Chamberlain and his Liberal Unionist pledges on land reform. Indeed, while the crofters, generally, were dissatisfied with the perceived shortcomings of the Crofters Act, they still sought individual occupancy rights, not state ownership of the land. During his second tour, Davitt urged Highland audiences to demand 'the land for the people', but he did not explicitly preach land nationalization as he had done in 1882. In criticizing the Crofters Act as 'practically valueless', he did declare his support for Napier's recommendation for the resurrection of the communal crofter township. At a demonstration at Uig Bay, Skye, he argued for new legislation to give effect to the proposals, especially by way of providing land for cottars.[25] But, as Dewey points out, the communal experience was alien to the contemporary crofting community: 'Whatever Celtic Revivalists might wish to believe, the "virus of systematic selfishness" had already done its work'.[26]

Davitt nevertheless continued to view the Highlands as an important arena in the conflict with landlordism and Toryism, and as the agrarian unrest continued, he returned to the region in July 1887.[27] The economic crisis in the

---

21 *Oban Times*, 30 Apr. 1887. **22** *Glasgow Observer*, 30 Apr. 1887. **23** Hunter, 'The politics of highland land reform', p. 58. **24** Davitt to McGhee, 1 and 3 May 1887; quoted in Máirtín Ó Catháin, 'Michael Davitt and Scotland', p. 24. **25** *Oban Times*, 7 May 1887. **26** Dewey, 'Gaelic agrarian legislation', p. 68. **27** *Oban Times*, 9 July 1887.

Highlands had deteriorated with a serious slump in the herring fishing industry, and, due to the sharp fall in non-agricultural earnings, the issue of land
availability became even more urgent, especially with the onset of winter in
1887. In Lewis, where the depression was felt most severely, crofters and cottars resorted to land raids. In November, the 80,000 acre deer forest at Park,
which had become a sporting reserve, was attacked over a period of three days,
the raiders killing over a hundred deer. The leaders were subsequently arrested and brought to Edinburgh for trial.[28] However, over the course of the next
year, raids and violent unrest continued. In January 1888 Davitt noted in his
diary, 'Movement in Lewis goes well'.[29] The following day he sent £25 to
Ferguson towards the legal defence of the leading Lewis raider, Donald
MacRae, and his co-defendants. He told Ferguson not to disclose the source
in case it might prejudice the crofters' case. The money had come from the
Western Islands Fund, but Davitt reasoned, 'Lewis it is true is not a Western
Irish Island, but it is a Western *Celtic* one, and I feel that subscribers will agree
with my so disposing of the above sum'.[30]

The Celtic periphery to which Davitt alluded figures centrally in the 'internal colonial' model adopted by Michael Hechter in his study of British national
development from the early sixteenth century. Hechter presents the classic 'underdevelopment' case in arguing that, despite formal acts of union, Wales, Scotland
and Ireland were not, in effect, integrated into the United Kingdom; rather, the
'Celtic fringe' was culturally denigrated and materially exploited by the metropolitan core, England. He argues that the economies of the peripheral regions
became specialized and highly commercialized in order to facilitate the expansion of the English market. This was reflected in agricultural practice and output, banking practices, and in the lack of English capital invested in the peripheral regions, other than those investments which promoted English industries.
Industrialization resulted in the development of railways, but, Hechter points
out, this followed a specific pattern in the Celtic regions: 'In most cases the rail
routes linked the productive centres of the periphery to England [...] Railway
extension was much less responsive to population density in Wales, Scotland and
Ireland than in England'. English hegemony was also reflected in the assimilation of English culture by indigenous elites (although Hechter acknowledges that
the gentry in Ireland were largely of English origin in any case).[31] In her more
recent work, Linda Colley observes that in the late eighteenth century, after the
loss of the American colonies, the 'Celtic elites' became more closely integrated
with their English counterparts, 'reinvigorating the power structure of the British
empire and forging a unified and genuinely British ruling class'.[32]

28 Hunter, *The making*, pp 170–5. 29 Davitt's diary, 13 Jan. 1888, DP, TCD, MS 9548. 30 See
ibid., 14 Jan. 1888. 31 Michael Hechter, *Internal colonialism: the Celtic fringe in British national
development, 1536–1966* (London, 1975), pp 81–95, 109–23, 149. 32 Colley, *Britons*, p. 166.

In Davitt's correspondence with Tom Ellis during the agrarian unrest in Wales in 1886, he commented that his recent visit to the principality had been 'but a manifestation of a sympathetic interest in the affairs of a people who are kindred to my own race'.[33] Expressions of pan-Celtic solidarity also featured prominently in his second Highland tour, during which he was labelled 'The tribune of the Celtic Race' by the *Glasgow Observer*.[34] He certainly linked metropolitan hegemony with the underdevelopment of the Celtic regions, especially Ireland and the Scottish Highlands. At Helmsdale he declared that 'it ought to be the ambition of every Celt [...] to war against that [landlord] system [...] which has been the fell instrument in England's hand for the extermination and enslavement of the Celtic race'.[35] Later, at Stromferry, he remarked, 'The exterminator's hand which has depopulated Ireland has also been busy with destruction here [in the Highlands]'.[36] And speaking at Wick, at the outset of his tour, he referred to the demand for Irish self-government in the context of the revolt of British 'colonies and dependencies'.[37]

It is significant that Davitt was most popular in Scotland. Yet, pan-Celticism notwithstanding, it is important to note that his intervention in both the Highlands and in Wales was ultimately part of that much broader scheme to forge an alliance between the democratic masses of Britain and Ireland. Marx had argued that the interests of the working class in Britain depended on a resolution of the Irish question, and he, too, called for such an alliance. According to Strauss, Davitt was 'the most important practical spokesman of this policy'.[38] Speaking at St James's Hall, London, in October 1883 for the English Land Reform Union, he delivered what he considered 'a sort of proletarian manifesto'.[39] Adopting the term 'proletariat' loosely to mean the 'masses', he said,

> The only economic use of the proletariat, according to some writers, is to provide riches and luxury for the superior class of mortals, supply data for the support of the Malthusian theory of population, and to occasionally become the object of aristocratic pity and charity [...] But the proletarian Sampson is beginning to discover that he has intelligence as well as brute qualities, and it will be well for the landlord and capitalist Philistines to recognize [...] in time, that justice is due to him.[40]

From his land nationalization campaign of 1882–3 and his subsequent involvement with William Small and others in organizing Lanarkshire miners, Davitt

---

33 Davitt to Ellis, 1 Mar. 1886, DRD, NLW, MS 63.   34 *Glasgow Observer*, 7 May 1887.   35 Ibid., 30 Apr. 1887.   36 Ibid., 7 May 1887.   37 Ibid., 30 Apr. 1887.   38 Strauss, *Irish nationalism*, p. 188.   39 Davitt to McGhee, 23 Oct. 1883, DP, TCD, MS 9328/[180/4].   40 DP, TCD, MS 9601/69. On the printed copy of Davitt's speech, he crossed out the term 'proletariat' and pencilled in the word 'masses'.

increasingly came into closer contact with trade unionists, radicals and socialists in Britain. He was one of the principal speakers at a huge labour demonstration in Hyde Park on Easter Monday, 11 April 1887, at which Gladstone,
George Bernard Shaw, John Burns, Edward Aveling and Elanor Marx also
spoke.[41] A few months after the Hyde Park rally he responded to an open letter in *Reynolds's Newspaper*, a weekly radical organ, which urged him to advance
the organization of unskilled workers, many of whom were Irish, by following the example set by the American Knights of Labor. Henry Pelling points
out that the late 1880s constituted 'one of the few periods when the state of
political organization of the working class as such in America could be regarded as more complete as that of the British workers'.[42] Davitt himself duly travelled to the United States in October where he addressed the General
Assembly of the Knights in Minneapolis, during which he stated that 'the
struggle between the classes and masses in Ireland was but a counterpart of
the battles which were being fought in the cause of industrial humanity in
every land under the sun'.[43]

Founded originally as a clandestine fraternal order in 1869, the Knights
of Labor had a broad social and political programme designed to represent
the interests of all 'toilers'.[44] According to Pelling, it was reminiscent of the
'grandiose schemes of trades unionism in Owen's day'.[45] From 1879 the Order,
as it was known, was led by Terence V. Powderly, a Pennsylvanian machinist
of Irish descent. Under his leadership the organization grew rapidly and by
1886 had a membership of over 700,000.[46] Branches of the Knights were organized in Britain in the early 1880s and gradually secured a hold in the
Midlands. Through Powderly, Davitt was enlisted to address a specially convened meeting in the West Midlands in May 1888 in an effort to expand the

41 Yvonne Kapp, *Elanor Marx, ii, the uncrowned years, 1884–1898* (London, 1976), p. 198. In her
account of this demonstration, Kapp claims that Davitt refused to meet Aveling because the latter was an atheist. Kapp's source is a letter from Engels to Paul Lafargue in Paris; *Friedrich
Engels/Paul et Laura Lafargue: correspondence* (Paris, 1956), pp 28–9. In it, Engels wrote, 'Le grand
anarchiste Kropotkine, avant-hier, a accepté l'hospitalite de la Soc[ial] Dem[ocratic] Federation,
il était avec eux et Davitt sur leur *waggonnette*. Très caractéristique: quelqu'un vou-lait amener
Davitt chez Aveling, mais D[avitt] dit: I cannot meet him, because he is an Atheist!' ('The great
anarchist Kropotkine, the day before yesterday, accepted the hospitality of the Soc[ial] Dem[ocrat-
ic] Federation. He was with them and Davitt in their wagon (lorry/carriage). This is very characteristic: someone wanted to bring Davitt to Aveling, but D[avitt] said: I cannot meet him,
because he is an Atheist!'). In fact, this would have been very much out of character for Davitt,
both in terms of principle and, indeed, political expediency. He had, after all, consistently backed
Bradlaugh's right to be admitted to parliament.   **42** Henry Pelling, *America and the British left:
from Bright to Bevan* (London, 1956), p. 63.   **43** Young, 'Changing images', p. 83.   **44** M.A. Jones,
The limits of liberty (New York, 1992), p. 311.   **45** Henry Pelling, 'The knights of labor in Britain,
1880–1901', *Economic History Review*, 2nd series, 6 (1956), p. 313.   **46** Jones, *The limits*, p. 311.

organization in Britain. He was made the first District Master Workman of D.A. (District Assembly) 208, an area in the West Midlands comprising five Local Assemblies with at least 670 members. The title 'Master Workman' was grandly bestowed on the president of each Assembly, and in D.A. 208 Davitt proved instrumental in promoting the organization among unskilled Irish workers in the Birmingham area. At the special meeting, at which McGhee was also present, he remarked that the Knights embraced every form of skilled labour and every kind of labour known in the 'civilized world, from the scavenger in the street to the author at his mental task; from the agricultural labourer to the scientist at his laboratory; from the chimney sweep to the skilled engineer'.[47] In Ireland, the Knights established two branches in Belfast and Derry in 1889.[48] Davitt addressed the latter in January 1890 and afterwards wrote that it augured well for the future of the labour cause in Ireland.[49]

In fact, the Knights had reached their zenith in Britain and Ireland in 1888–9. Their rapid demise thereafter was, in Pelling's view, hastened by their failure to find 'a *raison d'être* [...] comparable to that of the "new unions" which managed to survive the depression of the early 1890s'.[50] Davitt had been observing the development of 'new unionism' with interest and was in close contact with McGhee who by now had established himself as a leading organizer of dock labourers. When the National Union of Dock Labourers in Great Britain and Ireland (NUDL) was founded in Glasgow in February 1889, McGhee and McHugh assumed the positions of president and general secretary respectively. They were both chiefly responsible for the subsequent expansion of the NUDL which recruited large numbers of dockers in Liverpool and Birkenhead within months of its foundation. In 1890 the union had a membership of almost 25,000, roughly half of which was concentrated in the five Merseyside branches.[51] Writing from Paris, Davitt excitedly congratulated McGhee on this organisational exploit: 'By my soul, but McH and yourself are about to monopolize all the dockers in these countries [...] The poor capitalists in Liverpool are in for a bad time'.[52]

It was as a result of strike action at the Liverpool and Birkenhead docks in March 1890 that McGhee called on the services of Davitt by requesting that he mediate in a dispute between the NUDL and the Liverpool Employers' Labour Association (ELA). The strike had broken out somewhat haphazardly and the workers' demands had not been officially drawn up by the union: some members emphasized the issue of wages, while others were more concerned with the hours of night work and the time allocated to meal breaks.

---

47 Pelling, 'The knights', 31–2; *FJ*, 9 May 1888. **48** Pelling, 'The knights', 331. **49** Davitt's diary, 23 Jan. 1890, DP, TCD, MS 9553. **50** Pelling, 'The knights', 328–9. **51** Eric Taplin, *The dockers' union: a study of the national union of dock labourers, 1889–1922* (Leicester, 1985), pp 28–9. **52** Davitt to McGhee, 13 Oct. 1889, DP, TCD, MS 9328/[181/6].

Davitt had several meetings with the ELA, and at the end of March a settlement was reached which ended the three-week old strike. The terms of the strike settlement favoured the employers: although night work was limited to nine hours, those who did work longer were to be paid according to new wage terms; likewise, those who worked during the designated dinner hour from 12 noon to 1.00 p.m. were to receive two hours' pay. Other aspects of the settlement – weekly contracts, union recognition of non-union labour, and the NUDL's guarantee that it would recognize the neutrality of Liverpool ships in other port disputes which did not concern Liverpool employers and dock labourers – bolstered the ELA's position.[53] However, one fact was not lost on the employers: the NUDL had not been broken during the strike and McGhee and McHugh retained their standing among the dockers.

Davitt acted as a mediator in a number of industrial disputes in the spring of 1890. Less than a week before his involvement in the negotiations in Liverpool, he had been instrumental in ending a strike in Dublin which had been called by the Dublin United Builder's Labourers' Trade Union to secure a pay increase for its members.[54] And in April he intervened in the largest railway strike to have then taken place in Ireland. This followed the dismissal of two Cork workers by the Great Southern and Western Railway (GSWR) company.[55] The strike was called on 20 April and several days later it spread to Dublin. A strike committee, headed by William Foreman of the Amalgamated Society of Railway Servants (ASRS), announced the extended strike action as a protest against the dismissal of the two Cork employees, the alleged breach of agreement by the company in the matter of porters' wages, and the refusal of the company to recognize the union.[56] Signalmen also struck, thus bringing rail traffic to a halt. Before meeting with GSWR officials, Davitt attended a meeting of the railwaymen in Dublin, where he stated that he was intervening not only out of sympathy with the workers but in the public interests of the country.[57] At a subsequent demonstration in Phoenix Park he argued that the signalmen, who 'have duties and obligations to the travelling public far transcending those of any other branch of the railway service', had acted irresponsibly by leaving their boxes without adequate notice.[58] Nevertheless, he expressed general support for the men's claims and welcomed their willingness to submit their case to arbitration.[59] Archbishop William Walsh of Dublin, A. Galbraith, Fellow of Trinity College, Dublin, and Edward Harford, general secretary of the ASRS, formally represented the workers in arbitration with the railway directors, and after a week of strike action an agreement was reached on 2 May. The settlement represented a victory for the compa-

---

53 Taplin, *The dockers' union*, pp 37–8.   54 Lane, *The origins*, pp 166–7.   55 *FJ*, 26 Apr. 1890.
56 *FJ*, 25 Apr. 1890.   57 *FJ*, 26 Apr. 1890.   58 *FJ*, 28 Apr. 1890.   59 *FJ*, 25 and 28 Apr. 1890.

ny. The workers themselves were forced to acknowledge that the strike had been called without sufficient notice.[60]

Davitt was alert to the possibilities of radicalized trade unionism. The *Labour World*, of course, paid tribute to the progress of 'new unionism'; and in the context of the demands of the labour movement, it warned, 'The old programme is played out, and we are all growing heartily sick of mere wire-pulling and routine party politics'.[61] However, by this time Davitt had grave misgivings about the degree to which strike policy was being employed, especially in Ireland. In early 1891 he expressed his concerns to Michael McKeown, the Belfast organizer and vice-President of the NUDL.[62] McKeown led the dockers' union with McGhee and Mc Hugh and all three were collectively known as the 'three Macs'.[63] In Ireland the union had been moving south from Belfast from the end of 1889. By the middle of 1891 it was established in fifteen ports and had some 2,000 members.[64] McKeown asked Davitt to become involved in a strike in Sligo in February 1891. Dockers there had organized themselves into the Mutual Protection Association in March of the previous year and had demanded a wage increase of a penny in order to secure 'the docker's tanner', six pence an hour. Within months the dockers amalgamated with the NUDL and when McKeown visited Sligo he found the members hot-headed and belligerent.[65] Davitt was sympathetic to the dock labourers, but he informed McKeown that, besides not having the spare time, he believed that 'the strike policy had been carried too far in the three countries in the last six months'.[66] He suggested that strikes be suspended for a year or so to give time to build up the financial resources of the movement and reinforce its organization.

This is consistent with a *Labour World* editorial in October 1890, in which Davitt advocated a greater consolidation of labour organization in England than had yet been attempted.[67] However, his response to McKeown's request could also have had something to do with his attitude to the spread of British unions in Ireland, an issue which surfaced when he found himself in conflict with Dublin socialists in 1890. In March of that year Adolphus Shields of the Irish Socialist Union had asked him to assist in advancing 'new unionism' in Ireland. Shields had been in contact with him for some weeks and had been hoping to encourage him to launch a labour paper in Dublin. As the recently appointed Dublin district secretary of the National Union of Gasworkers and General Labourers of Great Britain and Ireland, Shields specifically requested that Davitt preside at a labour demonstration in Phoenix Park on 30 March. Davitt replied that he would not be in the country at that time.

60 *FJ*, 3 May 1890. 61 *LW*, 21 Sept. 1890. 62 Davitt to McKeown, 20 Feb. 1891, NLI, MS 18,563. 63 Taplin, *The dockers' union*, p. 45. 64 O'Connor, *A labour history of Ireland*, p. 48. 65 John Cunningham, *Labour in the west of Ireland* (Belfast, 1995), pp 17–8. 66 Davitt to McKeown, 20 Feb. 1891, NLI, MS 18,563. 67 *LW*, 4 Oct. 1890.

However, when it emerged that he was in fact due to be in Dublin on the day of the demonstration, a very public altercation flared up. After realizing that he was still being billed as the chairperson of the forthcoming meeting, Davitt wrote an open letter to Shields in the Dublin *Evening Telegraph*, in which he registered his qualms about speaking at the demonstration.[68] He stated, rather implausibly, that he knew little of the organizing union, the Gasworkers' Union. His real concerns became apparent, however, when he stated that,

> all Irish labour bodies should have the right to the unfettered man-
> agement of their own funds, and should not be compelled to resort to
> a strike or any similar action because it may seem expedient or neces-
> sary to men unacquainted with the peculiar economic conditions in
> Ireland to order a resort to such a proceeding in England or Scotland.[69]

When the Phoenix Park rally was finally held Davitt's position was chal-
lenged by Edward Aveling who highlighted the value of the collaboration between the Irish and British working classes. This blatantly ignored the fact that such collaboration was one of the central planks of Davitt's radicalism and a recurring theme in his speeches. In his own address at the rally, Shields criticized Davitt's absence from the demonstration and accused him of identify-
ing with labour in England, Scotland and Wales at the expense of the Irish working class.[70] In January 1890, only two months before this altercation, Davitt had noted in a diary entry that the cause of Irish labour must be advanced;[71] and it was later that month that he set up the IDTLF in Cork. In November he also involved himself in talks with John Martin and John Simmons of the Dublin Trades Council – of which Davitt himself was an honorary member – in which he mooted the notion of an all-Ireland trade union. J.W. Boyle has suggested that in advancing such an idea, Davitt was probably motivated by a wish to see Irish trade unions exerting an influence on the Irish Party similar to that which British unions had on the Liberals in the area of social reform.[72] Nevertheless, Shields had a point: there was a certain irony in the fact that Davitt should have expressed reservations about the role of British trade unionism in Ireland when he himself was more active in Britain; indeed, the *Labour World* was based in London.

Shields's remarks anticipated by some years Connolly's criticism that Davitt had surrendered himself to the control of British labour interests and had therefore abandoned the 'industrial proletariat' in Ireland. It was on that basis that Connolly described Davitt's later career as a 'failure'.[73] Of course, Davitt

---

68 *ET*, 29 Mar. 1890; cited in Lane, *The origins*, p. 167. **69** Quoted in ibid., pp 167–8. **70** Ibid., p. 168. **71** Davitt's diary, 2 Jan. 1890, DP, TCD, MS 9553. **72** J.W. Boyle, *The Irish labour move-ment in the nineteenth century* (Washington, 1988), pp 137–8, 144–5. **73** Connolly, editorial in

– who had, after all, attempted to unionize agricultural and town labourers in the south of Ireland – might very well have argued that Connolly's own activism ignored the plight of the rural working class. The only reference to agriculture in the programme of the Irish Socialist Republican Party (ISRP) in 1896 was a call for the establishment of agricultural machinery depots for the purpose of lending improved machinery to the agricultural population at a low cost.[74] Connolly later acknowledged, to some degree, the importance of 'fraternal' co-operation between town and country in *The re-conquest of Ireland* (1915).[75] Yet, as Lee has pointed out, he remained ultimately reluctant 'to acknowledge the existence of rural Ireland', and was largely unfamiliar with the ideas which Lenin and other orthodox Marxist thinkers were formulating on the role of the peasantry.[76]

The dispute between Davitt and the Dublin socialists certainly suggests that Davitt's misgivings about the role of British unions in Ireland may very well have dictated his response to McKeown. However, Frederick Engels believed that Davitt had overcome such reservations by 1891. Just over a week before Davitt's letter to McKeown, Engels wrote to Friedrich Sorge, explaining that Davitt had changed his position after learning from Irish gas workers that their union's 'constitution secures them perfectly free home rule'.[77] Davitt was indeed concerned with autonomy even within the wider context of 'new unionism'. When, in his *Labour World* editorial, he recommended the greater and more disciplined organization of labour, he stipulated that it should be a federation of labour, where '[E]very trade would have perfect autonomy, each union would be self-governing'.[78] He must also have been genuinely concerned about the level of organization in the Sligo situation. After all, not only was the NUDL strike in Sligo broken, but others in Derry, Waterford and Dundalk suffered a similar fate that year.[79] John Cunningham states that Davitt's note of caution was quite soundly based, considering that the 'new unions […] recruited widely and among people who had not previously been organized'.[80]

Yet in all of this, it must also be borne in mind that Davitt was no labour militant. When he referred to social revolution and to revolutionary programmes he often prefaced his remarks with the term 'constitutional',[81] an adjective consciously used to set himself apart from the extreme left. Moreover, he distrusted undisciplined militancy. This was evident in the land war. Indeed, even as a Fenian, his activities were more conspiratorial than confrontation-

the *Harp*, Aug. 1908. **74** Greaves, *The life and times of James Connolly*, p. 61. **75** Connolly, *The re-conquest of Ireland*, in *James Connolly, collected works*, vol. i (Dublin, 1972), pp 267–8. **76** Lee, *The modernization*, p. 151. **77** Engels to Sorge, 11 Feb. 1891, quoted in *Marx and Engels on Ireland* (London, 1971), p. 353. **78** *LW*, 4 Oct. 1890. **79** O'Connor, *A labour history of Ireland*, p. 48. **80** Cunningham, *Labour in the west*, p. 24. **81** Davitt's diary, 7 Jan. 1888, DP, TCD, MS 9548; and diary entry, 7 May 1893, DP, TCD, MS 9554.

al. In February 1888 he presided at a meeting in London to welcome John Burns and R.B. Cunninghame Graham after their discharge from Pentonville prison where they had been serving a sentence for their part in a demonstration at Trafalgar Square three months earlier. At the meeting Burns was in a rebellious mood. He called for a rallying cry like that which had been made 'in Paris a hundred years ago [...] Trafalgar Square [could become a] revolutionary square and let the Bastille be Pentonville Prison'.[82] Davitt was irked by the incendiary nature of the meeting, especially as he was trying to lay down a practical programme for organizing London. He confided in his diary:

> [programme] Won't be acted upon, of course. Too many leaders and too much [?] for steady, disciplined work. English people generally slow crowd to rouse, but Londoners are damn too clever to do anything but assert egotistical doctrines [...] The Irish are a generation ahead of these self-conceited Cockneys.[83]

Davitt did have genuine concerns about discipline within the labour movement. But despite these practical considerations, there was also a certain ambivalence in his outlook. More precisely, he harboured a deeper concern that the 'proletarian Sampson' might become unmanageable and ultimately prove destructive. His fears were shared by Ferguson who, during the rise of the new unions, warned, 'There is [...] a blinded Sampson in our midst who has his hands upon the pillars of our civilization, and who in some grim revel may bury us in his ruins'.[84] Davitt employed class rhetoric but did so loosely. As McFarland remarks with regard to Ferguson, 'The "bourgeoisie" and "proletariat" [...] became interwoven with "the democracy" in his rhetorical tapestry. Yet this was a linguistic shift rather than an ideological conversion'.[85] Essentially, Davitt advocated a 'golden mean between the extremes of individualism and communism'.[86] He drew a sharp distinction between class warfare and aggressive agitation, and it was in the context of the latter that he understood the work of the progressive labour movement. When he remarked on the need to place 'a proper revolutionary (constitutional) programme before the working masses of Great Britain', he made specific reference to Jeremy Bentham's maxim, 'Make the ruling powers uneasy'.[87]

He was, therefore, extremely cautious about the employment of strike action. This was reflected in his advocacy of arbitration. Others, however, questioned the efficacy of this policy. Following the Builder's Labourers' strike in Dublin in 1890, the socialist monthly, *Commonweal*, slighted Davitt by claim-

---

82 Quoted in D.C. Richter, *Riotous Victorians* (London, 1981), p. 156. 83 Davitt's diary, 18 Feb. 1888, DP, TCD, MS 9548. 84 Quoted in McFarland, *John Ferguson*, p. 207. 85 Ibid., p. 193. 86 Davitt, *Leaves*, vol. ii, p. 117. 87 Davitt's diary, 7 Jan. 1888, DP, TCD, MS 9548.

ing that the men had gained little in the settlement; 'in fact', it commented, 'many of them will lose 1s. 6d.' Incensed, Davitt wrote to the paper, asserting that the deal had given the labourers an increase on the wage they had previously received.[88] Even McGhee questioned Davitt's role in the settlement of the Railway Servants' strike. He apparently accused Davitt of having subordinated the interests of labour in order to prevent any disruption to Irish trade, which would inevitably have resulted from prolonged railway strike. In reply, Davitt made two valid points: the men had, by their own admission, contravened the rules of their own organization by going on strike without due notice; and, ultimately, they themselves voted to return to work by an overwhelming majority. However, clearly angered by the serious criticism levelled by his own 'Awacato del Diavolo', he stated unapologetically:

> Your tirade against 'Trade' ('the brazen faced harlot, liar and hypocrite') is in strong contrast with the language used towards it by George in his discussion with the Melbourne Protectionist: 'Trade without which we would be barbarians […] utter savages' etc. etc. – I incline to George's view and I am not prepared to sacrifice what little Trade the South of Ireland possesses for the sake of a few hundred Railway porters who are by no means the worst paid section of the workers of Ireland […] You seem to think that if I had put myself at the head of the men and fought for their demands, they could have won. You are wrong. But even were I assured that such would be the outcome of such lead I would not take it in [this?] instance. I shall advocate strikes when labour organizations are *Federated* and when, consequently, a strike will be short, sharp and decisive. Until then you will never get me to lead a strike […] Call this 'conciliation' and 'weak' and whatever you like. It is my policy and those who don't like it will never have it thrust upon them, I assure you. All they have got to do is not to invite me to come to their assistance.[89]

In truth, Davitt was much more comfortable with arbitration as a means of resolving industrial disputes. During his Australasian tour he was particularly impressed by the way in which many of the Labour parties of the respective colonies had come to manage such disputes. After visiting New South Wales he paid tribute the character of the Labour Party there. He remarked that the Party had actually created success out of the region's maritime strike of 1890, for the defeat of the strike 'opened wide the eyes of working men to the folly of neglecting political means for reaching better ends than the strike failed to obtain'. Significantly, he endorsed what appears to have been an early example of social partnership, whereby 'the Trade Unions co-operated with the victorious capitalists and their government allies, through the means of a commission, in an effort to find a way of settling trades disputes'. Out of these developments, he remarked, 'a peaceful revolution has been created in the Parliamentary politics of New South Wales'. He afforded a special commendation for the colony's Trades Disputes Conciliation and Arbitration Act of March 1892, which provided an 'object-lesson' in the value of advancing the amelioration of working conditions through parliamentary means. The Arbitration Act was, he noted, inadequate in that it was not compulsory and was limited in its operation to only four years. However, he pointed to the much more 'skilfully drawn' Industrial Conciliation and Arbitration Act (1894) of New Zealand which was both permanent and possessed 'the element of gentle compulsion'.[90]

Davitt clearly recognized the right of labour to organize itself independently. In his Portland writings he had underscored the need for a wider distribution of political power. In considering the nature of representation in the house of commons, he wrote,

> It appears that 168 members are directly interested in the Army and Navy; 282 represent land; 122 represent law; 18 liquor; 25 banks; 84 literature and science; 113 railways, including 21 chairmen, 6 deputy chairmen, 85 directors and one contractor; 155 members represent commerce, *and two represent labour*.[91]

To redress this imbalance he made the case for an independent labour party in Britain. It is significant that he was formulating these ideas at least a decade before the formation of the Independent Labour Party (ILP) in 1893. Actually, at the time of his incarceration in Portland, the same case was being made by Engels in a series of articles in the *Labour Standard*.[92] In *Leaves from a prison diary*, Davitt stated his belief that, with the cultivation of a strong labour press which would serve to educate the working class, it was possible to secure the 'return [of a] party fifty or sixty strong to the [...] Commons, instructed to act independently of political parties, and with a view to the interests of labour'. He contended, moreover, that such a development would act as a catalyst in encouraging parliamentary labour organization in other European nations. He even went further by arguing that political power, democratically exercised, would check British imperialist policy because a party representative of the common masses would not 'stifle the legitimate aspirations of other peoples'.[93]

---

90 Davitt, *Life and progress*, pp 219–23, 375. 91 Davitt, *Leaves*, vol. ii, pp 146–7. 92 A.L. Morton and G. Tate, *The British labour movement* (London, 1956), pp 162–3. 93 Davitt, *Leaves*, vol. ii,

Later, in the *Labour World*, he outlined the cost of putting fifty working-men into the house of commons. With a salary of £200 per annum, together with £300 each on election expenses, he estimated a total of £45,000 over a three-year period, which would be met if the workingmen of the UK contributed 6*d.* per head every three years. He was confident that this could be done, although he pointed out that such direct representation would only be realizable when internal jealousies were put aside and there existed a united movement with a single purpose, as had been demonstrated by the middle classes when they secured their claims in 1832.[94] Indeed, at this point he was of the view that an independent course would be precipitate. This was not merely an organizational consideration. Given that the prize of home rule was firmly on the political agenda owing to the Gladstonian endorsement, he felt a particularly pressing need to back lib-labism. From his own perspective as an Irish nationalist, a rupture with the Liberals was simply too great a price to pay. He believed that he did not now have the luxury of preaching his earlier recommendation that Labour should adopt as its motto, '"He has most friends who has least need of them"'.[95]

However, Keir Hardie, though an ardent supporter of Irish home rule, felt no such constraints. Following a clash with the Liberals over the candidature for Mid-Lanark in a by-election in March–April 1888, it was he who embraced Davitt's dictum and ran as an independent. Although still a Liberal when the Mid-Lanark seat was declared vacant, Hardie had become a notable advocate of direct labour representation. When he made a bid to stand as the official Liberal candidate in the constituency, its significance was apparent, for he was determined to contest the election in any event. He quickly won the support of Ferguson and the Glasgow-based Home Government Branch of the INL.[96] Ferguson considered the by-election an important opportunity for mainstream Liberalism to recognize the interests of labour. He called for '"fair play" in this effort of Labour in Scotland to obtain representation'.[97] Davitt, too, became involved. He attempted to secure Parnell's endorsement of Hardie's candidature and even lobbied the secretary of the National Liberal Federation, Frederick Schnadhorst.[98] Hardie had, by now, forced the matter by declaring himself an independent labour candidate. On 20 April Schnadhorst had a meeting with him in Glasgow in an effort to win his acquiescence with the offer of a Liberal seat in the next general election.[99] Parnell wrote to Davitt that day remarking that there now appeared to be some prospect of an end of the dispute.[1] The Irish leader was conscious of the importance of the labour vote, but, as Moody points out, he was 'still more anxious not to stampede the timid,

pp 152–61. **94** *LW*, 19 Oct. 1890. **95** Davitt, *Leaves*, vol. ii. p. 160. **96** Morgan, *Keir Hardie*, p. 27. **97** McFarland, *John Ferguson*, p. 199. **98** Moody, 'Davitt and British movement', p. 66. **99** Morgan, *Keir Hardie*, p. 30. **1** Parnell to Davitt, 20 Apr. 1888, DP, TCD, MS 9378/1076.

monied element in Gladstone's following'.[2] His hopes of a speedy resolution were misplaced, however, because Hardie rejected Schnadhorst's offer.

In the end, Hardie was heavily defeated in a three-cornered contest in which the Liberal candidate, Wynford Philipps, won comfortably.[3] Hardie had officially stood as an independent 'labour and home rule' candidate, but that was not enough to secure the support of the estimated 1,200 Irish voters in the constituency.[4] Ferguson was actually condemned for his part in the campaign by other branches of the INL and by the staunchly Catholic *Glasgow Observer*.[5] Writing in his column in the *Melbourne Advocate* on the eve of polling day, Davitt criticized the home rule press for attacking Hardie so bitterly over his independent stance. He warned, 'It will be remembered by Scotch working-men (who were home-rulers before Gladstone) that Irish MPs were sent from London to oppose the labour candidate'.[6] Still, he himself was conscious, more so that ever, that what was at stake in this dispute and in any others that might arise was the potential for 'a falling off in the Liberal vote' and a victory for coercion.[7] Moreover, he was deeply suspicious of the role of Henry Champion in Hardie's campaign. He suspected Champion, editor of the *Labour Elector*, of being a conduit for Tory subsidies designed to split the Liberal vote. Champion had been involved in the 'Tory Gold' scandal in 1885, in which Conservative money was used to finance two socialist candidates in London to the same end.[8] In Hardie's own campaign, Champion made a contribution of £300 under decidedly dubious circumstances.[9]

Ultimately, Davitt's support for Hardie in the Mid-Lanark contest was a principled stand rather than a departure from lib-labism. This was also the case with Ferguson. Even when the latter became an honorary vice-president of the Scottish Labour Party (SLP), which was created out of Hardie's Mid-Lanark support base within weeks of the by-election, he did not consider it a breach with radical Liberalism. His official position within the SLP did not even require his resignation from the Liberal Party. As McFarland comments, he hoped that the new party 'would function as a […] force *within* the Liberal bloc, shifting the parameters of debate, so that his agenda of land and social reform would become incorporated as a mainstream demand'.[10] There was also, of course, that underlying fear that a conflict between the 'proletariat' and 'bourgeoisie' would undermine 'the foundation of our social edifice'.[11] At the official opening meeting of the party in Glasgow in August, at which

2 Moody, 'Davitt and British labour', p. 66. 3 Morgan, *Keir Hardie*, p. 30. 4 McFarland, *John Ferguson*, pp 199–200. 5 Morgan, *Keir Hardie*, pp 28–9. 6 *Melbourne Advocate*, 26 Apr. 1888; cited in Moody, 'Davitt and the British labour movement', p. 67. 7 Davitt to McGhee, sometime in Mar. or Apr. 1888, DP, TCD, MS 9328/[181/4]. 8 Pelling, *Origins*, p. 40. 9 Morgan, *Keir Hardie*, p. 26. 10 McFarland, *John Ferguson*, pp 204–6. 11 Quoted in Morgan, *Keir Hardie*, pp 33–4.

Cunninghame Graham presided, a far-reaching radical programme was adopted. Yet it was not a distinctively socialist one. According to Morgan, land
reform was the principal issue which linked the various political elements within the party. Land nationalization was, indeed, a central plank of the programme.[12] Former Scottish Land Restoration Leaguers, notably Shaw
Maxwell, Bruce Glasier and Murdoch, as well as G.B. Clark of the Highland
Land League, were all significant figures in the new organization.[13] Despite
his defiant speech at the inaugural meeting, even Hardie himself did not recognize the development as a definitive split with Liberalism.[14]

Nevertheless, when Hardie and others who were actively pursuing inde-
pendent labour action later became more strident, Davitt's attitude hardened.
Besides, by the spring of 1892 he was defending lib-labism on the basis that
Gladstone's party was 'no longer entirely under the control of capitalist members. Its programme is also wider, more democratic and essentially more pro-
labour than heretofore'.[15] This was undoubtedly an allusion to the so-called
'Newcastle programme', outlined in October of the previous year while
Gladstone was speaking at the annual meeting of the National Liberal
Federation. It included various points relating to labour representation, electoral reform and a vague reference to the eight-hour day. It had proposals for
disestablishment in Scotland and Wales and ultimately affirmed a commitment to home rule for Ireland. It attracted considerable attention as the most
radical position adopted by the Liberals. Hardie acknowledged Gladstone's
cautious recognition of the principle of the eight-hour day, but he argued that
the 'programme' was still too limited on social policy.[16] In fact, Gladstone actually found some of the measures difficult to accept.[17] As H.C.G. Matthew has
noted, 'On questions of political economy, Gladstone remained [...] a mid-
century free-trade retrencher. The role of the state was that of an enabling
agent in a society self-regulated by thrift'.[18]

In the general election in July 1892 Hardie stood as a 'labour' candidate
in West Ham South and won the seat by a comfortable margin. In his campaign he had declared that he was committed to addressing social issues beyond
the narrow parameters of the 'Newcastle programme'. His own programme
in the election was, however, essentially lib-lab in nature, and his return had
more to do with the support which he received from local Liberals than with
the working class. But in the wake of his victory he turned his attention to
other contests which were still in progress and proceeded to castigate those
Liberal candidates who were opposed to the eight-hour day. He even urged
Liberal electors to vote for unionists in the constituencies in question.[19] Davitt

12 Ibid., pp 33–5. 13 Moody, 'Davitt and British labour', p. 67. 14 Morgan, *Keir Hardie*, p. 34.
15 *Melbourne Advocate*, 14 Apr. 1892, DP, TCD, MS 9613. 16 Morgan, *Keir Hardie*, p. 49. 17
Jenkins, *Gladstone*, p. 582. 18 Matthew, *Gladstone*, p. 321. 19 Morgan, *Keir Hardie*, p. 51–2.

was scathing in his response, especially when Hardie recommended the Conservative candidate, C.F. Hamond, in Newcastle-on-Tyne. Morley, one of the two Liberal candidates in the constituency, was known for his doctrinaire opposition to an eight-hour bill, and Cunninghame Graham in particular singled him out for rebuke on this count. Plans to ensure that Morley was not returned in the general election had actually been afoot for some months. At a number of meetings in September 1891, Hardie, Cunninghame Graham and John Burns had rallied opposition to his candidature. Their intervention at the time of the general election significantly reduced Morley's share of the vote, and he fell behind the Conservative candidate in the two-seat constituency, his Liberal colleague, Craig, receiving the least amount of votes.

In August, when Morley ran again in a by-election in the constituency, a prerequisite for assuming the position of chief secretary for Ireland under the new government, he was resolutely opposed once more by Hardie, Cunninghame Graham and by Champion. In the contest, he was sufficiently anxious about the socialists in Newcastle to enlist Davitt's support. The Irish were a robust electoral force in the area, and it is interesting that in his electoral addresses Morley equated the success of home rule with the interests of workingmen in practically the same language as that used by Davitt.[20] During the campaign, Davitt argued that the eight-hour question was simply a distraction. Writing in the *Melbourne Advocate* he emphasized that there were clear divisions among workers on the issue:

> The majority of coalminers are in favour [...] The textile workers are opposed, as a rule [...] while in both these great branches of British industry there is a marked difference of opinion as between a voluntary application of the eight hours principle [...] and a putative enforcement through the means of statutory enactment.[21]

Davitt was right; opinion among the workers was divided. But even though he thought that Hardie and his associates were acting in an utterly reprehensible manner, he cannot have been unaware that by highlighting the divided opinion among workers he himself was serving a point often tendentiously made by Morley to justify his flat refusal to countenance such a bill. Morley had, after all, publicly expressed grave concern over important aspects of the 'Newcastle programme' relating to state regulation of industry.[22] The following year, Davitt was forced to note in his diary that 'Morley [was] still stubborn' on the issue.[23]

20 D.A. Hamer, *John Morley, liberal intellectual in politics* (Oxford, 1968), pp 276–9. 21 *Melbourne Advocate*, 19 Aug. 1892, DP, TCD, MS 9613. 22 Morgan, *Keir Hardie*, p. 52. 23 Davitt's diary, 3 May 1893, DP, TCD, MS 9554.

Yet, for Davitt, the overriding factor was home rule, especially given the significance of Morley's official appointment in Ireland. Addressing an audience in Newcastle, he stated bluntly that a vote against Morley was essentially a vote for 'the enemies of Ireland'.[24] His role in the campaign, no doubt, had a significant impact on the successful outcome for the Liberals. Morley certainly thought so. Shortly after the contest he wrote thanking Davitt, 'the man to whom my friends say I owe most'.[25] Less than a week later he invited him to dine at the chief secretary's residence in the Phoenix Park.[26] Davitt declined the invitation on the grounds that he was not a 'society man' and, more seriously, because he believed that his presence at the chief secretary's lodge would have political ramifications.[27] T.W. Heyck has claimed that Davitt did attend a luncheon at Morley's residence in Dublin.[28] But that was clearly not the case on this occasion; and, indeed, it seems unlikely that he would have visited at any other time during Morley's chief secretaryship between 1892 and 1895. As Patrick Maume states, nationalist politicians avoided social contacts with British officials in Ireland because they were conscious of the potential political liabilities.[29]

In Davitt's case, he was concerned that his attendance at the chief secretary's lodge might compromise Morley's own standing with Parnellites, especially in Dublin. In the general election, the Parnellites held nine seats, of which three were in Dublin city and another in Dublin county.[30] The capital was, as Callanan states, 'the jewel the anti-Parnellite crown lacked'.[31] Davitt explained to Morley that emotions had been raw since the acrimonious North Kilkenny by-election of December 1890, and 'If [...] the Dublin Parnellites saw me going to the Lodge they might be induced to attack you over it in the papers'.[32] It was Davitt who had engineered the anti-Parnellite campaign in Kilkenny by organizing 'a sort of flying column [...] to dog Parnell's footsteps'. Scenes during the election actually became ugly and Davitt himself was physically assaulted.[33] It was understandable, then, that he should have considered it judicious to 'content myself with other channels of communication' with Morley,[34] although the chief secretary himself later managed to run foul of many Parnellites in Dublin city council by revealing his opposition to the amnesty cause.[35] But even beyond his concerns for the chief secretary's standing with nationalist Ireland, Davitt had other possible reasons for avoiding too close an

---

24 Quoted in Hamer, *John Morley*, p. 279. 25 Morley to Davitt, 6 Sept. 1892, DP, TCD, MS 9335/317. 26 Morley to Davitt, 12 Sept. 1892, DP, TCD, MS 9335/318. 27 Davitt to Morley, 13 Sept. 1892, DP, TCD, MS 9335/319. 28 T.W. Heyck, *The dimensions of British radicalism: the Irish case, 1874–95* (Chicago, 1974), p. 222. 29 Maume, *The long gestation*, p. 93. 30 O'Brien, *Parnell*, p. 315, fn. 2. 31 Callanan, *T.M. Healy*, p. 400. 32 Davitt to Morley, 13 Sept. 1892, DP, TCD, MS 9355/319. 33 Callanan, *The Parnell split*, p. 67. 34 As above, fn. 32. 35 McGee, *The IRB*, pp 25–6.

association with Morley. When the latter offered him a position on the Congested Districts Board in October 1892 he flatly refused it,[36] perhaps fearing the accusation of place-hunting, a charge which had threatened to damage or ruin the reputations of nationalist politicians since the 1850s when John Sadlier and William Keogh took posts in the Whig-Peelite administration.[37]

During the Newcastle by-election, Morley had informed Gladstone that the demand for the eight-hour day in the constituency was only 'a *drapeau* for a small clique of vanity and spite'.[38] Davit knew, however, that disillusionment with the Liberal Party was not a mood exclusive to a particular group of disaffected labour figures. Still, he had convinced himself that Hardie and others, who were now preparing to inaugurate the ILP,[39] were attempting to 'boss the Labour movement', and that they represented a direct threat to the prospect of Irish self-government.[40] Ferguson and McGhee were of the same opinion.[41] At this time, Davitt also found himself in conflict with the Fabians following an attack on Liberal social policy by Bernard Shaw and Sidney Webb. In an article written in defence of the government, and particularly in response to the Fabians assertion that they did 'not care a dump' about home rule, he highlighted progressive measures which had been introduced by the Liberal administration, such as the Railway Servants' Hours Act and the Employers' Liability bill, and rounded on the Fabians for what he considered their blatant political opportunism.[42] He was clearly single-minded in his commitment to the home rule cause and was therefore prepared to defend the Liberals on a number of fronts. However, his criticism of Hardie was particularly misguided, given that the latter actually voted in favour of the second home rule bill when it was introduced in the commons in September 1893.

In February 1894 Davitt himself was asked by local Liberals in Newcastle to stand in the constituency with Morley.[43] He 'refused for obvious reasons', jokingly assuring Dillon, 'I am not a Liberal yet'.[44] Moreover, he was of the view that labour had some claim to the second seat in Newcastle. This did not indicate a change in his opinion of Hardie and the ILP. He was still adamant that 'Hardie and Co' were 'secret enemies' of home rule.[45] And in response to the claims made by Fred Hammil of the ILP in an article in the *Fortnightly Review* that Irish nationalism was demanding that labour must 'Wait!', he argued that there was no inherent antagonism between labour and the home

36 Morley to Davitt, 25 Oct. 1892, DP, TCD, MS 9355/326. 37 Maume, *The long gestation*, pp 90–1. 38 Quoted in Hamer, *John Morley*, p. 279. 39 Morgan, *Keir Hardie*, pp 62–3. 40 Davitt to McGhee, 2 Sept. 1892, DP, TCD, MS 9521/5989. 41 Moody, 'Davitt and British labour', p. 72. 42 Davitt, 'Fabian fustian', *Nineteenth Century* (Dec. 1893), in King (ed.), *Michael Davitt*, vol. ii, pp 3–4. 43 Davitt's diary, 19 Feb. 1894, DP, TCD, MS 9555. 44 Undated letter from Davitt to John Dillon (sometime in Feb. 1894), DP, TCD, MS 9404/1625. 45 Davitt's diary, 11 Feb. 1894, DP, TCD, MS 9555.

rule cause, provided that 'labour' was not understood to mean the 'narrower interests [...] of a particular Socialist body'.[46] He now considered it impera-tive that the Liberals be encouraged to go farther along a progressive path – 'payment of members and election expenses; state ownership of minerals; municipalization of land; eight hours; taxation of land values; abolition of the House of Lords and kindred measures' – in order to neutralize what he per-ceived as the threat of the 'K. H. Party'.[47]

The bitterness between Davitt and the ILP intensified in the spring of 1894, notably during a second by-election in Mid-Lanark following the res-ignation of Wyford Philipps. When Davitt visited the constituency he endorsed the candidature of the Liberal, James Caldwell, despite the fact that Hardie had attempted to enlist his support for the independent labour candidate, Robert Smillie. Shortly before the poll, Davitt actually had a meeting with Smillie, whom he found most amiable,[48] and informed him that he had inter-vened in the contest on behalf of the Liberal interest because he had been advised by Ferguson that he (Smillie) had no hope of being returned, even with the full weight of the Irish vote behind him. Smillie confidently chal-lenged this forecast, and Davitt apparently ended the meeting by giving assur-ances of his support in any future contests.[49] He certainly viewed Smillie in a different light from Hardie. Several days after their meeting he noted in a diary entry, 'Smillie is an honest Home Ruler. Hardie is not'.[50] It was a curi-ous statement, given Hardie's support for the home rule bill only months ear-lier, and considering that Smillie was apparently sympathetic to Orangeism.[51] Ultimately, Caldwell was returned in the by-election and Smillie was left aggrieved by the involvement of the Irish nationalists, especially 'Glasgow's adroit wire-puller', Ferguson. In a few lines of verse, the *Labour Leader* lam-pooned both Ferguson and Davitt:

> Writes Johnnie av Benburb to Mick of Ballybrack,
> 'Yez might send us down a line to keep the bhoys on track;
> And if yez can cam o'er yourself, it may be just as well,
> For Hardie, Small and Smillie's like to damage dear
> Caldwell.[52]

Despite Davitt's preoccupation with home rule and the Liberal alliance, he nevertheless remained committed to the principles of the labour cause, even if it involved criticizing the Liberals, or indeed the Irish Party, as he did

---

46 Davitt, 'Home rule and labour representation', *Speaker*, 28 Apr. 1894. **47** As above fn. 45.
48 Davitt's diary, 3 Apr. 1894, DP, TCD, MS 9555. **49** Smillie, *My life*, pp 105–6. **50** Davitt's diary, 6 Apr. 1894, DP, TCD, MS 9555. **51** Young, 'Irish immigrants' contribution', p. 94. **52** Quoted in McFarland, *John Ferguson*, p. 255.

during a by-election in Sheffield in the summer of 1894 when the local Liberal Association rejected the nomination of a trade unionist, Charles Hobson.[53] It must be noted, however, that Davitt had not had the same personal experience of the British industrial system as some other notable labour figures, such as Hardie and Smillie, whose working lives directly shaped their politics. Admittedly, as a boy, Davitt had sustained an horrific injury in the cotton mill in Lancashire. But it was his consequent disability that removed him from the harsh life of Britain's industrial masses, and placed him in the much more favourable circumstances of attending the Wesleyan school in Haslingden, and later working in the printing-house of Henry Cockcroft. Hardie, on the other hand, had worked as a collier from the age of ten until he was twenty-three. As Morgan explains, 'The working-class world that he knew [...] was a miner's world, with its private, close-knit loyalties. It was the miners' cause that led him into trade union activity, into the movement for an eight-hour day [...]'[54] Similarly, Smillie began work in collieries while in his teens and remained in the mines into his twenties. His experiences in the pit made him 'look back with a shudder' in his later years.[55] Davitt's understanding of mining conditions was, therefore, not based on first hand knowledge. The same may even be said with regard to the land: gardening, one of his favourite occupations along with reading, was the closest he ever got to toiling the soil.[56] Writing decades after the land war, F.H. O'Donnell observed that the 'father of the Land League' had possessed no 'special knowledge whatever of Irish agriculture'.[57]

Davitt clearly had some sympathy with Smillie in the Mid-Lanark contest. However, he considered Hardie an egotistical demagogue. During the Newcastle by-election he wrote to McGhee, 'Lord if you were here to see Keir Hardie, you would be tempted to curse the political Gods or die or become a capitalist or a landlord'.[58] In the course of the by-election campaign he even accused Hardie of being in the pay of the Tories.[59] Hardie, of course, was not particularly impressed by Davitt either, especially since the O'Shea divorce scandal, and Davitt's remarks only served to compound their mutual antagonism. Morgan remarks that Hardie's attitude towards Morley during the Newcastle contest was entirely consistent with his long-standing position on the eight-hour question. It was, moreover, a 'completely logical' outcome of his estrangement from the Liberals since 1888.[60] Nevertheless, Hardie's decision to recommend a Conservative to voters was seriously misguided. It not only provoked Davitt but also incurred the criticism of Marxists. It was

53 Moody, 'Davitt and British labour', p. 72. **54** Morgan, *Keir Hardie*, p. 6. **55** Smillie, *My life*, p. 21. **56** See Davitt's diary, 15 Jan. 1888, DP, TCD, MS 9548. **57** O'Donnell, *The history*, vol. i, p. 366. **58** Davitt to McGhee, 7 Aug. 1888, DP, TCD, MS 9521/5988. **59** See Hardie, 'Michael Davitt', p. 416. **60** Morgan, *Keir Hardie*, pp 52–3.

from this time that Engels began to distrust Hardie. He even alleged that the *Labour Leader* was financed by Tory and anti-home rule elements.[61]

Davitt held that the position adopted by Hardie *vis-à-vis* the Liberals was 'crude and inexperienced' and the programme of the ILP impracticable.[62] Yet as Moody has shown, the enmity that existed between Davitt and Hardie up until the turn of the twentieth century was essentially driven by a mutual misunderstanding of each other's politics.[63] Hardie's position following the Mid-Lanark dispute in 1888 was actually quite an ambivalent one. It was, according to Morgan, a tentative move away from lib-labism, an 'uncertain lurch towards socialism [...] shot through with hesitations and contradictions'; in fact, his 'Liberal heritage never left him'.[64] Davitt's pronouncements on the ILP were perhaps an example of his misreading of Hardie, for, rather than being inflexible, the ILP was a broad coalition. Hardie himself later stated that although the party was dedicated to the interests of the working class, it had 'never had a hard and dry creed of membership'. Its aim was to 'blend the classes into one human family'.[65]

Davitt also believed that the ILP was doctrinaire on economic matters, that it was collectivist and utopian. That was enough in itself to convince him that Hardie's politics were fundamentally flawed. There was, he argued, 'a vast amount of difference between [...] a wise and practicable state and municipal joint stock socialism, and the proposal that all the means of production, distribution and exchange should be in the hands and under the absolute control of the government'.[66] After hearing the socialist, William Morris, speak for the first time at the Labour Day demonstration in Hyde Park in 1893, he noted in his diary, 'Speech incoherent. Plans utterly impracticable'. In Davitt's view, communism was predicated on the fallacy that human nature is essentially altruistic. Ultimately, then, the 'Socialist Commonwealth of Britain', which he viewed as the ideal of the ILP, would 'not materialize [...] as Mr Keir Hardie and his friends confidently predict as possible when the Socialist Party shall number one hundred members within the House of Commons'.[67] But in this, too, Davitt was mistaken in his assessment of Hardie. Morgan's study has shown that Hardie's socialism was never dominated by 'the one overriding objective of the public ownership of the means of production, distribution and exchange. Indeed [...] the long-term objective of a socialist commonwealth receded in importance. It was a symbol of faith, but not much more'. V.I. Lenin himself considered Hardie's 'revisionism' as contemptible as the outlook of the Mensheviks.[68]

---

61 Ibid., p. 71. 62 Davitt's draft lecture, 'Trend of the labour movement in Great Britain', intended for publication (written some time between 1893 and probably 1900), DP, TCD, MS 9526/6102. 63 Moody, 'Davitt and British labour', p. 72. 64 Morgan, *Keir Hardie*, pp 31–2. 65 Quoted in ibid., pp 212–13. 66 Davitt, 'Trend of the labour movement', DP, TCD, MS 9526/6102. 67 Davitt's diary, 7 May 1893, DP, TCD, MS 9554. 68 Morgan, *Keir Hardie*, p.

Some Irish nationalists had joined the ILP. For example, James Sexton, the trade unionist and former president of the INL branch in Newcastle, was one of the party's founding members.[69] Yet Davitt, for his part, believed that the Irish movement itself was 'an advanced as well as a home rule party',[70] and in the general election in 1892 he recommended seven labour-nationalist candidates to Irish constituencies.[71] In one of his articles in the *Melbourne Advocate* he celebrated the endorsement of 'Home Rule and Labour' candidates,[72] although he felt the need to write to Dillon on the same day expressing concerns about the potential for a poor response from the 'business people' in Waterford if the trade unionist, Eugene Crean, was fielded there.[73] Crean, as it happens, was returned in the general election, together with his fellow trade unionist, Michael Austin.[74] In April 1891, Austin had been appointed to the Royal Commission on Labour. This had caused some mixed feelings in Cork, where Austin was secretary of the Democratic Labour Federation. The President of the City United Trades' Association stated plainly that Austin had exaggerated the degree to which he represented the interests of workingmen in the south of Ireland. In wider political circles, Justin McCarthy challenged the government's failure to nominate Davitt to the Commission. Davitt certainly considered himself qualified, but he believed that the Conservative government had taken a 'purely political' decision in not selecting him.[75] The *Labour World* strongly protested against the exclusion.[76]

Of the labour-nationalist candidates fielded in the general election, four were returned: Crean and Austin; the Parnellite, William Field; and Davitt himself, after standing in North Meath. However, North Meath was one of the most bitterly fought contests between Parnellites and anti-Parnellites, and following a petition by the unsuccessful Parnellite candidate, Pierce Mahony, Davitt was unseated in December 1892 on the grounds of 'undue influence and intimidation [...] by and through [...] Roman Catholic clergymen'. Shortly before the election, the bishop of Meath, Thomas Nulty, who had formally nominated Davitt, issued a pastoral letter in which he urged the Catholic laity to vote for Davitt and his anti-Parnellite colleague, Patrick Fulham, who was running in South Meath. The pastoral address stated that Parnellism struck at the foundation of the Catholic faith, and warned that 'those who refuse to accept [this] deprive themselves of every rational ground or motive for believ-

216. **69** Wollaston, 'The Irish nationalist movement', p. 176. **70** Davitt's diary, 11 Feb. 1894, DP TCD, MS 9555. **71** O'Connor, *A labour history of Ireland*, p. 57. **72** *Melbourne Advocate*, 3 Dec. 1891, DP, TCD, MS 9613. **73** Davitt to Dillon, 3 Dec. 1891, DP, TCD, MS 9403/1567. **74** O'Connor, *A labour history of Ireland*, p. 57. Davitt later regretted having recommended Austin because he discovered in 1894 that he (Austin) was using his position as an MP to back a 'fraudulent' business venture; see Davitt's diary, 25 June 1894, DP, TCD, MS 9556. **75** *FJ*, 10 Apr. 1891. **76** *FJ*, 11 Apr. 1891; *LW*, 18 Apr. 1891.

ing in the truth of any of the other doctrines of their religion'.[77] When the election petition was finally about to come to trial, Davitt wrote to Dillon, acknowledging, 'The case against some priests is absolutely conclusive'.[78]

In January 1893 Davitt wrote an article in the *Nineteenth Century* entitled 'The priest in politics', in which he defended his position. He distanced himself from Bishop Nulty's pastoral and expressed his agreement with the decision reached by the judge who had tried the Meath petitions. But, while he insisted that the Irish clergy had no right to exert spiritual pressure to influence political opinion, he contended that the 'priesthood' nevertheless had a right to participate in 'political warfare'. He argued, moreover, that in successive popular movements during the nineteenth century, the priest was 'on the side of constitutional right, and an advocate of progressive reform'. He claimed, furthermore, that, 'nourished as they have been by the social democratic movement of the past twenty years in a wider political atmosphere', Irish priests were Christian socialists rather than adherents of political Ultramontanism.[79] Davitt's article, it must be stated, was directly aimed at his Tory and unionist critics who seized upon the Meath elections to bolster their case against home rule. But the issue of clerical interference also added to the questions raised by some on the left regarding the extent of Davitt's radicalism. Even as early as 1885 William Morris had queried whether Davitt would be 'as dangerous a rebel' once Irish self-government was obtained.[80] Connolly's later verdict was that from the time of the O'Shea divorce scandal, Davitt had 'fought with all his force and aggressiveness to establish the priesthood in full control of secular affairs in Ireland'.[81]

At the beginning of 1893 Davitt became an honorary secretary of the National Federation, the anti-Parnellite organization, although he was extremely reluctant to attend meetings of the Irish Party.[82] Dillon had been encouraging him to become more involved, especially given the increasing threat posed by Healy. In September, Davitt himself actually cautioned Dillon that Healy was 'paving the way for a "clerical" (a Healy) party at the next general election'.[83] It was in the context of the mounting political rivalries within nationalism, and owing to the fact that the Gladstone's government was about to introduce the second home rule bill in the house of commons, that Davitt decided to run for another parliamentary seat, this time in North-East

77 Quoted in C.J. Woods, 'The general election of 1892: the catholic clergy and the defeat of the Parnellites' in F.S.L. Lyons and R.A.J. Hawkins (eds), *Ireland under the union, varieties of tension: essays in Honour of T.W. Moody* (Oxford, 1980), p. 297.   78 Davitt to Dillon, 30 Nov. 1892, DP, TCD, MS 9403/1554–1570.   79 Davitt, 'The priest in politics', *Nineteenth Century*, 33 (Jan. 1893), 151–2.   80 Quoted in Lane, *The origins*, p. 116.   81 Connolly, editorial in the *Harp*, Aug. 1908.   82 Lyons, *The Irish parliamentary party, 1890–1910* (CT, 1975), pp 187–8.   83 Lyons, *John Dillon*, pp 152–3.

Cork, where a by-election had opened up. This was not without personal risk, for he told Dillon that Mahony and other Parnellites were threatening to hold the costs of the Meath petition 'over my head' if he decided to contest the seat.[84] This was a financial burden he could ill afford. In the end, he did stand in Cork in February 1893, and only several days after securing the seat he made his maiden speech in the commons, in which he defended the home rule bill. In his speech, which was later published as a pamphlet by the Liberal Publication Department, he referred to the bill as a compromise 'between absolute independence such as I once believed could be won for Ireland, and government by force and unconstitutional means on the other hand'. He declared that Protestant civil and religious liberties would be secure in a home rule Ireland, although he argued that 'Ulsteria' was part of a Tory strategy to thwart democracy. The underlying issue in the home rule debate was, he asserted, 'the question of the supremacy of the masses or the classes in the Constitutional government of these three islands'.[85]

Davitt's parliamentary career was, however, short-lived. After only three months he was declared bankrupt, a ruling which automatically disqualified him from sitting in parliament. This had come about after his failure to meet the costs of the Meath petition. He was, in any case, a reluctant parliamentarian. When, in May 1893, he noted in a diary entry, 'The constitutional revolution marches on', he meant it not simply in terms of the home rule cause but in the much wider context of the democratic agenda.[86] Shortly before his disqualification, he wrote, 'One good may result from it [bankruptcy] – I may escape from parliamentary penal servitude'.[87] Still, he paid dearly for his brief role in parliamentary politics. His bankruptcy cost him over £1,000, and at the end of the year he reflected, 'Neither the priests or the people of Meath who got me into this mess have offered to pay me one cent of the money which I have lost in this business'.[88] There were also political costs. In 1898 he reminded Dillon that he had 'all but alienated *almost all* my staunch American friends through entering the British parliament'.[89] Indeed, his decision to take his seat cannot have been arrived at lightly. After all, he was essentially still a republican. He had laboured over the idea of entering parliament for some time, and certainly ran it past McGhee.[90]

During his short time in Westminster, he was dogged by political enemies. At the time of the Meath election, and subsequently during the bankruptcy proceedings, he had had to endure a sustained attack from Devoy in America,

84 Davitt to Dillon, Jan. 1893, DP, TCD, MS 9404/1575. **85** *The settlement of the Irish question: a speech by Michael Davitt, MP* (London, 1893), in King (ed.), *Michael Davitt* vol. ii, pp 7, 20. **86** Davitt's diary, 7 May 1893, DP, TCD, MS 9554. **87** Ibid., 30 Mar. 1893 **88** Ibid., 31 Dec. 1893. **89** Davitt to Dillon, 29 Oct. 1898, DP, TCD, MS 9409/1766. **90** Ó Catháin, 'Michael Davitt and Scotland', p. 22, p. 25, fn. 23.

who was determined to sabotage his political career. Devoy actually accused him of having been partly responsible for the murder of a prominent Clan na Gael official, Dr Patrick Cronin, who was killed by Clansmen in Chicago in 1889 on the basis that he was a possible British agent, a suggestion once made by Davitt.[91] Davitt slammed Devoy's claims as 'diabolical falsehoods', and he considered it 'fortunate for [Devoy] and perhaps for me too that the Atlantic rolls between us just now'.[92] But there was an attack of a similar nature from another quarter. Only weeks before his disqualification, he had been referred to favourably by H.H. Asquith, the home secretary, in a speech in the commons on the home rule bill. Before Asquith had finished his remarks, in which he welcomed Davitt's support for the bill, Lord Cranbourne, on the opposite benches, muttered 'murderer' in relation to Davitt. This was a reference to the 'pen letter' and to Davitt's old conspiratorial days of the late 1860s. The following day Davitt wrote to Cranbourne, stating that he expected him to be in the commons after the weekend to take a question on the 'atrocious allegation which you made against me in the House last evening'.[93] Despite being outraged, Davitt ultimately let the matter drop, on the basis that the Speaker had directed Cranbourne to apologize to the house shortly after the slanderous remark had been made.[94]

Davitt was, no doubt, glad to be out of Westminster, but his bankruptcy had left him impecunious. Matters were not helped by the fact that in recent years he had found it difficult to settle down to the steady literary work from which he normally earned a living.[95] It was, therefore, largely as a result of these financial worries that he decided to embark on the tour of Australia. He also felt a particular need to provide for his wife and children whom he was hoping to move from the Land League cottage in Ballybrack – where the annual cost of maintenance was £200 – to the coast of Mayo.[96] His wife occasionally received some financial assistance from a wealthy aunt in California,[97] but it was clearly not enough to sustain the costs of living in Ballybrack. Davitt was naturally eager to embark on a tour for these reasons, but he was also troubled by the idea of having to exit the Irish political stage, given the growing antipathy between Dillon and Healy.[98] In September 1894 he wrote in his diary, 'There is absolutely no lengths to which this miserable little wretch [Healy] is not prepared to go in his game of splitting up the party'.[99] So concerned was he that his departure might 'wear the appearance of deserting the ranks' that he effectively sought Dillon's blessing before he made a final deci-

91 Golway, *Irish rebel*, pp 271–2; McGee, *The IRB*, pp 185–6. **92** Davitt to Sabina, 4 Jan. 1894, DP, TCD, MS 9325/97. **93** Davitt to Cranbourne, 15 Apr. 1893, DP, TCD, MS 9341/431. **94** DP, TCD, MS 9341/434. **95** Davitt's diary, 12 Aug. 1894, DP, TCD, MS 9556. **96** Ibid., 12 Aug. and 11 Nov. 1894. **97** Moody, *Davitt*, p. 552. **98** See Callanan, *T.M. Healy*, pp 422–7. **99** Davitt's diary, 3 Sept. 1894, DP, TCD, MS 9556.

sion to embark on a tour.[1] Dillon duly obliged, perhaps influenced to some extent by the fact that he himself had left Ireland ten years earlier during that other critical juncture when Davitt required his support in facing Parnell.[2] However, when Davitt left for the Antipodes in April 1895, he did not 'disappear out of history', as Lyons puts it in describing Dillon's departure;[3] despite learning of the tragic death of his young daughter, he engaged in fund-raising for the Irish Party in the course of his lecturing tour.[4]

In Australia, he was also able to examine more closely the reforming achievements of the respective Labour parties which he had acknowledged as an inspiration when he recommended labour-nationalist candidates for the 1892 general election.[5] In Brisbane, he had a meeting with the seventeen members of the Queensland parliamentary Labour Party with whom he had a friendly exchange of views. He found the members 'quite up to the best-informed of English trade union leaders, both in political education and in general knowledge of economic questions'. He observed that the Labour Party contained its share of utopian socialists, as distinct from what he termed 'the more numerous progressive section'. However, despite the potential for a 'coming cleavage' between the two elements, he acknowledged the importance of the Party as an independent entity:

> The present Opposition in Queensland is the Labour Party. What was the Opposition in pre-Labour times has all but vanished. It was, I believe, a nominal Liberal Party, with no special mission or aspiration beyond that of getting into office by votes of the working classes. It has practically ceased to exist since the Labour Party succeeded in capturing some twenty constituencies by its more distinct issues and policy.[6]

Davitt was honoured by the Australian trade union movement during his tour, and it is ironic that during his addresses he was most loudly cheered for his outline of the rising figures in British labour politics, notably Keir Hardie.[7]

Before leaving Ireland, Davitt had confidentially informed Dillon of the possibility of his running for parliament again at the next general election.[8] He detested the formal atmosphere at Westminster, but his commitment to Dillon and to the anti-Parnellite faction of the Irish Party probably determined his decision to accept the South Mayo seat to which he was elected in his absence in the general election in July 1895. Moreover, his observations

1 Davitt to Dillon, 16 Feb. 1895, DP, TCD, MS 9406/1693. 2 Davitt to Dillon, 22 Feb. 1895, DP, TCD, MS 9406/1695. 3 Lyons, *John Dillon*, p. 70. 4 On 15 July 1895 he cabled £1000 to Justin McCarthy; Davitt's diary/notebook, DP, TCD, MS 9562. 5 *Melbourne Advocate*, 3 Dec. 1891, DP, TCD, MS 9613. 6 Davitt, *Life and progress*, pp 252–3. 7 O'Farrell, *The Irish in Australia*, pp 232–3. 8 Davitt to Dillon, 22 Feb. 1895, DP, TCD, MS 9406/1695.

of parliamentary labour politics in the Australasian colonies may have given him an added sense of purpose in considering the prospect of re-entering parliament. It may even have played at least some part in his later *rapprochement* with Hardie. However, in the mid-1890s he was still highly critical of Hardie and considered him as unscrupulous as Healy. In the wake of the general election, he wrote to McGhee,

> What a pity that Redmond [...] Healy and [...] Hardie did not find themselves parties in the running of one parliamentary group. For monumental egoism and political cussedness, I question whether any other people can equal these products of Ireland and Scotland.[9]

Davitt was still focused on the prospects of Irish self-government via the Liberals, and this shaped his view of Hardie. In October 1896 he even cautioned Dillon against making support for the amnesty cause a condition of Liberal–nationalist co-operation. It would be a 'tactical blunder', he warned, '[...] the issue was not even a "test question" in Parnell's day; and ultimately amnesty would not be advanced by making it an issue in the election "over here", and it would set back the home rule agenda'.[10] Hardie, for his part, identified Davitt with Bradlaugh and Burns, whom he accused of having compromised their principles in order to work with the Liberals.[11]

During the Australian tour, Davitt found that the factionalism of the Irish movement was causing him some difficulties, notably in fund-raising.[12] Writing to Dillon from Sydney, he underscored the need for a re-union of the Irish Party. He outlined a plan in which James O'Kelly would assume the position of chairman of the Party with Dillon himself acting as vice-chairman.[13] Davitt argued that this would render Healy powerless, even though he might enjoy the support of a small number of priests. And, given that Kelly was 'Parnell's favourite lieutenant', Redmond's rejection of a reunion under these terms would be tantamount to political suicide. Ultimately, a united party would, Davitt insisted, not only renew the Liberal–nationalist alliance but 'spell unlimited financial support for our movement' in Australia and America. Yet when he returned to Ireland at the beginning of 1896, the conflict within the Party was even more evident. Healy had expressed himself indifferent to the defeat of the Liberals in the general election, and before the end of the

9 Davitt to McGhee, 30 Aug. 1895, DP, TCD, MS 9521/6001. 10 Davitt to Dillon, Oct. 1896, DP, TCD, MS 9407/1729. This did not stop Davitt himself agitating on the amnesty issue. He raised the question of remaining Irish political prisoners in the house of commons in Feb. 1897; see *Hansard*, 4th series, 46, col. 1138, 25 Feb. 1897. 11 Moody, 'Davitt and British labour', p. 73. 12 Davitt to McGhee, 30 Aug. 1895, DP, TCD, MS 9521/6001. 13 Davitt to Dillon, 23 Sept. 1895, DP, TCD, MS 6728/47.

year he was removed from the executive of the Irish National League of Great Britain and from the National Federation.[14] At a Party meeting in January 1897, Davitt made a proposal on Party discipline which was specifically designed to check Healy's activities. His resolution contained provisions which forbade members to publicly contest party decisions or to subscribe to a rival fund, the 'People's Rights Fund', which began with subscriptions which Healy had received from supporters, many of whom were priests.[15] Davitt's resolution was passed. However, Healy now led a small but formidable faction, which not only proved a drain on anti-Parnellite funds but also posed a constant political challenge.

Divisions in Ireland had a significant impact on the Irish movement in Britain. When Healy addressed an audience in Glasgow in the summer of 1897, violent scenes erupted between Dillonites and Healyites. According to McFarland, individual Scottish INLGB branches, including the 'John Ferguson', found it difficult to remain intact. Davitt was depressed by the whole political situation. He even found himself having to intervene in a bitter dispute in Glasgow between Ferguson and his other political ally, Charles Diamond. As manager of the *Glasgow Observer*, Diamond, who had given favourable coverage to Ferguson's work as a local councillor in Glasgow, had become distrustful of the latter's association with the ILP, and was generally concerned by the numbers of Catholic workers joining the Party.[16] Young comments that, as far as the workers were concerned, agitation for the nationalization of the means of production was only a logical extension of the demand for the nationalization of land and mineral royalties, that campaign which had been backed by the Catholic clergy in the west of Scotland in the mid-1880s. Yet, editorials in the *Glasgow Observer* argued that Catholicism and socialism were incompatible.[17] When the animosity between Diamond and Ferguson grew more heated at the beginning of 1898, Davitt asked Dillon to intervene. He told Dillon that the Glasgow dispute and the general state of political affairs made him 'feel very much tempted to "clear out" as you did in 1883'.[18]

However, he did not 'clear out'. With the resumption of his parliamentary career, he was now based in Battersea, London, where he and his family rented a house at 67 Park Road 'for three years at £45 a year' in March 1896.[19] In parliament, he worked on a number of social reform and political fronts. As a member of the Select Committee investigating the alleged non-observance of the Fair Wages Resolution, he kept in contact with E.L. Richardson, secretary of the Irish Trade Union Congress, to ensure that the Irish unions had

14 Callanan, *T.M. Healy*, p. 425. **15** Lyons, *The Irish parliamentary party*, pp 64–5. **16** McFarland, *John Ferguson*, p. 275. **17** Young, 'Working class and radical movements', pp 227–30. **18** Davitt to Dillon, 1 Feb. 1898, DP, TCD, MS 6728/91. **19** Davitt's diary, 26 Mar. 1896, DP, TCD, MS 9567.

the best opportunity to air their case against the particular government departments in Ireland which were most in breach of the spirit and terms of the Resolution.[20] Years later, after Davitt's death, Richardson wrote to Mrs Davitt acknowledging the role her husband had played as an MP in attempting to secure direct representation for the trades councils of Dublin, Belfast and Cork on the Board of Technical Instruction, which was then under consideration as part of what later became the Agricultural and Technical Instruction (Ireland) Act (1899).[21]

In his capacity as an MP, Davitt also became involved in the inspection of prisons, the issue in which he had maintained a keen interest since the time of his submission before the Kimberley Commission in the late 1870s, and on which he had written and lobbied. From the early 1880s he had argued that the existing classification, discipline and sentencing of prisoners only reflected a regime which was nothing more than a 'punishing machine [...] which mechanically reduces [prisoners] to a uniform level of disciplined brutes'.[22] He had visited prisons during his Australian tour,[23] and had also shown an interest in the conditions of prisoners in Honolulu during a brief visit there in December 1895.[24] Now, in 1898, he undertook a series of inspections of British prisons to 'see if statements about "great change" from the past to the present system was a reality'. During April, he visited Wormwood Scrubs and the prisons of Bedford, Birmingham and Bristol. He also made it his business to visit the more familiar Dartmoor and Portland. Generally, he found some significant changes for the better, in terms of diet, reduced frequency and severity of punishments, and, notably, in the segregation of first-time offenders, 'star-class men', from seasoned prisoners. After inspecting Dartmoor, he wrote in his diary, 'Today! What a contrast? [...] went down to where the boneshed was. It is no longer there. Has been swept away along with the prison cesspool'.[25] There was, however, still much that remained to be done, in his view, including an end to long periods of confinement in solitary after sentencing, corrugated iron-cells, and more exercise and further improvements in diet. In fact, some aspects of the diet and the accommodation of prisoners had changed for the worst.

Another Select Committee on which he sat during his time at Westminster was that set up in February 1899 to inquire into the question of old age pensions. It gave him the chance to highlight what he considered to be three of the main causes of poverty: the Poor Law, land monopoly and the liquor indus-

20 Davitt to Richardson, 22 and 30 June 1896, DP, TCD, MS 9375/106,108. 21 Richardson to Mrs Mary Davitt, 13 Sept. 1907, DP, TCD, MS 9375/1010. 22 Davitt, 'Criminal and prison reform', *Nineteenth Century* 36 (Dec. 1894), in King (ed.), *Michael Davitt*, vol. i, p. 15; Moody, *Davitt*, pp 211–20. 23 Davitt, *Life and progress*, pp 452–70. 24 DP, TCD, MS 9644. 25 'Notes on visits to prisons', 9 Apr. 1898, DP, TCD, MS 9571.

try. In his own paper which he submitted to the Committee, he proposed radical social welfare legislation, fundamental to which would be a 'thorough reform' of the existing Poor Law system. Workhouses, he proposed, would be replaced by 'Labour Hospitals' for the care of 'worn-out workers'. On this new statutory welfare model, a labour pension scheme would be instituted whereby pensions, administered by local authorities, would be advanced to claimants who could prove that their earnings as a worker had been impaired by age, feebleness, an industrial accident or the care of dependents. Half of the cost of this provision would come from local rates, specifically for pensions, and the other half, for the 'Labour Hospitals', would be chargeable to the imperial exchequer which would meet the cost through a tax upon land values and on the sale of intoxicating liquors. These specific interests would be subject to such a tax on the grounds that,

> a. [...] the existing system of class ownership of land has worked injuriously to the welfare of labour in the country and town; limiting opportunities of employment to workers in rural districts, through the operations of rent and of arbitrary tenure, adding thereby to the congestion of population in industrial centres, on the one hand, and to the unearned increment of ground-rent values in such places, on the other. And,
> b. That the consumption of intoxicating drinks by the industrial classes has been, and is likely to continue, a main contributory cause of that poverty, and an insidious hindrance in the way of more general efforts being made to provide for the necessities of labouring old age; the profits from these two great state-created monopolies being, therefore, fair and opportune sources from which to claim funds for Labour Hospitals for invalid workers.[26]

Outside Westminster, Davitt continued to involve himself in labour politics and agitation in Britain. A few months after he had informed Dillon that he felt like clearing out, he was in north Wales in support of the Penrhyn quarrymen who had been involved in a protracted dispute with Lord Penrhyn over wages and working conditions.[27] In September 1896 the workers had gone on strike when Penrhyn had suspended seventy-one men and refused to recognize the Quarrymen's Committee which was demanding a minimum wage of 4*s*. 6*d*. per day.[28] During the strike, Davitt was in contact with the leading

---

26 Davitt, 'Pensions for worn-out workers', DP, TCD, MS 9416[1939/17]. In 1908 legislation, pensions were advanced to the strictly deserving poor over the age of 70, and it was not until the Old Age Pensions Act of 1919 that the provisions were expanded; see Royle, *Modern Britain*, pp 201–5.   27 Davitt to D. R. Daniel, 4 May 1898, DRD, NLW, MS 954.   28 Morgan, *Wales*, pp 211–12.

spokesman of the workers, D.R. Daniel, a close friend of Tom Ellis.[29] Daniel distinguished himself as a skilled organizer during the dispute and played a large part in building a strike fund which eventually totalled over £19,000. Indeed, he became something of a national figure.[30] However, after eleven months, the strike could not be sustained and terms were ultimately agreed in which the Penrhyn quarries offered the Quarrymen's Committee minimal recognition but still refused to meet the workers' demands.[31] Discontent among the workers persisted, and it was in this context that Davitt attended a large demonstration of quarrymen at Bethesda (Bangor) in May 1898.[32] Some of those in the union, including Daniel, had wanted to continue the strike, despite the lack of funds.[33] Nevertheless, in October 1900 another strike was called after twenty-six workers were prosecuted following disorder in the quarry. The management of the quarry responded by locking out the men and a stalemate prevailed until the summer of 1903 when the strike ended, again with the workers failing to secure their demands.[34]

The Penrhyn quarry industry itself was also damaged in the dispute. During the lock-out, Lord Penrhyn had even alleged in a letter to the *The Times* (London) that Davitt had instigated the strike as part of a 'deliberately-planned scheme of Socialistic aggression'. He claimed that he had been informed by J. Gibson, editor of the *Cambrian News*, that Davitt had previously remarked that a decision had been taken by socialists to 'take possession of [...] the Penrhyn quarries, and to work it in the interest of the people'.[35] Davitt described the accusations as a 'miserable invention'.[36] He responded in a letter of reply to the *The Times*, in which he acknowledged that while addressing meetings in Wales in the mid-1880s he had certainly advocated the abolition of landlordism and the nationalization of mines and quarries; but he stated categorically that he had not been involved in any socialist organizations in Britain and had therefore not been in a position to launch such a plan.[37] The *Aberystwyth Observer* also cast doubt on the allegations.[38] Ultimately, in a damage-limitation exercise, Gibson himself was forced to retract the basis of the charges.[39] Daniel wrote to Davitt, congratulating him on the effective way in which he had dealt with the matter. He expressed a hope that the issue of the quarry dispute could be raised in the house of commons.[40] A couple of weeks later, Davitt wrote to Redmond, now chairman of the re-united Irish Party, requesting that he sup-

29 Davitt to Daniel, 8 Feb. 1898, DRD, NLW, MS. 951.   **30** K.W. Jones-Roberts, 'D.R. Daniel, 1859–1931', *Journal of the Merioneth Historical and Record Society* 5 (1965), 65.   **31** Grigg, *The young*, pp 213–14.   **32** See Davitt to Daniel, 4 May 1898, DRD, NLW, MS 954.   **33** Grigg, *The young*, p. 214.   **34** Jones-Roberts, 'D.R. Daniel', pp 67–8.   **35** *The Times*, 21 Mar. 1903, DP, TCD, MS 9395/1429–1440.   **36** Davitt to Daniel, 9 Apr. 1903, DRD, NLW, MS 957.   **37** *The Times*, 26 Mar. 1903.   **38** *Aberystwyth Observer*, 26 Mar. 1903.   **39** *The Times* (London), 1 Apr. 1903.   **40** Daniel to Davitt, 7 Apr. 1903, DP, TCD, MS 9395/1436.

port a motion against Lord Penrhyn. He impressed upon Redmond the dangers of alienating staunch Welsh home rulers and of identifying 'a progressive Irish Party with the worst possible kind of Welsh landlordism'.[41] Redmond clearly did not oblige, for in May, Davitt wrote to McGhee, 'Fancy Redmond and O'Brien refusing to vote on the Penrhyn motion'.[42]

By this stage, Davitt was on much better terms with Hardie. Despite all the years of enmity, relations between the two improved for a number of reasons by the turn of the century. Their shared pro-Boer sympathies in the second Anglo–Boer war had brought them closer, especially after Davitt's protest resignation from parliament.[43] Although the re-united Irish Party itself was supportive of the Boer cause, Davitt can only have taken note that Hardie's use of parliamentary time to raise issues surrounding the South African war[44] was in stark contrast to the lacklustre approach of some Irish members.[45] Moreover, from Davitt's point of view, the principle upon which the Labour Representation Committee (LRC) was formed in February 1900 was a much more pragmatic approach to independent labour politics. 'The object of the [founding] conference', Hardie later remarked, 'was not to discuss first principles but to endeavour to ascertain whether organizations representing different ideals could find an immediate and practical common ground'.[46] Hardie and the ILP had played a decisive role in the proceedings of the conference. While alliances along the lines of lib-labism were rejected, it was agreed that any prospective labour candidates would not be required to be socialists or even workingmen. Indeed, Morgan notes that '[t]he very concept of socialism never intruded itself on any of the new [LRC] platforms'.[47] In any case, Davitt had grown disenchanted with the Liberals. With the Lords' rejection of the second home rule bill in September 1893, the Liberal Party had begun to retreat from the home rule imperative. In the early months of 1894 Morley desperately appealed to Gladstone to remain as leader of the Party, but to no avail. When the Earl of Rosebery succeeded Gladstone as premier in March he declared that home rule could not be granted until it enjoyed the overwhelming support of the people of England, given that England was 'the predominant member of the Three Kingdoms'.[48]

But the real *rapprochement* between Davitt and Hardie came during the run-up to the 1906 general election. Hardie responded enthusiastically to an appeal made by Davitt in Glasgow in May 1905 for co-operation between Irish nationalists and the LRC in the forthcoming election.[49] He commend-

41 Davitt to Redmond, 9 Apr. 1903, JRP, NLI, MS 15,179. 42 Davitt to McGhee, May 1903, DP, TCD, MS 9521/6014. 43 Moody, 'Davitt and British labour', pp 73–4; Morgan, *Keir Hardie*, pp 107–8. 44 Morgan, *Keir Hardie*, p. 121. 45 For Davitt's criticism of such members see his letter to Alfred Webb, 30 Oct. 1899, DP, TCD, MS 9490/4953–4986. 46 Quoted in Morgan, *Keir Hardie*, p. 109. 47 Ibid., p. 110. 48 Hamer, *John Morley*, pp 297, 285–6. 49 Moody, 'Davitt

ed Davitt on his stance and requested that he work against any opposition that might come from the Irish Party towards Labour candidates.[50] It was expected that around eighty workingmen would stand in the election, and Hardie was ultimately anxious to forge an understanding with the Irish movement.[51] He considered it a significant development, therefore, when Redmond declared, during a rally in Glasgow in November, that, 'whenever possible', Irish electors should give a preference to Labour candidates over Liberals who had 'openly, defiantly, and insolently repudiated their pledges to the Irish'. A *Labour Leader* editorial warmly welcomed Redmond's pronouncements, but it took issue with his remarks that Liberal Party managers had a duty to facilitate the return of more Labour candidates in the election.[52] In fact, only two years previously, the LRC secretary, Ramsay MacDonald, had entered into a secret agreement with the Liberal chief whip, Herbert Gladstone, to secure up to thirty seats for LRC candidates in the next election. Hardie was also aware of this pact, but neither he nor MacDonald ultimately considered it a compromise of the independence of the LRC.[53] In December, Hardie wrote to Redmond, highlighting the advantages of a direct working arrangement between Labour and Irish nationalism. He noted that the only area on which they would probably diverge in the next parliament would be education, and in this he accepted that they would each go their own way.[54]

The education question was certainly one on which Davitt and Hardie were on common ground. They were both firm advocates of secular education, and, on that basis, each had opposed the Tory Education bill of 1902, which was framed with the intention of creating a national school system in England, and of protecting the position of denominational schools.[55] Davitt had reacted angrily to the efforts of members of the Catholic hierarchy in England, notably Cardinal Vaughan, to have the Irish Party represent the educational interests of the Catholic church. During the commons debates on the Education bill, Dillon had spoken in favour of denominational schooling.[56] Davitt was dismayed, not least because the Irish Party also passed a celebratory resolution marking the pope's jubilee:

> I really don't know where we are drifting [he protested in a letter to Dillon]. What with your own exertions for Vaughan and co., and the growing clerical treason against the national cause all over Ireland, and now the making of the Irish "national" party a Catholic party (for that

and British labour', p. 74. **50** Hardie to Davitt, 4 May 1905, DP, TCD, MS 9330/190. **51** Ibid. The *Labour Leader*, 8 Dec. 1905, listed seventy-seven labour candidates. **52** *Labour Leader*, 17 Nov. 1905. **53** Morgan, *Keir Hardie*, pp 131–2. **54** Hardie to Redmond, 26 Dec. 1905, DP, TCD, MS 9485/4776. **55** Morgan, *Keir Hardie*, p. 118, p. 136. **56** Lyons, *John Dillon*, p. 220.

is how the resolution will be understood everywhere) it begins to look as if we are drifting into a modern imitation of the historic "brass band". After all Irish people have done for the Catholic Church, it will be the cruel irony of fate to find England successfully strangling Irish National Freedom with a Catholic rope.[57]

Davitt did not agree with those whom he called 'Ultra-democrats', who were opposed to any kind of religious instruction in state schools. In his opinion, it was a difficult issue in a democracy; he himself had extolled the culture of learning which he encountered in Catholic schools in Australia.[58] However, while he was not against religious teaching, he was, as a matter of principle, opposed to state-subsidized religious instruction. Even during his time as an MP, he had made his position clear to Dillon. In 1896 he wrote to him on the question of Catholic universities:

> There are enough of Catholic colleges for the manufacture of British civil servants in Ireland at present. The question of a C. University can afford to wait [...] Moreover, I am no lover of universities, on principle. Those who can afford to go there are pretty able to look after their own educational requirements. With me one educational problem is the *workers*. Let the idlers fight their own battle.[59]

He only refrained from attacking the scheme at that time in order to avoid putting Dillon in a difficult position *vis-à-vis* his political enemies.

However, by 1906 Davitt's priorities had changed. Conscious of the political designs of the English Catholic hierarchy, which was calling on Catholics to vote against Liberal and Labour candidates because of their opposition to denominational schools, he adopted secular education as one of the central planks of his campaign during the general election.[60] In December 1905 he wrote to H. Mitchell, secretary of the General Federation of Trade Unions, requesting a full list of 'Labour and Socialist' candidates to whom he could lend his support. He expressed the view that 'Those [constituencies] in which the Irish vote is strong, and where the priests are counted upon as openly or semi-hostile, would [...] be the places for me to go'.[61] He was also determined to assist labour opposition to Liberal imperialist candidates. He urged MacDonald to put forward a candidate in Leith to stand against the staunch Roseberyite, Munroe Ferguson. Davitt and Hardie had already tried to per-

---

57 Davitt to Dillon, 1 Aug. 1902, DP, TCD, MS 9413/1901. 58 Davitt, *Life and progress*, pp 126–8. 59 Davitt to Dillon, Nov. 1896, DP, TCD, MS 9407/1733. 60 Moody, 'Davitt and British labour', p. 75. 61 Davitt to Mitchell, 19 Dec. 1905, LRCP, JRLUM, MS LRC 28/93.

suade Cunninghame Graham to run for the Leith seat, but the latter was unable to do so because of financial difficulties.[62] Ferguson was also involved in the concerted effort to find a suitable candidate for this contest.[63] Elsewhere, Davitt himself had been asked to stand as a Labour candidate in Mid-Lothian, the 'premier constituency in Scotland', where Rosebery's son, Lord Dalmeny, was standing.[64] He refused, however, on the grounds that he could not cover the election expenses and also because of his abiding aversion to the political culture at Westminster.[65]

Davitt became actively involved in the general election campaign at the beginning of December 1905 when he travelled to London to address a number of meetings. In Stepney he spoke on behalf of Will Thorne, secretary of the Gasworkers Union, who was standing in West Ham South; and in Battersea he endorsed the candidature of John Burns.[66] Burns had been criticized for his increasing alignment with the Liberals from the early 1890s and, latterly, for his acceptance of the position of president of the Local Government Board in the Liberal administration which was formed by Sir Henry Campbell-Bannerman at the end of 1905. Although Burns's opposition to the Boer war had won him praise in the ILP press during the Anglo–Boer conflict,[67] the *Labour Leader* now drew attention to the £2,000 annual salary which he would receive as a cabinet minister, and his £1,200 a year pension. It commented, 'John Burns, the "man of the red flag", the "working engineer", is now the Right Honourable John Burns, P.C., M.P.'.[68] On the far left, Burns was condemned by Hyndman, who warned Davitt, 'You do not and cannot know him as we [his former labour associates] do [...] I tell you[,] he has been Asquith's tool for many years'.[69] Years later Hyndman reflected, '[Davitt] never would believe what I told him about John Burns, for example – that he was merely a self-seeker, whose one object was to get well-paid office on one side or the other'.[70] Hyndman considered Davitt sympathetic to a fault. Yet when the latter engaged in a more intensive series of meetings on behalf of Labour on the eve of the election, he did so on the understanding that he would be free not only to support Burns and Henry Broadhurst but also Hyndman who represented that other extreme of the labour movement.[71] Hyndman certainly appreciated the support, as he acknowledged in correspondence with Davitt.[72]

62 Davitt to MacDonald, 28 Dec. 1905, LRCP, JRLUM, MS LRC 28/94; see also Hardie to Davitt, 28 Dec. 1905, DP, TCD, MS 9485/4777. **63** McFarland, *John Ferguson*, p. 318. **64** J.F. Paterson to Davitt, 25 Nov. 1905, DP, TCD, MS 9330/202. **65** McFarland, *John Ferguson*, pp 318–19. **66** Moody, 'Davitt and British labour', p. 74. **67** Morgan, *Keir Hardie*, p. 107. **68** *Labour Leader*, 15 Dec. 1905. **69** Hyndman to Davitt, 21 Dec. 1905, DP, TCD, MS 9330/198. **70** Hyndman, *Further reminiscences*, p. 51. **71** Hardie, 'Michael Davitt', p. 415. **72** Hyndman to Davitt, 28 Dec. 1905, DP, TCD, MS 9330/199.

From the early 1890s Burns had identified less with the unemployed, whose cause he had formerly championed, and gradually distanced himself from the broader concerns of independent socialism in favour of local social issues such as free meals in schools. Nevertheless, according to Chris Wrigley, 'in his liblabism, his brand of municipal socialism, his Battersea working-class particularism, Burns was very much in line with the working-class sentiment in the trade union branches and in Batteresa as a whole'.[73] Davitt, for his part, was committed to assisting the Burns campaign in the 1906 election. On 10 January, shortly before the poll, he issued a statement to Irish voters in Battersea urging them to vote for Burns on the basis of his record on the Irish question and on his work for 'the people's cause, Irish as well as British'. 'John Burns', he stated, 'remains John Burns although he has become a cabinet minister'. In particular, Davitt cautioned the Irish in the constituency

> not to be influenced or seduced in this contest by insidious English clerical advice to vote for the Tory candidate under the pretext of defending Catholic schools [...] The man who is prepared to do justice to Ireland will be guilty of no injustice to the schools of the Irish poor in England.[74]

The Education bill of 1902 had not applied to Ireland, but the possibility of future legislation on education under the Liberals led members of the Irish Catholic hierarchy to join with their counterparts in England in calling on Catholics to vote for the Tories. On 15 January, on the eve of the general election, the bishop of Limerick, Edward O'Dwyer, had a letter published in the *Freeman's Journal*, in which he argued that a prospective Liberal administration would ultimately seriously undermine Catholic education in England. There was also the fear, of course, that the Liberals would turn their attention towards educational reform in Ireland. A week later, Davitt responded with a letter of his own to the same paper. Challenging O'Dwyer's 'alarmist predictions', he made a case for secular education with separate provision for religious instruction by 'ordained instructors' from the different denominations. He pointed out that under a secular system of education in Australia and America, the 'Catholic faith [was] progressing by leaps and bounds'.[75] His views were of no great surprise to the Irish Catholic hierarchy. Indeed, just over a year earlier, he had published his article on an imagined future assembly in 1910, with state control of education having been secured with the electoral success of a radical democratic party.[76] His intervention against bishop

73 C. Wrigley, 'Liberals and the desire for working-class representatives in Battersea, 1886–1922', in Kenneth D. Brown (ed.), *Essays in anti-labour history: responses to the rise of labour in Britain* (London, 1974), pp 137–8, 154. **74** DP, TCD, MS 9420/2101–2195. **75** *FJ*, 22 Dec. 1906. **76** Davitt, 'The Irish national assembly', p. 297.

O'Dwyer was bitterly resented by many Catholics, including the archbishop of Dublin, William Walsh.[77] But even after the election, Davitt continued to challenge the church's position on the question. In one of a number of letters to the *Freeman's Journal* in February, he asked,

> In connection with this real or affected clerical antagonism to non-Catholic colleges, perhaps your correspondent will kindly inform me where the Lord Peter O'Brien's, the Judge Kenny's, the Sir Anthony McDonnell's [...] and a host of other shining Dublin Catholic lights were educated? Have their subscriptions or patronage for Church bazaars been scornfully refused because the donors had passed through the 'Protestant atmosphere' of Trinity or the 'Godless' classes and philosophy of the Queen's Colleges? [...] When have the 4,000 Catholic students who have passed through the Cork, Galway, and Belfast Colleges been admonished or condemned? Or, is it that the Episcopal boycott of these seats of learning is only intended for the children of the poor, and not for the boys of the 'nobility and ginthry' for whose family and 'station' so many of our eminent Churchmen have so preferential, and so deferential, an esteem?[78]

In the weeks leading up to the general election, Davitt had committed himself to a gruelling schedule of speaking engagements in England and Wales on behalf of Labour. He began his campaign on 3 January by addressing an audience in Birmingham in support of J.B. Glasier, the candidate for the Bordesley division, and his 'old friend and colleague' from the days of the land agitation in Scotland.[79] Two days later he delivered a speech in St Helen's where the Labour candidate, Thomas Glover, was standing against the Conservative, H. Seton-Karr. This was a straight contest between Labour and the Conservatives, courtesy of the deal made between Herbert Gladstone and MacDonald.[80] During his endorsement of Glover, Davitt spoke of the affinity which he believed existed between British labour and the home rule cause. And, referring to the need for strong labour representation, he remarked,

> You will never get old-age pensions, you will never get the extended franchise, you will not get the measures you are clamouring for, until you send enough men from your own class, who understand your social conditions; you will never get full justice until men from your own ranks are sent to Westminster.[81]

77 King, *Michael Davitt*, p. 77. **78** *FJ*, 6 Feb. 1906. **79** *Birmingham Daily Post*, 4 Jan. 1906. **80** Henry Pelling, *Social geography of British elections, 1885–1910* (Hampshire, 1994), p. 266. **81** *St Helen's Newspaper and Advertiser*, 9 Jan. 1906.

In all, Davitt addressed nineteen meetings in January,[82] in the course of which he gave his backing to other Labour candidates, such as John Robert Clynes and G.D. Kelley (Manchester), Walter Hudson (Newcastle), Fred Jowett (Bradford), and James O'Grady (Leeds).[83]

Towards the end of his tour, he visited Leicester, and in his sixteenth address in almost as many days, he spoke on behalf of Broadhurst and MacDonald. Acting under the influence of Herbert Gladstone following his pact with MacDonald, the Liberals had made a decision to put forward only one candidate in the two-seat constituency, the lib-lab, Broadhurst, who had sat there since 1894.[84] This ensured that there would be no split between the Liberals and Labour. Davitt, then, could comfortably recommend both candidates to Irish voters in the area, which he did. He was reported speaking alongside both men during his visit. In an effort to counter Conservative propaganda on home rule, he connected the demand for Irish self-government with the democratic agenda in Britain. Home rule, he declared, 'was not responsible for [...] unemployment; and [...] it had not filled [...] workhouses with a million of broken down English workers'.[85] He also reiterated the importance of working-class representation in parliament.

One of his final speeches in the election campaign, or indeed in any other such campaign, was delivered on behalf of Hardie in Merthyr Tydfil where there was a substantial Irish population. He joined Hardie on a platform where others speakers included local nonconformists and Annie Kenny of the women's suffrage movement. Hardie's election manifesto included the abolition of the house of lords, women's suffrage, old age pensions, a cut in expenditure on armaments, Welsh disestablishment, and general home rule, particularly for Ireland. In addition, he argued for the public ownership of key industries.[86] Hardie had maintained a keen interest in contesting a seat in Merthyr for some time. He, like Davitt, believed that the Welsh were predisposed to socialism.[87] Eager to secure the Irish vote for his erstwhile adversary, Davitt stated in his address that he had it from Redmond and Dillon that 'it was their desire that wherever a Labour candidate was standing, he was to get Irish support'.[88]

In fact, the Irish policy was much more qualified. It is true that in the pre-election manifesto which the Irish Party issued at the beginning of January, Irish electors were advised to vote for Labour. However, it was stated that exceptions should be made if Liberal candidates were 'old and tried friends of home rule', or if a vote for Labour ran the risk of returning a unionist.[89] It

---

82 Sheehy Skeffington, *Michael Davitt*, p. 195. **83** Moody, 'Davitt and British labour', p. 74. **84** Pelling, *Social geography*, p. 210. **85** *Leicester Daily Post*, 15 Jan. 1906. **86** Morgan, *Keir Hardie*, pp 150–1. **87** Morgan, *Wales*, p. 212. **88** *Merthyr Express*, 13 Jan. 1906. **89** Quoted in Wollaston, 'The Irish nationalist movement', p. 189.

must be noted that only two months earlier Redmond and T.P. O'Connor had had a meeting with Campbell-Bannerman to discuss home rule. Within days of their meeting, the Liberal leader made a speech in Stirling in which he announced that he aimed to secure a measure of Irish self-government 'consistent with and leading up to the larger policy'.[90] The ILP was deeply disappointed by the manifesto with which the Irish Party approached the general election. It was strongly criticized in the *Labour Leader* where it was viewed as

> a case of thank-you for nothing when we get down to details. In every case [the Irish League] ha[s] made the claims of the Labour candidate subordinate to the interests of Liberals or has only supported the Labour man because he was punishing some anti-Home Rule Liberal.[91]

The *Clarion* also found 'this continual solicitude for the interests of the Liberal Party [...] astounding'.[92] Indeed, the Irish policy resulted in a situation whereby Irish support was given to candidates from different parties in neighbouring divisions. For example, when Davitt was campaigning for Jowett in the West division of Bradford, Irish support was mobilized for the Liberal, Ald. Priestly, in the East.

Davitt himself was naturally more committed to Labour than any of the other Irish leaders. He had, in fact, opposed Irish Party policy before. For instance, during a by-election in Dewsbury in January 1902, he lent his support to Harry Quelch, the editor of the SDF organ, *Justice*. Shortly before the election, the *Dewsbury Reporter* published a letter from J.F.X. O'Brien endorsing the Liberal candidate, Runciman, who was a Roseberyite. Quelch, however, was able to use a letter of support which he had received from Davitt to bolster his campaign.[93] During the general election campaign, Davitt's speeches were, for the most part, consistent with the policy of the Irish Party. Yet a dispute arose over the three-cornered contest in Burnley where Hyndman was standing. Davitt had informed Redmond of his intention to speak in Burnley on Hyndman's behalf. He appealed to the Irish leader to ensure that T.P. O'Connor did not promise the Irish vote in the constituency to the Liberal, Fred Maddison.[94] It was with considerable surprise, then, that just a week later he learned that the executive of the United Irish League (UIL), the organization originally established by William O'Brien in 1898 but now largely under the control of the Irish Party, had passed a resolution endorsing Maddison's candidature. Davitt wrote to Redmond in protest, registering his determination to back Hyndman in any event. Not only had he made a

90 Lyons, *The Irish parliamentary party*, p. 113. 91 Quoted in Wollaston, 'The Irish nationalist movement', p. 190. 92 Quoted in ibid., p. 190. 93 Ibid., pp 188–9. 94 Davitt to Redmond, 28 Dec. 1905, JRP, NLI, MS 15,179.

promise to do so, but he considered the SDF leader a personal friend 'of 25 years standing'. By way of resolving the conflict of interests, he recommended that the Burnley branch of the UIL continue on its course of supporting Maddison while he would proceed to back Hyndman 'without referring to the local branch, or its action […] or to the manifesto either'. He warned, however, that if the executive publicly or privately issued a mandate for Maddison, he would consider it a refusal of his compromise and resign from the Party's directory and the UIL.[95]

Two days after his letter to Redmond, he accordingly addressed a meeting at the Gaiety Theatre in Burnley, where he spoke in support of Hyndman. He did not make any deprecating references to Maddison, but he noted that the Liberal had not been recommended by any of the labour or trade union bodies.[96] As with all his speeches during this campaign, he took the opportunity to advance the home rule cause. He also again touched on the education question and defended secular control of schools. He advised Irish voters to 'never to put their country or their faith in antagonism with popular or democratic forces'.[97] His appearance on behalf of Hyndman lent some weight to the Labour campaign in Burnley where a strong socialist organization had already been established by the local SDF organizer, Dan Irving. However, despite Davitt's intervention, Hyndman was unsuccessful at the polls. His defeat was compounded by the fact that he tailed Maddison, the winner, by only 350 votes.[98] Clearly frustrated, he immediately blamed the Irish vote.[99] According to Chsuhichi Tsuzuki, Hyndman had not campaigned on a revolutionary socialist agenda. His policies included free trade, secular education, an end to Chinese labour in South Africa, and Irish home rule. Yet, as Tsuzuki points out, Hyndman was not 'a thoughtful strategist'.[1] Although the Irish manifesto undoubtedly worked against him, he also damaged his campaign by allowing himself to be drawn into a debate on religion and socialism. During a meeting in the Mechanics' Institute in Burnley he identified the Catholic church with the forces of capitalism, and in an exchange with a Fr Cobb he injudiciously asserted that Christianity was 'played out'.[2] It was this lack of tact which, in Davitt's view, cost him the seat. 'Hyndman lost Burnley', Davitt informed Redmond, 'by his damned bad manners and scientific socialism. If he had adopted my advice he would have been member for Burnley now'.[3]

Although Hyndman valued Davitt's support and considered him an outstanding political activist, he later wrote that the 'great Irishman […] never

95 Davitt to Redmond, 2 Jan. 1906, DP, TCD, MS 9420/2157. Davitt dated this letter 1905, but it must have been 1906. **96** *Burnley Express*, 10 Jan. 1906. **97** Ibid. **98** Pelling, *Social geography*, p. 262. **99** *Burnley Express*, 17 Jan. 1906. **1** Chushichi Tsuzuki, *H.M. Hyndman and British socialism* (Oxford, 1961), pp 157–8. **2** *Burnley Gazette*, 16 Dec. 1905. **3** Davitt to Redmond, 14 Jan. 1906, JRP, NLI, MS 15,179.

perhaps understood what [socialism] meant'.[4] During the general election campaign, while speaking on behalf of Will Thorne at Canning Town, Davitt himself remarked, 'I am not a Socialist [...] I am content to be an Irish Nationalist and Land Reformer; but there are many articles in the political creed of Socialism to which I willingly subscribe'.[5] Sheehy Skeffington would have accepted this as an accurate description of Davitt's radicalism.[6] According to Hardie, however, Davitt had privately declared himself a socialist shortly before this speech but was reluctant to 'proclaim the fact too loudly' during the general election campaign because he believed that it would have interfered with the prospects of Labour candidates such as Thorne.[7] Blunt claimed, indeed, that Davitt had described himself as a 'Christian Socialist' during the 1880s.[8] It is certainly the case that Davitt campaigned for Labour on the basis of personal conviction, and he ultimately viewed the return of twenty-nine Labour members as hugely significant, particularly as the landslide victory for the Liberals had effectively removed the prospects of a home rule bill. In a final analysis, he reflected,

> When the Labour representation in the House of Commons is a hundred and fifty strong, as probably will be in the next Parliament, then we will talk about Home Rule. I am convinced that the balance of power will rest with the Labour Party in the next Parliament.[9]

Ultimately, it is difficult to locate Davitt securely on an ideological spectrum. A clearer understanding of his view of socialism is gained from his notes for a speech which was to be delivered to the parliamentary Labour Party after the general election. In these notes, entitled 'Socialism', he identified the Industrial Revolution and its concomitant capitalism with the exploitation of the modern worker. Like William Morris, he pointed to a pre-industrial era when 'craftsmen owned their own tools and had their wages regulated by custom or municipal law'.[10] Morris, as Thompson observes, was not nostalgic for the medieval society of handicraftsmen; rather, his problem with modern society related to the way in which machinery was employed by capitalists 'to reduce the skilled labourer to the ranks of the unskilled [...] to intensify the labour of those who serve the machines'.[11] McGhee and McHugh also shared the view that mechanization was a refinement of the exploitation of the industrial worker.[12] Davitt, too, remarked in his draft speech that the worker had

4 Hyndman, *Further reminiscences*, p. 53. 5 Quoted in Hardie, 'Michael Davitt', p. 415. 6 See Sheehy Skeffington to Mr Rothstein, 19 Sept. 1908, SSP, NLI, MS 40,741/6. 7 As above, fn. 5. 8 Blunt, *The land war*, p. 93. 9 *Irish People*, 10 Feb. 1906; cited in Bew, *Conflict*, p. 124. 10 Davitt, 'Socialism', DP, TCD, MS 9345/4662. 11 Quoted in Thompson, *William Morris*, pp 649–50. 12 William Kenefick, *'Rebellious and contrary': the Glasgow dockers, 1853–1932* (East Lothian, 2000),

been transformed into the 'human attendant upon labour-saving devices'. He was also particularly conscious that 'Capital now owns both machinery, tools and land, workers can only obtain access to these agencies of production on such terms as capitalism will dictate'. In considering the inevitable question of the just society, he noted the socialist argument that such a society was predicated on the state's control of the means of production and exchange, and the 'complete dethronement of private capital'. Yet, in this context, he introduced Mill to make the point that there was a 'middle [ideological] position'.[13]

Davitt was uncompromising in his commitment to state ownership of land. But, as we have seen, he was not prepared to 'pronounce a dogmatic opinion' when it came to the question of state control and ownership of other resources and core utilities. In *Leaves from a prison diary* he remarked that it was 'for every successive generation in any given community to say what duties shall be discharged independently by individuals or collectively by the state'.[14] As a radical democrat, he was driven by the pursuit of social justice based on egalitarian principles. He worked against structures of privilege and attempted to raise counter-hegemonic consciousness. There is no doubt that he had socialist tendencies, and he was highly respected by many on the left. In 1892 he, along with Hyndman and Dr Robert Spence Watson of the Society of Friends of Russian Freedom, arbitrated at a revolutionary court of honour to settle a dispute between Russian and Polish revolutionaries in London.[15] These courts were conceived of in the mid-nineteenth century by exiled European radicals, whose principles, as E.H. Carr explains, 'precluded [them] from submitting their differences to the established courts; and from whom could one expect justice, and a sense of revolutionary values, if not from a jury of revolutionaries themselves?'[16] However, despite Davitt's leftist activism in Britain during his later political career, and his being identified with revolutionary ideals, he did not embrace socialism. He rejected the socialist commonwealth, not only because he feared that liberty would be compromised in such a society but also because he believed that competition – which he distinguished from monopoly capitalism – was relatively efficient.

p. 138. **13** Davitt, 'Socialism', DP, TCD, MS 9345/4662. **14** Davitt, *Leaves*, vol. ii, p. 128. **15** John Slatter, 'An Irishman at a revolutionary court of honour: from the Michael Davitt papers', *Irish Slavonic Studies* 5 (1984), 32–42. **16** E.H. Carr, *The romantic exiles* (London, 1998), p. 98.

6 / Internationalist and independent witness

W HILE AN ENGAGEMENT WITH international issues and causes was a
distinctive feature of Davitt's later political career, particularly during
his last ten years, it is nevertheless significant that even during the land war he
situated the cause of social and political justice in Ireland in an international
context. In a speech in his native Straide, in February 1880, he declared, 'The
cause of Ireland today is that of humanity and labour throughout the world'.[1]
Of course, it was not until his release from Portland that he began to extend
his range of political activity and to adopt a broader political agenda. Yet there
was clearly an international dimension to his own personal sense of mission
even before his second term of imprisonment. In a diary entry in December
1880, he noted, 'Hope my work for the [coming] year may prove beneficial to
Ireland and its people and tend to advance the cause of humanity and labour
in every affected country'.[2] According to F.H. O'Donnell, Davitt 'had a call to
preach a covenant; and his covenant would have stood most things on their
heads'.[3] O'Donnell shared Davitt's later working interest in international affairs,
especially those pertaining to British imperial policy, but he was in no way sympathetic to Davitt's social radicalism. Nevertheless, his remarks reflected a more
general view, held even by prominent figures on the left, that Davitt, the freelance activist, was something of an anomalous agitator.

Even during his early years growing up in Britain, Davitt seems to have had
a keen interest in global events. This, perhaps, accounts for his later passion
for travel. During his tour of Europe in 1885, he referred to Louis Kossuth as
'one of my favourite heroes when doing my boyish reading'.[4] He probably first
read about Kossuth in the library or the newsroom of the local Mechanics'
Institute in Halslingden.[5] In fact, it was in the Institute's library that he 'first
[learned?] of Ireland' through the books at his disposal.[6] In his later teens, he
also gleaned information on current international events from newspaper
reports which he read during his time as a 'printer's devil' and newsboy in

---

1 Quoted in Moody, *Davitt*, p. 366. 2 Davitt's diary, 31 Dec. 1880, DP, TCD, MS 9534; see
also his diary for 1879–80, DP, TCD, MS 9529/8. 3 O'Donnell, *The history*, vol. i, p. 452.
4 Davitt's diary, 24 Jan. 1885, DP, TCD, MS 9544. 5 Moody, *Davitt*, pp 20–1. 6 Davitt,
Jottings, p. 86.

Haslingden, where he sold 'my *Manchester Guardians* and *Examiners* and *Bury Times*, hawking the news' of the battles of the American Civil War and of the Maori wars in New Zealand.[7] Of course, as he himself later acknowledged, he was heavily influenced by English working-class radicalism in these formative years.[8] It is safe to assume, therefore, that he would have been familiar with *Reynolds's Newspaper*, which was published in London by former Chartists with a circulation of 350,000 in 1861. This paper, together with the smaller weekly, *Beehive*, identified with radical movements in the United States, the latter referring to the eight-hour movement there as 'Our American brethren'.[9]

Internationalism was an essential element of the Jacobin heritage,[10] and as John Newsinger remarks, the 'longest-lived of the Chartist sentiments'.[11] Besides expressions of solidarity with the cause of labour in the United States, the English radical movement's interest in international issues was also evidenced by its support for Italian nationalism and for independence movements in Poland and Hungary. The young Davitt must have read about Garibaldi's visit to England in 1864, during which the Italian patriot was greeted by a procession of 50,000 men from different labour organizations.[12] One of the first to meet Garibaldi on this occasion was Joseph Cowen, who had fêted other revolutionary leaders, such as Kossuth and Mazzini, during their visits to England.[13] Cowen also later became supportive of Davitt during the land war.[14] Indeed, English radicalism had historic connections with revolutionary Irish nationalism, the most significant point in case being the alliance between Chartists and Irish Confederates in the late 1840s when plans were drawn up for simultaneous popular risings.[15] Attempts to effect a *rapprochement* with the British left were undertaken by the Fenian leader, James Stephens, in the mid-1860s.[16] The essentially proletarian social base of Fenianism was, as Tom Garvin has observed, 'reminiscent' of the Chartist base.[17] Yet English radicals were divided on the question of an alliance with militant Irish republicanism at this time. Ultimately, despite issuing an appeal for clemency for Fenian prisoners on trial for the murder of a policeman during a Fenian raid on a prison van in Manchester in September 1867, the Reform League rejected the idea of an alliance.[18]

Members of the first International Workingmen's Association, notably George Odger and Benjamin Lucraft, were among the strongest supporters of the Fenians on the Reform League executive.[19] At a meeting of the League's

7 Davitt, *Life and progress*, p. 344. 8 Davitt, *The Times-Parnell Comm*, p. 30. 9 Pelling, *America and the British left*, pp 25–6. 10 Thompson, *The making of the English*, pp 911–12. 11 John Newsinger, 'Old chartists, fenians, and new socialists', *Éire-Ireland*, 17 (Spring 1982), p. 26. 12 Ibid., p. 27. 13 Duncan, *Life of Joseph Cowen*, pp 8–9. 14 Ibid., p. 127. 15 Thompson, *The making of the English*, pp 183–5, 481–2, 903–4; Rachel O'Higgins, 'The Irish influence in the chartist movement', *Past & Present*, 20 (1961), 91. 16 Newsinger, 'Old chartists', 25–31. 17 Tom Garvin, *Nationalist revolutionaries*, p. 34. 18 Newsinger, 'Old chartists', 39. 19 Ibid., p. 39.

general council, Odger even declared that had he been Irish he would have joined the Fenians.[20] Marx extolled their position; for, as he stated in a letter to Engels, he 'sought in every way to provoke this manifestation of the English workers in support of Fenianism'.[21] James Stephen himself had joined the International while in New York in 1866, although his level of involvement was negligible, given that he devoted most of his time to internal IRB matters, not least the security of his own leadership position. Marx referred to him as 'the most doubtful of our acquisitions'.[22] However, the International was to have important, if short-lived, links with Fenianism in the early 1870s. The Irish section of the International in the United States was dominated by IRB émigrés, including John Devoy; and largely owing to the work of the Fenian, Joseph Patrick McDonnell, branches were formed in Ireland and in Irish communities in England in 1871–2.[23] The branches in Ireland lasted only a matter of months after encountering serious opposition generated by the Catholic clergy. Still, it is significant that most members of the International in Ireland and England were almost certainly either Fenians or former Fenians.[24]

Davitt had joined the IRB, and was imprisoned for his subversive activities, shortly before Irish branches of the International were organized in England.[25] However, even in his later political career he never did become affiliated with any formal international structures. While the *Labour World* provided information on trade union movements in other countries, it is significant that it gave no information on the Second International, or on socialist movements. Davitt's internationalism was based more on an instinctive identification with the principle of democratic–republican liberty than on a settled ideology. Having committed himself to the campaign for land nationalization after his release from Portland in 1882 – a campaign which was itself, of course, informed by the international premise of George's critique of land monopoly – he had set the stage for his freelance career and an engagement with issues of justice and liberty outside the Irish–British connection. It was this aspect of his activism that provoked early criticism from Matt Harris in the months following the Kilmainham 'treaty'. Harris bitterly opposed efforts to promulgate 'cosmopolitan' agrarian ideas in Ireland. Alluding to Davitt, he stated, 'Is it time for any Irishman, except one who has lost himself in dreams of world reform, to float a new agitation. I say no whoever says yes [*sic*]'.[26] Harris was not the only one of Davitt's contemporaries to view his

20 Royden Harrison, *Before the socialists: studies in labour and politics, 1861 to 1881* (London, 1965), p. 141. 21 Quoted in Newsinger, 'Old chartists', p. 40. 22 Quoted in J. Newsinger, *Fenianism in mid-Victorian Britain* (London, 1994), p. 68. 23 Seán Daly, *Ireland and the first international* (Cork, 1984), pp 17–18, 130, 141. 24 Cormac Ó Gráda, 'Fenianism and socialism: the career of Joseph Patrick McDonnell', *Saothar*, 1:1 (May 1975), 35. 25 Moody, *Davitt*, pp 43–4. 26 *CT*, 1 July 1882.

political role as anomalous. F.H. O'Donnell wrote that Davitt was 'a mere Lancashire Radical compounded of Chartism and the French Revolution'.[27] In his obituary to Davitt in 1906, Blunt remarked that he was always 'too much of a theorist [...] in some ways Davitt was less Irish than cosmopolitan, and at times identified himself, in spite of his strong patriotism and hatred of English rule, perhaps too much with English party politics'.[28] W.B. Yeats's verdict was that he 'had wrecked his Irish influence by international politics'.[29] And on the extreme left, Hyndman concluded that he 'would never accept socialism as possible of realization [...] So he had a Utopia of his own for Ireland and other countries'.[30]

It was, perhaps, the freelance nature of Davitt's later activism and his lack of reference to an ideological framework that left him with such a reputation. It is interesting that internationalism formed an important aspect of Hardie's politics at a time when the British labour movement was insular. Hardie attended congresses of the Socialist International and even intervened in ideological debate at the Amsterdam congress in 1904. Yet, while his internationalism was peculiar in the context of British labour and even drew criticism from contemporaries, it did not damage his legendary standing on the British left. Ultimately, he was not a political loner, certainly not in the sense that Davitt was. According to Morgan, he viewed the International as 'a kind of world-wide equivalent of the Labour Representation Committee at home'[31] For Moody, however, it was precisely Davitt's attempts to apply the 'internationalist' principle of land nationalization to Ireland that have proved most problematic. As a fundamentally 'socialistic and internationalist' doctrine, contends Moody, land nationalization was incompatible with the historicist narrative of nationalism. Davitt, he argues, never faced this 'contradiction'.[32] However, Davitt, for his part, did not sense any such inconsistency. In 1884 he wrote,

> The cause of labour like that of religion can be international without being unpatriotic. Religion wars against the vice and sin not of one country but of humanity, and the forces of industry likewise should not only be directed against the injustice of monopoly in one nation but the combined in, at least, an international bond of sympathy against all those laws and vested interests and enterprises which rob the workers of human society of the reward of their industry – the wealth which labour alone produces.[33]

27 O'Donnell, *The history*, vol. i, p. 367. 28 *Speaker*, 9 June 1906. 29 W.B. Yeats, *Autobiographies* (London, 1970), p. 140. 30 Hyndman, *Further reminiscences*, p. 53. 31 Morgan, *Keir Hardie*, pp 180, 198–9. 32 Moody, *Davitt*, pp 524–5. 33 Davitt's diary, 1884 (no precise date), DP, TCD, MS 9540/76.

It is important to note that Davitt's nationalism identified landlordism not only with the English conquest of Ireland but, more broadly, with British imperialist structures of enslavement which extended to India and other dependencies. In his writings in Portland he pointed to the historical context of British rule in Ireland and India and to the self-serving 'British Interests' which 'are made the *primum mobile* alike of [Britain's] conquests, rule of the conquered, and relations towards other powers and peoples'. In the case of India, he made reference to the 'rapacious East India Company';[34] and in *Leaves from a prison diary* he characterized the Castle administration in Ireland as a repressive, alien regime. To better inform English popular opinion about the true nature of British 'centralized despotism' in Ireland he hypothesized a state of affairs in which the relative positions of Ireland and England were reversed and a coterie of Irish officials governed Britain through Whitehall, and presided over an administration in which 'anti-English principles and sentiments' were prevalent.[35]

H.V. Brasted has pointed to three distinct Irish nationalist perspectives on the British empire in the late nineteenth century. In the early 1870s Isaac Butt argued for a federal arrangement in which Ireland, as a self-governing entity, would reap the benefits of empire as a recognized partner of Britain. This pro-imperial view was the converse of the physical force republican perspective, particularly the advanced position adopted by Patrick Ford and articulated in the *Irish World*, which aimed to effect the downfall of the British empire by acting in solidarity with other subject nations and peoples, especially India, as part of a broad insurrectionary strategy. Between these two diametrically opposed views, Brasted has identified the 'compromise' position of the Parnellites, which critiqued imperial expansion and sought internal reform of the empire. According to Brasted, this policy was initially formulated by F.H. O'Donnell who highlighted the need for Irish nationalists to act as the voice of 'the unrepresented nationalities of the Empire'.[36] Like Ford, although for different reasons, O'Donnell advocated the forging of bonds of solidarity with other nationalists in Asia and Africa. This 'universalism', as Brasted terms it, appealed to Davitt. However, Davitt's line of thinking cannot be conveniently categorized: by the end of the land war he had, of course, distanced himself from the use of political violence, such as was central to Ford's strategy; and even though he became associated with constitutional nationalism from

---

34 Davitt, *Jottings*, pp 19, 26. **35** Davitt, *Leaves*, vol. ii, pp 169–210. Davitt's critique of Castle rule, which he restated in a lecture in London shortly after his release from Portland, was later published as a pamphlet entitled *The Castle Government in Ireland* (1882); repr. in King (ed.), *Michael Davitt*, vol. i. **36** H.V. Brasted, 'Irish nationalism and the British empire in the late nineteenth century', in Oliver McDonagh, W.F. Mandle and Pauric Travers (eds), *Irish culture and nationalism, 1750–1950* (Canberra, 1983), pp 83–98.

the early 1880s, he ultimately remained committed to republicanism as a political ideal.

Parnellites adopted an anti-imperialist stance, but, according to Brasted,
most, including Parnell, were not prepared to embrace 'universalism' as a matter of principle. O'Donnell and a few other notable individuals, such as Alfred
Webb, were the exceptions.[37] The strength of O'Donnell's conviction was evident in his statement in the house of commons in March 1884 when he bluntly asserted,

> English tyranny in Ireland [is] only a part of that general system of the
> exploitation of suffering humanity which made the British Empire a
> veritable slave empire [...] Parliamentary agitation [he argued] would
> not be very effective until the Irish people [...] effected a coalition with
> the oppressed natives of India and other British dependencies.[38]

O'Donnell had addressed himself to Indian grievances from an early stage
in his parliamentary career and was known for his reports on Indian affairs as
the London correspondent of the *Bombay Gazette*.[39] By the end of the 1870s
the condition of India was, as Mary Cumpston has noted, a '"Raw" that
Parnellites delighted to rub'.[40] Britain's difficulties in other areas, notably South
Africa, were also celebrated and exploited by Irish nationalists. Davitt paid
tribute to the Zulu king, Cetshwayo, for his fierce resistance to British hegemony in the Anglo-Zulu war of 1879.[41] Parnell himself described the conflict,
which had been precipitated to serve British imperial interests,[42] as 'an unjust
and flatigious war', and he lamented that 'At least half of the regiments now
at the Cape are composed of young men from Connemara [...] sent to
Zululand to become the holocaust of the imperialism which has lately become
so much the fashion'.[43]

Nationalists particularly responded to the defiance of the South African
Boers in the face of British imperial consolidation. Seven Irish parliamen-
tarians, including Parnell and O'Donnell, had obstructed the passage of the
South African Confederation bill which followed the annexation of the
Transvaal republic in April 1877.[44] According to O'Donnell, none of his fel-

---

37 Ibid., pp 94–5. **38** Quoted in Mary Cumpston, 'Some early Indian nationalists and their
allies in the British Parliament, 1851–1906', *EHR*, 76 (Apr. 1961), 297, fn. 1. **39** O'Donnell, *The
history*, vol. i, pp 423–4. **40** Compston, 'Some early Indian nationalists', p. 297. **41** Davitt,
Jottings, p. 28. **42** Thomas Pakenham, *The scramble for Africa, 1876–1912* (London, 1992), pp
51–5. **43** Quoted in Robert Kee, *The laurel and the ivy, the story of Charles Stewart Parnell and
Irish nationalism* (London, 1993), p. 186. **44** The other Irish MPs were Joseph Biggar, E.D. Gray,
G.H. Kirk, Captain J.P. Nolan and J. O'Connor Power; see Donal McCracken, *Forgotten protest:
Ireland and the Anglo–Boer war* (Belfast, 2003), pp 3–8.

low filibusterers knew 'whether the Transvaal was a town or a mountain' at this point.[45] Nevertheless, their opposition in the commons was significant, because, as Parnell acknowledged, Irish members did not normally interfere in debates on imperial matters.[46] Their actions were certainly not in keeping with the parliamentary conduct of Butt. In the months that followed the South Africa debate, Parnell and other like-minded parliamentarians watched with what Donal McCracken describes as 'smug satisfaction' as the British faced mounting disaffection among the Boers, a political climate which would later result in open armed conflict in 1880.[47] Davitt later wrote that a no-rent strike should have been called in Ireland in February 1881 to coincide with the hugely significant Boer victory over the British at Majuba Hill.[48] It was, indeed, during the first Anglo–Boer war that Gladstone and the majority of his cabinet came to appreciate the potentially far-reaching implications of local insurgency within the empire. In the weeks preceding the battle of Majuba, the colonial office received reports that Afrikaner disaffection was spreading beyond the Transvaal. D.M. Schreuder maintains that while there was certainly much sympathy between the Cape Dutch and the republican Boers in 1880–1, it is unlikely that this was anything other than an ephemeral 'unity' produced by the reality of the war. However, it was enough, especially given the simultaneous unrest in Ireland, to prompt a *volte-face* by the Liberal administration, from a policy of coercion to one of conciliation. As Schreuder points out, the decision was taken to 'kill the problem of the Afrikaner by kindness', a policy that would later be applied to Ireland.[49]

In his writings in Portland, Davitt drew parallels between Ireland and other subject nationalities of the empire; but it was in his capacity as a freelance activist from the early 1880s that he began to engage with international issues on a practical level. India was of particular interest to him. He was convinced that the overthrow of British rule there was 'only a question of time'.[50] Like other nationalists, he recognized the importance of Britain's premier colonial possession. In 1876, during debates on the Royal Titles bill, which would make Queen Victoria the Empress of India, Disraeli had told his lord chancellor, Lord Cairns, 'The Empress-Queen demands her Imperial Crown'.[51] However, despite being considered the jewel in that Crown, India had no political representation at Westminster. This democratic deficit was identified by some Irish nationalists, including Davitt, as a basis for Irish–Indian co-operation. In 1878, after receiving an appeal for political support from the British Indian Association, O'Donnell presented Butt with a proposal for an alliance in which

45 O'Donnell, *The history*, vol. i, p. 216. 46 McCracken, *Forgotten protest*, p. 4. 47 Ibid., p. 11. 48 Davitt, *The fall*, p. 309. 49 D.M. Schreuder, *Gladstone and Kruger, liberal government and colonial 'home rule', 1880–85* (London, 1969), pp 103–4, 160–1, 471–4. 50 Davitt, *Leaves*, vol. ii, p. 156. 51 Quoted in Robert Blake, *Disraeli* (London, 1998), p. 562.

the Irish Party would field Indian candidates in exchange for the 'political and pecuniary support of a great Indian movement'.[52] Butt was not persuaded. Later, in 1883, Davitt put the same question before Parnell. He suggested that the Party find a seat in Ireland for Dadabhai Naoroji, an eminent Indian leader living in London. Naoroji, a mathematician by profession, was known for his scientific critique of Britain's economic drain on India.[53] Davitt urged Parnell to seize the opportunity to 'have the honour of giving direct voice in the house of commons to countless millions of British subjects who were ruled despotically and taxed without votes'. Parnell, it seems, was 'very much taken' by the proposal but ultimately feared that it would give rise to disagreement within the Party.[54]

It was shortly before his imprisonment in Richmond jail in 1883 that Davitt discussed the Naoroji issue with Parnell, along with a number of other measures which, if adopted by the Irish Party, would, in Davitt's view, have established closer links between Irish nationalism and British democracy.[55] These discussions represented Davitt's last serious effort in the post-Kilmainham climate to encourage Parnell along a radical path. Yet Parnell had already begun to advance his own conservative agenda by this point, which resulted in a radically changed movement within a few short years. According to McCracken, he also began to adopt a more moderate attitude towards the empire by 1885. This was reflected in the agreement which he reached with the leading imperialist and South African mining magnate, Cecil Rhodes, in 1888. Rhodes believed that the retention of Irish MPs at Westminster in the event of a home rule settlement was critical to the realization of a federated empire. After the defeat of the home rule bill of 1886, which had provided for total exclusion of Irish members, he made it clear to the Irish Party that if it agreed to argue for the retention of Irish representation at Westminster, he would donate £10,000 to the Party. He held discussions with the Irish leader in the summer of 1888, and while Parnell stopped short of agreeing to insist on such a provision during future negotiations, he agreed in principle to support continued Irish representation in the imperial parliament after home rule. This was enough to secure a donation of £11,000 from Rhodes.[56] In an article in the *Fortnightly Review* in December 1898, the Birkenhead journalist and later biographer of Chamberlain, J.L. Garvin, remarked that if home rule had been realized in Parnell's day, 'he would have become at once an imperial force as strong as Mr. Rhodes'.[57] For C.C. O'Brien, there is little doubt that Parnell would have opted for 'imperial federation', with a self-governing Ireland acting as 'a

---

52 O'Donnell, *The history*, vol. i, p. 428. **53** S.R. Singh, *Dadabhai Naoroji, 1825–1917, the grand old man of India* (New Delhi, 1985), pp 11–14. **54** Davitt, *The fall*, p. 447. **55** Ibid., pp 444–7. **56** McCracken, *Forgotten protest*, pp 20–2. **57** Quoted in O'Brien, *Parnell*, p. 349, fn. 1.

willing partner in the British empire'.⁵⁸ McCracken remarks that in the short term 'the Rhodes money was to strengthen Parnell's hand in controlling the advanced men' within the Irish movement.⁵⁹

When Davitt returned from his European tour in 1885, he and Blunt discussed possibilities for broadening the campaign against the British empire. In this context, Davitt again raised the issue of setting aside Irish seats for Indian representatives.⁶⁰ It was a measure of his restored confidence after this tour that in May 1888 he intervened directly by writing a letter to the *Freeman's Journal* in which he proposed the selection of Naoroji for a forthcoming election contest in South Sligo. It was, he opined, a suggestion which should recommend itself to all Irishmen sympathetic to every people 'rightly struggling to be free'. He hoped that both Parnell and the electors of Sligo would 'rise equal to the occasion'.⁶¹ Evidently, his views were not widely shared by his fellow nationalists. The *Sligo Champion*, while acknowledging his 'philanthropic' work on behalf of 'the tithe payers of Wales, the Crofters of the Highlands, the coolies of India, and the fellahs of Egypt', failed to understand how the representation of an Irish constituency by an Indian would advance the home rule cause.⁶²

Despite the earnest efforts of a few to find a seat for an Indian representative in Ireland in the 1880s, Naoroji's eventual election to the British parliament was as the member for Central Finsbury in 1892.⁶³ This, however, did not provide him with a stable political platform. He lost this seat during the 1895 general election and was again forced to turn his attention to Ireland. In January 1896 he appealed directly to Davitt, with whom he had been friendly now for over a decade, but was informed that there was 'no hope' of his being selected for an Irish constituency.⁶⁴ Davitt shared the general Irish nationalist preoccupation with the political goal of home rule. To a certain extent, he was even prepared to tolerate Liberal imperialist rhetoric in order to expedite that end. In a diary entry in November 1894 he noted that Lord Rosebery was proving to be Salisbury's 'equal' in his concerns for England's interests abroad.

> [Rosebery's] imperialism and semi-jingoism are [he wrote] detestable from an Irish nationalist point of view, but if he can carry the next General Election by this sort of thing and thereby carry Home Rule afterwards, he may jingo and imperialize to his heart's content – in his speeches.⁶⁵

---

58 Ibid., p. 349. 59 McCracken, *Forgotten protest*, p. 24. 60 Blunt, *The land war*, p. 318. 61 *FJ*, 28 May 1888. 62 *Sligo Champion*, 2 June 1888. 63 Singh, *Dadabhai Naoroji*, p. 22. 64 Quoted in King, 'Michael Davitt, Irish nationalism and the British empire in the late nineteenth century', in Peter Gray (ed.), *Victoria's Ireland? Irishness and Britishness, 1837–1910* (Dublin, 2004), p. 122. 65 Davitt's diary, 10 Nov. 1894, DP, TCD, MS 9556.

Yet Davitt was not simply motivated by the Irish question; he supported Naoroji as a matter of principle and advocated justice for India on its own terms. Indeed, his contribution to Indian nationalism was recognized in October 1894 when he was asked to preside at the Tenth Indian National Congress in Madras. He declined the invitation on the grounds that his acceptance would prove 'a big risk for the Congress' because it would be exploited by sections of the press.[66] In the end, it was his old friend, Webb, who presided.[67]

Writing to Webb in the course of his visit to Rome in 1885, Davitt had remarked that he looked forward to the day when the British empire would meet the same fate as the imperial system of ancient Rome.[68] However, despite his principled opposition to imperial structures, he was intrigued by the progress of Canada and the Australasian colonies as autonomous entities within the empire. When he visited Canada in the autumn of 1891, he was struck by the ethnic diversity of the colonists, their industriousness, and the political institutions of the Dominion. 'Hereditary legislators are', he remarked, 'as ridiculously absurd to the Canadian mind as to that of Uncle Sam over the border'. He noted that Canada had the opportunity to make a bid for independence, but he accepted that if it seceded from the empire, it would be vulnerable to annexation by the United States. He himself was of the view that such territorial expansion by the US would only compromise its 'free institutions'. In any case, he acknowledged that most of the Canadians with whom he spoke had no appetite for secession.[69]

He found a similar attitude among Australasian colonists during his tour of the Antipodes. In most of the colonies, he observed an almost theatrical allegiance to the Crown, although he pointed out that such loyalty was conditional upon the preservation of the colonies' tariff autonomy. He was bemused to discover the same sentiment of attachment to the empire among the Irish in Australia. While visiting the homes of compatriots, especially those of Catholic clerics, he noticed 'the picture of the Queen [...] flanked by that of Mr. Gladstone, and, not unfrequently [*sic*], by either Mr Parnell, Mr Dillon, or Mr O'Brien – a somewhat incongruous association'.[70] If the Irish affection for Queen Victoria was one aspect of life in the relatively new Antipodean communities which made Davitt uneasy, he could take some consolation from the fact that his fellow countrymen had established a 'good record' for themselves in the policing profession, despite racist broadsides from 'jackeroo journalists'. In describing the role of Irish colonists he was eager to affirm the Irish capacity for self-government, as was designated a prerequisite by Mill in his

---

66 Quoted in King, 'Michael Davitt, Irish nationalism and the British empire', p. 123. 67 Webb, *Alfred Webb*, p. 67. 68 Davitt to Webb, 5 Mar. 1885, DP, TCD, MS 9490/4953–4986. 69 Davitt, 'Impressions', pp 631–47. 70 Davitt, *Life and Progress*, pp 130–1.

thinking on the good society. He did acknowledge, however, that the Irish were not free from prejudice, and he recounted how an Irish policeman, a Francophile, had actively harassed German colonists in 1870 during the Franco–Prussian war.[71] Irishmen did, indeed, constitute a sizable percentage of the colonies' police forces, especially in Victoria where, in 1874, as much as eighty-two per cent were Irish-born.[72] One feature of Irish representation in the profession, certainly one which Davitt would, no doubt, have been less inclined to mention, was that many Irish recruits had previously served with the RIC. Irish policemen in Australia were, moreover, not only sometimes 'mix[ed] up [in] racial antipathies' with colonists of other nationalities, as Davitt put it,[73] but were also at times at odds with the working-class Irish. Referring to the Irish parentage of Ned Kelly, Elizabeth Malcolm remarks that what is 'less often remembered [about Kelly] is that most of the policemen he killed and most of those who pursued him were Irish born, as indeed was the judge who sentenced him to death'.[74]

Dillon had toured Australasia in 1889–90 and had taken a keen interest in the evolution of self-government in the region.[75] However, the pioneering nature of the social and political development of the colonies made a much greater impression on Davitt. Although he had committed himself to a lecturing programme during his long-awaited tour, his real aim was to study progress in the colonies. Australasia was, he later wrote, 'an industrial empire of unfederated Labour nations, where neither wars nor foreign policies intrude their demoralizing influences upon the peaceful programmes and progress of domestic government'.[76] He was impressed by the laws and institutions of the new states and by their respective Labour parties. He considered South Australia and New Zealand particularly progressive because of their regulation of labour[77] – or, as he termed it, their 'judicious application of the principle of State Socialism'[78] – and their extension of the franchise to women. South Australia had gone even further than New Zealand by giving women the right to become members of the Legislative Assembly.[79] Davitt's attitude to women was, in many respects, typically Victorian; the qualities which he favoured most in the opposite sex were 'modesty and domesticity'.[80] Nevertheless, he believed that a recognition of the right of women to participate fully in political life was the mark of a mature democracy. He had earlier written in Portland that,

71 Ibid., p. 136. 72 E. Malcolm, '"What would people say if I became a policeman"?: the Irish policeman abroad', in Oonagh Walsh (ed.), *Ireland Abroad: politics and professions in the nineteenth century* (Dublin, 2003), p. 101. 73 Davitt, *Life and progress*, p. 137. 74 Malcolm, '"What would people say "' p. 102. 75 Lyons, *John Dillon*, p. 103. 76 Davitt, *Life and progress*, p. viii. 77 Ibid., pp 51–2, pp 373–4. 78 Ibid., p. ix. 79 Ibid., p. 49, p. 366. 80 See his answers on a novelty questionnaire, DP, TCD, MS 9344/458.

[in] the near future, we may depend upon it, women will be a far more important factor in both the industrial and political mechanism of society than they are now, and it would be well that this should be the case [men …] have no moral right to refuse to women the opportunity of achieving their independence […] in the struggle for existence.[81]

In the last year of his life, when campaigns for women's suffrage were gaining momentum in Ireland and Britain, he put his name to a memorial calling on Irish Party MPs to back a Women's Suffrage bill which had been introduced to the house of commons.[82]

Australasia was, for Davitt, a land of opportunity which offered better 'conditions of existence to the average man'. He noted that employment opportunities for artisans and general labourers were extremely limited in large cities such as Melbourne and Syndey, but he pointed to the 'boundless areas of land' which were available for cultivation and to the huge potential for employment in the mining of the colonies' natural resources, namely gold, silver and coal. The existing gold mines of the region had already generated much employment; although in his survey of the goldfields, Davitt objected to the lack of safety measures for miners, and drew attention to the glaring difference between miners' wages and the fortunes amassed by mine proprietors, such as at Mount Morgan in Queensland, the most lucrative of all the mines in operation.[83] He also became particularly exercised by the employment of Kanakas, South Sea islanders, in the sugar industry of Queensland. The issue of cheap Kanaka labour had become particularly contentious, and, after observing conditions on some of the plantations,[84] Davitt concluded that the 'enlistment' of such workers was simply a case of exploitation rather than economic necessity. The argument that the islanders were being Christianized was, in his opinion, 'a piece of disgusting capitalistic hypocrisy'. The food, climate and general working environment of the plantations were alien to the Kanakas, and this, Davitt argued, accounted for a death rate of fifty out of a thousand 'in a country boasting so low a rate of mortality among the white population as fifteen in the same number'. He recommended the break up of the large plantations and the division of the land among small cane cultivators.[85]

The conditions of the Aboriginal population were also of particular interest to him. He praised Catholic missionaries in Western Australia for their work in attempting to end the mistreatment of the indigenous race. He predicted, however, that the physical marginalization of the Aborigines, and the brutal punishments meted out to them for encroachments upon settlers' lands

81 Davitt, *Leaves*, vol. ii, p. 29. **82** Sheehy Skeffington, *Michael Davitt*, pp 217–18. **83** Davitt, *Life and progress*, pp 266–7, 290, 408–9 **84** Davitt's diary, 28 July 1895, DP, TCD, MS 9563/7. **85** Davitt, *Life and progress*, pp 275–8.

in search of game, would inevitably result in their disappearance as a people. They were, he claimed, victims of imperialism:

> The white man's law justifies him in stealing the black man's country, his wife and daughters whenever he wants them; but to take a sheep from this moral professor of the ten commandments is to earn the penalty of a bullet![86]

Indeed, during his visit to New Zealand, Davitt was mindful of the British imperialist advances in the region in the 1860s and of the Maori resistance, the accounts of which he first read in his youth. He drew parallels between the Land League and the passive agrarian campaign of the Maoris in the 1870s, in which hundreds of natives were imprisoned without trial for violating land laws in order to secure recognition of their ancient rights. Davitt referred to the leading Maori figure, Te Whiti, as the 'Maori Land Leaguer'.[87]

The New Zealand which Davitt experienced and learned of during his visit was, as he later put it, 'probably the most progressive country in the world'.[88] In praising its progress he paid particular tribute to the former Liberal prime minister of the colony, John Ballance, an Irishman from Co. Antrim, and to his cabinet colleague, John McKenzie, a Scottish Highlander.[89] Both were land reformers intent on sub-dividing New Zealand's large pastoral estates in order to provide land for ordinary farmers. As the minister of Lands and Agriculture in the 1890s, McKenzie secured the passage of a series of legislative reforms which opened up crown lands for leasing based on the principle of lease-in-perpetuity. Under an Advances to Settlers scheme in 1894 he also provided state credit, at a low interest, to small farmers for the clearing of land and the equipment of holdings. However, it was apparent from his Lands Improvement and Native Land Acquisition Act of 1894 that he was committed not only to the 'burst up' of the large estates but also to buying Maori lands in order to facilitate further land settlements, particularly on the North Island.[90] Maori members of parliament opposed key elements of the new legislation, and were particularly critical of the fact that Maori landowners would have made more profit if they had been permitted to sell on the open market. More seriously, Maori farmers were excluded from the Advances to Settlers scheme. The Maori MP, H.K. Taiaroa, whom Davitt noted as an important parliamentary representative of 'the remnants of the Maori people',[91] informed the legislative council that the Liberal administration aimed to 'get the land from the Natives as quickly as possible in order to settle Europeans upon it'.[92] Tom

86 Ibid., p. 34. 87 Ibid., p. 378. 88 Ibid., p. 366. 89 Ibid., p. 388. 90 Tom Brooking, *Lands for the people? the highland clearances and the colonisation of New Zealand: a biography of John McKenzie* (Otago, 1996), pp 121–2, 128. 91 Davitt, *Life and progress*, pp 368–9. 92 Quoted in Brooking,

Brooking comments that while McKenzie and his Liberal colleagues had not calculatingly planned to dispossess the Maoris, their 'unfair' policies demonstrated a commitment to 'completing the process of colonization'. He observes that it was with 'unintentional irony' that, while crediting Ballance and McKenzie with land laws based on the principle of 'the land of a country for the people of a country', Davitt added that the Maoris had resisted British land confiscations in defence of the same principle.[93] Indeed, while focusing largely on British imperialism as the reason for the demise of the Australian Aborigines, Davitt also tended to ignore the role which the Irish and their descendants played in that process of dispossession.[94]

Despite the social justice issues which gave Davitt cause for concern during his tour, his work, *Life and progress in Australasia*, was written essentially a celebration of the colonies as self-governing entities. He believed that the progress of the new polities highlighted the anomaly of Ireland under the Union. He commented on the 'astounding inconsistency' in granting 'the freest possible Home Rule (with power to tax British products in the bargain)' to the 45,000 colonists of Western Australia in 1890, 'after denying in 1886 a cribb'd, cabined, and confined self-governing constitution to five millions of people in Ireland'.[95] In an early speech in London in 1882, he had argued that, unlike Canada and Australia, both Ireland and India were effectively ruled outside a 'British Constitution so often lauded as the guarantee and guardian of personal liberty'.[96] Later in 1897, he questioned the nature of British rule in India during a debate in the commons. He stated that Britain's 'only justification for holding India by the sword would be in making a prosperous country'. This, he asserted, was evidently not the case, for out of a population of 250,000,000 Indians 'at least 170,000,000 [remained] absolutely illiterate 150 years after the commencement of British domination'.[97]

Davitt's return from Australasia at the beginning of 1896, and his subsequent re-entry to parliament, signalled a more public stand on international issues. He was 'a somewhat silent Member' during his career at Westminster between 1896 and 1899,[98] but he did make notable interventions in which he challenged and attacked British imperial policy. Noel McLachlan remarks that he effectively became 'the parliamentary conscience of the whole British Empire'.[99] In January 1897 he stood in parliament and asked if the Royal Niger Company had been acting independently in a recent expedition to Benin, or

Lands for the people?, p. 143. **93** Ibid., pp 141–3, 241. **94** See Bob Reece, 'The Irish and the Aborigines' in Tadhg Foley and Fiona Bateman (eds), *Irish-Australian studies: papers delivered at the ninth Irish-Australian conference, Galway, April 1997* (Sydney, 2000), pp 192–203. **95** Davitt, *Life and progress*, pp 26–7. **96** Davitt, *The Castle Government in Ireland*, p. 14. **97** *Hansard*, 4th series, 52, cols. 447–8, 5 Aug. 1897. **98** Ibid., cols. 443–4, 5 Aug. 1897. **99** Noel McLachlan, 'Michael Davitt and passive resistance: the path not taken', *TLS*, 12 Feb. 1999.

whether it was effectively shaping British imperialist policy in commanding the prosecuting of a war.[1] A week later, he questioned the colonial secretary, Chamberlain, on the conduct of British soldiers in the overthrow of Prempeh, the King of the West African kingdom of Ashanti.[2] At the beginning of his colonial secretaryship in 1895, when he joined Salisbury's Conservative government, Chamberlain had referred to Britain as 'a great landlord' with an unexplored and underdeveloped estate,[3] a metaphor that would not have been lost on Davitt. It was only months after taking office, then, that he ordered the invasion of Ashanti in an effort to thwart French advances on the West African gold coast. The British take-over of the Ashanti kingdom was largely effortless, the capital, Kumasi, falling without so much as one shot being fired. Prempeh and other prominent chiefs were exiled and a war indemnity of 50,000 ounces in gold was imposed on the country.[4] In the house of commons, Davitt challenged Chamberlain to disclose whether Prempeh had agreed to make a full submission and accept British terms before the invasion; and to explain why, after having reached Kumasi, British troops 'looted the King's house and dug up the graves of dead chiefs in search of treasure'.[5] When Davitt again raised the issue of Ashanti the following year he did so in the context of a broad critique of British and French colonial expansion in West Africa:

> We have heard a great deal [...] about French interests and English interests, but we have heard nothing about the inhabitants of this [West] part of Africa. Nobody had ventured to say a word in support of the interests of the dark people of this African continent. I want to know when the inhabitants of the regions invited either England or France to steal their country and rob them of their liberties. No such petition from these people had been presented to this House, and I am sure I am stating what is true when I declare that you have gone to these parts of Africa despite the protests of these people, whom you declare you want to civilize.[6]

Less than two months after this intervention Davitt caused the government some embarrassment when he questioned the grounds on which the Chinese revolutionary leader, Sun Yat Sen, had been banished from Hong Kong.[7] In 1895 Sun had used the colony as a base from which to plan the overthrow of the government in Canton in southern China. Sun himself was no stranger to Hong Kong: he had had a largely Western education and indeed

---

1 *Hansard*, 4th series, 45, col. 188, 21 Jan. 1897.   2 Ibid., col. 678, 28 Jan. 1897.   3 Quoted in Denis Judd, *Radical Joe: a life of Joseph Chamberlain* (London, 1977), p. 190.   4 Pakenham, *The scramble*, p. 513.   5 *Hansard*, 4th series, 45, col. 678, 28 Jan. 1897.   6 Ibid., 53, cols 1632–33, 24 Feb. 1898.   7 Ibid., 56, cols 219–20, 5 Apr. 1898.

had graduated from the Hong Kong College of Medicine. Together with other young republican revolutionaries living in the colony and in certain parts of southern China, he was familiar with Western political concepts and seemed to have been influenced to some extent by the ideas of Mill.[8] The ultimate aim of the plot against the Canton government was to destabilize and ultimately bring down the traditional Manchu dynasty and to introduce democratic and liberal reforms which would modernize and strengthen China. Although the attempted coup in October 1895 proved unsuccessful, the fact that it had been plotted in Hong Kong forced the colony's government and its governor, Sir William Robinson, to treat the matter as an international issue. Opposed to the revolutionaries' use of Hong Kong as a refuge, Robinson banned Sun from returning to the colony. This decision became particularly controversial in Britain later in 1896 when the exiled Sun became the object of much publicity following his abduction by the Chinese legation in London, and his detention at the Chinese embassy for almost two weeks before his release was negotiated by the British foreign office.[9]

Davitt's parliamentary question on Sun's exclusion followed a letter which he had received from Roland Mulkern, Sun's agent in London. Mulkern sought Davitt's co-operation in forming a committee in Britain which would highlight the Chinese reform agenda and work to prevent any 'unjust intervention' on the part of the British government in the event of an uprising in China.[10] Davitt readily gave his support. In the summer of 1898 he again challenged Chamberlain on the exclusion of the 'Chinese reformer'. He questioned why the decree of banishment was still in place when no breach of British law had been committed on British territory. When the colonial secretary replied that the press had reported that Sun was 'now leading rebels in China', Davitt interjected, 'I hope he will be successful'.[11] The coded shorthand which Davitt used in his correspondence with Mulkern indicates that he kept abreast of developments in the East and was himself kept informed of revolutionary developments by both Mulkern and Sun who considered him an important ally.[12] It seems that he was even planning a visit to China and

8 Eric Hobsbawm, *The age of empire, 1875–1914* (London, 2002), pp 282–3. 9 Frank Welsh, *A history of Hong Kong* (London, 1997), pp 337–8. 10 Mulkern to Davitt, 26 Mar. 1898, DP, TCD, MS 9488/4920. 11 *Hansard*, 4th series, 62, cols 76–77, 18 July 1898. 12 DP, TCD, MS 9488/4936. In this list of coded shorthand terms for correspondence (written in Davitt's handwriting), Davitt is known as 'Stephen'; his effects in parliament – 'Stephenson'; Mulkern – 'James'; Sun Yat Sen – 'John'; revolutionary party led by Sun – 'Johnson'; Chamberlain – 'William'; China – 'Edward'; Chinese government – 'Edwardson'; Hong Kong – 'Monaco'; Hong Kong government – 'Patrick'; Japan – 'White'; Russia – 'Green'; American – 'Brown'; England – 'Black'; France – 'Red'; Germany – 'Blue'; Italy – 'Yellow'; revolutionary forces and means – 'Tea'; arms, ammunitions etc – 'Sugar'; Chinese fleet – 'Coffee'; a Chinese man of war – 'Opium'; assistance from Japan – 'Health'; assistance from Russia – 'Benefit'; assistance from America – 'Cotton';

Japan.[13] His contribution was certainly recognized by Sun who wrote to him in 1899 thanking him for his support, in and out of parliament. The attention which Davitt's parliamentary questions focused on Britain's Far East policy was crucial, for, as Sun himself remarked, 'If we could gain the sympathy and support of England and free from the molestation of other European Powers, our success would be a most probability [*sic*]'.[14]

As the *Freeman's Journal* noted, Davitt's commentary on the government's foreign policy incensed many within the British political establishment.[15] In an editorial in *St James's Gazette* it was argued, indeed, that his public utterances and writings were tantamount to subversion and that he should therefore be denied unlimited licence as a parliamentarian. Concern was also expressed that his 'ravings' carried considerable weight with the readership of the foreign press.[16] This was a direct response to the publication of a letter which Davitt wrote in April 1899 to Wilhelm Liebknecht, leader of the Social Democratic Party in the German Reichstag, on the international dispute over the Samoan islands.[17] Davitt declared a particular interest in the issue, having visited Samoa in 1895 at the end of his extended tour that year.[18] Britain, Germany and the United States had established a tripartite protectorate over the islands in 1889 after years of rivalry, but tensions soon resurfaced.[19] In 1899, during a civil war between Samoa's native chiefs, the German foreign office became alarmed when British and American warships were dispatched to the region. The foreign secretary, Bernhard von Bülow, warned against any Anglo–American attempts to engineer a political settlement. He made it clear to London and Washington that the existing provisional government of king Mataafa, 'having been recognized by the three Consuls', must be maintained 'as the legal status quo' until an alternative had been jointly agreed by the three signatory powers.[20]

Davitt shared this distrust of American and British interests in Samoa. He advised Liebknecht that the dispute had been instigated by a body known as the London Missionary Society which, as an agent of British imperial interests, was responsible for promoting an Anglo–American alliance in order to establish English predominance in western Samoa. The Missionary Society aimed to have Mataafa deposed, Davitt maintained, 'because he has the support of the Germans in [*sic*] the Island and on account of his being a Catholic'.

---

assistance from England – 'Wine'; assistance from France – 'Oil'; unprepared for attack – 'Sick'; no forward movement for present – 'Holiday'; may strike a blow soon – 'Medicine'. See also Sun Yat Sen to Davitt, 2 Nov. 1899, DP, TCD, MS 9488/4919.   **13** Sun to Davitt, 2 Nov. 1899, DP, TCD, MS 9488/4919.   **14** Sun to Davitt, 25 May 1899, DP, TCD, MS 9488/4918.   **15** *FJ*, 17 Apr. 1899.   **16** *St James's Gazette*, 22 Apr. 1899.   **17** The letter was published in *FJ*, 17 Apr. 1899.   **18** 'Visit to Samoa', DP, TCD, MS 9644; also *Life and progress*, p. 397.   **19** Gordon A. Craig, *Germany, 1866–1945* (Oxford, 1981), p. 242.   **20** *FJ*, 15 Apr. 1899.

In his controversial letter, which was widely published,[21] Davitt attacked Britain and urged Liebknecht not to identify the American people with the conduct of 'one or two of those who are acting disloyally in the name of the Great Republic'. This was an allusion to the administration of President McKinley who was identified with imperialist expansion. D.K. Fieldhouse points out that the United States was an unlikely imperialist power, given the egalitarian nature of its Declaration of Independence and the fact that as a nation it was born out of resistance to British rule. However, the reality was that by the end of the 1890s it had become an imperial power in its own right.[22] Leading political and literary figures in the US, such as Mark Twain – whose company Davitt had enjoyed on his voyage from Melbourne to New Zealand[23] – opposed a policy of expansionism, believing it to be unconstitutional.[24] The same view was shared by Davitt's old Land League colleague, Patrick Egan, who had become prominent in Irish–American politics after his departure from Ireland in 1883 and who eventually served as the US minister to Chile between 1889 and 1903.[25] Quoting Abraham Lincoln's statement that 'The bulwark of our nation's safety lies not in its fortresses or in its navy, but in the spirit which recognizes the heritage of men in all lands, everywhere', Egan argued that imperialism was 'un-Republican and un-American'. He attacked the policy of McKinley and his government, particularly the decision to annex the Philippines, and called for 'the return of the country to true old-time Americanism'.[26]

During 1897 and 1898, Irish–Americans protested against a proposed Anglo–American arbitration treaty, which they viewed as an effective alliance that would influence the US administration's attitude towards the Irish national question. Davitt joined in the protest. He wrote to various American papers and even crossed the Atlantic to agitate on the issue. He petitioned senators in Washington and ultimately contributed to the defeat of the proposal.[27] In May 1898 he told William O'Brien that he was 'working so hard against this Anglo–American alliance' and that he considered McKinley 'thoroughly pro-English'.[28] He ultimately believed that his writings on the matter had made him unpopular in England, and that even '[m]y book on Australia was virtu-

---

21 The letter was published in European papers such as *Vorwärts* and *Le Figaro*; see Davitt's press-cutting book, DP, TCD, MS 9492/5041–5061. 22 D.K. Fieldhouse, *The colonial empires: a comparative survey from the eighteenth century* (London, 1966), pp 341–2. 23 Davitt, *Life and progress*, pp 337–42. 24 Jones, *The limits*, p. 402. 25 Alan J. Ward, *Ireland and Anglo–American relations, 1899–1921* (London, 1969), p. 39, fn. 19; also p. 278. Davitt and other Irish nationalists had viewed Egan's appointment as a significant boost for their cause; see *Irish World*, 6 Apr. 1889. Egan wrote to Davitt after his appointment, remarking that he valued his new role 'as an American citizen and also for "our cause"'. 'I wouldn't', he continued, 'be surprised if English Toryism would try to make trouble for me in Santiago'; Egan to Davitt, 20 Apr. 1889, DP, TCD, MS 9368/839. 26 *FJ*, 30 Oct. 1899. 27 Ward, *Ireland*, pp 44, 55. See also *FJ*, 31 May 1906. 28 Davitt to O'Brien, 18 May 1898, NLI, MS 913.

ally boycotted' because of it.[29] Yet it was the mooted 'alliance', rather than American expansionism itself, that was his main preoccupation. Only several months before the Samoan crisis erupted he openly criticized McKinley for proposing joint co-operation with Britain in the building of a canal through Nicaragua.[30] The Clayton-Bulwer Treaty of 1850 required that the construction of any isthmian canal by either of the two powers should be jointly controlled and left unfortified.[31] But Davitt argued that the recent Spanish–American war, out of which the United States had acquired territories in the Western Pacific and Latin America, effectively rendered the treaty obsolete. He pointed out that America now admitted that an interoceanic canal was a matter of national security. The idea of joint co-operation was, he protested, 'tantamount to adding the United States to the British Colonial Office'.[32] Ultimately, the proposal was never acted upon in the form which Davitt feared: the Hay-Pauncefote Canal Treaty of 1900 provided that the US could build the canal without British support, but could not fortify it.[33] And, despite Davitt's fixation on British imperial designs in the Samoan crisis, the islands were divided between Germany and the United States in October 1899.[34] Salisbury had, in fact, considered Samoa more trouble than it was worth, and by making certain concessions to Germany in the resolution of the dispute he managed to secure German non-intervention in the affairs of southern Africa.[35]

It was the outbreak of the second Anglo–Boer war in October 1899 that occasioned Davitt's protest resignation from Westminster and the most dramatic speech of his parliamentary career. On 25 October, during a commons debate on an army estimates bill, he denounced the aims of the British war effort as 'the meanest and most mercenary [...] which ever prompted conquest or aggression'. Expressing his solidarity with the Boers, he declared that he would be prepared to reject a government offer of Irish independence if it were conditional upon his 'voting against liberty in South Africa'. Then, announcing his resignation in a peroration clearly designed to remind Britain that disaffection with British rule was not confined to Africa, he provocatively stated,

> When I go I shall tell my boys, 'I have been some five years in this House, and the conclusion with which I leave it is that no cause, however just, will find support, no wrong, however pressing or apparent, will find redress here, unless backed up by force.'[36]

29 Davitt to Sabina, 10 Dec. 1890, DP, TCD, MS 9325/102. **30** *FJ*, 10 Dec. 1898. **31** Jones, *The limits*, p. 407. **32** As above, fn. 30. **33** Ward, *Ireland*, pp 42–3. **34** Fieldhouse, *The colonial empires*, p. 342. **35** Andrew Roberts, *Salisbury: Victorian titan* (London, 1999), pp 719–20. **36** Davitt's speech of resignation, 25 Oct. 1899 in King (ed.), *Michael Davitt*, vol. ii, pp 8–9.

The *Irish People* described his decision as the most momentous event in 'our Irish world since the death of Mr. Parnell'.[37]

In the weeks leading up to his resignation, Davitt had championed the cause of the Boers, in and out of parliament, and was one of the few nationalist MPs to become a member of the recently formed Irish Transvaal Committee.[38] In July, several months before the war, he and Dillon had stood in the house of commons and condemned the future use of the new soft-nosed 'dum-dum' bullet, a round which exploded on impact.[39] The supply of such ammunition to serving British soldiers in South Africa was an issue on which Davitt had earlier challenged the under-secretary of state for war.[40] His efforts in raising the issue of 'dum-dums' in the summer of 1899 were applauded by W.T. Stead who was then in the Netherlands reporting on the first international peace conference at The Hague.[41] The conference, which met between 18 May and 29 July, was convened for the purposes of reaching international agreement on arms reductions and on conventions of military warfare. Another main objective was to establish a formal framework for the pacific settlement of international disputes through arbitration.[42] The sessions of the conference were initially closed, but Stead, who was there as the correspondent of the *Manchester Guardian*, was able to use his close contacts to gain inside information and report on the debates. Even the *Dagblad*, the main newspaper of The Hague, provided him with a page of his own.[43] Towards the end of the conference, he was able to provide Davitt with an insight into the position which the British representatives were adopting on the controversial 'dum-dum' bullet.[44]

When the peace conference had first been proposed by Czar Nicholas II in August 1898, Stead used his journalistic influence to raise public interest in the idea. He launched a new weekly paper in London, *War Against War*, and organized an International Peace Crusade. He was already well known for his campaigns against Bulgarian atrocities, child prostitution, and slavery, and for his support for causes such as housing for the poor. He had advocated arms limitations in the early 1890s and was a proponent of international arbitration.[45] During the peace conference, Davitt praised him for his stand 'for humanity and for liberty'.[46] Davitt himself had highlighted the need for

37 *Irish People*, 4 Nov. 1899; cited in McCracken, *Forgotten protest*, p. 49. 38 McCracken, *Forgotten protest*, p. 43. 39 Roberts, *Salisbury*, p. 741. 40 *Hansard*, 4th series, 74, cols. 687–88, 8 Feb. 1898. 41 Stead to Davitt, 12 July 1899, DP, TCD, MS 9450/3620. 42 Shabtai Rosenne (ed.), *The Hague peace conferences of 1899 and 1907 and international arbitration: reports and documents* (The Hague, 2001), pp xv–xvi. 43 Barbara Tuchman, *The proud tower: a portrait of the world before the war, 1890–1914* (New York, 1996), 257. 44 Stead to Davitt, 20 July 1899, DP, TCD, MS 9450/3621. 45 Tuchman, *The proud tower*, pp 245–8. 46 Davitt to Stead, 18 July 1899, SP, CAC, MS 1/19.

an international tribunal as early as 1882. As Carla King has noted, he was ahead of his time in this regard.[47] In Portland he wrote,

> The progress in Government has been generally from the despotic towards the responsible and the popular, from restriction towards freedom – from incapacity towards skill. There is still room for vast improvement in this department of civilization. Wars, or the reckless sacrifice of human life – often in pursuit of immoral ends, generally to attain questionable advantages for the people who have to pay for them, should be abandoned in favour of Arbitration. When the mass of all nations become educated and see the criminal folly of these wholesale murders of the human species, it will be an easy task to compel civilized governments to submit their disputes to the adjudication of an International Arbitration Tribunal instead of to the sword.[48]

Although The Hague conference failed to achieve agreement on arms reductions, a Permanent Court of Arbitration was nevertheless established; and one of the 'Declarations' accepted by the conference was a prohibition on the use of the 'dum-dum'.[49] British delegates did not sign the military convention, although they accepted that it had a certain moral validity, at lest for 'a white man's war'.[50] This acceptance resulted in the later decision not to use reserve supplies of the 'dum-dum' in the Anglo–Boer conflict. Yet it is significant that it was against the backdrop of the historic peace conference that Britain took the decision to go to war in South Africa in the first instance. Davitt believed it was a decision that would 'rank in history as the greatest crime of the nineteenth century'.[51] The war even seemed to have led him to despair of universal arbitration. He told Dillon that he was only prepared to believe in its efficacy if 'England is compelled to disgorge some of her burglar nation plunder'.[52]

In the flurry of speculation on Davitt's motives for resigning his parliamentary seat, it was cynically suggested by Tim Healy that he had taken umbrage at his failure to secure a nomination to the secretaryship of Mayo county council.[53] Redmond also apparently accused him of 'playing to the gallery'.[54] There

---

47 Davitt, *Jottings*, p. 255. 48 Ibid., p. 120. 49 Rosenne, *The Hague*, p. 138. 50 Quoted in T. Pakenham, *The Boer war* (London, 1992), p. 251. 51 Davitt's speech of resignation, 25 Oct. 1899, in King (ed.), *Michael Davitt*, vol. ii, p. 6. 52 Davitt to Dillon, 11 Dec. 1900, DP, TCD, MS 9411/1828. It is significant that only a few months before this letter, Stead had attempted to get Davitt involved in a new, international campaign for arbitration; see Stead to Davitt, 21 Sept. 1900, DP, TCD, MS 9450/3362. 53 *FJ*, 27 Oct. 1899. Davitt had earlier denied that he had any intention of putting himself forward for the post; see *FJ*, 15 Sept. 1899. 54 Davitt to Dillon, Sept. 1901, JDP, TCD, MS 6728/113.

is no doubt, however, that Davitt was genuinely outraged by the war. Moreover, as he himself told Webb, it was precisely the conduct of nationalist members who remained away from the war sessions in parliament, and the 'action of Healy in trying to turn the occasion into a disgraceful row among the few who attended', that led him to his decision. He found that he simply 'could no longer work with such men'.[55] Webb himself had resigned in 1895 over the Party's failure to check Healy. Shortly after his resignation he told Dillon, 'For some years my happiness or unhappiness in life have [*sic*] to a not inconsiderable degree depended upon the vagaries of Mr. Healy'. He later experienced bouts of nostalgia for parliamentary life, but these were 'cleared […] away' by his experience of Britain's 'force, fraud and brutal imperialism' in South Africa.[56] Indeed, if Webb had been an MP in 1899 he would most probably have followed Davitt's lead.

The RIC believed that Davitt had actually decided to resign even before the war.[57] It is certainly true that he detested Westminster as much as ever. Only a year earlier he had told the house of commons that he considered membership the continuation of 'a punishment not too richly deserved, and I frequently sigh, while sitting helpless on the Benches, for the days when, instead of vainly trying to make laws, I might have built up a lasting reputation in Dartmoor as a stonebreaker'.[58] He viewed his parliamentary career as a personal sacrifice which was made to advance the constitutional agenda and to support Dillon. But he was desperate to extricate himself from his responsibilities to the Party, and as early as November 1896 he told Dillon that he must be allowed to retire 'altogether'.[59] By the turn of the century, particularly with the reconciliation within the movement, he believed that he had fulfilled his role. He told Dillon, 'I have done my duty to the League and Party in what I have already done. I don't feel called to do any more and I will not'.[60] McCracken is accurate in his observation that, 'Standing between the advanced men and the parliamentarians, [Davitt] had found himself on the periphery of both nationalist movements'.[61] It is important to note, indeed, that Davitt had begun to actively encourage a broader level of co-operation between constitutional nationalists and separatists.[62] The Dublin police observed that he 'never fails to do anything he can to attract the extreme party and constitute himself as a connecting link between the two parties'.[63] His resignation speech

---

55 Davitt to Webb, 30 Oct. 1899, DP, TCD, MS 9490/4962. **56** Webb, *Alfred Webb*, pp 10, 73. **57** McCracken, *Forgotten protest*, p. 89. **58** *Hansard*, 4th series, 53, col. 1095, 18 Feb. 1898. **59** Davitt to Dillon, Nov. 1896, DP, TCD, MS 9407/1733. **60** Davitt to Dillon, Sept. 1901, JDP, TCD, MS 6728/113. **61** McCracken, *Forgotten protest*, p. 89. **62** See Matthew Kelly, 'The end of Parnellism and the ideological dilemmas of Sinn Féin' in Boyce and O'Day (eds), *Ireland in transition, 1867–1921* (London, 2003), pp 149 (and note 39), pp 264–5. **63** Quoted in ibid., p. 149.

certainly had the whiff of cordite about it and could be said to have constituted an appeal to the 'hillside men'.

Having resigned, he committed himself fully to pro-Boer activities. When he learned that Chamberlain was to pay a high-profile visit to Dublin in December to receive an honorary degree from Trinity college he seized the opportunity to attack both the war and Chamberlain as its 'prime author'.[64] The Irish Transvaal Committee organized a protest demonstration to be held at Beresford Place on Sunday 17 December, the day before the colonial secretary's planned visit. This proved to be the scene of a running battle between the police and protestors when the committee's main activists, John O'Leary, James Connolly, Maud Gonne and Arthur Griffith, decided to lead crowds of Boer supporters to the designated venue in defiance of a ban by Dublin Castle.[65] When the demonstration was eventually moved to the offices of the Transvaal Committee in Abbey Street, Davitt and Willie Redmond arrived, and, along with other members of the committee, addressed a highly charged, but exultant, crowd. Proclaiming a victory for the protestors, Davitt lampooned Dublin Castle officials for their 'imbecility' in highlighting the pro-Boer cause by banning the Beresford Place meeting in the first instance. He castigated the authorities of Trinity college, that 'academic Orange Lodge', and described their decision to bring Chamberlain to Dublin as being in keeping with a tradition of 'anti-Irish' sentiment and religious and political bigotry. In his attack on Britain's 'criminal conspiracy' in South Africa, he challenged a recent speech by Chamberlain in which the latter claimed Germany and the United States as allies.[66] The German and American governments were certainly both sympathetic to Britain; the Kaiser even suggested ways in which the British might defeat the Boers.[67] But Davitt pointed to the popular anti-war and pro-Boer feeling in Germany and to the prevalence of such sentiment among Irish–Americans and other European immigrant communities in the United States. He pointed out that 'even President McKinley was compelled' to deny an Anglo–American alliance within forty-eight hours of Chamberlain's claims.[68]

Irish nationalists were gripped by 'pro-Boer fever', especially after 'Black Week' in mid-December 1899, during which the British suffered three consecutive defeats in major battles at Stormberg, Magersfontein and Colenso. Davitt went so far as to assert that the Boer successes had brought Britain as a military power 'to the dust [...] out of which it is not likely to rise again in our generation'. He roused his Dublin audience to laughter when he stated that the only other European power that now considered Britain a threat was the prince

64 *FJ*, 18 Dec. 1899. **65** McCracken, *Forgotten protest*, pp 54–6. **66** As above, fn. 64. **67** Donal Lowry, '"The Boers were the beginning of the end"?: the wider impact of the South African war' in Donal Lowry (ed.), *The South African war reappraised* (Manchester, 2000), pp 215–18. **68** *FJ*, 18 Dec. 1899.

of Monaco and his 'army of six Generals and fifty men'.[69] In fact, notwithstanding the events of 'Black Week', the Boers had already begun to suffer a reversal of fortunes in the wider context of the war. Still, Davitt's jubilation was understandable: the British public were stunned by the news of the losses suffered at the hands of the small Boer nations; and in his despondency and humiliation, Chamberlain himself could only describe 'Black Week' as Britain's 'darkest hour'.[70] The David-and-Goliath aspect of the war appealed directly to Davitt's imagination. As he told Stead before the outbreak of hostilities, 'Just think of it! The British Empire against – 130,000 God-fearing Boers!'.[71] Davitt depicted the Boers as virtuous, Christian yeomen, resisting the tyranny of a corrupt empire. Acutely aware of the international focus on the conflict, he was determined to offset any British propagandistic portrayals of the Boers as 'wanting in "civilization"'. They were, he argued, only destitute of the civilization peculiar to 'Anglo-Saxon countries – that of a godless culture, of refined vice, of divorce courts and immorality, of drunkenness and prostitution'.[72] Rather than a 'semi-savage foeman', president Kruger was a 'sincerely religious man' of unimpeachable integrity who was committed to his country and his family. The Boer General, Louis Botha, was 'a gentleman farmer' and 'a man of conspicuous natural culture'. Davitt even attributed British military defeats to the 'superiority' of the Boer character. Of the battle at Colenso he later remarked,

> Physically, mentally, and morally the veldt Dutchman, reared on the farms of the country for which he was fighting as head of a family, was, for a South African campaign, as much more capable than the uniformed anaemic product of British city and slum life, trained under a brainless military system which teaches a soldier to do nothing except as he is ordered by his "superiors", as a finished athlete is in strength and muscle above a factory operative disguised in Tommy Atkins's toggery. In health and strength, in powers of endurance, in clearness of vision and consequent accuracy of aim, in nerves free from the shaky effects of dissipation, in the capacity of individual initiative, and, above all, in the consciousness of moral manhood sustained by religious conviction, the average Boer of Botha's little army on the Tugela was a match for any five of the kind of men whom Buller had, tho these were accounted the crack regiments of the British army.[73]

Davitt's involvement in the pro-Boer cause was his most serious anti-imperialist engagement. He believed that the Boer resistance had potentially far-

---

69 Ibid. **70** Pakenham, *The Boer war*, p. 247. **71** Davitt to Stead, 14 July 1899, SP, CAC, MS 1/19. **72** Davitt, *The Boer fight for freedom: from the beginning of hostilities to the peace of Pretoria* (New York and London, 1902), p. 37. **73** Ibid., pp 29–31, 36, 163, 280.

reaching consequences for the future of the empire. Following his parliamentary resignation he made plans to visit the Tranvaal. After organizing his personal finances,[74] he duly sailed from Marseilles to Portugese East Africa on the 25 February 1900. He travelled in an official capacity as a war correspondent, having been commissioned as a reporter by both the *New York American* and the *Freeman's Journal*.[75] Sailing on board the *Oxus*, he learned that the ship's complement included thirty volunteers for the Boers.[76] He also soon came to suspect that two young Englishmen on board, one of whom had looked 'hard' at him in Mersailles, were British agents.[77] In all, his journey took twenty-nine days, and he arrived in Pretoria on 26 March, the day after his fifty-fourth birthday.[78] On his arrival he met Major John MacBride and learned that there had been a 'split' within the ranks of the Irish Transvaal Brigade under the command of Colonel John Blake. He was not at all surprised. As he told Dillon, '[t]his is inevitable in every Irish concern, military or civil. Col. Blake is, I am told[,] fond of the bottle, and it is alleged MacBride keeps him good company'.[79] Despite Blake's apparent liking for 'the bottle', Davitt later acknowledged his bravery in the war.[80]

Although the trip had taken its toll on him, Davitt was clearly excited to have the opportunity to witness events at first hand, and after spending only one day in the Transvaal capital he set out for the Orange Free State after being told that 'important events were pending' there.[81] He wrote to Dillon, 'Make no mistake about it, this war has scarcely yet begun'.[82] Given his reputation as a Boer sympathizer, Davitt had no difficulty in securing interviews with the Boer leaders. When he first reached Pretoria he was briefed on the course of the war by the Transvaal state secretary, F.W. Reitz, and was then brought to meet President Kruger.[83] Two days later he had an impromptu meeting with the Orange Free State president, Marthinus Steyn, as they journeyed together *en route* to Kroonstad.[84] In just over a week after his arrival in South Africa, Davitt had managed to cover over five hundred miles, visiting Boer camps and interviewing the main political leaders, as well as other

---

74 He borrowed £250; see King, 'Davitt, Irish nationalism and British empire', p. 128. **75** On the back of the front cover of his hard-back diary for 1900 (Feb. – June) Davitt wrote, 'Received a telegram from Stead at Marseilles saying the "New York Journal" will accept letters from me during my stay in the Transvaal'. In the same entry he also noted, 'The Directors of the "Freeman's Journal" sent me a request before I left London to write letters for their paper'; Davitt's diary, 1900, DP, TCD, MS 9572. He left South Africa at the end of May 1900, but his correspondence was delayed in reaching the *Freeman's Journal*. His letters were subsequently published in that paper on 6, 8, 11, 16, 19, 23, 26, 28, and 30 June 1900. **76** Davitt's diary, 25 Feb. 1900, DP, TCD, MS 9572/1. **77** Davitt's diary, 27 Feb. 1900, DP, TCD, MS 9572/7. **78** McCracken, *Forgotten protest*, p. 132. **79** Davitt to Dillon, 4 Apr. 1900, DP, TCD, MS 9411/1803. **80** Davitt to Dillon, 29 Aug. 1902, DP, TCD, MS 9413/1909. **81** *FJ*, 19 June 1900 (Davitt's letter is dated 28 Mar.). **82** Davitt to Dillon, 4 Apr. 1900, DP, TCD, MS 9411/1803. **83** *FJ*, 19 June 1900. **84** Ibid.

members of the respective Volksraads.[85] He also had meetings with leading military figures, such as General J.H. De la Rey,[86] who, along with General Christiaan De Wet, had begun to formulate guerrilla principles for military engagement with the British.[87] Davitt reported that in the key areas of morale, ammunition and food supplies the Boers had the ability to sustain their campaign for another two years.[88] During a sojourn in Kroonstad he met De Wet and was shown the wagons, field-telegraph appliances and food luxuries which the latter had confiscated after his recent victory at Sannah's Post (31 March).[89] Eager to acquire first-hand information on the war and to visit front-line Boer camps, Davitt travelled south from Kroonstad to Brandfort in the second week of April. On the journey he observed a train-load of imprisoned British troops whom he photographed with his Kodak camera.[90] At Brandfort he interviewed Botha[91] and General Tobias Smuts.[92] In his notes on his visit to this Boer camp, he alluded to the Boer character in a very romanticized account:

> Games: favourite one tossing of men in bullocks hide – some men sent as high as 20 feet. All games simple and manly. Did not see a single group (out of 1,000 men) playing at cards. Not a single man with least sign of drink. No rowdyism, no fighting or quarrelling; all enjoying themselves as [if] at a picnic [...] Not a single woman in camp. A Boer family came to visit today with one handsome girl of 14. Attitude of young Boers towards [them] most gentlemanly. Excited very little noise, except from those [the] family came to see.[93]

Davitt's columns made for interesting reading, especially given his attention to detail and his thumbnail sketches of the Boer leaders. Yet his admiration for the Boer character and his sympathy and solidarity with the cause of the two republics were apparent throughout. As Donal Lowry points out, the telegraph had globalized world news by the end of the nineteenth century and both the British and the Boers understood from the beginning that they were involved in a propaganda war.[94] Davitt realized that his own coverage of the war would not go unnoticed in Britain. He told Dillon that 'jingo spies' in Pretoria and Johannesburg had threatened to have him arrested when he returned home. He took this threat seriously and asked Dillon to inform him 'how feeling is in my regard in the London press and otherwise owing to my visit out here'. He believed that '[a]ny trumpted up charge against a pro-Boer

85 *FJ*, 26 June 1900 (Davitt's letter is dated 5 Apr.). 86 *FJ*, 19 June 1900. 87 Pakenham, *The Boer war*, pp 387–90. 88 *FJ*, 26 June 1900. 89 *FJ*, 8 June 1900 (Davitt's letter is dated 14 Apr.); see Pakenham, *The Boer war*, pp 392–5. 90 Ibid. 91 *FJ*, 6 June 1900 (Davitt's letter is dated 12 Apr.). 92 *FJ*, 8 June 1900. 93 Davitt's account of visit to Boer camp, 15 Apr., 1900, DP, TCD, MS 9645/1–4. 94 Lowry, "'The Boers were the beginning'", p. 203.

– myself especially – would be enough for a London jury, under the prevailing jingoism', to condemn him to another period of imprisonment. To avoid such a fate, he was prepared to relocate himself and his family to America for a few years, if there was a sign of 'any *real* danger'.[95] He wrote to Dillon again with the same fears were playing on his mind.[96] Nevertheless, he continued to travel throughout the Boer states and to report on events up until mid-May. By the beginning of May the British had captured Bloemfontein, and Field-Marshall Lord Roberts had resumed his advance north towards Pretoria.[97] Due to inadequate defences, the Transvaal executive decided not to defend the capital against the imminent British offensive, and on 7 May the last meeting of the Volksraad was held. It was with a certain poignancy that Davitt wrote of this final session, which he himself attended. The assembly struck him as 'painfully suggestive of a funeral ceremony over the body of what would soon be a slain Republic'.[98] If the event was funereal, Davitt was a bona fide mourner. On 15 May, as he made preparations to depart from South Africa, he wrote,

> Farewell Pretoria! You will soon cease to be [the] capital of a Nation. The enemy will make you another of his "centres" of civilization. Brothels, paupers, hypocrites, gospel mongers in the pay of British mammon [...] will replace the kind of life you have been familiar with.[99]

Pretoria eventually fell on 5 June.

Despite his anxiety about the possibility of arrest, Davitt returned to Ireland on 1 July.[1] By this stage, the hit-and-run guerrilla tactics of De Wet and De la Rey had resulted in a series of military coups for the Boers. De Wet's brother, Piet, won a notable victory at the end of May when he forced the surrender of a battalion of Irish Yeomanry at Lindley; De Wet himself followed this up a week later with another win at Roodewal. The inability of the British to pin down the Boers left Roberts frustrated, and soon disabused him of the view that the war was practically over. Not for the first time, the British public were astonished and unsettled by the tenacity of the Boers.[2] Salisbury, for his part, found it 'painful' to learn of such British defeats.[3] But in Ireland, the news only served to galvanize the pro-Boer movement throughout the summer months.[4]

In October, Davitt drafted an address to be presented to Kruger who was *en route* to Europe after a dramatic exit from the Transvaal.[5] Having been com-

95 Davitt to Dillon, 25 Apr. 1900, DP, TCD, MS 9411/1805. **96** Davitt to Dillon, 23 June 1900, DP, TCD, MS 9411/1811. **97** Pakenham, *The Boer war*, pp 371–2. **98** Davitt, *The Boer fight*, p. 422. **99** Quoted in McCracken, *Forgotten protest*, p. 132. **1** *FJ*, 2 July 1900. **2** Pakenham, *The Boer war*, pp 435–7, 445, 449. **3** Roberts, *Salisbury*, p. 767. **4** McCracken, *Forgotten protest*, pp 71–2. **5** *FJ*, 20 Oct. 1900; Pakenham, *The Boer war*, p. 458.

missioned by the *New York American* to cover the event and to report on the 'important revelations' which were expected of Kruger, Davitt travelled to Marseilles in November.[6] The Irish Transvaal Committee, out of which Griffith's Cumann na nGaedheal organization had just emerged, also prepared an address and sent a delegation to greet the Transvaal president on his arrival.[7] It is significant that after his return from South Africa, Davitt sometimes put in an appearance at Dublin meetings of the Griffithite Celtic Literary Society,[8] a debating club of advanced nationalists which became openly critical of the parliamentary approach of the Irish Party.[9] However, it was with an address signed by nationalist MPs, as representative of the Irish nation, that he met and welcomed Kruger in Europe.[10] Irish MPs keenly sought meetings with the Boer leaders in Europe, even though quite a number, including Healy, Redmond and even Dillon, had had qualms about signing the address.[11] Davitt himself often arranged such meetings. He was recognized by the Boer leaders as an important ally and they stayed in close contact with him. At The Hague in August 1902, he dined with De la Rey and his family. He also spent time with De Wet on this occasion, jokingly informing him of the Irish legend which alleged that he (De la Rey) was Parnell. On departing at the end of his visit, Davitt was 'warmly thanked [...] for his services' by the Boer generals.[12] Interestingly, while stopping in Paris on his return journey, he wrote to Dillon, 'Maud Gonne and MacBride found poor old Dr Reitz here [...] and obtained an advertisement for themselves out of the visit which was duly cabled to New York'.[13]

Since his return to Ireland immediately after the war, Davitt had been working on a book on the conflict in the hope of making 'a couple of hundred pounds out of my six months' labours'.[14] The finished work, *The Boer fight for freedom*, was published in America in May 1902. It did not enjoy substantial sales: although there was, curiously, an order placed for a dozen copies by the British vice-consul of 'one of the ports in Puerto Rico', there was only a demand for 250 copies from South Africa and 'stray orders' from Australia.[15] This was, no doubt, due partly to the fact that the Boer leaders themselves, De Wet, Botha, and De la Rey, were having their own accounts of the conflict published.[16] Davitt's book was based on his own observations and primary sources, and, for the latter part of the war, on secondary reports from which he constructed a war narrative up until the final peace of Pretoria. Though

6 Davitt to Dillon, 12 Nov. 1900, DP, TCD, MS 9411/1823. 7 McCracken, *Forgotten protest*, p. 72. 8 Kelly, 'The end of Parnellism', p. 149. 9 Brian Maye, *Arthur Griffith* (Dublin, 1997), p. 95. 10 McCracken, *Forgotten protest*, p. 72. 11 Ibid., 95. 12 DP, TCD, MS 9645/5–14. 13 Davitt to Dillon, 29 Aug. 1902, DP, TCD, MS 9413/1909. 14 Davitt to Dillon, 12 Nov. 1900, DP, TCD, MS 9411/1823. 15 Funk and Wagnalls to Davitt, 1902, DP, TCD, MS 9480/4573. 16 McCracken, *Forgotten protest*, 146.

described as a potboiler by McCracken, the work has also been claimed as a classic.[17] As its title implies, it was written from an unashamedly pro-Boer perspective. It was dedicated to the late General Philip Botha,[18] brother of Louis Botha, and in its preface Davitt paid thanks to the Boer officers and officials 'who were my travelling and tent companions in my visits to the various camps'.[19] Davitt was, of course, only present in South Africa for a limited period, but he depended on Boer testimonies and official reports for the material for his work. His account of the war was clearly intended to offset the 'Falstaffian exaggeration' of the British 'Jingo' press.[20] Even while writing the book, he found himself in conflict with the London *Daily Mail*.[21] Yet, despite his attack on 'anti-Boer falsehoods',[22] his own treatment of events was no less questionable. He argued, for instance, that British 'inhumanity' during the war had extended to violations of the Red Cross, notably at Dundee in October 1899, where Boer doctors were apparently attacked and imprisoned. He unquestioningly relied on reports in the Boer press to support his case.[23] However, a more recent, thoroughgoing account has conversely claimed that the Boers themselves had contravened the Geneva Convention by shelling British field hospitals at Dundee with a Krupp 40-pounder Long Tom, despite the presence of a twelve-foot-high Red Cross flag.[24] As Stephen Howe has observed, Davitt was 'predisposed credulously to swallow any and every story of British atrocities'.[25]

In his coverage of the war, Davitt also gave scant regard to British allegations of Boer oppression of the indigenous population. British imperialists had attempted to justify the war by arguing that it was being waged in the interests of the rights of native Africans. This claim did not carry much weight. As Lowry remarks, the portrayal of Salisbury, Chamberlain and Sir Alfred Milner as moral crusaders 'made very unconvincing propaganda material'.[26] Nevertheless, Davitt failed to seriously investigate the allegations in the way in which he had dealt with the 'black labour problem' in Australia.[27] During his time in South Africa he raised the issue of the alleged maltreatment of natives with Boers leaders and others whom he met and interviewed. He was told by General Smuts that the 'loyal' conduct of the 'Kaffir population' in the context of the war was 'the strongest human proof that a people who can act in this manner [...] are not a race upon whom we trample or whom we maltreat in ordinary times'.[28] Davitt, curiously, seemed convinced by this dubious line

17 Ibid., p. 132; Stephen Howe, *Ireland and empire: colonial legacies in Irish history and culture* (Oxford, 2000), p. 46. **18** At the same time that the book was published, Davitt and Alfred Webb opened a fund for Botha's widow; *FJ*, 15 May 1902. **19** Davitt, *The Boer fight*, preface. **20** Ibid., p. 96. **21** *FJ*, 22 Oct. 1900. **22** Ibid. **23** Davitt, *The Boer fight*, p. 138. **24** Pakenham, *The Boer war*, p. 143. **25** Howe, *Ireland and empire*, p. 46. **26** Lowry, '"The Boers were the beginning"' p. 205. **27** Davitt's diary, 28 July 1895, DP, TCD, MS 9563/7. **28** *FJ*, 8 June 1900.

of reasoning. He himself had observed native Africans on the land, and in a brief diary entry he commented that their passivity in the absence of their "'Masters'", who were away at war, was in itself 'very strong evidence of the considerate way in which they are treated by the Boers in times of peace'.[29] Ultimately, he refused to accept the British allegations as anything other than propaganda. His general acceptance of the viewpoint of figures such as Smuts can probably be explained by wilful naiveté.

Davitt viewed the Anglo–Boer conflict very simply: he unconditionally accepted the Boers as the true nation of South Africa and simultaneously dismissed the Uitlanders as a British garrison; the indigenous black population did not figure at all in the political equation. His indifference towards native Africans was typical of the attitude prevalent among pro-Boer activists in Ireland, and among small-nation nationalists and leftist movements in Europe.[30] There were exceptions, however, such as Hyndman and the Polish socialist, Rosa Luxemburg, both of whom remarked on the fact that the native majority had no stake in the conflict.[31] Keir Hardie romanticized the Boers during the war,[32] but he, too, later became critical of the failure of the Afrikaners to concede political rights to the majority population. He raised the 'native question' in the house of commons and argued that the customary land rights of black tribes should be recognized.[33] Yet these issues were flatly disregarded by Davitt. Indeed, in his account of the war, he repeatedly referred to native Africans as 'savages'. In highlighting the merits of Johannesburg's civic culture before the outbreak of the war, he remarked on the 'enlightened administration in its cities and towns' and praised the police and magistracy for ensuring that '[e]ighty thousand savages [mine workers] were kept under orderly control [...] and made subject to civilized laws and customs'.[34] No mention was made of working conditions in the mines or of the Transvaal's discriminatory racial laws which forbade natives to walk on the pavement. When the British forces captured Johannesburg in May 1900, Lord Roberts himself utilized these existing racial laws to impose the same style of law and order on the local native population.[35]

It is significant that the area of British military conduct which Davitt singled out for particular condemnation was the employment of Africans as combatants in the war. Natives had been employed by both the Boers and the British in a variety of unarmed functions, such as scouts and spies, but Colonel R.S.S. Baden-Powel set a precedent during the siege of Mafeking when he

29 Davitt's diary, Feb.–June 1900, DP, TCD, MS 9572/105.   **30** Howe, *Ireland and empire*, p. 57.
31 Lowry, "'The Boers were the beginning'", pp 210–11.   **32** Morgan, *Keir Hardie*, p. 105. The race issue in South Africa was also dealt with in the *Labour Leader*; see, for example, *Labour Leader*, 23 June 1905.   **33** Ibid., p. 197.   **34** Davitt, *The Boer fight*, pp 12–13.   **35** Pakenham, *The Boer war*, p. 429.

equipped 300 Africans with rifles.[36] Davitt's account of the attack by black combatants on a Boer laager at Derdepoort in the north-west of the Transvaal in the early stages of the war evoked something of what Pakenham describes as 'the spectre of a black peril', which later 'rode with every Boer commando'.[37] Colonel G.L. Holdsworth and Africans of the Beuchuana chief, Linchwe, had attacked the Derdepoort laager in November 1899, but as the British column retreated, Linchwe's men continued their strike on the Boer camp and then turned their attack on a nearby white community.[38] In recounting the event, Davitt stated that

> the Kaffirs [...] killed a lady, an American by birth, in bed, and mortally wounded her husband, who was in the act of rising when the savages burst into the room. A German trader was disembowelled and otherwise tortured, while an English photographer named Early was hacked to death with spears.[39]

In fact, two white civilians were murdered in the 'massacre', not four.[40] Yet for Davitt there was no 'blacker' or 'more repulsive deed to be found in the annals of this war'. He condemned the British for having 'armed savages to help her in a war which had its origins in the motives as base and as odious as ever prompted the Sultan of Turkey to burn an Armenian village or to massacre his rebellious subjects'.[41]

Davitt's attitude to the South African natives was clearly not consistent with a crusade for international justice and liberty. Of course, his opposition to the British campaign was visceral, and it could be argued that he was, to some extent, blinded by his loyalty to the Boers. However, the racist tone of his language, not only in relation to native Africans but also in reference to indigenous races elsewhere, raises a more fundamental question about his own cultural prejudices, and even his attitude to imperial encounters. It is true, he not only attacked British rule in Ireland but also denounced British and French imperial expansion in West Africa. However, he still later described West Africans as 'savages'.[42] The term was also applied to the Australian Aborigines,[43] the Maoris[44] and native North Americans,[45] albeit without the harsh overtones which were reserved for South Africans. Davitt apparently saw no contradiction in using such language

36 Davitt, *The Boer fight*, pp 169–71; see also Pakenham, *The Boer war*, p. 402. 37 Pakenham, *The Boer war*, p. 472. 38 Fransjohan Pretorius, 'Boer attitudes to Africans in wartime' in Lowry (ed.), *The South African war reappraised* (Manchester, 2000), p. 106. 39 Davitt, *The Boer fight*, p. 174. 40 Pretorius, 'Boer attitudes', p. 106; Pakenham, *The Boer war*, p. 472. 41 Davitt, *The Boer fight*, pp 171, 593. 42 Davitt, 'What I think of the English', *Universal Magazine*, July 1900, in King (ed.), *Michael Davitt*, vol. ii, p. 3. 43 Davitt, *Life and progress*, p. 36. 44 Ibid., p. 383. 45 Davitt, 'Impressions' , p. 635.

while at the same time attacking the British for subjugating 'so-called savage races'.[46] An entry in his diary during his visit to Samoa in 1895 indicates that he was certainly conscious of the pejorative nature of the term. He noted that it was hardly applicable to the 'courteous and agreeable' natives whom he encountered on the island.[47] However, while he objected to the use of the term as part of the standard language of imperialism, he appears, at the same time, to have been largely oblivious to the fact that his own frequent references to 'savages' betrayed a certain sense of cultural superiority.

It seems that even though Davitt was staunchly opposed to aggressive empire-building – which is the context within which he viewed the Anglo–Boer war – he was nevertheless open to white European, even imperial, encounters with 'savage' peoples which were not part of obvious structures of enslavement. In describing the 'enlightened' work of Catholic missionaries among Aborigines in Western Australia, he commented that the native children connected with the Benedictine monastery at New Norica, eighty miles north of Perth, were 'eminently teachable', and that, through the instruction of the brothers of the missionary community, the girls had a good command of the English language and the young native men were 'very fond of cricket, and are excellent players'.[48] Catholic missionaries, Spanish Benedictine brothers and Irish Sister of Mercy, had had a presence in the colony since 1846 when they were brought to the region by the first Catholic bishop of Perth, Irishman John Brady. Brady had been critical of the oppression of natives by European colonizers. But even though he argued that the human dignity of the Aborigine should be recognized and respected, his missionary project did not involve the restoration or protection of Aboriginal culture. Catherine Kovesi Killerby points out that while Brady and early Irish missionaries 'may not have subscribed to the nineteenth-century attitudes of biological and ethical superiority of white Europeans, they did believe in their own cultural superiority'.[49] Observing the work of the Christian community in the colony half a century later, Davitt, likewise, did not question the cultural values which were being inculcated in the natives. It is clear that by describing Aboriginal children as 'eminently teachable' he essentially meant that they were civilizable.

This attitude was also evident in his commentary on progress in Canada. He was impressed by the way in which native Indians had been 'induc[ed]' by the Canadian government to 'put off the customs of savage for the habits of civilized life'. One of the 'prettiest' scenes which he witnessed during a visit

46 Davitt, *The fall*, p. 723. **47** 'Visit to Samoa', 5 Dec. 1895, DP, TCD, MS 9644. **48** Davitt, *Life and progress*, pp 35–6. **49** Catherine Kovesi Killerby, '"Never locked up or tied": early Irish missionary attitudes to the Aboriginal people of Western Australia' in Philip Bull, Frances Devlin-Glass and Helen Doyle (eds), *Ireland and Australia, 1798–1998: studies in culture, identity and migration* (Sydney, 2000), pp 125–31.

to Vancouver was 'that presented by an Indian village of white houses, with a white church in the centre, peeping out from a forest of pines on the banks of the Burrand Inlet'. The Canadian policy of culturally assimilating the indigenous population was, he argued, more 'enlightened' than the 'system of extermination' adopted by the United States administration.[50] Less than a year before his visit to Canada, almost 300 Sioux men, women and children had been massacred by US soldiers at Wounded Knee, in the battle which concluded the US conquest of the North American Indian.[51] Yet by simply describing the Canadian policy on natives as 'far *more* humane' than that of the United States (my italics), and only briefly alluding to the US 'system of extermination', Davitt betrayed his own cultural prejudices and an inconsistency in addressing issues of justice and liberty. He was much more exercised by the murder of white Christian civilians at Derdepoort in his later account of the Anglo–Boer war. Ultimately, he never questioned the cultural superiority of white Europeans. In his early writings in Portland, he even remarked that in its early involvement in India, Britain had had an 'opportunity of substituting a Christian and modern civilization for that of a barbarous and declining one, and of planting the religion of the Gospel in the heart of Asia', but had decided instead to satisfy its own narrow economic interests.[52] Again, there is evidence here of the distinction which he drew between positive European influences and encounters, and structures of enslavement. In the case of the South African conflict, he was unable to conceive of the native population as oppressed because the Afrikaners were, in his view, involved in a counter-hegemonic struggle. He seemed to consider the African natives who were combatants on the British side all the more 'savage' because they were, as he understood it, colluding with imperialists and capitalists.

For Davitt, the British war in South Africa was a capitalist war, designed to serve the specific interests of the Uitlander 'capitalist kings' on the Rand. He lamented that 'unfortunate "Tommies" had to die' in a conflict fought for 'the capitalists and schemers of London and Johannesburg'.[53] As it happens, he himself had had investment interests in South African mining since 1896 when he, Charles Diamond and T.P. O'Connor formed a mining syndicate. In January 1896 he 'paid £100 in to Diamond's hand', with another £150 to follow, several months before the latter sailed for South Africa in search of investment opportunities.[54] In September, Diamond reported back from Johannesburg, 'The place is the happy hunting ground for capitalists with colossal fortunes and without a single scruple. Corruption is rampant, and one

---

50 Davitt, 'Impressions', p. 635. 51 The battle of Wounded Knee occurred on 29 Dec. 1890; see Dee Brown, *Bury my heart at wounded knee: an Indian history of the American west* (London, 1991), pp 440–5. 52 Davitt, *Jottings*, pp 19–20. 53 Davitt, *The Boer fight*, pp 28–9, 116. 54 Davitt's diary, Jan. 1896, DP, TCD, MS 9568/2.

has to buy everything'.[55] Given Davitt's attack on 'capitalist kings' on the Rand, his own involvement in such a venture appears highly hypocritical. Although F.H. O'Donnell was inaccurate in his later description of Davitt as a communist, he nevertheless made an interesting observation when he remarked, 'Like other communists, Mr Davitt could be inconsistent. I remember the pleasure and profit which he derived from a favoured allotment of Lipton shares that he was enabled to sell in the rising market, just like any capitalist speculator at Capel Court or on Wall Street'.[56] Indeed, in March 1898 Davitt wrote to William O'Brien, 'You will I know be glad to learn that Lipton has given me a thousand shares. T.P. has got another thousand. I am now a bloated capitalist and so am likely to start for New York [...]'[57] Davitt's remarks were made somewhat tongue-in-cheek, but his entrepreneurial undertakings were significant all the same. He seemed, however, to have had no ethical qualms about his investments, not even in South Africa. Of course, he essentially ignored the abject working conditions of black miners in Johannesburg, and in this he was hypocritical. But against such a charge as that levelled by O'Donnell, he would have justified his speculative dealings by drawing a distinction between the small shareholder and the large, monopoly capitalist.

In his famous pamphlet, *Imperialism, the highest stage of capitalism* (1916), Lenin wrote that capitalism had undergone a significant transformation in the later decades of the nineteenth century, during which a coalescence of bank and industrial capital had resulted in the prevalence of monopoly capitalism and the creation of a 'financial oligarchy'. He contended that the lack of investment opportunities in economically advanced countries, where capitalism had become 'overripe', had necessitated imperialist expansion as a means of securing new, external arenas of profitable investment. 'It is beyond doubt', he asserted, 'that capitalism's transition to the stage of monopoly capitalism [...] is *connected* with the intensification of the struggle for the partition of the world'.[58] Capitalism at its highest stage had, therefore, 'been transformed into imperialism'.[59] While Davitt certainly identified the causes of the Anglo–Boer war with the demands of large capitalists, his assessment was not based on a

---

55 Diamond to Davitt, 6 Sept. 1896, DP, MS 9478/4469–4492. **56** O'Donnell, *The history*, vol. i, p. 502. **57** Davitt to William O'Brien, 31 Mar. 1898, NLI, MS 913. McFarland, *John Ferguson*, claims, p. 263, that Sir Thomas Lipton's 'gift' of 1000 shares to Davitt was only discovered after Davitt's death. However, the letter to O'Brien proves that the 'gift' was not exactly a secret. **58** Lenin, *Imperialism, the highest stage of capitalism* (Peking, 1975), pp 52–3, 72–5, 92. **59** Ibid., p. 20. Lenin's argument was challenged after the Second World War. D. K. Fieldhouse, for instance, rejected the idea of an obvious correlation between colonial acquisitions and the export of capital; Fieldhouse, '"Imperialism": an historiographical revision', *Economic History Review*, 80 (1965). On the same point, Agatha Ramm has, incidentally, remarked that Germany's East-African colony cost more than it was worth and also failed to receive much financial investment; Ramm, *Europe in the twentieth century, 1905–1970* (London, 1987), p. 184.

thoroughgoing analysis of capitalism. Like Hardie, he simply pointed to the machinations of certain capitalists in his diagnosis of the causes of the conflict. Hardie's analysis of the war was, according to Morgan, based on 'traditional radical arguments [and …] differed very little in kind from Bright and Cobden's denunciation of the Crimean War almost fifty years earlier'.[60]

In his attack on the Rand's 'capitalist kings', Davitt named and specifically singled out over forty prominent Jewish speculators whom he considered guilty, along 'with Mr Cecil Rhodes, [of] hav[ing] succeeded in enforcing [their own commercial interests] by the arbitrament of war – at a cost to the British people of over £150,000,000 in taxes, and 30,000 lives'.[61] Davitt's portrayal of Jewish magnates as instigators of imperialist expansion was indicative of the strain of anti-Semitism which coloured the arguments and rhetoric of many pro-Boers and anti-war campaigners, notable among whom were John Burns and the English economist, J.A. Hobson.[62] Yet, despite his expressed views, Davitt had earlier written, in a letter which was published in the *Freeman's Journal*, that Ireland could boast of having never had a 'share in this black record [of …] un-Christian and barbarous treatment of [the] unfortunate [Jewish] people'. He even identified the plight of the Jews with the Irish experience of emigration and exile. Moreover, he condemned 'Tory protectionists' for blaming low wages and trade depression in London's East End on the influx of Jewish immigrants.[63] As King has pointed out, the apparent contradiction in Davitt's outlook reflected the clear distinction which he made between affluent, influential Jews and the ordinary Jewish masses who were periodically subjected to oppression and persecution.[64] In *Within the pale*, his 1903 work on the persecution of the Russian Jew, he made his position clear when he wrote,

> Where anti-Semitism stands, in fair political combat, in opposition to the foes of nationality, or against the engineers of a sordid war in South Africa, or as the assailant of the economic evils of unscrupulous capitalism anywhere, I am resolutely in line with its spirit and programme. Where, however, it only speaks and acts in a cowardly racial warfare, which descends to the use of an atrocious fabrication responsible for odious and unspeakable crimes […] it becomes a thing deserving of no more toleration from right-minded men than do the germs of some malady laden with the poison of a malignant disease.[65]

It was in May 1903 that the *New York American* commissioned Davitt to travel to Russia to investigate and report on the anti-Semitic pogrom in Kishinev

60 Morgan, *Keir Hardie*, pp 105–6. **61** Davitt, *The Boer fight*, pp 28–9. **62** Lowry, '"The Boers were the beginning"', p. 205. **63** *FJ*, 13 July 1893. **64** King, 'Davitt, Irish nationalism and British empire', p. 129. **65** Davitt, *Within the pale*, pp ix–x.

in the province of Bessarabia. Davitt's international profile, especially his journalism, undoubtedly made him a candidate for the assignment. King suggests
that he was probably the first choice.[66] He had, of course, already reported on
the Anglo–Boer war for the *New York American* only a few years earlier.
Predictably, he quickly accepted the Kishinev commission and set out for
Russia in mid-May.[67] While travelling to Constantinople and Odessa he had
a chance encounter with Hyndman, with whom he journeyed by train for two
days. According to Hyndman, Davitt's initial comments on their meeting were,
"'We might swear all the oaths we liked, Hyndman, but there is not a police
bureau in Europe would believe that this is an accidental meeting'".[68] Davitt
eventually reached Kishinev on 22 May and spent just over a week in the town.
His reports were widely printed in Europe and America, after their initial publication in the *New York American*, and served as material for *Within the pale*,
his fifth major work.[69] In his various visits to other countries, he generally had
a future publication in mind as a source of income. He told Hyndman that he
had been drawn to the Russian assignment for financial reasons.[70] However,
his intense interest in international affairs was, without doubt, the real moti-
vating factor in his decision to undertake the mission. Indeed, it must be pointed out that there is no evidence to suggest that in his various journalistic com-
missions, Davitt was ever guilty of self-censorship, or of having tailored his
reports to conform to the line taken by a particular paper.

In the preface to *Within the pale*, he made the claim of balanced reporting:
'While in Russia I tried to find both sides of the anti-Semitic Question, so
as to give expression to all views which could throw light upon the crimes that
had shocked the public mind in America and in Europe [...]'[71] It is apparent
from his written account that he took a thoroughly investigative approach to
the claims of persecution. Although on the ground for only a short time, he
exhaustively interviewed all the parties concerned, the Jewish community and
the government officials, and considered all the existing evidence.[72] This is
confirmed in a recent, authoritative examination of the pogrom by Edward
Judge who acknowledges Davitt's findings as 'Perhaps the most objective testimonies' of the time.[73] Davitt's reportage of the massacre was certainly much
in contrast to his coverage of the war in South Africa. He concluded that the
attacks on the Jews had been orchestrated by local anti-Semitic leaders, principally Pavolachi Kroushevan, editor of the *Bessarabetz*, who used his paper to
inflame tensions in the town, especially after the recent murder and suicide
of a young boy and girl, respectively, in what Kroushevan claimed to have been

66 King, 'Michael Davitt and the Kishinev pogrom', p. 24. 67 Ibid., p. 20. 68 Hyndman, *Further
reminiscences*, p. 52. 69 King, 'Michael Davitt and the Kishinev pogrom', pp 26, 32–3. 70
Hyndman, *Further reminiscences*, p. 52. 71 Davitt, *Within the pale*, p. v. 72 Ibid., pp 102–6. 73
Edward H. Judge, *Easter in Kishinev: anatomy of a pogrom* (New York & London), 1992, p. 129.

ritual Jewish blood sacrifices. The massacre of over fifty people and the serious injury of hundred more had, Davitt also found, been carried out with the 'passive connivance' of the police chief and certain officers.[74]

Davitt's time in Kishinev was extremely emotionally demanding. Even Hyndman acknowledged that the assignment was one that would have to pay well, given the 'arduous and distressing character of the work'.[75] Evidence of murder, mutilation and the rape of women and girls left Davitt dismayed and appalled.[76] Writing to Webb from Berlin on his return home, he remarked that what he had seen would 'haunt me to my dying days'.[77] He had found that anti-Semitism was endemic in Russian society. He argued that the 'genesis' of the pogrom was to be found in the 'special' anti-Semitic laws, at least one hundred in total, which coerced the Jews in all aspects of their lives.[78] He also encountered a general feeling of 'competitive prejudice and jealousy' towards the Jewish population. During his visit to Odessa he was unable to elicit a favourable opinion of the Jews from either merchants or otherwise 'independent impartial observers'.[79] His experiences convinced him that the only solution to the 'Jewish Question' was that proposed by the Zionist movement, the re-settlement of Jews in a new Jewish polity in Palestine.[80] During his own visit to Palestine in 1885 he had found the absence of Jews 'strange'.[81]

The Zionist idea of re-settlement had latterly been formulated by the Austrian journalist, Theodore Hertzl, who produced a pamphlet in 1896 entitled *Der Judenstaat* (*The Jewish State*). The following year the Zionist Congress was founded at Basle.[82] Davitt argued that a 'courageous plan of repatriation' should be supported by the leading world nations, and that, in regard to the Russian Jew, the government of Russia had a direct responsibility in facilitating the process of re-settlement. This included assisting 'the wealthy Jews of Christendom' in financing the scheme. He made reference to his early visit to Palestine and to the opportunities for settlement in the region.[83] Hertzl's Zionist plan was not universally welcomed by Jews. Davitt's own espousal of Zionism was criticized in an editorial in the *American Israelite*, which argued against 'the tame submission of the Russian Jews and emigration from the land of their birth'.[84] Yet Davitt was wholly convinced that emigration to Palestine was the only viable solution. In fact, *Within the pale* was not only written in order to highlight the nature of the Kishinev pogrom but also to 'put forward a plea for the objects of the Zionist movement'.[85] Davitt had actually opposed

74 Davitt, *Within the pale*, pp 122–6. **75** Hyndman, *Further reminiscences*, p. 52. **76** See Davitt's diary, 1903, DP, TCD, MS 9577/6 **77** Davitt to Webb, 3 June 1903, DP, TCD, MS 9490/4970. **78** Davitt, *Within the pale*, pp 94–5. **79** DP, TCD, MS 9503/5418 **80** Davitt, *Within the pale*, pp 82–90. **81** Davitt's notes on Palestine, 1885, DP, TCD, MS 9544. **82** J.M. Roberts, *Europe, 1880–1945* (London, 1978), p. 77. **83** Davitt, *Within the pale*, pp 86–8. **84** *American Israelite*, 20 Aug. 1903. **85** Davitt, *Within the pale*, p. v.

a proposal by the publishers in America, Barnes & Co., to have Lord Rothschild of the Jewish banking dynasty write an introduction to the book. 'He is', Davitt remonstrated, 'opposed to the Zionist movement; he is opposed to denunciations of Russia'.[86]

In January 1904, less than a year after experiencing the horrors of Kishinev, Davitt found himself defending the rights and liberty of the ordinary Jew in Ireland, after a priest in Limerick, Fr John Creagh, used his position as spiritual director of Catholics in the city and as head of the arch-confraternity of the Holy Family – an association comprising 6,000 members – to launch an attack on the local Jewish community. It seems that Creagh had initially been contacted by Limerick retailers who were stirred by that very 'competitive prejudice and jealousy' which Davitt observed in the Christians of Odessa. At a meeting of the arch-confraternity on 11 January, Creagh accused the Jews of insinuating their way into every aspect of commercial life in the city and of buying most of their goods from their co-religionists in Europe, to the detriment of local Irish trade and industry. He then effectively instructed his congregation to resort to a boycott of Jewish traders. The day after the sermon, the local rabbi, Elias Bere Levin, appealed to Davitt to intervene in an effort to forestall a general boycott and to prevent a serious outbreak of violence. Davitt lost no time in responding. In a letter to the *Freeman's Journal* several days later, he hit out at Creagh's anti-Semitic diatribe and criticized him for introducing 'the spirit of barbarous malignity' into Ireland on the pretext of concern for the interests of Irish workers. Conscious of the sequence of events that had led to the pogrom in Kishinev, he also moved to discredit any suggestion that the Jews practised ritual murder.[87]

At the next meeting of the arch-confraternity on 18 January, Creagh took the opportunity to respond to Davitt. He declared himself opposed to violence against the Jewish community and insisted that he had never insinuated that Jews were guilty of ritual killings. However, he suggested that Davitt's views were 'against the common good', and he again exhorted Limerick Catholics to continue the boycott. He warned that if the Jews were permitted to operate unchecked, 'the people would become their absolute slaves – and slavery to them was worse than the slavery to which Cromwell condemned the Irish when he shipped them to the Barbadoes'. He referred to Davitt as a 'self-constituted advocate of the Jews [who would] injure his country by nurturing such an evil state of things'.[88] Davitt also incurred the censure of sections of the local and provincial press;[89] and a trade union body in the city even

---

86 Davitt to Author's Syndicate, 8 July 1903, NLI, MS 18575. 87 Dermot Keogh, *Jews in twentieth-century Ireland: refugees, anti-Semitism and the holocaust* (Cork, 1998), pp 27–32. 88 *FJ*, 20 Jan. 1904. 89 Keogh, *Jews*, pp 251–2, fn. 27.

passed a motion condemning his involvement.[90] Support for Creagh's stance was, notably, expressed in Griffith's *United Irishman*, which attacked the 'journalistic hacks' and 'uninformed sentimentalists' who challenged the boycott.[91] No explicit reference was made to Davitt or his stance in the dispute, but it is significant that Griffith had harboured a dislike of Davitt since the Parnell split and was averse to the Davittite project of forging links with British democracy.[92] Nevertheless, Davitt remained steadfast in his solidarity with the beleaguered Jews. The anti-Semitic crusade lost its momentum before the end of the year; but, ultimately, the boycott and the bitter feelings which it engendered heralded the gradual departure of the Jews from Limerick.[93] Davitt wrote to McGhee, 'The Jew as you know is not a favourable subject with some class of Irishmen. Liberty and justice are the prerogatives of ourselves; though we sometimes cheer for the Boers to share our constituency'.[94] Davitt's own role in the episode was, however, remembered by the wider Jewish community in Ireland, and when he died two years later, a wreath was sent to his funeral as a mark of respect.[95]

In the months that followed his intervention in the Limerick boycott, he refocused his attention on the international stage. He travelled to the United States to campaign against renewed proposals for an Anglo–American arbitration treaty. As well as lobbying senators, as he had done in 1897, he also used his column in the *Irish World* as a platform to articulate Irish opposition to greater Anglo–American co-operation.[96] He had already put his case in his pamphlet, *Ireland's Appeal to America*, published in 1902 and based on an earlier speech in Chicago, in which he alerted Americans to the need to prevent 'the Anglo-maniacs of the United States' from 'lowering this Republic's dignity to the level of a diplomatic puppet for Great Britain in the hierarchy of nations'.[97] He had considerable influence in American political circles; in fact, he was on quite good terms with president Theodore Roosevelt. The latter had supported the British in the Boer war, despite being sympathetic to the Boers, and was also a strong supporter of arbitration with Britain; but he had declared himself supportive Irish home rule, and this left many Irish favourably disposed towards him.[98] After arriving in America in 1904, Davitt received a letter from the president, who thanked him for the gift of 'two blackthorns', which he accepted as 'a good omen' at the beginning of the presidential year. 'It is always a real pleasure to see you', Roosevelt wrote, 'You must never go through Washington without letting me know'.[99] The following year, when Roosevelt was scheduled

90 Ibid., p. 39. **91** Cited in ibid., p. 42. **92** Maume, *The long gestation*, p. 51. **93** Keogh, *Jews*, pp 50–1. **94** Davitt to McGhee, 10 Aug. 1903, DP, TCD, MS 9328/[181/32]. **95** Sheehy Skeffington, *Michael Davitt*, p. 214. **96** Ward, *Ireland*, p. 55. **97** Davitt, *Ireland's appeal to America*, *Denvir's Monthly Irish Weekly*, Mar. 1902, in King (ed.), *Michael Davitt*, vol. ii p. 17. **98** Ward, *Ireland*, pp 41–3. **99** Roosevelt to Davitt, 17 Feb. 1904, DP, TCD, MS 9454/3705.

to take part in a St Patrick's day banquet, Davitt appealed to him to use the occasion to speak in favour of Irish self-government.[1] There was clearly a rapport between them, despite their differences on international politics. Indeed, Roosevelt later described Davitt as a personal friend.[2]

Davitt had been bitterly opposed to the suggestion of a Permanent Board of Arbitration between Britain and the United States since it was first mooted. As an MP in 1896 he refused to sign a memorial in favour of such a body, believing that its realization would render 'Uncle Sam [...] a diplomatic donkey'.[3] During much of 1904, he campaigned with the same vigour in opposing the renewed proposal. His agitation ultimately proved instrumental in securing the eventual defeat of the arbitration treaty in February 1905. Reflecting on the outcome, the British consul-general in New York, Sir Percy Saunderson, later commented, 'There is no doubt in my mind that the Irish, helped on by Michael Davitt's presence, exerted a strong influence on Congress at the time that the [...] negotiations for an arbitration treaty were under way'.[4] Davitt considered it a significant victory, and later wrote triumphantly of the Treaty's unsuccessful passage through the Senate.[5] The US administration had also negotiated treaties with Japan, Germany and other European nations. However, the Irish–American political offensive was directed solely at Britain. The Irish constituency was not prepared to entertain the idea of an Anglo–American *entente cordiale*, certainly not in the absence of Irish independence. Of course, Irish nationalists had historically sought to exploit Britain's international difficulties and to cultivate links with its enemies. During the debate over America's relationship with Britain, there was, predictably, strong Irish support for Russia in the Russo-Japanese War of 1904-5. Two years previously, Britain and Japan had forged an alliance which was designed to serve their respective interests in the Far East and to frustrate Russian expansion in the region. Writing in the *Irish World*, Davitt attacked the alliance and charged Japan with 'playing England's game' in the Far East. Irish–Americans rallied support for Russia, and at mass meetings Russian flags were now flown in the place of Boer flags.[6]

Davitt's pro-Russian sympathies were reflected in his reports on industrial unrest in Russia, which he covered during visits there in 1904 and 1905, having been commissioned, once again, by the *New York American* as an investigative journalist. Towards the end of May 1904, after receiving his commission, he set out for Russia on his first assignment, furnished with a letter of

1 Davitt to Roosevelt, 4 Mar. 1905, DP, TCD, MS 9454/3709. 2 *FJ*, 8 June 1906. 3 See Davitt's draft of an open letter to W.T. Stead, 4 Apr. 1896, DP, TCD, MS 9459[371/15]. 4 Saunderson to British ambassador, James Bryce, 23 Feb. 1907, in Bryce to Hardinge, 7 Mar. 1907, FO 371/359; quoted in Ward, *Ireland*, p. 55. 5 Davitt, 'The Irish national assembly', pp 293–4. 6 Ward, *Ireland*, pp 44, 52.

introduction from Count Cassini, the Russian ambassador in Washington.[7] After reaching his destination, he engaged the services of an interpreter before making his way to St Petersburg, where he arrived on 5 June.[8] His brief was to investigate claims, specifically those made in the *London Standard*, that Russia's campaign against Japan was suffering because Russian troops were tied down in European parts of the empire dealing with widespread unrest among industrial workers. While in St Petersburg, Davitt visited the industrial districts of the city himself, interviewing 'numbers outside the [industrial] works, in the tea houses, in the streets, and near the Churches'. After more than two weeks of interviewing workers who 'spoke quietly, intelligently and freely', he concluded that there was 'not a trace' of any such discontent. In fact, he implied that the workers were more concerned with the reports of the Russian campaign in the East.[9] In conducting these interviews, he could not divorce the newspaper reports of serious political unrest from what he considered to be British government propaganda and press intrigue.

His resentment towards the British political establishment and his abiding preoccupation with the Irish national question were very much in evidence, indeed, when he met the Russian author, Tolstoy, towards the end of his tour. After a few days in Moscow, during which he viewed the Kremlin and marvelled at the 'vastness, strength and beauty' of the city,[10] he travelled to interview Tolstoy at Yasnaya Polyana in the Tula province. He was quite piqued when Tolstoy mistook him for an Englishman. 'Oh no', Davitt corrected his host, 'I am Irish, not English in any sense'.[11] Davitt had clearly read *Resurrection*, Tolstoy's last great novel, published only several years before their meeting, and it was some of the themes dealt with in this work which provided a basis for their discussion. The later part of the novel highlighted the conditions of prisoners in Siberia, and when Tolstoy asked for an account of Britain's treatment of political prisoners, Davitt readily obliged. 'All this was evidently new and unsuspected to the author of "Resurrection"', Davitt later wrote, 'and his eyes soon began to express a knowledge of why an Irishman should resent being taken for an Englishman'.[12] Davitt then gave the celebrated author an account of the Irish nationalist struggle and ended with the appeal, 'You have the ear of the reading world as possibly no living layman has today. Say a word for Ireland's right to rule herself whenever you can'.[13]

When Davitt left Russia at the end of June, he was convinced that the reports of serious industrial and political unrest had been grossly exaggerated for political purposes. However, in January 1905, following the events of

7 See letters and papers relating to Russia tour, DP, TCD, MS 9507/5477. 8 Ibid., 3 June 1904, MS 9580. 9 Ibid., MS 9507/5493. 10 Ibid., MS 9580/45 11 Ibid., 'Davitt's meeting with Tolstoy, 22 June 1904', MS 9647 12 Ibid., 9580/59. 13 DP, TCD, MS 9647.

'Bloody Sunday' (22 January), when troops shot pacific demonstrators after a strike in St Petersburg, he was requested by the *New York American* to return to investigate. Immediately after the shootings, he received a wire from E.F. Flynn, the head of the journal's bureau in London, asking him to 'start at once for Moscow'.[14] Within days, Davitt was back in St Petersburg. He wrote to the Tsar requesting a short interview, but he was informed of the protocol which required such applications to be made to the Russian ministry of foreign affairs through a foreign embassy.[15] He did, however, manage to secure an interview with the deputy Minister of the Interior and chief of police, General Tropov, at the Winter Palace on 28 January. Tropov told him that while there was a desire for better conditions among the workers, there was no sympathy with revolutionary ideas. 'All civilized nations', Tropov stated, 'experience these economic disturbances with disorder and often bloodshed – following result conflict between workers and law'. Davitt himself noted in his diary that he shared the suspicion, circulated from official Russian sources, that Japan and its European allies 'had scattered millions among revolutionaries [to create?] disturbances so as to embarrass Russia [...]'[16]

The events of 'Bloody Sunday' had been quickly followed by strikes and violent clashes in Warsaw, and by agitation in Finland for political autonomy. In early February, Davitt's mission took him to Helsinki and later to the Polish capital. From the early nineteenth century, Finland had enjoyed autonomy within the empire under the special status of a Grand Duchy. However, after 1899 its constitution and special rights were abolished against the background of a new policy of Russification. During a five-day stay in Helsinki between 6 and 10 February, Davitt noted that socialism had only a 'slender hold' on the Finnish workingmen, and that 'Marxian doctrines' were mainly confined to the better educated class of wage earners. However, he remarked on the 'great national and political agitation' which was widespread. He welcomed the agitation, and supported the demand for the restoration of the constitution of the grand duchy. It is clear that he was comfortable addressing the Finnish constitutional question, but he viewed the industrial unrest in Warsaw, where he spent three days after leaving Helsinki, with the same circumspection with which he treated the Russian interest, believing that the strikes there had not represented genuine revolutionary upheaval.[17] In May, after he had returned from Russia, he received a letter from Hardie who remarked on how the Russian situation 'stirs one's pulses [sic] and also rouses one's indignation. It is the great object lesson of our day what a united people can accomplish'.[18] Shortly after 'Bloody Sunday', a *Labour Leader* editorial had, indeed, 'rejoice[d] in the widespread insurrection'

14 'Russian tour', 23 Jan. 1905, DP, TCD, MS 9582/1. 15 Ibid., 28 Jan. 1905, MS 9582/2; MS 9508/5496. 16 Ibid., MS 9582/2–5. 17 Ibid., MS 9508/5502; MS 9508/5503. 18 Hardie to Davitt, May 1905, DP, TCD, MS 9330/191.

and declared, 'All hail! then to the Russian Revolution that is or is to be'.[19] Davitt, for his part, could not deny the genuine labour demands behind the various incidents of strike action. However, after having had the opportunity 'of learning the truth on the spot', he maintained that Russia's internal problems had been deliberately overstated. In his view, the strikes would eventually lead to 'far-reaching' democratic reforms which, if conceded, and if preceded by the restoration of the Finnish constitution, would 'make Russia the day following their concession, the greatest and strongest power among the World-Empire of today'. He accused leading London papers and also the European press, which 'is, owned or controlled by Stock-Exchange influences, and especially by Jews', of 'imaginative invention'.[20] In the end, he refused to accept the uncomfortable fact that, propaganda aside, the newspaper reports had actually highlighted serious underlying political problems which threatened the Russian empire from within. The day after his meeting with Tropov, he received a typed copy of a revolutionary manifesto which was a call to arms, urging workers to 'raid gun-shops', 'build barricades', to avenge their brothers' blood which 'flows' in Manchuria. Workers were also urged to bring industry to a halt, to 'attack [prisons] and release comrades'. But in pencil at the bottom of the page of this manifesto, Davitt wrote, 'Did not use this. Manifesto written for consumption [of] English correspondents'.[21] Of course, Davitt's own investigation was contemporaneous with the unfolding events, and the revolutionary nature of the situation was much more difficult to assess. Yet it is important to note, as Sheehy Skeffington did, that his 'normally revolutionary sympathies were warped [...] by a distrust of English intrigue'.[22]

By the beginning of the twentieth century, Davitt had established himself as a formidable international activist, and was widely known for his involvement in international campaigns and for his journalistic coverage of political and humanitarian crises. From the early 1880s he identified with a broad international agenda which challenged structures of enslavement and privilege. In his writings, his practical engagements, and even in his capacity as a parliamentarian, he principally confronted the British empire, his *bête noire*. Stephen Howe, in his assertion that '[e]arly Irish nationalists hardly ever identified their situation or cause with that of other, non-European subject peoples in the British Empire or beyond',[23] too readily overlooks Davitt's unique role as an agitator and activist outside the Irish–British nexus, and indeed the anti-imperialist stance of other nationalists such as Webb. Yet, while Davitt did not assert, as Dillon had during his tour of New Zealand in 1889, that the Irish had a right to self-government 'because we are white men',[24] he still harboured

---

19 *Labour Leader*, 27 Jan. 1905. **20** DP, TCD, MS 9508/5506. **21** DP, TCD, MS 9508/5499. **22** Sheehy Skeffington, *Michael Davitt*, pp 185–6. **23** Howe, *Ireland and empire*, p. 44. **24** Quoted

a certain ambivalence towards non-European peoples. On the one hand, he believed that every people had the right to exist free from imperialism and hegemonic control; but, on the other hand, he tended to view the influence of European culture as a civilizing one, and this determined his benign attitude to forms of cultural domination, even within the context of empire. Moreover, in his fixation on undermining the British empire, he was sometimes guilty of double standards in addressing issues of justice and liberty, most notably in the case of South African natives but also during the Russia crisis. While Howe does not give due consideration to the anti-imperialist strain in late nineteenth-century Irish nationalism, King's statement that Davitt 'sympathized with the downtrodden everywhere', and her view that he might be viewed as 'a pioneer of the idea of an ethical foreign policy', equally fails to fully recognize the nature of the complexities and the inconsistencies which were apparent in his later political activism.[25]

in Lyons, *John Dillon*, p. 105. Lyons (p. 105) rather too casually explains Dillon's reference to race by remarking that he was 'only stating a political cliché', which reflected the prevailing view at that time that 'self-government was likely to be the preserve of white-settled colonies'. 25 King, 'Davitt, Irish nationalism and British empire', p. 130.

7 / Conciliation and the new Ireland

DAVITT MAINTAINED THAT THE Act of Union was central to the British imperialist mentality, given that Englishmen had been 'schooled in the faith' that the very existence of the empire was dependent on a single parliament for Britain and Ireland.[1] British imperialism was represented in Ireland, he argued, by 'a horde of unsympathetic officials' in Dublin Castle and by what he termed a 'garrison of anti-Irish landlords'.[2] In his later years, even when he came to accept that land nationalization had no significant appeal among the Irish peasantry, he continued to view the land question as critical to the nationalist and social reform agendas and remained fundamentally at odds with the idea of a British-sponsored scheme of land settlement. He was one of the principal critics of the 1902 Land Conference report which served as a basis for the subsequent Wyndham Act (1903). In recent historiography on the agrarian war, it has been argued that he, along with Dillon and Thomas Sexton, stymied the potential for political progress at a critical juncture in the history of modern Ireland by opposing the far-reaching land legislation introduced by the chief secretary, George Wyndham, and by attacking the 'new politics of conciliation' on which the Land Conference was based.[3] Davitt's radical social agenda certainly determined his attitude to the Wyndham Act. Yet he himself had openly endorsed the idea of a land conference when it was first mooted and, indeed, had put forward proposals for a settlement. Ultimately, it was not the conference, or even negotiating with landlords, that concerned him; it was his abiding preoccupation with both the social question and the national question, always inextricably linked, and his belief that the latter in particular would not be advanced within the overall political context of 'conciliation', as it came to be championed principally by William O'Brien and the Co. Limerick landlord, Lord Dunraven.

Davitt once remarked, with more than a hint of 'sneaking' satisfaction, that Irish landlords were 'more Bourbon than the Bourbons in learning nothing from their own experience or misfortunes, or from the progressive march of ideas and events'.[4] However, by the early years of the twentieth century a more

---

1 Davitt, *The fall*, p. 499. 2 Davitt, *Leaves*, vol. ii, p. 169. 3 Bew, *Conflict*, p. 220; Bull, *Land*, pp 169–75; Jackson, *Home rule*, pp 191–3. 4 Davitt, 'Retiring the landlord garrison', p. 779.

pragmatic and challenging approach had been adopted by some landlords, which not only reflected divisions within the ranks of their own class but which also highlighted serious differences among nationalists on the strategic importance of the land question and on the nature of a definitive settlement. While the official landlord organization, the Landowners' Convention, was hostile to the idea of negotiating with the tenantry, and put forward an impossible precondition to talks by demanding the exclusion of the option of compulsory purchase,[5] the initiative taken by a small group of landlords in 1902 in calling for a historic conference was viewed by Davitt himself as a clever political move which ultimately secured 'a counter revolution in the value of landlord property which is without a parallel in the history of agrarian or political reform'.[6]

This initiative came against a background of heightened agrarian agitation which had been organized by the United Irish League (UIL). When the League was first founded by William O'Brien in Mayo in 1898, it resolved to force the redistribution of large grazing lands among smallholders. After the Land Act of 1881, landlords had begun letting their untenanted land on an eleven-month lease basis, which meant that the transaction was not subject to the rent-fixing authority of the land courts. This arrangement attracted large graziers who, as Fergus Campbell points out, had a close, lucrative economic relationship with landlords.[7] The grazing issue was a particularly sensitive one in Connacht, and Davitt himself took an active part in organizing the new agrarian campaign – unlike other nationalist parliamentarians, including Dillon[8] – and even managed to draw on Fenian support, as he had done with the Land League in 1879-80. By 1901, O'Brien had adopted a new policy for the UIL. Conscious that the anti-grazier campaign appealed mainly to the peasantry in the west, and aware of the need for the League to adopt a national campaign, he included the demand for compulsory land purchase as part of the organization's objectives. The campaign, notably its tactic of boycotting, now not only targeted graziers but also landlords, and O'Brien used this to apply pressure on the government. Branches of the League grew by eighteen per cent between July 1901 and March 1902, and as a result there was an increase in the number of unlet grazing farms.[9] Both the government and the landlords responded to the agitation.

The first sign in the new landlord approach came in the summer of 1902 when a Kerry landlord, Lindsay Talbot-Crosby, wrote a letter to the *Freeman's Journal* proposing a conference of men 'representative of the several parties' to negotiate a resolution to the land question.[10] This was followed in

5 Bull, *Land*, p. 147. 6 *FJ*, 26 Sept. 1903. 7 F. Campbell, *Land and revolution: nationalist politics in the west of Ireland, 1891–1921* (Oxford, 2005), p. 19. 8 Bew, *Conflict*, p. 39. 9 Campbell, *Land and revolution*, pp 58–61. 10 Quoted in Bew, *Conflict*, p. 96.

September by an intervention by Captain John Shawe-Taylor, the son of a Galway landlord, who not only proposed a conference but also put forward the names of representatives. Nationalist leaders, especially O'Brien who had rejected Talbot-Crosby's original proposition, responded favourably to the new invitation by Shawe-Taylor, which, significantly, had the backing of Wyndham. Indeed, it was made known to O'Brien that the chief secretary was of the view that parliament would 'do a big thing' if the prospect of agreement existed.[11] The landlords initially named in Shawe-Taylor's letter to the press – Lord Barrymore, the duke of Abercorn, Colonel Saunderson and the O'Conor Don – refused to participate in the proposed forum, and the Landowners' Convention itself remained firmly set against the initiative. However, the idea of a conference was not without appeal to many ordinary landlords, and after a ballot organized by an independent provisional committee formed by Shawe-Taylor and other like-minded landlords, four nominees for the proposed conference emerged, the earl of Dunraven, the earl of Mayo, Colonel Hutcheson-Poë and Colonel Nugent-Everard. Their counterparts on the tenants' side were O'Brien, Redmond, Timothy Harrington and the radical northern unionist, T.W. Russell, all of whom had been originally nominated by Shawe-Taylor and later endorsed by the Irish Party.[12] With Dunraven as chairman and Shawe-Taylor as secretary, the conference was eventually convened at the Mansion House, Dublin, on 20 December.

Davitt had made a contribution to the debate on the land conference proposal in October 1902 with the publication of his pamphlet, *Some suggestions for a final settlement of the land question*. In it, he acknowledged that his land nationalization scheme had not appealed 'to the strong human desire or passion to hold the land as "owner" which is so inherent in the Celtic nature'. However, he remained committed to the principle of state ownership of the land and still held that it was impossible, in any real sense, to own land 'as a ship or any moveable [...] object is owned'.[13] Land, in other words, could never be viewed as a market commodity. Indeed, when he later met Tolstoy, he was encouraged to learn that the renowned author had read *Progress and poverty*, and that after reading it had written a letter to the emperor urging him to nationalize the land of Russia.[14] Land, in fact, was central to the social message of Tolstoy's *Resurrection*, and a familiarity with the works of Henry George was cited as one of the redeeming features in the character of the dissolute prince, Nekhlyudov. A landlord, Nekhlyudov gradually reaches a critical point of social consciousness, during which 'the fundamental doctrine of [...] George came vividly to mind, and he remembered his former enthusiasm and won-

---

11 Quoted in Bull, *Land*, p. 146. **12** Ibid., p. 150. **13** Davitt, *Some suggestions for a final settlement of the land question* (Dublin, 1902), pp 6–7. **14** Davitt's visit to Tolstoy, 22 June 1904, DP, TCD, MS 9647.

dered how he could ever have forgotten it all'.[15] Still heavily influenced by Georgeite principles, Davitt insisted, in his pamphlet on the land question, that the concept of 'occupying ownership' had to be qualified. While 'owners' had rights, they also, he argued, had a responsibility to meet a certain 'obligation, or duty or tax to the State' which recognized that the nation as a whole had a stake in the land. This assertion was reflected in his view that any future conference had to be representative not only of the classes most immediately interested but 'as far as possible, of the country also'. He welcomed the chief secretary's statement that the Irish land question should be settled by Irishmen, although he could not resist describing the latter's declaration as something of an acknowledgement of England's failure to rule Ireland.[16]

In his pamphlet, Davitt called for a conference in the form of a National Council at which all classes would be represented and all proposals open to debate. The Council would have thirty-two-county local government representation; ten members each from the Landowners' Convention and the UIL; five from the Land and Labour Associations which represented the interests of rural labourers;[17] and a representative each from the trades councils of Dublin, Belfast, Derry, Limerick and Cork. The make-up, as outlined, not only reflected Davitt's insistence that *national* interests, however disparate, should be represented, but also his belief that social partnership was a basis for future social and economic progress. In all, the Council, which would meet in Dublin, would have 72 delegated representatives. As a mechanism to redress any 'manifestly unfair balance' of class representation, especially against the landlords, a further 28 members would be co-opted.[18]

Denying that he was 'the most intransigent of the "agitators"', as apparently implied by Colonel Saunderson, Davitt moved to refute claims that he had previously argued against compensating landlords for their estates.[19] He was able to make reference to the proposals for compensation which he had publicly outlined in his keynote Liverpool speech twenty years earlier. He noted that some of the calculations in that plan had been excessive, such as his estimate that the total annual rental of Ireland was £15,000,000. In his new proposals he put the figure at £7,000,000. He recommended a compensation package of twenty-one years' purchase of this amount, £147,000,000, or, as a round figure, £150,000,000. Outlining a scheme in which the payment of the landlords' compensation would come from taxation raised as Ireland's contribution to the imperial exchequer, he proposed that the government constitute an Irish 'local authority', or a permanent administrative 'National Land

15 L. N. Tolstoy, *Resurrection* (London, 1966). p. 287.   16 Davitt, *Some suggestions*, pp 7, 32, 34.
17 O'Connor, *A labour history of Ireland*, p. 53, p. 62.   18 Davitt, *Some suggestions*, pp 31–8.   19 Ibid., p. 1. Despite their differences, Davitt and Colonel Saunderson had a grudging respect for one another; see Jackson, *Colonel Edward Saunderson*, pp 99–100.

Council', which would be empowered to give existing tenants rights of 'own-ership', subject to a basic rent-charge on the land which would be much lower than the existing judicial rents. The government would loan the capital sum of compensation to the proposed 'local authority' which would liquidate the debt by charging tenants three-and-a half per cent annually on £100,000,000 of the loan (an annual payment of £3,500,000), and by charging 'Ireland' three-and-a-half per cent on the remaining £50,000,000 (which would amount to £1,500,000 per annum). Once the debt had been liquidated, the sum of £1,500,000 would continue as a perpetual rent-charge. Davitt accepted that many would demand that the 'predominant partner' (Britain) should pay the £50,000,000 which was expected of 'Ireland'. However, he argued that Britain would be more likely to loan the full amount for the land settlement if it was not required to pay one-third of the amount. He also believed that 'Ireland' itself would benefit by paying this amount, because the revenue gained from the perpetual rent-charge would represent 'a solid National asset, which would enable the country to promote and foster her industrial welfare'.[20]

In stating his proposal, Davitt made reference to the plan outlined in an article in the *Statist* in 1886 by the economist, Robert Giffen, who proposed the transfer of land ownership in Ireland to local authorities. Davitt had viewed Giffen's ideas as enlightened and constructive, especially because the latter had envisaged the municipalization of the land of Ireland as part of a home rule settlement. It prompted Davitt to write an article shortly afterwards in the *Contemporary Review*, in which he outlined a scheme of land nationaliza-tion under an Irish national state.[21] In his 1903 article, he did not discuss his proposed scheme in the strict context of the national question. He did, how-ever, *implicitly* connect a land settlement with future political institutional structures. The ideas, as formulated in his pamphlet, were reminiscent of the 'local authority' scheme put forward by Chamberlain in the mid-1880s. However, it is apparent, on a close reading, that he viewed the National Land Council as a first step to more extensive political powers. The nation's pay-ment of the perpetual rent-charge would, he explained, not come from taxa-tion but would be diverted from expenditure on areas such as policing, the judiciary and the workhouse system.[22] He shrewdly avoided any explicit ref-erences to a future political framework. Yet he did allude to an 'Irish Republic': in the course of explaining that Britain would be unlikely to contribute to the cost of buying out the landlords, owing to its lack of 'conscience where money is concerned', he gratuitously remarked that an appeal for an 'Irish Republic' would stand more chance of success.[23] It was a throw-away comment, but his

---

20 *Some suggestions*, pp 21–8. 21 Davitt, 'Mr Giffen's proposed solution to the Irish question', *Contemporary Review*, 49 (Apr. 1886). 22 Davitt, *Some suggestions*, pp 22–3. 23 Ibid., pp 27–8.

reference to the 'Republic' was significant all the same, given that there was no mention of home rule at all.

Davitt believed that his land settlement offered the incentive to the tenantry to effectively own their land. The payment of a basic ground charge, which would be so low compared with existing rents, would give tenants an opportunity to build on their interest; and for the poorer tenants it would provide a basic security net. Davitt did not state what penalty would be incurred if the rent-charge was not paid; he simply noted that evictions would all but disappear. But, ultimately, the tenant, and the land as a national asset, would be protected by a Homestead Law. Tenants would own their land, subject to certain conditions, such as not mortgaging the land 'in reckless borrowing of money'; and there would be a law against sub-letting, except in certain circumstances. To bring the land scheme into effect, Davitt proposed a Representative Commission,[24] comprising Dillon; Sexton, the Irish Party's financial expert; the O'Conor Don; T.W. Russell; Murrough O'Brien of the existing Land Commission; Lord Castletown, an associate of Shawe-Taylor and a supporter of the Land Conference initiative; and James McCann, a former unionist who became the independent nationalist MP for St Stephen's Green in 1900.[25]

Davitt left for a tour in the United States with Dillon shortly after the publication of his pamphlet.[26] When he returned at the beginning of 1903, the Land Conference under Lord Dunraven had already been held and had produced a short report, which was signed on 3 January. It recommended land purchase on a huge scale, facilitated by the provision of treasury loans to tenants, the annual repayment of which would be considerably less than the existing rent. It was not a scheme of compulsory purchase, but landlords were guaranteed a fair price based on judicial rents; and, as an incentive to sell, they would receive a treasury 'bonus' on the sale price of their estates.[27] In the wake of the conference, O'Brien championed the recommendations and the new policy of 'compulsory attraction', as he called it.[28] Davitt, however, was critical of the report and began to take issue with its details, especially the financial proposals which, in his view, were ambiguous.[29] Declaring his 'somewhat old-fashioned Land League convictions', he cautioned against 'unreasoning zeal' for the new recommendations and pointed out that, pending a judgement on the report by a national convention, the only authorized land reform programme before nationalists was that contained in the constitution of the UIL, namely, the abolition of landlordism by means of the compulsory sale of the landlords' interest, and the provision of cottages and one-acre allot-

---

24 Ibid., p. 25. 25 For more on McCann, see Maume, *The long gestation*, p. 234. 26 Lyons, *John Dillon*, p. 227. 27 Bull, *Land*, pp 152–4. 28 *FJ*, 2 Feb. 1903. 29 Ibid.

ments for agricultural labourers and adequate dwellings for the urban working classes.[30] Compulsory purchase was not Davitt's ideal solution, but he
insisted that it was what the UIL demanded and, as such, should therefore be
legislated for. His critical attitude clearly had some influence on Dillon, who,
by the beginning of February, was growing more convinced that the conference had been a 'mortal blunder'.[31]

O'Brien later suggested that Davitt and Dillon's opposition to the new land
proposals had resulted from a sense of indignation at not having been named
in Shawe-Taylor's original call for a conference.[32] Yet Davitt's pamphlet was
written as a response to Shawe-Taylor's initiative; and, as Lyons has shown,
there is nothing in Dillon's correspondence to indicate that he was piqued.[33]
Indeed, shortly before his departure to America, Dillon had supported
Redmond, Harrington and O'Brien in their engagement with the landlords,
despite having had reservations about the proposed conference.[34] Like Davitt,
he was deeply suspicious of the role of the government in the moves towards
a land settlement. Even O'Brien had his own doubts about Wyndham in the
early months of 1903, and harboured fears that the expected new land bill
would be substantially different from the proposals in the Land Conference
report.[35] The bill, when introduced on 25 March, embodied the Conference's
recommendations, but O'Brien still had major difficulties with particular provisions. Designed to encourage landlords to sell their entire estates, the bill
made provision for the full price of the land to be advanced to tenants at three-
and-one-quarter per cent interest, repayable over sixty-eight-and-a-half years.
A 'bonus' on the sale of each landlord estate was also to be given at twelve per
cent of the total purchase price. Nationalists were incensed that the £12 million to be provided for the landlords' bonuses was to be paid out of Irish rev-
enues. There were also objections that the higher purchase prices on first-
term rents (rents settled by the land courts under the Land Act of 1881) and
on second-term rents (rents fixed after the Land Act of 1896) were excessive.[36]
O'Brien was keenly aware of the resentment which fellow nationalists felt
towards certain aspects of the bill. Davitt met him at Westminster during the
parliamentary debate on the new measure and found him dejected.

> After Wyndham's speech [Davitt wrote to Dillon] I came down to the
> lobby and I could not refrain from the human temptation of saying 'I
> told you so', to both O'Brien and Redmond. They were both keenly
> disappointed at the bonus being levied altogether on Ireland and the

30 *FJ*, 27 Jan. 1903. 31 Quoted in Lyons, *John Dillon*, p. 229. 32 Warwick-Haller, *William*
O'Brien, p. 230. 33 Lyons, *John Dillon*, p. 228. 34 Ibid., p. 228. 35 Warwick-Haller, *William*
O'Brien, p. 230. 36 Lyons, *John Dillon*, pp 229–30. For a detailed account of the provisions of
the Wyndham Act, see Bull, *Land*, pp 152–8.

landlords getting the whole of it. O'Brien's manner was entirely changed. He hinted at the rejection of the Bill.

Despite O'Brien's despondency, however, Davitt discerned that he was ultimately prepared to accept the bill, 'faults and all, with some talk of amendments'.[37]

At a national convention, held in April to reach a determination on the matter, O'Brien acknowledged that the measure had 'faults' which would have to undergo 'radical and sweeping' amendments, especially in regard to the outstanding question of evicted tenants, those 'gallant wounded soldiers' of the agrarian campaign. However, he joined with Redmond in underlining the historic importance of the bill in its objective of bringing about the end of landlordism. He warned that by denouncing the measure 'within an inch of its life', nationalists ran the risk of sealing its fate in England. Referring to the perpetual rent-charge proposed by Davitt, he remarked that such a provision would make a mockery of the concept of peasant ownership and be tantamount to simply 'substituting Dublin Castle for the landlords'.[38] This, of course, was a criticism that had been levelled against Davitt's ideas on a land settlement in the early 1880s. O'Brien knew well that any allusion to land nationalization would stand in his favour in confronting Davitt, especially at an assembly largely made up of tenant farmers who were fixed on the principle of land ownership. In defending the idea of a perpetual rent-charge, Davitt, for his part, insisted that it was imperative that the nation had the power to prevent any form of Irish landlordism. He also argued that the administration of the new land code under Wyndham's legislation would, in any case, be in the hands of Dublin Castle. Significantly, he remarked that there could be no end of the land struggle until the administration of the land of Ireland was in 'the hands of an Irish Department responsible to Irish National feeling'.[39]

From the outset, Davitt had protested that, under the recommended land scheme, landlords would receive too high a price.[40] At the convention, he focused on this issue, arguing that the price which the landlords would receive would be based on the purchase of the valuation of the nominal rental of their estates, not the net rental which was considerably lower. This, he told his audience, made the landlord bonuses totally unjustifiable; and to emphasis the point, he referred to the particularly sensitive fact that the £12 million subsidy would be 'not British but Irish money'. He followed up these critical remarks on the 'financial God-send' for the landlords with a mention of the agricultural labourers for whom the bill made no specific provisions. Indeed, even the Landowners' Convention was now firmly behind the bill, confident

37 Davitt to Dillon, 29 Mar. 1903, JDP, TCD, MS 6728/131. **38** *FJ*, 17 Apr. 1903. **39** Ibid. **40** *FJ*, 2 Feb. 1903.

of the benfits which would accrue to landlords.[41] It is interesting that it was around this time that Davitt was also agitating against mine-owning landlords in Wales,[42] where Dunraven himself owned mines.[43] Davitt did not propose outright rejection of Wyndham's measure – such a proposition would have been futile, especially given the expectations which had been excited among the peasantry, even farmers on the margins – but he did propose that the Irish Party should work to have the convention's proposed amendments included during the committee stage of the bill, and that later in the legislative process, the convention should be reconvened to consider the Party's report on the results of the amendments, and to ultimately reach a verdict on the amended bill. This proposal was made as an amendment to O'Brien's resolution that the Irish Party should have the power to reach a final decision on the bill. Davitt agreed to withdraw his resolution if either O'Brien or Redmond viewed it 'in any sense' hostile.[44] It so happened that Redmond, the chairman, took the view that the resolution involved the question of confidence in the Party, and Davitt duly withdrew it.

Davitt was obviously conscious of being outnumbered at the convention, especially with Dillon absent due to ill health.[45] Even John Ferguson had come to take a favourable view of the bill, although, as McFarland remarks, 'he felt his retreat from Georgeite ideals keenly'.[46] Sheehy Skeffington later maintained that Davitt's proposal would have been carried if he had not decided to withdraw it. A second convention would, it is argued, have highlighted the 'defects' of the bill and 'the country would have been spared the infliction of the Wyndham Landlord Relief Act'. Davitt's decision to effectively make his proposal subject to the sanction of Redmond or O'Brien was, in Sheehy Skeffington's view, typical of the 'magnanimity' which characterized his political dealings.[47] It seems, however, that Davitt was eager to offset the widespread view that he was simply intent on wrecking the bill. The nationalist MP, Thomas Condon, remarked that Davitt's resolution 'bears on its face the willing-to-wound-but-afraid-to-strike principle'.[48] Indeed, Davitt was wary of taking up an extreme stance against the bill. When the UIL was established he had viewed it as an opportunity to give shape to 'a *real* nationalist and democratic Irish party'.[49] The League's leadership had then hoped that the Irish Party, as the elected representative body of the Irish nation, would become linked with the League's broad agrarian and nationalist agenda, and act much

---

41 Campbell, *Land and revolution*, p. 79. **42** See Davitt to McGhee, May 1903, DP, TCD, MS 9521/6014. **43** Maume, *The long gestation*, p. 67. **44** *FJ*, 17 Apr. 1903. **45** Lyons, *John Dillon*, p. 227. **46** McFarland, *John Ferguson*, p. 301. **47** Sheehy Skeffington, *Michael Davitt*, pp 180–2. **48** Quoted in Bull, *Land*, p. 158. **49** Davitt to O'Brien, 6 Apr. 1899; quoted in P. Bull, 'The United Irish League and the reunion of the Irish Parliamentary Party, 1898–1900', *IHS*, vol. 26:101 (1988), p. 63.

as an alternative government. When, after a year of the organization's existence, it became clear that many parliamentarians were not amenable to such a strategy, the UIL sought to exert more control over the Party, and, in particular, to influence the selection of parliamentary candidates. The re-union of the Party under Redmond in 1900 interrupted this work, and it was for this reason that Davitt, O'Brien and others had a difficulty with the re-union arrangement itself.[50] However, by the time of Wyndham's land bill, Redmond and O'Brien were closely aligned, largely because of the latter's intense commitment to conciliation, and Davitt feared the implications of an open breach with them at this point.

Only Davitt and Patrick White, the MP for North Meath, publicly opposed the land bill before it became law.[51] When the Act was passed in August, however, open opposition quickly mounted. The *Freeman's Journal*, under the control of Sexton, had previously been reserved in its criticism of the bill, but with the passage of the new legislation it became highly critical and was used by Sexton to highlight what he viewed as the unsound aspects of the Act's financial clauses.[52] Dillon, who had been convalescing in Egypt for several months, returned home at the end of April, and less than two weeks after the enactment of Wyndham's measure, he took the lead with Davitt and Sexton in launching a fierce, concerted attack on the Act. In a speech in Swinford on 25 August he stated that the price which landlords were getting was well in excess of the market value of their estates. Then, in remarks which would put him on a collision course with O'Brien, he declared his utter scepticism towards the 'doctrine of conciliation'. Landlords, he bluntly claimed, were only interested in conciliation at a price: '25 years' purchase price of the land'.[53] Like Davitt, he did not hold out any hope of the rural poor benefiting from the new settlement. Indeed, despite a provision for the redistribution of the land, Paul Bew points out that the western question was never really addressed.[54] Although the ideal of land nationalization clearly failed to appeal to the imagination of the peasantry, Travers makes the important observation that in Davitt's favour it can be argued that he 'recognized the limits of land purchase as a solution [his ...] romance with nationalization was less ideological than an emotional prescription for a malaise which he had diagnosed more accurately than any of his contemporaries'.[55]

On 8 September, at a meeting of the National Directory of the UIL, resolutions approving of the new land legislation were passed, and a strategy for testing the Act was devised. Davitt and Dillon did not attend.[56] Their antag-

50 Ibid., pp 52–78; see also Bull, *Land*, pp 131–3. 51 Maume, *The long gestation*, p. 68. 52 Lyons, *John Dillon*, p. 230. 53 Quoted in ibid., p. 236. 54 Bew, *Conflict*, p. 102. 55 Travers, 'Davitt after the Land League', p. 88. 56 Lyons, *John Dillon*, p. 237; see Davitt to Dillon, 15, 19, 23 Aug. 1903, JDP, TCD, MS 6728.

onism towards O'Brien was fundamentally based on differences over the political implications of accepting the land settlement. For them, land agitation
was fundamental to the nationalist agenda, and in Davitt's case, also to the
cause of radical social reform. At the end of his speech at the National
Convention in April, O'Brien had signalled his departure from Davitt and
Dillon's line of thinking by declaring that the policy of 'conference and conciliation' was the way forward in resolving Ireland's political troubles.[57] Writing
to Dillon a week after the meeting of the UIL Directory, Davitt attacked
O'Brien for 'knif[ing] the movement'. The constitutional nationalist movement was, he told Dillon, dead, 'poisoned by O'Brien with a big dose of
Dunravenism'.[58] However, despite this rather exaggerated pronouncement,
the campaign against O'Brien's policy continued. In a letter to the *Freeman's
Journal*, Davitt remarked that the landlords were reluctant to openly extol the
Wyndham Act because its terms had been, in his view, so blatantly framed in
their favour. '"Conciliation"', he asserted, 'was a wholly one-sided business'.[59]
By the end of October, O'Brien was putting serious pressure on Redmond to
'discipline' Dillon.[60] Yet, while Redmond himself was still firmly committed
to the policy of conciliation, he was understandably unwilling to move against
Dillon who enjoyed considerable support, and who could count in particular
on the loyalty of the strong nationalist organization in Belfast under the leadership of Joe Devlin.[61] After becoming MP for North Kilkenny in 1902, Devlin
came to prominence within the general secretaryship of the UIL and was
strongly opposed to O'Brien's policy of conciliation.[62]

According to Philip Bull, there existed in 1903 an opportunity for a realignment in nationalist politics based on a shared economic interest between the
substantial class of 'large' farmers in Ireland and the capitalist former landlord class. A political departure centred on class alliance would also build upon
the 'natural alliance' that existed between Catholic tenant farmers and their
Presbyterian counterparts in the northern counties.[63] He contends, however,
that the triumph of Davitt, Dillon and Sexton over O'Brien, who resigned
from the Irish Party in November, kept the nationalist movement wedded
to land agitation as a political weapon and ensured the 'primacy of ethnic and
sectarian divisions'. This line of argument was taken up by the *Irish Times* in
the immediate aftermath of O'Brien's resignation when it condemned Davitt,
'who still has theories regarding "prairie-value", and cannot bear the thought
of agrarian agitation, "the engine that draws the Home Rule train", coming
to an end'.[64] The role which Devlin and the exclusively Catholic Ancient Order

57 *FJ*, 17 Apr. 1903. 58 Quoted in Lyons, *John Dillon*, p. 238. 59 *FJ*, 26 Sept. 1903. 60 Bew,
Conflict, pp 116–18. 61 Bull, *Land*, p. 167. 62 Eamon Phoenix, *Northern nationalism: nationalist politics, partition and the Catholic minority in Northern Ireland, 1890–1940* (Belfast, 1994), p. 3.
63 Bull, *Land*, pp 188–90. 64 *Irish Times*, 6 Nov. 1903.

of Hibernians (AOH) played in strengthening Dillon's hand was, Bull claims, an indication in itself of the direction in which the movement was moving, that is, down a cul-de-sac of traditional sectarian politics.[65]

Bull takes issue with the neat distinction which Paul Bew makes between 'radical agrarians' and 'conciliationists' in his analysis of the nationalist divide over the Land Conference and the Land Act. Bull argues, conversely, that O'Brien did not simply shift from an agrarian to a political agenda, as Bew suggests, but rather clearly identified the UIL with a nationalist agenda from the beginning; and Dillon, for his part, was not exactly a 'radical agrarian' in the sense that Davitt was.[66] However, Bull does share with Bew the view that the development of a policy of conciliation in the early years of the twentieth century, as championed by O'Brien, opened up the possibility of a major shift in Irish politics which might have broken down traditional political divisions, particularly as they developed and became concentrated in the north.[67] The same case is made by Alvin Jackson who tentatively suggests, in fact, that the Belfast political talks of 1997–8 'had a distant ancestor in the Land Conference of 1902' and in the 'centrist' agenda of O'Brien.[68] The Land Conference was certainly of historic significance. Yet it does not follow that O'Brien's solution at that time was a panacea for wider political conflict. Co-operation on the basis of economic logic was not necessarily enough to create and sustain a common political ground. While O'Brien certainly played a pivotal role at a popular agrarian level – indeed, Campbell argues that this has been historiographically neglected as a determinant in bringing about the Land Conference and the land legislation[69] – there is no convincing reason to believe that he was a significant enough player in 'high' politics to advance an overall political shift. Those who argue along these lines have tended to be too sanguine about such a prospect. Ultimately, while it may be tempting to speculate on the course which history might have taken if the 'conciliationist' approach had been adopted before 1914, the reality was that the particular political agenda of O'Brien and Dunraven was not embraced by their contemporaries. O'Brien's efforts left him sidelined within the nationalist movement, and Dunraven became a particularly isolated figure within unionism.

For Bull, the uncompromising stance taken by Davitt and Dillon on O'Brien's policy of conciliation can be explained by their 'acclimatization' to the radical side of British politics, to which many Irish MPs had become exposed as a result of the Liberal–nationalist alliance in 1886. Davitt and Dillon's fierce opposition to the 'Conservative-enacted Land Act' demonstrated, in Bull's view, 'the extent to which their outlook had shifted from

---

65 Bull, *Land*, pp 171–2. 66 Ibid., pp 167–9. 67 Ibid., pp 190–1; Bew, *Conflict*, p. 220. 68 Jackson, *Home rule*, p. 323. 69 Campbell, *Land and revolution*, pp 82–4.

nationalism to class, from a priority for Irish autonomy to a multi-British alliance against privilege and old elites'.[70] While this may, perhaps, be said of Dillon, Bull fails to recognize that Davitt was very much influenced by the British radical tradition from an early point, and was himself, in important respects, a product of British working-class life. Moreover, at least from the time of the land war he identified Irish landlordism with imperialism and with structures of privilege. Indeed, although Davitt adopted a hard-line attitude towards landlords in his speech at the national convention,[71] he previously indicated that he envisaged a political role for former landlords in a new political dispensation, when the landlords had been extricated from what William Feingold calls the 'whole complex of privileges' in Ireland.[72] In this context, Davitt suggested that landlords could remain in the country for the 'discharge of other and more useful functions, national and municipal, than they have ever performed as the "English Garrison"'.[73]

Only a few years before the Land Conference, he had actually adopted a conciliatory approach to Lord Dunraven during a local government election campaign in Croom.[74] The need for nationalist representation on boards of guardians had, from the early days of the evolution of the Land League campaign, been underlined by Davitt. At a central meeting of the League in December 1880, he and Patrick Egan urged support for sympathetic candidates. Egan stated that the people 'had too tamely submitted to the landlord conspiracy, especially in the matter of the boards of guardians'.[75] King has perhaps overstated the case in suggesting that Davitt seemed 'keen to seize the opportunity for a peaceful expansion of a nationalist proto-state';[76] but the strategy of contesting elections was, without a doubt, crucial to the development of the nationalist movement. It was, then, with a strong measure of incredulity that the *Limerick Leader* reported on Davitt's speech at Croom in March 1899, in which he declared himself in favour of the local council, when elected, 'co-opting [Dunraven] as a resident of the county and a man of some distinction'.[77] Davitt, it must be stated, was not averse to working with those from a unionist background, especially in creating conditions for industrial development in the country. The woollen company which he started in 1887 had the financial backing of Dublin businessmen who differed with him 'as wide as possible' on the land and the national questions.[78] It is possible that,

70 Bull, *Land*, pp 169–70. **71** *FJ*, 17 Apr. 1903. **72** William L. Feingold, *The revolt of the tenantry: the transformation of local government in Ireland, 1872–1886* (Boston, 1984), p. 11. **73** Davitt, 'Retiring the landlord garrison', p. 794. **74** See Michael V. Spillane, 'The 4th earl of Dunraven, 1841–1926: a study of his contribution to the emerging Ireland at the beginning of the twentieth century' (PhD thesis, University of Limerick, 2003), pp 36–7. **75** Feingold, *The revolt*, p. 113. **76** King, introduction to Davitt, *Jottings*, p. xxi. **77** *Limerick Leader*, 29 Mar. 1899; quoted in Spillane, *The 4th earl*, p. 37. **78** *FJ*, 18 Apr. 1887.

given the safe return of a Conservative government in 1886, certain liberal unionists in the capital were prepared to support him in an enterprise aimed at reviving industry in the city at that time. The woollen company was, Davitt noted, established to facilitate all woollen manufacturers, including those of an Orange persuasion.[79]

Davitt's attitude towards Dunraven in Croom clearly amounted to a conciliatory gesture. But, ultimately, he could not countenance conciliation as promoted by O'Brien, especially given that it was based on a land settlement which he viewed as one-sided. 'Conciliation' along constructive unionist lines echoed, in a number of important respects, Chamberlain's devolution ideas and schemes of the mid-1880s. It sought generous devolution for Ireland, with incremental administrative responsibilities for practical 'good government' within the framework of the Union. Davitt's ambition for Ireland could not be confined to strategies and structures, the definitive 'end' of which was 'devolution' in such terms. His conciliatory impulses and actions, and the practical forms of ameliorative state initiatives for Ireland, particularly as they concerned the most disadvantaged and historically abused elements of Irish society to which he gave his support, were required always to permit, indeed to advance, forward movement towards the ultimate end of Irish popular sovereignty. The 'march of the Irish nation', however measured the pace or however inclusive its version of 'the nation' might be, could not, for him, be accommodated within the conciliation strategy of 1903, as he understood it. He remained suspicious of any political moves towards co-operation in the context of Dublin Castle rule. In a letter to T.D. Sullivan in July 1904, he expressed his 'disbelief in O'B[rien]'s attempts to succeed where O'Connell, Butt, Parnell and others have failed'.[80]

In his later article, 'The Irish national assembly (Session of 1910)', Davitt imagined a future pluralist political settlement which would be born out of the failure of 'conciliation'.[81] This was a direct reference to the aborted proposals for devolution which had been produced in September 1904 by Wyndham's under-secretary, Sir Anthony MacDonald, and the Irish Reform Association, a body formed by Dunraven, Talbot Crosbie, Shaw-Taylor and other landlords out of the defunct Land Committee. MacDonald, who had only recently been appointed to Ireland, had essentially drafted the proposals, and this resulted in a crisis among Conservatives, and especially Ulster unionists, not only because MacDonald was a Catholic, but also because he had drawn up his secheme for devolution with the implicit approval of Wyndham. This perceived treachery from within Dublin Castle precipitated

79 *FJ*, 5 May 1888. **80** Davitt to Sullivan, 28 July 1904, TDSP, NLI, MS 8237. **81** Davitt, 'The Irish national assembly', pp 286–91.

the formation of the Ulster Unionist Council and ultimately forced Wyndham's resignation in March 1905.[82] Davitt, whose article appeared within weeks of the chief secretary's resignation, viewed the whole affair with derision, and also a hint of amusement. He had never doubted what he considered to be the pernicious constructive unionist basis of conciliation. In the lead up to the introduction of Wyndham's land bill in March 1903, he had received a number of letters from Shaw-Taylor who was eagerly attempting to 'discuss matters' with him. In one such letter, Shaw-Taylor referred to an initiative by Talbot Crosbie, who had issued a circular in which he suggested that landlords should 'forward a movement for Private Bill legislation in Ireland'. Shaw-Taylor remarked to Davitt, 'I don't quite known whether this is [a] delicate way of handling H[ome] R[ule]'. He felt that it may have been 'unwise', given the level of unionist opposition it could have invited. However, he believed that it would show Davitt 'how genuine is the sentiments that the *ex*-landlords mean to take their part in national life'.[83] In another letter two weeks later, he assured Davitt:

> [...] Dunraven is working hard – as the future will soon show to organize and lead those who at present represent the landlord element so that when the Land Question is settled they may be ready to play their part in the national uplifting of the Irish race.[84]

In fact, a week before the formation of the Irish Reform Association, Shawe-Taylor also wrote to Dillon along the same lines, holding out the hope of a new understanding between landlords and tenants in a new Ireland, once 'this wretched land business' was out of the way.[85] However, Shaw-Taylor's political creed was unionism, and this was underlined with the enunciation of the principles of the new reform association. In its preliminary report, it affirmed:

> While firmly maintaining that the parliamentary union between Great Britain and Ireland is essential to the political stability of the empire, and to the prosperity of the two islands, we believe that such union is compatible with the devolution to Ireland of a larger measure of local government than she now possesses.[86]

This was not a framework within which Davitt was prepared to consider a settlement, or indeed Dillon for that matter. Davitt viewed the devolution

---

82 See F.S.L Lyons, 'The Irish unionist party and the devolution crisis of 1904–5', *IHS*, 6:21 (1948), 1–22. **83** Shaw-Taylor to Davitt, 1 and 5 Mar. 1903, DP, TCD, MS 9448/3609. **84** Shaw-Taylor to Davitt, 17 Mar. 1903, DP, TCD, MS 9448/3612. **85** Shaw-Taylor to Dillon, 18 Aug. 1904, cited in Campbell, *Land and revolution*, pp 76–7. **86** Quoted in Lyons, 'The Irish unionist party', p. 2.

proposals of Wyndham and MacDonald as having had one principle design, to 'strangle the Irish Nationalist movement'.[87] While he accepted the benefits that flowed from legislation brought about through constructive unionist policies, he nevertheless challenged and criticized their shortcomings, and always made sure to underline his view that they were passed for reasons of political expediency. For example, the Local Government Act (Ireland) of 1898, which provided for the creation of democratically elected county and district councils, proved instrumental in advancing the UIL strategy of gaining control of local government. Almost immediately after the passage of the Act, O'Brien noted in a diary entry that if every county in Ireland was as organized as the UIL in Mayo, then '30 of the County Councils would be simply 30 Irish Parliaments'.[88] Davitt himself later described the legislation as having represented 'another reeling blow' to feudalism in Ireland, but he also stressed that the central local government board was a department of Dublin Castle, was independent of Irish local opinion, and had a veto on local and administrative matters.[89] He took the same qualified stance on the Agricultural and Technical Instruction bill in 1899. He had, of course, argued for provision for technical instruction for artisans and labourers since the early 1880s. However, he attacked the bill, not only as a transparently inadequate measure, but also because he considered it to have been crudely framed in the spirit of 'killing home rule with kindness'. Writing in the *Melbourne Advocate*, he stated:

> A Board of Agriculture for Ireland is one of the latest proposals of our Unionist Ministry [...] Coercion or kindness, concession or repression, it all comes to the same in the end [...] Its finance is bad, the extent of the popular representation which is to be admitted to the new Board in unsatisfactory, while the general scope and character of the proposed institution suggests a stronger desire to create a number of new offices for hungry loyalists and clamouring partisans than any honest desire to extend a real helping hand to Irish agricultural industry.[90]

Nevertheless, despite this scathing attack, Davitt still worked as an MP to amend the bill, and to secure direct representation for the trades councils of Dublin, Belfast and Cork on the Board.[91]

Ireland, as depicted in Davitt's article on the future national assembly, would have been granted home rule in 1908, following sustained international pressure on Britain by the US, Canada and Australasia, thereby giving Ireland the

87 Davitt, 'The Irish national assembly', p. 288. 88 Quoted in Bull, *Land*, p. 134. 89 Davitt, *The fall*, pp 686–7. 90 *Melbourne Advocate*, 12 May 1899, cited in McNeil, 'Land, labor and liberation', p. 397. 91 See E.L. Richardson to Mrs Davitt, 13 Sept. 1907, DP, TCD, MS 9375/1010.

'full freedom to develop her own genius, industries, institutions, education, Gaelic ideas, and progress in her own way'.[92] In the 1910 elections to the new Irish assembly, a 'National Democratic Party' would have come to power with the backing of the progressive wing of the 'Ulster Party' and the 'Independent Labour Party'. The proposed programme of the new administration would embody some of the features which Davitt considered essential for a just society and a new political dispensation in Ireland: changes in the 'defects' of the Land Purchase laws, better housing for the rural and urban working classes, measures for the construction of harbours and piers, and secular education. One of the first measures to be taken by the new government would be to protect the marching rights of Orangemen, as a way of upholding the democratic privileges of all 'classes and creeds', even if it involved deploying the police to ensure that these rights were exercised. Another 'tactful' measure to be adopted would be to defray all local rates paid by Harland and Wolff for twenty-years in recognition of the credit which the company had given Ireland as an major industrial base.[93]

Davitt obviously had his own ideas for a policy of constructive nationalism. He was, indeed, encouraged by recent signs of dissent within official unionism. Throughout the latter part of the 1890s, T.W. Russell, as a prominent member of the Unionist Party, had pressed the issue of radical land reform. In September 1900 he declared himself in favour of compulsory land purchase and led a tenant-farmer movement which subsequently ran against official unionist candidates in East Down and North Fermanagh.[94] Davitt later identified Russell with a conservative agenda because of his role in negotiating the Wyndham Act,[95] although it is still significant that Russell had been proposed as a member of the Representative Commission in Davitt's earlier pamphlet on the solution to the land question. The whiggish politics of the unionist leader, Saunderson, also clashed with the populist Belfast shipworker, T.H. Sloan, who led a revolt against the leadership of the Party in the summer of 1902, eventually winning a by-election contest in South Belfast in August where he ran as a candidate of the militant Belfast Protestant Association. Largely owing to pressure brought to bear by Saunderson, Sloan was dismissed from the Orange Order in October. However, he responded by joining with Robert Lindsay Crawford, a journalist from Lisburn and editor of the *Irish Protestant*, in forming the Independent Orange Order some months later. Davitt himself was to describe Sloan as a 'thoroughly honest Irishman' and a 'sincere democrat' (although Sloan would return to the official Unionist

---

92 Davitt, 'The Irish national assembly', pp 294–5. 93 Ibid., pp 285–6, 296. 94 See Alvin Jackson, 'Irish unionism and the Russellite threat, 1894–1906', *IHS*, 25:100 (1987). 95 Davitt, 'The Irish national assembly', p. 285.

Party by 1906).⁹⁶ At his last ever public speech at the Town Tenants' Conference in Dublin in March 1906, Davitt also paid a warm tribute to Lindsay Crawford.⁹⁷

In 1879–80, the Land League had made a concerted effort to involve Ulster farmers in agrarian agitation;⁹⁸ and later in 1882, when there was growing popular unionist unrest in response to the mobilization of the nationalist movement, Davitt made frequent visits to the north where, as Frank Thompson has observed, he always showed greater 'sensitivity to northern protestant interests [...] than other nationalist leaders'.⁹⁹ Davitt was, of course, still a nationalist, and his expressions of solidarity with Ulster democracy were not always welcome. During a meeting in Ballymoney, Co. Antrim, in November 1882, Orangemen pounded their drums outside the hall where he was speaking, and he had to depend on the assistance of the police, who 'bludgeon[ed] the "loyal" [...] roughs on my account'. He later wrote in his diary, 'Orangeism thy name is ignorance'.¹ Nevertheless, given his background in Lancashire, he, more than most nationalists, would have been sensitive to the divisiveness of sectarianism, and his appeals to Ulster unionists were genuine. But he was too sanguine about the possible alignment of future political groups, as he imagined it in his 1910 assembly article. He certainly would have clashed with Ulster unionists generally in their more militant opposition to home rule by that time. During a visit to Rockhampton in Queensland, during his 1895 Australian tour, he was asked by a deputation from a Separation League to endorse their campaign for decentralization from Brisbane, and to support their efforts to establish a new northern colony. He refused to lend his support, explaining that it was a domestic matter. Yet he also remarked that the Separation League's case was as 'weak' as one which might easily be put by Ulster unionists in asking for separation from a home rule Ireland.²

In writing the article on the imagined national assembly, Davitt had not, however, intended to explore future relations with unionism, but rather to highlight differences within nationalism. It is significant that the party, whose defeat at the polls in the 1910 election was forecast, was the 'National Conservatives' under Sir John Waterford (Redmond). O'Brien, described as Sir William O'Westport, was identified as the chief secretary of the outgoing conservative government.³ Davitt knew he was being provocative in this article. Before it was published he wrote to McGhee,

---

96 See J.W. Boyle, 'The Belfast Protestant Association and the Independent Orange Order, 1901–10', *IHS*, 13 (1962–3), pp 117–52. 97 Quoted in Sheehy Skeffington, *Michael Davitt*, p. 194. 98 Moody, *Davitt*, pp 424–5. 99 Thompson, *The end of Liberal Ulster*, p. 283. 1 Davitt's diary, 17 Nov. 1882, DP, TCD, MS 9535. 2 Davitt, *Life and progress*, p. 264. 3 Davitt, 'The Irish national assembly', p. 285.

> I think I will provide you with a laugh, over the whole conciliation busi-
> ness if you only invest in a copy of the 'Independent Review' for April.
> There will be a row over the same article, or I am very much mistaken,
> but no matter.[4]

From 1903 O'Brien had argued that Davitt had failed the tenants and labourers, and essentially the nation, by attacking Wyndham's Act and also conciliation. Davitt, for his part, held that O'Brien had capitulated to the landlords
and Dublin Castle,[5] and that he and Redmond were place-hunters. He referred
to O'Brien as 'pig-headed and more autocratic than the average Tsar'.[6] Later,
in a letter to John O'Leary in 1906, he wrote that the description of O'Brien
as 'a historic lunatic' was 'very apt [...] For the last three years I considered
him a hopeless ego-maniac'.[7] As for Redmond, Davitt had had a problem with
him since the early 1890s, describing him to Dillon as 'undisciplined as he is
morally a coward';[8] and although Redmond had ultimately failed to back
O'Brien's position after the Wyndham Act, Davitt's assessment of him was that
he was still in full sympathy 'with O'Brien's pro-west British policy, and it is
only a fear of losing the Chair of the Irish Party, that keeps him from going
back to where they both started, from the spirit and policy of the Land
Conference'.[9] For Davitt, the land and the national questions always remained
linked. Even though important aspects of the radical agrarian programme of
the early 1880s were never realized, or indeed his own land nationalization
scheme, he nevertheless celebrated the agrarian revolution in *The fall of feudalism*, essentially because it had expedited the demise of the 'landlord garrison', the symbol of British rule in Ireland. However objectionable he had found
the details of the 1903 land act, he still acknowledged that 'It drives a few more
nails into the coffin of Irish landlordism, and it will help to bring the land of
the country under the control of the remnants of our Celtic people'.[10]

4 Davitt to McGhee, 23 Mar. 1905, DP, TCD, MS 9521/6020. 5 Davitt to Dillon, 18 July 1904, JDP, TCD, MS 6728/212. 6 Davitt to T.D. Sullivan, 28 July 1904, TDSP, NLI, MS 8237. 7 Davitt to O'Leary, 12 May 1906, DP, TCD, MS 9377/1061. 8 Davitt to Dillon, n.d. DP, TCD, MS 9414/1914. 9 Davitt to McGhee, 15 Apr. 1905, DP, TCD, MS 9521/6021. 10 *Melbourne Advocate*, 23 July 1903, cited in McNeil, 'Land, labor and liberation', p. 444.

Epilogue

URING HIS LATER political life, Davitt never experienced poverty in any real sense, certainly not as he had known it in his youth, but his single-minded commitment to political agitation, over financial considerations, often left him impecunious. By his late fifties, however, he found himself and his family in much more favourable circumstances, his wife having been left a substantial inheritance in 1904 by her wealthy Californian aunt, Mary Canning.[1] The Davitt family had moved to Dalkey, Co. Dublin, after Davitt's resignation from parliament in 1899, and with their later financial windfall, he and his wife had security in their Dalkey residence,[1a] where they could now comfortably rear their four children, Michael, Eileen, Cahir and Robert Emmet.[2] This settled life, however, did not signal Davitt's retirement from political activism. Up until his death in May 1906 he was, typically, planning campaigns and embroiled in controversy. In his final weeks, he had two meetings at his home with Alfred Webb on the controversial education question. Both were opposed to denominational education, and, against the backdrop of Davitt's recent clash with Bishop Edward O'Dwyer of Limerick on the issue, each had apparently received a letter from Dillon and Redmond, requesting that they refrain 'from publicly giving utterance to our views on the subject'.[3] In one of Davitt's letters to the *Freeman's Journal* during his altercation with the bishop, he championed secular education, and warned,

> Make no mistake about it, my Lord Bishop [...] Democracy is about to rule in these countries; and if you are wise you will cease to uphold the class dominance, in state and in Universities, of the Dukes of Norfolk and Lords Dunraven, and try to find in government by the people the best and surest safety for the religious and educational rights and privileges of all faiths.[4]

It was indicative of Davitt's distinctive role as a freelance agitator that, as Patrick Maume has observed, his death 'saved the Irish Party from considerable embarrassment'.[5]

1 Moody, *Davitt*, p. 552. 1a In 1899 the family moved to Comber House, Mount Salus, Dalkey, and later lived at St Justin's, Victoria Road, Dalkey; see Bernard O'Hara, *Davitt* (Mayo, 2006), p. 72. 2 Michael b. 1890; Eileen, b. 1892; Cahir, b. 1894; Robert Emmet, b. 1899. 3 Webb, *Alfred Webb*, pp 74–5. 4 *FJ*, 22 Jan. 1906. 5 Maume, *The long gestation* p. 83.

Davitt's death at the age of sixty was an untimely one, having been caused by septicaemia, which he contracted after complications brought on by an earlier tooth extraction. It had been his wish, as expressed in his will, that he be buried alongside his mother in Manayunk, near Philadelphia, if he should die in America, and in his native Straide, if he should die in Britain.[6] His insistence that he be buried anywhere other than Britain reflected his abiding hatred of everything which he considered the British ruling class and the British empire to represent. He had always taken great exception to being taken for an Englishman. He had, of course, politely but firmly corrected Tolstoy on this count during their meeting in 1904; and in the early 1890s, when W.T. Stead was planning to compile an album of portraits of the most notable political figures in Britain, Davitt wrote in a friendly but slightly earnest manner,

> My dear Mr Stead, how do I come under the above heading of your proposed album of Potraits? Or, are you thinking of changing 'Ireland' into 'West Britain' and thereby solving England's difficulty over here by merging us all in your British name? You may make the Pope an Englishman and bring St Peter's to the Thames Enbankment, but you will find the other job a far more difficult one.[7]

Davitt believed himself to be of true Celtic pedigree, descended 'from the O'Doherty's, all black Celts'.[8] He considered it one of the distinguishing features of Parnell that he 'was really more English than Irish in everything except political feeling and conviction. There was not a fraction of Celt in his composition, cast of mind, mode of thought or imagination'.[9]

Despite Davitt's request for the 'simplest possible ceremony', his remains, laid in state in a Dublin church before their removal to Straide, attracted thousands of mourners. His passing was reported in the press throughout Ireland and in Britain, Europe, America and Australia, a reflection of his international standing.[10] President Theodore Roosevelt sent a letter expressing his condolences.[11] In Britain, Keir Hardie wired the LRC in London, advising that the party 'should be well represented' at the funeral.[12]

In a later appreciation, Hardie remarked that, had Davitt been in parliament in the 1870s, he would have been an obvious choice as leader of Irish nationalism.[13] Yet Davitt never envisaged himself in a conventional leadership position. In the mid-1880s, once he had cut his political teeth in mainstream nationalist politics, he came into his own as a freelance radical, a role which

---

6 Sheehy Skeffington, *Michael Davitt*, p. 212. 7 Davitt to Stead, 24 Oct. 1894, SP, CAC, MS 1/19. 8 Davitt's diary, 24 Jan. 1890, DP, TCD, MS 9553. 9 Davitt to R.Barry O'Brien, 6 Dec. 1893, DP, TCD, MS 9377/1063. 10 See the four volumes of obituary notices in the Davitt Papers, TCD, MS 9626. 11 *FJ*, 8 June 1906. 12 Hardie to LRC, London, 1 June 1906, LRCP, JRLUM, LRC, MS LP GC5/104. 13 Hardie, 'Michael Davitt', p. 416.

suited his broad political agenda and also his temperament. His gravitation towards radical politics in Britain, and his identification with an international-alist agenda of social justice and liberty, was in many respects a natural pro-gression for someone who had experienced the injustice of the landlord sys-tem and who had been reared in a working-class immigrant community in Britain. He was first and foremost an Irish nationalist, but the influence of the British radical tradition, to which he was exposed as a young man in Haslingden, was also apparent and enduring in his thinking. His personal com-mitment to uniting Irish nationalism and British democracy was a manifesta-tion of this. Nevertheless, his eclectic politics and his freelance activism left him something of an outsider. Without his journalism, his main political plat-form, he would not have had the same later career or political impact.

He was not a particularly original thinker, but, as Moody has noted, he was a 'skilful adapter and transmitter of ideas'.[14] He was also a fiercely indepen-dent thinker and a highly intelligent and astute political tactician. Except for occasion when his own prejudices blinded him to political realities, he was quick to identify political opportunities and to seize them. J.J. Lee has recently suggested that Davitt was something of a prisoner of politics, given not only his intense dislike for parliamentary life but also his expressed yearning in diary entries and in personal correspondence for a quieter existence, beyond the realm of politics.[15] Indeed, in many ways, Davitt was a very private man, and at times found pleasure and satisfaction in nothing more than quiet peri-ods of reading or gardening, or travelling independently, without political commitments. But he was always drawn back into the grind of political work, and one suspects that he would ultimately have found it unbearable to be divorced from such a life, however demanding or frustrating that life might be. The allure of politics as an agent of progress or change always compelled him to commit himself totally to exacting schedules and campaigns, often without due consideration to his financial state or even his health.

From the mid-1880s, he embraced the role of a freelance radical, and in much of his political campaigning he identified with Henry George. However, he still remained very much independent of George. The latter had always stressed the international social agenda over particular national preoccupations, but Davitt himself remained a firmly committed Irish nationalist. Indeed, in 1886 when George unsuccessfully ran for the post of Lord Mayor of New York he felt 'deeply grieved' that Davitt, who was in America at the time, did not actively support him, but instead seemed more concerned by how such expres-sions of support would play with Parnell and other members of the Irish Party.

---

14 Moody, *Davitt*, p. 555.   **15** Lee made these remarks in his opening lecture at the Michael Davitt Centenary Conference, St Patrick's College, Drumcondra, Dublin, 26–8 May 2006.

George wrote to McGhee, 'I did not think it possible that [Davitt] could be in the country where the standard of the land for the people was raised without saying a single word for it'.[16] In his own defence, Davitt explained to George that any expressions of support for the campaign on his part would have been detrimental to George in the long term, because of the reaction it would have provoked from Parnell and others. In any case, Davitt felt that 'the hopeless task of cleaning out [New York] City Hall' was fraught with political risks for George.[17] However, by 1886 Davitt had an even greater reason to hitch himself to the Irish constitutional wagon, given the Liberal–nationalist alliance and the possibility for home rule, and this was undoubtedly also a factor in his decision not to openly back George. Davitt also acted independently in his relations with McGhee. He had, of course, taken a very different stance from McGhee during the railway strike in Ireland in 1890; and even in regard to 'new unionism' itself, it must be stated that Davitt never really immersed himself in the movement, despite his genuine support for the work of McGhee and McHugh.

Davitt's association with constitutional nationalism after the land war has led to his often being neatly situated within that tradition, notwithstanding his radical impulses. Carla King has remarked that he 'made the transition between two political traditions in Ireland, the physical-force approach of the Fenians and the constitutional one of the Irish Parliamentary Party'.[18] It is true, he did reject the use of political violence in the early 1880s, certainly by the time of the Phoenix Park murders. However, his politics straddled a number of ideological and political junctions during his later political career, and his involvement with the Irish Party in the 1880s and 1890s had less to do with a fundamental political conversion than with his belief in the efficacy of moderate political agitation. In 1893, he wrote to R. Barry O'Brien,

> To answer your question about my 'conversion' to 'constitutionalism' we would have to arrange our terminology. First, I am modest enough to claim that I am the most radical 'revolutionist' produced by the Fenian movement, if by revolutionist we are to understand one who goes in for fundamental change and in war against the older order of things. I 'left' the Fenians when I was expelled for having joined Parnell in the Land League. I am more a revolutionist than I was 30 years ago, in my opinion. I believe that constitutional media is infinitely more effective in these countries for real revolutionary work than conspiracies or secret societies. This is the extent of my 'conversion' to constitutionalism [...][19]

Davitt, it must be said, retained strong emotional ties with the Fenian tradition. In 1901 he appealed to Dillon to make £100 available to the old Fenian

16 George to McGhee, 7 Feb. 1887, HGP, NYPL. **17** Davitt to George, 4 Nov. 1886, HGP, NYPL. **18** King, *Michael Davitt*, p. 8. **19** Davitt to R. Barry O'Brien, 6 Dec. 1893, DP, TCD,

leader, James Stephens, who in his old age was 'in want of some comforts' before he died. Davitt asked Dillon to keep the matter private.[20] Significantly, it was one of Davitt's final requests, shortly before his own death, that his remains should be taken to St Theresa's church, Clarendon Street, Dublin, the only church which would admit the body of the Fenian, Charles McCarthy, who died suddenly after his release from prison in 1878.[21] The hierarchy had objected to the remains of Fenians being held in Catholic churches, and it was only due to the Carmelite fathers at St Theresa's church that McCarthy's body was accommodated there. Despite campaigning for home rule during his later career, Davitt always remained attached to the republican ideal. He often made reference to the radical agenda of a future democratic party in a home rule parliament, and in doing so he sometimes made it clear that such an agenda would have a separatist dimension.[22] In the *The fall of feudalism*, he argued that Ireland should be 'a state in the freest and fullest sense in which Holland, Denmark, Belgium, Switzerland, Bulgaria, Servia and Greece are'.[23] In this, Davitt was making a point about self-determination rather than republican-ism, but his particular affection for the Boers during the Anglo–Boer war owed something to the fact that the 'David' in that battle was represented by two small *republics*, defiantly resisting the encroachments of a hegemonic 'Goliath', the British empire. In 1896, when he had just reluctantly assumed his parlia-mentary position as the constitutional nationalist politician for South Mayo, Davitt told Stead that he was a 'republican by creed and conviction'.[24]

Of course, for many Fenians, Davitt had abandoned his nationalism. John O'Leary wrote that he had become 'not a nationalist at all in any real sense intelligible to us [Fenians], but only some sort of internationalist or socialist, in some sense not intelligible even to himself'.[25] This was a sentiment shared even by some constitutional nationalists; and among significant figures on the left, Davitt was simply viewed as something of an anomaly. Indeed, his polit-ical thought is not easily situated in an obvious ideological or political frame-work. There is a temptation to describe him as a 'Jacobin radical' at first. However, even this is inadequate, for, as we have seen, he was much less rad-ical than is often supposed. The most useful approach to understanding him is to view him as a universal figure, not in any ideological context but as some-one driven by an egalitarian mission to address issues affecting industrial humanity, everywhere. Viewed from this perspective, he is better understood as a nationalist, social reformer, educationalist, crusading journalist. Indeed, rather than having any place in ideological structures such as the first or sec-ond International, he can be identified – although without any exact parallels

MS 9377/1063. **20** Davitt to Dillon, 14 Jan. 1901, DP, TCD, MS 9421/1838. **21** Sheehy Skeffington, *Michael Davitt*, p. 213. **22** See *FJ*, 17 Nov. 1887. **23** Davitt, *The fall*, 717. **24** Davitt to Stead, 4 Apr. 1896, DP, TCD, MS 9459/[3753/15]. **25** Quoted in Moody, *Davitt*, p. 521.

– with the radical democratic movement of political exiles in Europe in the 1840s and 1850s, the movement described by E.H. Carr as 'the romantic exiles', and among whom were figures such as Louis Kossuth.[26] When Davitt met Kossuth in Turin in 1885, the old Hungarian leader stated that he himself was not a socialist, but he stressed that the application of the egalitarian principles at the centre of the Christian gospel would address the social question.[27] While Davitt was, contextually, a political figure in and of his own time and place, it is nevertheless possible to identify him with that broader tradition of international radicals, and in Ireland with that tradition which represented the 'men of no property', from the United Irish radicals of the 1790s to the social republicanism of Liam Mellows and Peadar O'Donnell in the twentieth century. James Hope, one of the most radical of the United Irishmen, expressed views on the 'main cause of social derangement' which would not be out of place in Davitt's writings.

> It was my settled opinion [he wrote] that the condition of the labouring class, was the fundamental question at issue between the rulers and the people, and there could be no solid foundation for liberty, till measures were adopted that went to the root of the evil, and were specifically directed to the restoration of the natural rights of the people, the right of deriving a subsistence from the soil on which their labour was expended.[26]

Davitt was, however, still very much a complex character. On the one hand, considering his campaigns for social justice and especially his international interventions, there can be no questioning his instinctive sympathy, and support, for the 'oppressed', the underdogs in any struggle with imperialist or despotic rule. But, as we have seen, he was also quite capable of partisan advocacy and, indeed, of occlusion of awkward evidence, when multiple levels of 'oppression' and multiple 'rights' were involved, as in the case of the black population in South Africa. His deep-seated instincts and the presiding preoccupation with national sovereignty and social justice which marked his political thought and activism cannot be shoe-horned neatly into a consistent and uncomplicated political career. There are paradoxes, personality factors, contradictions and inconsistencies which demand acknowledgement and explanation. Yet for all his contradictions, he can be understood as a product of his time, with many of the concomitant preoccupations and prejudices. His political life and thought may, moreover, be viewed as a prism through which many of the contradictions and complexities of Ireland's predicament in this historically critical 'time of choice', between 1890 and 1916, can be better understood.

26 Carr, *The Romantic*, passim. 27 DP, TCD, MS 9544. 28 R.R. Madden (ed.), *The United Irishmen: their lives and times*, 3rd series, vol. 1, *The autobiography of James (Jemmy) Hope* (London, 1846, repr. Belfast, 1998), p. 14.

Bibliography

MANUSCRIPTS

Trinity College Dublin
Michael Davitt papers
John Dillon papers

National Library of Ireland
Rosamund Jacob papers
J.F.X. O'Brien papers
John Redmond papers
Francis Sheehy Skeffington papers
T.D. Sullivan papers
Davitt's letter to William O'Brien, MS 913
Davitt's letter to Michael McKeown, MS 18,563
Davitt's letter to Author's Syndicate, MS 18,575

Davitt Archive, Straide
Davitt-Collins correspondence

Churchill Archive, Cambridge
W.T. Stead papers

John Rylands Library, University of Manchester
Labour Representation Committee papers

National Library of Wales, Aberystwyth
D.R. Daniel papers

New York Public Library
Henry George papers

OFFICIAL PUBLICATIONS

Hansard, Parliamentary Debates, 4th series, 1897–98

PRIMARY NEWSPAPERS AND JOURNALS

American Isarelite
Birmingham Daily Post
Burnley Gazette
Burnley Express
Connaught Telegraph
Evening Telegraph (Dublin)
Freeman's Journal
Gaelic American
Glasgow Observer
Irish Times
Irish World
Merthyr Express
Melbourne Advocate

Nationist
National Democrat
Oban Times
Pall Mall Gazette
Pilot (Boston)
Sligo Champion
Speaker
The Times (London)
Contemporary Review
Independent Review
Nineteenth Century
Socialist Review
Today

BOOKS, PAMPHLETS, ARTICLES AND THESES*

Arnstein, Walter, *The Bradlaugh case: a study in late Victorian opinion and politics* (Oxford, 1965).

Barker, C.A., *Henry George* (New York, 1955).

Bew, Paul, *Land and the national question in Ireland, 1858–82* (Dublin, 1978).

—, *Charles Stewart Parnell* (Dublin, 1980).

—, *Conflict and conciliation in Ireland, 1890–1910* (Oxford, 1987).

—, 'Parnell and Davitt' in D. George Boyce and Alan O'Day (eds), *Parnell in perspective* (London, 1991).

Blake, Robert, *Disraeli* (London, 1998).

Blunt, W.S, *The land war in Ireland: being a personal narrative of events* (London, 1912).*

Boylan, Thomas and Timothy Foley (eds), *Political economy and colonial Ireland* (London, 1992).

Boyle, J.W., 'The Belfast Protestant Association and the Independent Orange Order, 1901–10, *IHS*, 13 (1962–3).

—, *The Irish labour movement in the nineteenth century* (Washington, DC, 1988).

Brady, L.W., *T.P. O'Connor and the Liverpool Irish* (London, 1983).

Brasted, H.V., 'Irish nationalism and the British empire in the late nineteenth century' in Oliver McDonagh, W.F. Mandle and Pauric Travers (eds), *Irish culture and nationalism, 1750–1950* (Canberra, 1983).

Brooking, Tom, *Lands for the people? The highland clearances and the colonization of New Zealand: a biography of John McKenzie* (Otagon, 1996).

Brown, Dee, *Bury my heart at wounded knee: an Indian history of the American West* (London, 1991).

---

* Primary works and writings, other than Davitt's main texts, articles and pamphlets, are identified by an asterisk.

Buckland, Patrick, *Irish unionism i: the Anglo-Irish and the new Ireland, 1885–1922* (Dublin, 1972).

—, *Irish unionism ii: Ulster unionism and the origins of Northern Ireland, 1886 to 1922* (Dublin, 1973).

Buckley, David N., *James Fintan Lalor: radical* (Cork, 1990).

Bull, Philip, 'The United Irish League and the reunion of the Irish Parliamentary Party, 1898–1900', *IHS*, 26:101 (1978).

—, *Land, politics and nationalism: a study of the Irish land question* (Dublin, 1996).

Cahalan, J.M., 'Michael Davitt: the preacher of ideas, 1881–1906', *Éire–Ireland*, 11:1 (1976).

Cambrensis, Geraldus, *Expugnatio hibernicus*, ed. A.B. Scott and F.X. Martin (Dublin, 1978).*

Callanan, Frank, *The Parnell split, 1890–91* (Cork, 1992).

—, *T.M. Healy* (Cork, 1996).

Campbell, Fergus, *Land and revolution: nationalist politics in the west of Ireland, 1891–1921* (Oxford, 2005).

Canny, Nicholas, *Making Ireland British, 1580–1650* (Oxford, 2003).

Carr, E.H., *The romantic exiles* (London, 1998).

Cashman, D.B., *The life of Michael Davitt, founder of the land league* (London, 1882), repr. in Carla King (ed.), *Michael Davitt: collected writings, 1868–1906* (Bristol, 2001), vol. i.*

Clark, Samuel, *Social origins of the land war* (Princeton, 1979).

Colley, Linda, *Britons: forging the nation, 1707–1837* (London, 1996).

Collinson Black, R.D., *The statistical and social inquiry society of Ireland, centenary volume, 1847–1947* (Dublin, 1947).

—, *Economic thought and the Irish question, 1817–1870* (Cambridge, 1978).

Comerford, R.V., *The fenians in context: Irish politics and society, 1848–82* (Dublin, 1998).

Connolly, James, *The re-conquest of Ireland*, in *Connolly: collected works*, I (Dublin, 1972).

—, editorial on Davitt in the *Harp*, August 1908,* in O.D. Edwards and Bernard Ransom (eds), *James Connolly, selected political writings* (London, 1973).

Connolly, S.J., *Priests and people in pre-Famine Ireland, 1780–1845* (Dublin, 2001).

Craig, Gordon A., *Germany, 1866–1945* (Oxford, 1981).

Cronin, Mike and Darly Adair, *The wearing of the green: a history of St Patrick's day* (London, 2002).

Crowley, D.W., 'The crofters' party, 1885–1892', *SHR*, 25 (1956).

Cumpston, Mary, 'Some early Indian nationalists and their allies in the British parliament', *EHR*, 76 (Apr. 1961).

Cunningham, John, *Labour in the west of Ireland, working life and struggle, 1890–1914* (Belfast, 1995).

Curtis, L.P., 'On class and class conflict in the land war', *IESH*, 3 (1981).

—, *Apes and angels: the Irishman in Victorian caricature* (London, 1997).

Daly, Sean, *Ireland and the first international* (Cork, 1984).

Daniel, T.K., 'Griffith on his noble head': the determinants of Cumann na nGaedheal economic policy, 1922–32, *IESH*, 3 (1976).

Davis, Richard, *Arthur Griffith and Non-Violent Sinn Féin* (Kerry, 1974).

Davies, Alun, 'Ireland's Crystal Palace, 1853' in J.M. Goldstrom and L.A. Clarkson (eds), *Irish population, economy and society* (Oxford, 1981).

Davis, Graham, 'The Irish in Britain, 1815–1939', in Andy Bielenberg (ed.), *The Irish diaspora* (Essex, 2000).

Davitt, Michael, *Leaves from a prison diary; or, lectures to a 'solitary' audience*, 2 vols (London 1885), repr. in King (ed.), *Michael Davitt: collected writings, 1868–1906* (Bristol, 2001), vol. iii.

—, *Jottings in solitary* (ed.) Carla King (Dublin, 2003).

—, *The Times-Parnell commission: speech delivered by Michael Davitt in defence of the land league* (London, 1890), repr. in King (ed.), *Michael Davitt*, vol. iv.

—, *Life and progress in Australasia* (London, 1898).

—, *The Boer fight for freedom, from the beginning of hostilities to the peace of Pretoria* (New York and London, 1902).

—, *Within the pale: the true story of anti-Semitic persecutions in Russia* (repr. New York, 1975).

—, *The fall of feudalism in Ireland; or, The story of the land league revolution* (London, 1904).

—, *The prison life of Michael Davitt, related by himself* (London, 1878), repr. in King (ed.), *Michael Davitt*, vol. i.

—, *The land league proposal: a statement for honest and thoughtful men* (Glasgow, 1882).

—, *Land nationalization; or, National peasant proprietary. Michael Davitt's lectures in Scotland: the principles of radical reform in the land laws* (Glasgow, 1882).

—, *The castle government in Ireland: a lecture by Michael Davitt* (Glasgow, 1882).

—, *Speech of Michael Davitt at a meeting in favour of land nationalization, St James Hall, 30 October 1883* (London, 1883).

—, 'The punishment of penal servitude', *Contemporary Review*, 44 (1883).

—, 'The Irish social problem', *Today*, 4 (Apr. 1884).

—, 'Irish Conservatism and its outlooks', *Dublin University Review* (September, 1885).

—, 'About our artisans and industries', *Evening Telegraph* (Dublin), 14, 21 Nov., and 12, 19, 26 Dec. 1885, and 9 Jan. 1886.

—, *Landlordism, low wages and strikes* (London, 1884).

—, 'Remedies for Irish distress', *Contemporary Review*, 58 (Nov. 1890).

—, 'Mr. Giffen's proposed solution to the Irish question', *Contemporary Review* 49 (Apr. 1886).

—, *Reasons why home rule should be granted to Ireland: an appeal to the common sense of British democracy* (London, 1886).

—, 'Home rule: speech at Glasgow, April 20 1886 in support of Mr Gladstone's Home Rule bill', in King (ed.), *Michael Davitt*, vol. i.

—, 'Retiring the landlord garrison', *Nineteenth Century*, xxvii, May 1890.

—, *Revival of the Irish woollen industry. Brief historical record: how England endeavoured to destroy Irish manufacture. How Irish leaders propose to accomplish its revival. The Irish Woollen Manufacturing & Export Company* (Dublin,1887).

—, 'Impressions of the Canadian north-west', *Nineteenth Century*, 31 (Apr. 1892).

—, 'The priest in politics', *Nineteenth Century*, 33 (1893).

—, 'Fabian faustian', *Nineteenth Century* (Dec. 1893).

—, 'Home Rule and labour representation', *Speaker*, 28 Apr. 1894.

—, 'Criminal and prison reform' *Nineteenth Century*, 36 (Dec. 1894).

—, *Ireland's appeal to America, Denvir's Monthly Irish Weekly* (Mar. 1902).

—, *Some suggestions for a final settlement of the land question* (Dublin, 1902).

—, 'The Irish national assembly (session of 1910)', *Independent Review*, 5 (Apr. 1905).

Devine, T.M., *Clanship to crofters' war: the social transformation of the Scottish highlands* (Manchester, 1994).

Devoy, John, 'Michael Davitt's career', pts i–vii, *Gaelic American* (9 June–3 Nov. 1906).*

Dewey, Clive, 'Gaelic agrarian legislation and the Celtic revival: historicist implications of Gladstone's Irish and Scottish Land Acts, 1870–1886', *Past & Present*, 64 (Aug. 1974).

Donnelly, S.J., *The land and the people of nineteenth-century Cork, the rural economy and the land question* (London, 1975).

Duncan, William, *Life of Joseph Cowen (M.P. for Newcastle, 1874–86)* (New York, 1904).*

Dunleavy, John, *Davitt Haslingden* (Haslingden, 2006).

Feingold, W. L., *The revolt of the tenantry: the transformation of local government in Ireland, 1872–1886* (Boston, 1984).

Fieldhouse, D.K., *The colonial empires: a comparative survey for the eighteenth century* (London, 1966).

Fisher, Trevor, *Scandal: the sexual politics of late Victorian Britain* (Gloucestershire, 1995).

Fitzgerald, David, '"A peculiar tramping people": the Irish in Britain, 1801–70', in W.E. Vaughan (ed.), *A new history of Ireland; v, Ireland under the Union 1* (Oxford, 1989).

Foster, R., *Charles Stewart Parnell, the man and his family* (Sussex, 1979).

Garvin, Tom, *Nationalist revolutionaries in Ireland, 1858–1922* (Oxford, 1987).

Geary, Laurence M., *The plan of campaign, 1886–91* (Cork, 1986).

George, Henry, *Progress and poverty* (London, 1881).

—, *The Irish land question: what it involves and how alone it can be settled: an appeal to the land leaguers* (London, 1881).

Glasier, John F., 'Parnell's fall and the nonconformist conscience', *IHS*, 12 (1960–1).

Golway, Terry, *Irish rebel: John Devoy and America's fight for Ireland's Freedom* (New York, 1998).

Greaves, C. Desmond, *The life and times of James Connolly* (London, 1961).

Grigg, John, *The young Lloyd George* (London, 1973).

Hamer, D.A., *John Morley, Liberal intellectual in politics* (Oxford, 1968).

Hammond, J.L., *Gladstone and the Irish nation* (London, 1938).

Hanham, H. J., 'The problem of highland discontent, 1880–1885', *RHST*, 5th series, 19 (1969), 21–65.

Hardie, James Keir, 'Michael Davitt: the democrat', *Socialist Review*, Aug. 1908.*

Harding, Keith, 'The Irish issue in the British labour movement, 1900–1922' (PhD thesis, University of Sussex, 1983).

Harding, P., 'John Murdoch, Michael Davitt and the Land question: a study in comparative Irish and Scottish history' (MLitt thesis, University of Aberdeen, 1994).

Haslip, Joan, *Parnell: a biography* (London, 1936).

Healy, T.M., *Letters and leaders of my day*, vol. i (London, 1928).*

Hechter, Michael, *Internal colonialism: the Celtic fringe in British national development, 1536–1966* (London, 1975).

Heyck, T.W., *The dimensions of British radicalism: the Irish case, 1874–95* (Chicago, 1974).

Hobsbawn, Eric, *The age of empire, 1875–1914* (repr. London, 2005).

Hope, James, *The autobiography of James 'Jemmy' Hope* in R.R. Madden (ed.), *The United Irishmen: their lives and times*, 3rd series, i (repr. Belfast, 1998).*

Howe, Stephen, *Ireland and empire: colonial legacies in Irish history and culture* (Oxford, 2000).

Hunter, James, 'The politics of highland land reform, 1873–1895', *SHR*, 53 (Apr. 1974).

—, 'The Gaelic connection: the highlands, Ireland and nationalism, 1873–1922', *SHR*, 54 (Oct. 1975).

—, *The making of the crofting community* (Edinburgh, 1988).

Hyndman, H.M., *Further reminiscences* (London, 1912).*

Jackson, Alvin, 'Irish unionism and the Russellite threat, 1894–1906', *IHS*, 25:100 (1987).

—, *Colonel Edward Saunderson, land and loyalty in Victorian Ireland* (Oxford, 1995).

—, *Home rule: an Irish history, 1800–2000* (London, 2003).

Jenkins, Roy, *Gladstone* (London, 1995).

Jones, David S., 'The Cleavage between graziers and peasants in the land struggle, 1890–1910' in Samuel Clark and James Donnelly (eds), *Irish peasants: violence and political unrest, 1870–1914* (Manchester, 1983).

Jones, J. Graham, 'Michael Davitt, David Lloyd George and T.E. Ellis: the Welsh experience, 1886', *WHR*, 18 (1996–7).

Jones, M.A., *The limits of liberty: American history, 1607–1980* (New York, 1992).

Jones-Roberts, K.W., 'D.R. Daniel, 1859–1931', *Journal of the Merioneth Historical and Record Society*, 3 (1965).

Jordan, Donald E., *Land and popular politics in Ireland: county Mayo from the plantation to the land war* (Cambridge, 1984).

Judd, Denis, *Radical Joe: a life of Joseph Chamberlain* (London, 1977).

Judge, Edward H., *Easter in Kishinev, anatomy of a pogrom* (New York, 1992).

Kabdebo, Thomas, *Ireland and Hungary: a study in parallels with an Arthur Griffith bibliography* (Dublin, 2001).

Kane, Robert, *The industrial resources of Ireland* (Dublin, 1845).*

Kapp, Yvonne, *Elanor Marx*, vol. ii: *the uncrowned years, 1884–1898* (London, 1976).

Kee, Robert, *The laurel and the ivy: the story of Charles Stewart Parnell and Irish nationalism* (London, 1993).

Kelly, Matthew, 'The end of Parnellism and the ideological dilemmas of Sinn Féin', in D. George Boyce and Alan O' Day (eds), *Ireland in transition, 1867–1921* (London, 2003).

Kenefick, William, *'Rebellious and contrary': the Glasgow dockers, 1853–1932* (East Lothian, 2000).

Kennedy, Liam, *Colonialism, religion and nationalism in Ireland* (Belfast, 1996).

Keogh, Dermot, *Jews in twentieth-century Ireland: anti-Semitism and the holocaust* (Cork, 1998).

King, Carla, 'Michael Davitt and the Kishinev pogrom, 1903', *Irish Slavonic Studies*, 17 (1996).

—, *Michael Davitt* (Dundalk, 1999).

— (ed.) *Michael Davitt: collected writings, 1868–1906*, vols 1–8 (Bristol, 2001).

—, 'Michael Davitt, Irish nationalism and the British empire in the late nineteenth century' in Peter Gray (ed.), *Victoria's Ireland? Irishness and Britishness, 1837–1901* (Dublin, 2004).

Kerr, Donal A., 'Priests, pikes and patriots: the Irish Catholic church and political violence from the Whiteboys to the fenians' in Stewart J. Brown and David W. Millar (eds), *Piety and power in Ireland, 1760–1960, essays in honour of Emmet Larkin* (Belfast, 2000).

Kettle, T.M., 'Michael Davitt: the nationalist', *Socialist Review*, Aug. 1908.*

Kinealy, Christine, *This great calamity: the Irish famine, 1845–52* (Dublin, 2006).

Koss, Stephen, *Nonconformists in modern British politics* (London, 1975).

—, *The rise of the political press in Britain* (London, 1981).

Kovesi Killerby, Catherine, '"Never locked up or tied": early Irish missionary attitudes to the Aboriginal people of Western Australia' in Philip Bull et al. (eds), *Ireland and Australia, 1789–1998: studies of culture, identity and migration* (Sydney, 2000).

Krause, Davitt, 'The conscience of Ireland: Lalor, Davitt and Sheehy Skeffington', *Éire-Ireland*, 28:1 (Spring 1993).

Kunina, V.E., *Maikl Devitt, sun irlandskogo naroda: stranitsy zhizni I borby, 1846–1906* (Moscow, 1973).

Lane, Fintan, *The origins of modern Irish socialism, 1881–96* (Cork, 1996).

Larkin, Emmet, *The Roman Catholic church and the plan of campaign in Ireland, 1886–1888* (Cork, 1978).

Larkin, Felix. M, '"A Great daily organ": the *Freeman's Journal*, 1763–1924', *History Ireland*, 14:3 (May/June 2006).

Lawrence, E.P., *Henry George and the British Isles* (East Lansang, MI, 1957).

Lee, Joseph, *The modernization of Irish society, 1848–1918* (Dublin, 1989).

—, 'On the birth of the modern Irish state: the Larkin thesis' in Stewart J. Brown and David W. Millar (eds), *Piety and power in Ireland, 1760–1960, essays in honour of Emmet Larkin* (Belfast, 2000).

Lenin, V.I., *Imperialism: the highest stage of capitalism* (Peking, 1975).*

Lowe, W.J., *The Irish in mid-Victorian Lancashire: the shaping of a working-class community* (New York, 1989).

Lowry, Donal, '"The Boers were the beginning of the end"?: the wider impact of the South African war' in Donal Lowry (ed.), *The South African War reappraised* (Manchester, 2000).

Loughlin, James, 'The Irish Protestant home rule Association and nationalist politics, 1886–93', *IHS*, 24:95 (May 1985).

—, 'Constructing the political spectacle, Parnell, the press and the national leadership, 1879–86', in D. George Boyce and Alan O'Day (eds), *Parnell in perspective* (London, 1991).

—, 'Nationality and loyalty: Parnellism, monarchy and the construction of Irish identity, 1800–85', in D. George Boyce and Alan O'Day (eds), *Ireland in transition, 1867–1921* (London, 2004).

Lyons, F.S.L., 'The Irish unionist party and the devolution crisis of 1904–5', *IHS*, 6:21 (Mar. 1948).

—, 'The economic ideas of Parnell' in M. Roberts, *Historical Studies*, 2 (1959).

—, *John Dillon: a biography* (London, 1968).

—, *The Irish parliamentary party, 1890–1910* (CT, 1975).

—, *Ireland since the famine* (London, 1987).

MacRiald, Donald M., 'Crossing migrant frontiers: comparative reflections on Irish migration in Britain and the United States in the nineteenth and twentieth centuries', in MacRiald (ed.), *The great Famine and beyond: Irish migration in Britain in the nineteenth and twentieth centuries* (Dublin, 2000).

McCracken, Donal, *Forgotten protest: Ireland and the Anglo Boer war* (Belfast, 2003).

McFarland, E.W., *John Ferguson, 1836–1906, Irish issues in Scottish politics* (East Lothian, 2003).

McGee, Owen, *The IRB: the Irish Republican Brotherhood from the land league to Sinn Féin* (Dublin, 2005).

McHugh, Roger, 'Thomas Kettle and Francis Sheehy Skeffington' in C.C. O'Brien (ed.), *The shaping of modern Ireland* (London, 1960).

McLachlan, Noel, 'Michael Davitt and passive resistance: the path not taken', *TLS*, 12 (Feb. 1999).

McNeil, Laura, 'Land, labor and liberation: Michael Davitt and the Irish question in the age of British democratic reform, 1878–1906' (PhD thesis, Boston College).

Malcolm, Elizabeth, '"What would people say if I became a policeman"?: the Irish policeman abroad', in Oonagh Walsh (ed.), *Ireland abroad: politics and professions in the nineteenth century* (Dublin, 2003).

Marsh, Peter T., *Joseph Chamberlain: entrepreneur in politics* (London, 1994).

Marx and Engels, *Marx and Engels on Ireland* (London, 1971).

—, *The German ideology*, part one (ed.) C.J. Arthur (London, 1985).

Matthew, H.C.G., *Gladstone, 1875–1898* (Oxford, 1995).

Maume, Patrick, *The long gestation: Irish nationalist life, 1891–1918* (Dublin, 1999).

—, 'Standish James O'Grady: between imperial romance and Irish revival', *Éire-Ireland*, 39:182 (Spring/Summer 2004).

Maye, Brian, *Arthur Griffith* (Dublin, 1997).

Mitchel, John, *The last conquest of Ireland (perhaps)* (ed.) Patrick Maume (Dublin, 2005)*

T.W. Moody, 'Michael Davitt and penal servitude, 1870–77', *Studies*, 30:120 (December 1941).

—, 'Michael Davitt and the "pen" letter', *IHS*, vol. iv, no.15, Mar. 1945.

—, 'Michael Davitt and the British Labour Movement, 1882–1906', *RHST*, 5th series, 3 (1953).

—, 'Anna Parnell and the Land League', *Hermathena*, 117 (1974).

—, *Davitt and Irish revolution, 1846–82* (Oxford, 1982).

Moran, Gerard, 'Nationalists in exile: the National Brotherhood of St Patrick in Lancashire, 1861–5', in Roger Swift and Sheridan Gilley (eds), *The Irish in Victorian Britain: the local dimension* (Dublin, 1999).

Morgan, Kenneth O., *Wales in British politics, 1868–1922* (Cardiff, 1970).

—, 'Tom Ellis versus Lloyd George: the fractured consciousness of *fin-de-siècle* Wales', in Geraint H. Jenkins and J. Beverley Smith (eds), *Politics and society in Wales, 1840–1922: essays in honour of Ieuan Gwynedd Jones* (Cardiff, 1988).

—, *Keir Hardie: radical and socialist* (London, 1997).

Morley, John, *The life of William Ewart Gladstone*, 3 vols (London, 1904).*

Morton, A.L. and George Tate, *The British labour movement* (London, 1956).

Murphy, Maura, 'Fenianism, Parnellism and the Cork trades, 1860–1900', *Saothar, Journal of the Irish Labour History Society*, 5 (May, 1979).

Neal, Frank, 'Irish settlement in the north-east and north-west of England in the mid-nineteenth century', in Roger Swift and Sheridan Gilley (eds), *The Irish in Victorian Britain: the local dimension* (Dublin, 1999).

Newby, Andrew G., '"Shoulder to shoulder?" Scottish and Irish land reformers in the Highlands of Scotland' (PhD thesis, University of Edinburgh, 2001).

—, *The life and times of Edward McHugh (1853–1915): land reformer, trade unionist, and labour activist* (New York, 2004).

Newsinger, John, 'Old Chartists, fenians and new socialists', *Éire-Ireland*, 17 (Spring 1982).

—, *Fenianism in mid-Victorian Britain* (London, 1994).

O'Brien, Conor Cruise, *Parnell and his party, 1880–90* (Oxford, 1957).

—, 'Timothy Michael Healy' in O'Brien (ed.), *The shaping of modern Ireland* (London, 1960).

O'Brien, William, *Recollections* (London, 1905).*

ÓBuachalla, Brendan, 'From Jacobite to Jacobin', in Bartlett et al. (eds), *1798: a bicentenary perspective* (Dublin, 2003).

Ó Catháin, Máirtín, 'Michael Davitt and Scotland', *Saothar, Journal of the Irish Labour History Society*, 25 (1999).

—, 'Fenian dynamite: dissident Irish republicans in late nineteenth-century Scotland', in Oonagh Walsh (ed.), *Ireland abroad: politics and professions in the nineteenth century* (Dublin, 2003).

O'Connor, Emmet, *A labour history of Waterford* (Waterford, 1989).

—, *A labour history of Ireland, 1824–1960* (Dublin, 1992).

O'Connor, John, *The workhouses of Ireland: the fate of Ireland's poor* (Dublin, 1995).

O'Day, Alan, *The English face of Irish nationalism, Parnellites involvement in British politics, 1880–86* (Dublin, 1977).

— and John Stevenson (eds), *Irish historical documents since 1800* (Dublin, 1992).

— and N.C. Fleming, *The Longman handbook of modern Irish history since 1800* (Harlow, 2005).

O'Donnell, F.H., *The history of the Irish parliamentary party*, vol. i (London, 1910).*

O'Farrell, Patrick, *The Irish in Australia, 1788 to the present* (Cork, 2001).

Ó Gráda, Cormac, 'Fenianism and socialism: the career of Joseph Patrick McDonnell', *Saothar, Journal of the Irish Labour History Society*, 1:1, May, 1975.

—, 'Some aspects of nineteenth-century Irish emigration', in L.M. Cullen and T.C. Smout (eds), *Comparative aspects of Scottish and Irish economic and social history, 1600–1900* (Edinburgh, 1977).

—, *Ireland: a new economic history, 1780–1939* (Oxford, 1995).

O'Hara, Bernard, *Davitt* (Mayo, 2006).

O'Higgins, Rachael, 'The Irish influence in the Chartist movement', *Past & Present*, 21 (1961).

O'Shea, Katherine, *The uncrowned King of Ireland: Charles Stewart Parnell, his love story and political life* (Gloucestershire, 2005).

Ó Tuathaigh, Gearóid, *Ireland before the famine, 1798–1848* (Dublin, 1972).

—, 'The Irish in nineteenth century Britain: problems of integration', *RHST*, 5th series, 31 (1981).

Pakenham, Thomas, *The Boer War* (London, 1992).

—, *The scramble for Africa, 1876–1912* (London, 1991).

Parnell, Anna, *The tale of a great sham* (ed.) Dana Hearne (Dublin, 1986).*

Pelling, Henry, *America and the British left: from Bright to Bevan* (London, 1956).

—, 'The Knights of Labor in Britain, 1880–1901', *Economic History Review*, (1956).

—, *Origins of the Labour party* (Oxford, 1965).

—, *Social geography of British elections, 1885–1910* (Hampshire, 1994).

Phoenix, Eamon, *Northern nationalism: nationalist politics, partition and the Catholic minority in Northern Ireland, 1890–1940* (Belfast, 1994).

Pretorius, Fransjohan, 'Boer attitudes to Africans in wartime', in Donal Lowry (ed.), *The South African War reappraised* (Manchester, 2000).

Ramm, Agatha, *Europe in the twentieth century, 1905–1970* (London, 1987).

Reece, Bob, 'The Irish and the Aborigines', in Fiona Bateman and T. Foley (eds), *Irish-Australian studies: papers delivered at the ninth Irish-Australian conference, Galway, April 1997* (Sydney, 2000).

Reid, Fred, *Keir Hardie, the making of a socialist* (London, 1978).

—, 'Kier Hardie and the *Labour Leader*, 1893–1903' in Jay Winter (ed.), *The working class in modern British History: essays in honour of Henry Pelling* (Cambridge, 1983).

Richter, Donald C, *Riotous Victorians* (London, 1981).

Roberts, Andrew, *Salisbury: Victorian titan* (London, 1999).

Roberts, J.M., *Europe, 1880–1945* (London, 1978).

Rosenne, Shabtai (ed. and compiled), *The Hague peace conferences of 1899 and 1907 and international arbitration: reports and documents* (The Hague, 2001).

Royle, Edward, *Modern Britain: a social history, 1750–1985* (London, 1996).

Ryan, W.P., *The Irish labour movement* (Dublin, 1919).*

Schwartz, Pedro, *The new political economy of J.S. Mill* (London, 1972).

Sheehy, Ian, 'T.P. O'Connor and *The Star*, 1886–90' in George D. Boyce and Alan O'Day (eds), *Ireland in transition, 1867–1921* (London, 2004).

Sheehy Skeffington, Francis, *Michael Davitt: revolutionary, agitator and labour leader* (repr. London, 1967).*

Short, K.R.M., *The dynamite war: Irish–American bombers in Victorian Britain* (Dublin, 1979).

Shreuder, D.M., *Gladstone and Kruger, Ireland, government and colonial 'home rule', 1880–85* (London, 1969).

Singh, S.R., *Dadabhai Naoroji, 1825–1917: the grand old man of India* (New Delhi, 1985).

Slatter, John, 'An Irishman at a Russian revolutionary court of honour: from the Michael Davitt Papers', *Irish Slavonic Studies*, 5 (1984).

Smillie, Robert, *My life for labour* (London, 1924).*

Soutter, F.W., *Recollections of a labour pioneer* (London, 1923).*

Spillane, M.V. 'The 4th earl of Dunraven, 1841–1926: a study of his contribution to the emerging Ireland at the beginning of the twentieth century' (PhD thesis, University of Limerick, 2003).

Steele, E.D., 'J.S. Mill and the Irish question: reform and the integrity of the empire, 1865–1870', *Historical Journal*, 13 (1970).

Stenton, Michael and Stephen Lees (eds), *Who's who of British members of parliament, 1886–1918*, ii (Sussex, 1976).

Strauss, E, *Irish nationalism and British democracy* (London, 1951).

Takagami, Shin-ichi, 'The fenian rising in Dublin, March 1867', *IHS*, 29:115 (1995).

Taplin, Eric, 'Edward McHugh (1853–1915)', and 'Richard McGhee (1851–1930)', in J. Bellamy and J. Saville (eds), *Dictionary of labour biography*, vii (London, 1984).

—, *The dockers' union: a study of the national union of dock labourers, 1889–1922* (Leicester, 1985).

Taylor, Anthony, 'Commemoration, memorialisation and political memory in post-Chartist radicalism: the 1885 Halifax Chartist reunion in context', in Owen Ashton, Robert Fyson, and Stephen Roberts (eds), *The Chartist legacy* (Suffolk, 1999).

Taylor, Miles, *Ernest Jones, Chartism and the romance of politics, 1819–69* (Oxford, 2003).

TeBrake, Janet, 'Irish peasant women in revolt: the Land League years', *IHS*, 28:109 (1992).

Tierney, Mark, *Croke of cashel: the life of Archbishop Thomas William Croke, 1832–1902* (Dublin, 1976).

Thompson, E.P., *William Morris, romantic to revolutionary* (London, 1977).

—, *The making of the English working class* (London, 1980).

Thompson, Frank, *The end of Liberal Ulster: land agitation and land reform, 1868–1886* (Belfast, 2001).

Thompson, F.M.L., *The rise of respectable society in Victorian Britain, 1830–1900* (London, 1988).

Tolstoy, L.N., *Resurrection* (Middlesex, 1966).*

Travers, Pauric, 'Davitt after the Land League', in King (ed.), *Famine, land and culture in Ireland* (Dublin, 2000).

Tsuzuki, Chushichi, *H.M. Hyndman and British socialism* (Oxford, 1961).

Tuckman, Barbara, *The proud tower: a potrait of the world before the war, 1890–1914* (New York, 1996).

Walker, B.M., 'The 1885 and 1886 general elections – a milestone in Irish history', in Peter Collins (ed.), *Nationalism and unionism: conflict in Ireland, 1885–1921* (Belfast, 1996).

Wallace, Russel, 'How to nationalise the land: a radical solution to the Irish problem', *Contemporary Review*, 38 (November 1880).*

Ward, Alan J., *Ireland and Anglo–American relations, 1899–1921* (London, 1969).

Warwick-Haller, Sally, *William O'Brien and the Irish land war* (Dublin, 1990).

Webb, Alfred, *Alfred Webb: autobiography of a Quaker nationalist* (ed.) Marie-Louise Legg (Cork, 1999).*

Welsh, Frank, *A history of Hong Kong* (London, 1997).

Wollaston, E.P.M., 'The Irish nationalist movement in Great Britain' (MA thesis, London University, 1958).

Woods, C.J., 'The general election of 1892: the Catholic clergy and the defeat of the Parnellites', in F.S.L. Lyons and R.A.J. Hawkins (eds), *Ireland under the union, varieties of tension: essays in honour of T.W. Moody* (Oxford, 1980).

Wrigley, Chris, 'Liberals and the desire for working class representation in Battersea, 1886–1922', in Kenneth D. Brown (ed.), *Essays in anti-labour history: responses to the rise of labour in Britain* (London, 1975).

Yeats, W.B., *Autobiographies* (London, 1970).

Young, James D., 'Changing images of American democracy and the Scottish labour movement', *International Review of Social History*, 18 (1973).

—, 'Working class and radical movements in Scotland and the revolt from Liberalism, 1866–1900' (PhD thesis, University of Stirling, 1974).

—, 'The Irish immigrants' contribution to Scottish socialism, 1888–1926', *Saothar, Journal of the Irish Labour History Society*, 13 (1988).

Index

Sub-section entries are ordered chronologically, rather than alphabetically